Mastering

Microsoft Access

A Comprehensive Guide to Designing, Managing, and
Optimizing Your Databases with Step-by-Step Tutorials and
Expert Tips - From Novice to Database Guru

Thaddeus Locke

Disclaimer and Terms of Use
The author and publisher of this book and the accompanying materials have used their best efforts in preparing this book. The author and publisher make no representation or warranties with respect to the accuracy, applicability, fitness, or completeness of the contents of this book. The information contained in this book is strictly for informational purposes. Therefore, if you wish to apply the ideas contained in this book, you are taking full responsibility for your actions.

Printed in the United States of America

TABLE OF CONTENTS

v

xi

INTRODUCTION

All around the world, Microsoft Access is recognized as a database management system (DBMS) developed by the company that combines a graphical user interface (GUI), additional tools for software development, and the relational Access Database Engine (ACE). Included in the more expensive and professional editions of Microsoft 365, Access is available for purchase separately or as part of the suite of programs. Utilizing the Access Database Engine (formerly known as Jet Database Engine), it is capable of saving data in a format of its own. One more option available to you with this application is to directly link up with data stored in other databases and applications. Access features referential integrity, which includes deletes and cascading updates, as well as tables that support various field types. It also features reports that can be printed, as well as query interface forms that can be shown and data entered. The primary goal of obtains development was to give end users the ability to obtain data from nearly any source. Among this incredible program's many capabilities are the ability to import and export data to and from Outlook, Excel, dBase, Paradox, SQL Server, Oracle, and other formats. This program also gives you the option to link data exactly where it is and use it for reporting, viewing, editing, and querying purposes. With this, the data in existence changes and Access will make use of the latest data. Its compatibility with SQL (Structured Query Language) is another excellent feature of this application from the standpoint of a programmer. You can use SQL statements directly in Macros and VBA modules to make changes to Access tables, and you can view queries graphically or edit them as SQL statements. In addition, users can combine and utilize VBA and Bix macros for logic and programming forms, as well as object-oriented options.

Today's world has an abundance of data moving all around even at a very fast pace, which makes it necessary for data analysts to have some beneficial tools. This is where this book comes into play. There is an increasing demand for incredibly complicated data analysis. With the help of this book, you will become acquainted with Access and discover the various applications it can be used for, to enhance your daily data analysis and administration. This book is designed to help you demonstrate your abilities regardless of your current ability level (beginning, intermediate, or professional). It is advisable to start from the beginning if you are unfamiliar with Access and database administration in general. This will help you become comfortable with the program and construct other Access apps. Additionally, programming using Visual Basic for Applications (VBA) will be taught to you. Through all, this book has mind-engaging chapters that will help you get started properly and take you to the top. Enjoy, Learn, and Practice as you read along.

Overview of This Book

This unique book on Microsoft Access has been carefully written to ensure that readers can comprehend with ease all of the information contained in this book. In this book, you will learn all you need to know to make the best of Microsoft Access which also includes all necessary tips on VBA and macros.

Below is a sneak peek into what you will learn when you purchase this guide;

Chapter 1: Development of Databases

In this chapter, you will learn about the various vocabularies that are being used in Microsoft Access databases. In this section, you will learn about various databases, tables, records fields, and values and you will also learn about other relational databases. Objects in the Access Database which include tables, queries, display forms that include data entry, reports macros and VBA will also be discussed in detail in this chapter. Lately, you will learn about the various step design methods that should be embarked upon when making plans for database objects.

Chapter 2: Getting Started

Now you are ready to get started with the proper use of Microsoft Access. You will be introduced to the welcome screen, how to design an empty database, the interface which includes a panel for navigation, custom, object type tables and related views, data designed, tweaked date, and the ribbon and you will also learn about the toolbar for quick Access.

Chapter 3: Designing Access Tables

As you will get to understand later on when you are reading this book, the importance of tables in Microsoft Access, in this chapter, you will learn about the diverse types of tables used in Microsoft Access which include object tables, transaction tables, and join tables. You will also learn about the perfect way wherein you can design a New Table. This section includes learning about giving a field a name, knowing a type of data, giving a field description, and also getting to specify validation rules. This chapter will also introduce you to making use of the design tab where you will learn about the primary key, insert rows, delete rows, property sheet, indexes, and a host of others. You will also learn how to make a TBL customer as well as how best you can alter a table design which includes deleting a field you are no longer in use of and modifying the location of a field amongst others. Allocation of properties is another very important factor you will learn about in this chapter. Here you will learn about the common properties, format, custom numeric format, long and short text formats, input mask, and caption. Furthermore in this chapter, you will learn about indexing Access Tables which includes learning about the need for indexes, and multiple-field indexes, and you will also learn about when to index tables. Lastly in this chapter, you will learn about moving a table to a different database, adding records to a database table, having a perfect understanding of attachment fields, including an attachment field in the Datasheet view, and also including an attachment field in the design view.

Chapter 4: Knowing the Relationships between Tables

As earlier explained Access has a lot to do with tables, in this chapter, you will learn the various relationships that exist between tables. You will learn how to build bulletproof databases, and you will learn about the normalization and denormalization of data. Various table relationships will be discussed in detail in this chapter. Relationships like connecting data, one-to-one, one-to-many and so on will be discussed in this chapter. You will also learn about the various integrity rules, the creation of relationships, and the enforcing of referential integrity and you will also learn how you can get to view the relationships and how you can get to follow application-specific integrity rules.

Chapter 5: Working with Access Tables

So much about tables, yeah? In this chapter, you will learn about making effective use of Access Tables. You will learn about comprehending datasheets, looking at the datasheet window, moving in a datasheet, making use of the navigation buttons, and you will also learn about how best to check out the datasheet ribbon. Furthermore in this chapter, you will learn how to open a datasheet, insert new data, have a perfect understanding of how properties affect data entry, and gain an understanding of how properties affect data entry. In this chapter still, you will learn how to move between records to locate a particular value, getting values in the Datasheet. Making use of the undo feature, copying and pasting values, inclusion of new records, showing and deleting records, and altering display fonts are some of the other things you will be exposed to in this chapter. Arranging data in columns, saving the altered layout, filtering and organizing records in a datasheet, filtering a form, aggregating data, printing records, and previewing records are some of the other details you will get to learn in this chapter! Quite robust I must confess!

Chapter 6: Importing and Exporting Data

Data can be imported and exported. In this chapter, you will learn about the various ways in which Access works with external data. You will learn about the various types of external data, ways in which you can work with external data, when to import external data, and when to export it. You will also learn about the various options for importing and exporting which include importing from another Access database, importing from an Excel spreadsheet, importing data from text files, importing and exporting HTML documents, and lots more. You will also learn how to export external formats which includes exporting objects to other Access databases, exporting through ODBC drivers, and exporting through to Word.

Chapter 7: External Data Linking

In this chapter, you will learn about linking external data, getting to know tables that have been linked, linking to other Access database tables, linking to ODBC data sources, and linking to non-database data. Furthermore, you will learn about working with linked tables, configuring view properties, configuring relationships, optimizing linked tables, deleting a linked reference, viewing or altering information, refreshing a data source and its linked tables, and splitting a database. You will also get to learn about the various places to put certain objects and you will also learn how to make use of the edge browser control.

Chapter 8: Selecting Data with Queries

In this chapter, you will be introduced to queries where you will learn about what queries can do and what they return. You will also learn how to create a query, include various fields in your queries, run your query, work with query fields, and resize columns in the QBD grid which includes removing a field, inserting a field, and also concealing a field. You will also learn how best you can include criteria in your queries, you will gain more information on how to print a query record and save a query and you will also learn how to design multi-table queries. Furthermore in this chapter, you will learn about working with table pane, you will learn how to create and work with query joins and you will also be provided with sufficient information about joins which includes inner joins, outer joins, full outer joins, cross joins, specifying the type of join and you will learn how to delete join.

Chapter 9: Using Operators and Expressions in Access

In this chapter, you will be introduced to the use of operators. You will get to learn about the various types of operators which include mathematical, string, Boolean, etc. Operator precedence will also be discussed in this chapter where you will get to learn about the mathematical precedence, comparison precedence, as well as Boolean precedence. Furthermore in this chapter, you will learn about the use of operators and expressions in queries. You will gain insight into how to use query comparison operators, and have a perfect understanding of complex criteria, make use of functions in select queries, and reference fields in select queries. Entering IF single-value field criteria will also be discussed in this chapter which includes learning about the like operator and wildcards, specifying non-match values, and inserting true or false criteria. You will learn about the use of multiple criteria in a query which includes how to specify more than one value with the Or operator, making use of the Or cell or the QBD pane, making use of AND for the specification of a range, and using the between and And operator. Also in this chapter, you will learn how to insert criteria in various fields which includes making use of And and Or across diverse fields in a query, indicating OR criteria across fields in a query, and using And and Or simultaneously in different fields amongst others.

Chapter 10: Going Beyond Select Queries

In this chapter, you will be introduced to all other types of queries. You will learn about aggregate queries, and aggregate functions which include Group By, Sum, Avg, Count, Expression, Where, etc. You will also learn about action queries which include queries such as make table, append, update, crosstab, creating a crosstab query, making use of the query design in the creation of your crosstab query, and designing your crosstab queries. Also in this chapter, you will learn how to optimize query performance which will include normalizing your database design, making use of indexes on appropriate fields, optimizing by the improvement of query design, and compacting and repairing the database promptly.

Chapter 11: Transforming Data in Access

Here as the title of the chapter connotes, you will learn how to alter data. Things you will learn in this chapter include; finding and removing duplicate records, defining duplicate records, and removing duplicate records. You will also learn about common transformation tasks which include; filling in blank fields, concatenating, and concatenating fields. You will also learn about how to augment field values using your text by gaining knowledge on changing cases, removing leading and trailing spaces from a string, finding and replacing a certain text, and adding your text in key positions within a string.

Chapter 12: Working with Calculations and Dates

In this chapter, you will learn how to make use of a calculator when performing your analyses. Here you will learn about common calculation scenarios, how to make use of constants in calculation, make use of fields in calculations, make use of the results of aggregation in calculations, make use of calculation as an argument in a function, and will also learn how to construct calculations with the use of the Expression Builder. Furthermore in this chapter, you will learn about the various common calculation errors, and you will learn how to make use of dates in your analyses which includes learning about simple date calculations, advanced analysis with the use of functions, the date functions, and you will also learn about how to group dates into quarters.

Chapter 13: Performing Conditional Analyses

In this chapter, you will learn how to make use of parameter queries which includes gaining insight into how parameter queries work, learning more about ground rules of parameter query, working with parameter queries, combining parameters with operators, and making use of parameters as function arguments. The use of conditional functions will also be discussed in this chapter where you will get to learn about the IIF function, how to use the IIF function to avoid mathematical errors, getting to save time with IIF, and how to make use of the IIF functions for the creation of crosstab analysis. Lastly in this chapter, you will learn about the major difference between IIF and switch functions.

Chapter 14: The Fundamentals of Using SQL

In this chapter, you will learn about the basics of SQL which includes the Select statement, how to select all columns, the use of the Where clause, and making sense of joins(inner and outer joins). Furthermore, you will learn how to expand your search with the Like operator, and how to choose Unique values and rows without having to group and configure the sort order with the use of the ORDER BY clause. More in this chapter are details on how to show just the Select Top Percent, performing action queries with the use of SQL statements, making use of SQL-specific queries, and you will also learn how to manipulate columns with the use of Alter Table statement which includes how to add a column with the use of the ADD clause, altering a column with the use of the Alter Column clause, adding primary keys with the use of the ADD constraints clause, and you will also learn how to create pass-through queries.

Chapter 15: Subqueries and Domain Aggregate Functions

In this chapter, you will start by learning how to enhance your analyses with the Subqueries. Here you will get to know why Subqueries should be used, various subquery ground rules, how to create Subqueries without SQL statements, and how to make use of IN and NOT IN with Subqueries. Furthermore, you will learn how to make use of correlated Subqueries, uncorrelated Subqueries, and making use of Subqueries with action queries. Furthermore, you will learn about domain aggregate functions and you will gain insight as regards the various domain aggregate functions which include using no criteria, using text criteria, using domain aggregate function, creating a running count, and lastly, you will learn how to make use of a value from the previous record.

Chapter 16: Running Descriptive Statistics in Access

In this chapter, you will learn about basic descriptive statistics which includes executing descriptive statistics with aggregate queries, determining rank, mode, and median, ranking the records in your data set, getting the mode and median in a data set as well as pulling random sampling from your data set. Also in this chapter, you will learn about advanced descriptive statistics where you will be introduced to how to calculate percentile making, determine the quartile standing of a record, and create a frequency distribution.

Chapter 17: Creating Basic Access Forms

In this chapter, you will learn how to work with various form views, and you will get to learn more about the various types of forms which include the switchboard form, dialog box form, data entry form, record display form, etc. You will also be introduced to various controls in this chapter, you will learn how to categorize controls and add a control, and you will also learn how to make use of the control group. Using the field list, selecting and deselecting controls, selecting just one control, choosing various controls, manipulating controls, moving and aligning controls, altering the appearance of controls, grouping controls, deleting control, reattaching a label to control as well as introducing properties are sub-topics that will be discussed in this chapter.

Chapter 18: Working with Data on Access Forms

In this chapter, you will learn how to make use of the form views and you will also get to familiarize yourself with the ribbon where you will learn how to view groups, make use of the clipboard group, sort and filter groups, record group, find group, window group, and the text formatting group. You will also learn how to make use of pictures and OLE objects, enter data in a long text field, enter data in the date field, make use of the option group, make use of combo boxes and list boxes, switch to datasheet view, and save records. Printing form, adding a form header or footer, and dealing with section properties which include the visible property, back color property, and special effect property will all be discussed in these chapters. Modifying layout as well as the conversion of a form to a report will also be highlighted in this chapter.

Chapter 19: Working with Form Controls

In this chapter, you will get to learn about the use of form controls. You will learn how to configure control properties, make use of subforms, gain necessary tips on the design of forms, and make use of the tab stop property. Also in this chapter, you will learn how to deal with advanced form techniques which include making use of page number and the date or time controls, morphing a control, making use of the format painter, reducing the records shown on a form, and making use of the tab control. Lastly, you will learn about the use of dialog boxes to collect information where you will get to learn how to design query, configure the command buttons, set a cancel button, take off the control menu, create a form from scratch, design a subform, configuring forms properties, saving form record and also changing the appearance of the form.

Chapter 20: Data Presentation with Access Reports

In this chapter, you will be introduced to reports. Here you will learn how to perfectly identify the various types of reports which include tabular reports, columnar reports, and mailing label reports, and you will also learn how best you can differentiate between reports and forms. Creating a report from scratch and defining the report layout will also be highlighted in this chapter. Under this subtopic, you will learn how best to create a new report, choose the various grouping levels, choose the sort order, choose the summary options, choose a theme, make use of the print preview window, view the report in design view, print, and view report will also be discussed in this chapter in details. Banded report design concepts are also another aspect that will be discussed in this chapter. Under this subtopic, you will learn about the report header section, the page header section, the group header section, the detail section, the group footer section, the page footer section, and resizing a section will also all be discussed in this chapter.

Chapter 21: Advanced Access Report Techniques

In this chapter, you will get to know more about the grouping and sorting of data. You will learn how to group data alphabetically, group on date intervals, conceal repeating information, conceal a page header, and commence a new page number. Also in this chapter, you will learn how to format data which includes creating numbered lists, and bulleted lists, including an emphasis on the run time, including a blank line, making use of various formats in the same text box, centering the title, aligning control labels, and micro-adjusting controls. Adding data and adding more flexibility which deals with the display of all reports in a combo box, fast printing from queried data, making use of snaking columns in a report, and assigning unique names to controls will also be discussed in this chapter.

Chapter 22: Using Access Macros

In this chapter, you will be introduced to the use of macros. Here you will learn how to create a macro and assign a macro to an event. You will also gain more insight on the use of macro security where you will get to know how best to enable sandbox mode, utilize the trust center, and also employ the use of digital signature. Furthermore in this chapter, you will learn about multi-action macros, submacros, conditions, temporary variables, error handling, and macro debugging where you will also get to learn about OnError action, the macroError object, debugging macros, and embedded macros.

Chapter 23: Access Data Macros

In this chapter, you will be introduced to data macros and also have a perfect understanding of table events which include before events and after events. Furthermore in this chapter, you will learn how to make use of the macro builder for data macros, have a perfect understanding of the actin catalog, design your first data macro, manage macro objects which includes collapsing and expanding macro items, dragging macro items, saving macro as XML, and recognizing the limitations of Data macros.

Chapter 24: Getting Started with Access VBA

In this chapter, you will be introduced to Visual Basic for applications where you will get to learn VBA code basics, how to create VBA programs, working in the code window which includes the use of white space, and line continuation. Moving forward, you will learn about multi-statement lines which include intellisense, compiling procedures, and saving a module; you will learn about VBA branching constructs which include branching, making use of the If keyword, .looping, using the Do and Loop statement, and also making use of the For and the Next statement. Furthermore in this chapter, you will learn how to make use of the objects and collections, properties and methods, you will learn how best to explore the Visual Basic Editor and you will also learn how to make use of the object browser which includes VBE options, the editor tab of the options dialog box as well as the project properties dialog box.

Chapter 25: Mastering VBA Data Types and Procedures

In this chapter, you will learn about the use of variables which includes naming variables, declaring variables, the use of the Dim keyword, the public keyword, and the private keyboard. You will also learn how best to work with data types which includes forcing explicit declarations, making use of a naming convention, having a perfect understanding of variable scope and lifetime, examining scope, making use of constants, clearing constants, working with arrays, etc.

Understanding Subs and functions, calling VBA procedures, simplifying code with Named Arguments, and deploying an access application are some of the other topics that will be discussed in this chapter.

Chapter 26: Understanding the Access Event Model

In this chapter you will learn about various Access Events, you will learn about programming events, gain an understanding of just how events trigger VBA code, and create event procedures. You will also learn how to identify common events which include form event procedures, essential form events, and form data events. Also in this chapter, you will learn how to control event procedures, pay special attention to event sequence, write simple forms and control event procedures, and open a form with the use of an event procedure which also includes executing an event procedure when closing a form and also making use of an event procedure for the confirmation of the record deletion.

Chapter 27: Debugging Access Applications

In this chapter, you will learn how best to arrange VBA code, get your applications tested, employ the use of traditional debugging techniques, and you will also learn how best to make use of the Access debugging tools. Furthermore in this chapter, you will learn how to suspend execution with breakpoints, look at variables with the use of the local's window, make use of conditional watches, trap eros in your code, make use of the resume keyword and you will also learn how to include error handling in your procedures.

Chapter 28: Accessing Data with VBA

In this chapter, you will get to work with data, have a perfect understanding of DAO objects, and ADO objects, and learn how best to write a VBA code to get a table updated which includes updating fields in a record with the use of ADO, updating calculated control, checking the status of a record deletion, removing repetitive code, including a new record as well as deleting a record.

Chapter 29: Advanced Data Access with VBA

In this chapter, you will learn how to add an unbound combo box to s form to find data, filter a form which includes filtering with a code, filtering with a query, creating a parameter query, creating an interactive filter dialog box, and also you will learn how to migrate access data to Dataverse.

Chapter 30: Customizing the Ribbon

In this chapter, you will learn all that has to do with the use of the ribbon which includes editing the default ribbon, working with the quick access toolbar, developing custom ribbons, and making use of VBA callbacks and you will also learn about the basic ribbon controls.

Chapter 31: Preparing your Access Application for Distribution

In this chapter, you will learn how to define the current database choices and remove personal information from file properties on Save which includes making use of Windows Theme controls on forms and enabling layout view. You will also learn how to enable design change for tables in the datasheet view, how best to make use of the navigation options, ribbon, and toolbar options and you will also learn how to develop an application.

Chapter 32: Integrating Access with Sharepoint

In this chapter, you will be introduced to SharePoint, you will learn how to share data between Access and Sharepoint, Import SharePoint lists, export Access tables to Sharepoint, move access tables to SharePoint, and you will also learn how best to make use of Sharepoint templates.

PART 1

GET ACCESS TO FUNDAMENTAL INFORMATION

About what a building block is, this book has been designed to take you gradually from one step to another with each part containing chapters and also examples that are detailed and drive home the point. This section will cover several fundamental subjects that are required for you to successfully use a database. You will also learn how to make sure that data is properly implemented and normalized so that your table will function well. Make sure you give this section more time so you can gain all the necessary foundational knowledge. However, if you are already knowledgeable about database design, you may quickly go through the pages as a revision tool and perhaps pick up some new information.

CHAPTER 1
DEVELOPMENT OF DATABASES

Database development is unique and it is not the same way you play around with your computer. As against other applications like PowerPoint and Excel where you just have to be creative, there's a need for you to have basic foundational knowledge in database development. This chapter covers basic fundamental knowledge that you need to learn and cannot do without as it pertains to this application and the development of databases in general.

The vocabulary used in Access Databases

Nearly all of the fundamental terminology used in databases may be used with Access. Records, tables, fields, the database itself, and values that display a hierarchy from the smallest to the largest and vice versa are among these terms. Except for structured query language (SQL), all of the words listed above are equally utilized in practically all database systems.

Databases

An organized method of gathering data or data that has been electronically saved in a computer is known as a database. A database management system often oversees a database (DBMS). A database system, sometimes just referred to as a database, includes data and DBMSs as well as the numerous applications that are connected to them. Even though I've spoken about electronic databases, manual databases—also referred to as file systems or manual database systems—also exist. When using manual database systems, form completion is essentially limited to one method. Accessing information manually involves opening a filing cabinet, removing a file or folder, and then finding a specific piece of paper. Users will complete the forms using whichever approach is most convenient for them. Spreadsheets can also be used for data analysis or to present the data in an eye-catching way. To facilitate quick data processing and querying, data contained in the most popular databases used today are primarily arranged in rows and columns across a variety of tables. This will make it easy to access, alter, control, organize, and modify the data. It should be noted that most databases write and query data using the Structured Query Language (SQL). Different kinds of databases exist. The one you choose to utilize primarily depends on how the company intends to use the information.

In the sections below, you will find just a few databases that will be discussed in this book;

- **Relational database**: In the 1980s, this database gained popularity. A relational database is organized with its items in a well-organized set of tables with rows and columns. One of the most effective and versatile ways to access well-structured data is through relational database technology.

- **Object-oriented database**: Information found in an object-oriented database is represented in the form of objects similar to object-oriented programming.
- **Distributed databases**: This type of database has about two or more files that can be found in different locations. The database can be saved on various computers that are found right within the same location or diverged over various networks.

Access databases are merely an automated way to perform a paper file system's filing and retrieval tasks. Access databases make it easier to store information in an organized way. A database management system like Access can better transform data into really valuable information when it is stored in a very specific way. A database in Access is just more than a set of tables; it also contains other kinds of objects like forms, reports, macros, queries, and code modules. When you launch an Access database, you will be able to deal with the different objects. You can also choose to open various copies of Access at the same time and work at the same time with more than a single database if need be.

Tables

The main database object that contains all of the data in a database is a table. Data in tables is organized in a manner like a spreadsheet: rows and columns. A field on each record is displayed in a column, and each row represents a distinct record. For example, a table containing an employee's data for a corporation would have a row for each person and columns showing the employee's name, address, job title, and mobile number.

There are quite several things expected to be remembered when dealing with the use of tables. Below are some of these things;

- The number of tables that are in a database is limited only by just the number of objects that are allowed in a database. Primarily, a standard user-defined table can have up to about 1,024 columns. The storage capacity of the server helps to bring a limit to the number of rows in the table.
- To provide control over the data that is permitted, properties can be applied to different tables and each column inside the table. A key constraint in Table One ensures the enforcement of uniqueness or aids in the definition of a relationship that exists between tables. Alternatively, a constraint can be created on a column to prevent null values or to allow for a default value if the value is not indicated.
- Pages or rows can be used to compress data in tables. It is possible to store rows on a page by data compression.

In the sections below are the various types of tables that are available to you;

- **Partitioned Tables:** These tables are characterized by a horizontal data division that allows the data to be dispersed over multiple file groups. Because partitioning makes it possible to obtain or handle subsets of data quickly and effectively while simultaneously maintaining the integrity of the collection as a whole, it guarantees that enormous tables or indexes are relatively manageable.

- **Temporary Tables**: Here there are two types of tables which are local and global. They are quite different in terms of their names, availability, and visibility. Local temporary tables have just a single number sign(#) as the first character of their names they are visible basically to the current connection for the user and they are also deleted when the user disconnects. Since the first two characters of the names of global temporary tables are two number signs (##), users can only see them immediately after they are formed, and they are also deleted when all users who are referring to the table disconnect.

A table is recognized as an entity in Access. You need to consider how tables and other database objects reflect the actual things controlled by the database as well as the relationships between the entities when you are building tables and working on Access applications. Once the table has been constructed, it can be seen as a datasheet, or spreadsheet with rows and columns, just like a spreadsheet.

Records and Fields

The names of the database's fields are listed in the first row of an embedded datasheet, which is made up of rows and columns containing records and fields. There is just one record in the row, and within that record are fields that are related to each other. In a manual system (filling), the fields are the spaces that need to be filled in on a printed form, and the rows are separate forms, similar to sheets of paper. A field with a single column has multiple attributes that specify the kind of data that is embedded in it and also specify how Access should handle the field and day. The field name (company) and the data type (text) are two examples of these attributes. A field may also have additional characteristics, such as the Size attribute in the Address field, which informs Access of the maximum character limit for the address.

Values

Simply put, values can be defined as an intersection of both a record and a field. For example, the English Premier League can be a field, and then Chelsea Football Club can be the data entered to represent the value of the field. Certain basic rules control how data is infused into an Access table.

Relational Databases

You have a ton of access to current and reliable information when a database is properly built. When working with databases, a proper design is essential to achieving your objectives, therefore you should take the time to understand the fundamentals of design that make sense. It's possible that in the end, you'll have a highly adaptable database that satisfies all of your requirements. Access data is usually stored in related tables such that the data in one table is related to the data in another table. Access keeps the relationship between tables that are related thereby enabling easy access to have a customer and all of the orders of the customer extracted without having to lose any data or retrieving records that are not for the customer.

Data entry and reporting will be very simple when there are multiple tables because the amount of redundant data input will be reduced. For instance, if you are using an application that handles client information, you don't need to save the customer's name and address each time they place an order or make a purchase if you construct two tables. Since all records of a particular type are contained within the same table, data that is divided up into separate tables within a database makes the system easier to maintain. The design and time required will decrease when you allocate time for accurately entering data into various tables. It's common to refer to this procedure as normalization.

Objects in Access Database

Before starting to design databases, you must have a fundamental understanding of some concepts, regardless of your level of database experience. All the information and tools you need to utilize Access are contained in about six different sorts of objects. Table, query, form, report, macro, and module are examples of these tools.

Tables

As was previously said, tables play a crucial role in Access databases. Datasheets are the objects through which tables are interacted with. A datasheet, resembling an Excel sheet, facilitates the display of data in a table using a row-and-column structure. A datasheet presents data without any kind of filtration or change. Another name for it is the custom default mode, and it displays every field in a certain record.

Queries

You may easily add, remove, or modify data in your Access database by using a query. Utilizing queries can also help you find specific data quickly by requiring you to filter on some basic criteria. Finally, queries can be used to calculate or summarize data and automate data management tasks like regularly reviewing the most recent data. In a well-designed database, the data that should be presented through a form or a report is most times located in different tables. With the use of a query, you can extract the information needed from different tables and then bring them together to show it in the form of a report. A query can be either a request for data results from a database or for action on the specific data and at times it can also be both. A query can be used to add, modify, or remove data from a database, receive the response to a relatively straightforward inquiry, perform certain computations, and compile data from many tables. Because of their great versatility, questions come in a variety of forms, and their creation is contingent upon the nature of the work at hand. It is noteworthy to mention that virtually all forms and reports in Access are predicated on queries that combine filtering and sorting data before display. To modify, add, or remove database records, queries are frequently removed from macros or VBA routines.

Display forms including Data entry

A database item in Access called Forms can be used to create a user interface for a database application. A bound form may be used to insert, modify, or display data from a specific data source and has a direct relationship to a data source, such as a database or query. Alternatively, you may design an unbound form that lacks a direct connection to a data source but still includes all of the controls—such as labels and command buttons—that you might require to run your application. Data entry forms can be used to limit access to specific table fields. To verify the validity of your data before adding it to a database table, forms may also be used to improve data validation rules in VBA code. Datasheets are not always favored over forms. They often have a paper-like appearance and are incredibly helpful in helping users complete data entry chores quickly. Forms help ensure that data entry is simple and easy to understand by directing users through the field of the database that needs to be edited. A type of form known as the Read-only form is used for the sole purpose of the inquiry. These forms show some fields that are in a table. When some fields alone are shown and not all, this means that a user can be limited to data that are sensitive while also allowing access to other fields that are also in the same table.

Reports

In essence, reports give you a way to summarize and view the data in your Microsoft Access database in several formats. For example, you can make a very basic report that has the phone numbers of every contact on your phone, or you can make a summary report that shows the total amount of sales made in various nations or areas in a specific amount of time. Reports assist in displaying your data in a format similar to PDFs. Access gives you a remarkably high degree of flexibility when creating reports.

A report is quite helpful, particularly when presenting data from your database for any of the following purposes:

- Show or spread a summary of data.
- Archive snapshots of the data.
- Offer details about individual records.
- Having labels created.

You can use reports to compile several tables and visualize the intricate links between different data sources. Printing an invoice is a good example. The customer's name, address, and other pertinent information are all provided in the table, along with corresponding records from the sales table that may be printed to show the specific line item details for each product that the consumer has requested. Additionally, the report will compute the sales totals and publish them in a customized manner.

Macros and VBA

With the creation of a new database, you will have to start creating various database objects like tables, forms, and also reports. Eventually, you will get to a stage where you might have to include some sort of programming to have some processes automated and also help tie your database objects together. This is where the macros and VBA come into play. Programming in Access refers to extending the functionality of the database using Visual Basic for Applications code or Access macros. For example, suppose you have a form and a report, and you want to add a command button to the form that will open the report when it is clicked. In this context, programming refers to generating a VBA function or macro and then modifying the on-click event property of the command buttons. in a method that initiates the macro or procedure upon clicking the command button. If you are going through a very simple procedure like having to open a report, you can choose to make use of the Command Button Wizard to get all your work done or rather have the wizard turned off and then do the programming yourself. The approach you want to use for either database distribution or deployment will largely determine whether you choose to use VBA or macros. For example, if your computer is the only one you use and you have the database saved there, you might want to utilize VBA for practically all of your programming duties if you are comfortable using the code. However, let's say you want to use a file server to host your database so that other people may access it. In that scenario, you may need to refrain from utilizing VBA mostly for security-related concerns.

The functionality you require and, of course, security should be your two main considerations when deciding whether to utilize VBA or macros. Because VBA can be used to create routines that either damage computer files or jeopardize data security, security is a serious concern. If you are at all confident that the database you are utilizing comes from a reliable source, then you should be able to use VBA code when working with databases developed by others. When creating a database that other people will use, you should refrain from including programming features that need the user to explicitly grant the database trusted status. Macros on the other hand help with the provision of quite a straightforward way of getting to deal with so many tasks involving programming such as having to open and close forms and also getting to execute reports. Diverse object databases such as forms and reports that you must have designed in respect to the fact that there is just a little syntax that you ought to keep in mind can be assigned together swiftly. The arguments for every of the actions are displayed in the Macro Builder. In addition to increased security which is very important in today's world, macros also offer easy accessibility.

Planning for database objects

Several design chores must be completed after building database objects such as tables, forms, and reports. When your application is exceptional, your design will also seem unique. You can finish any system much faster and with greater success if you carefully consider your design. An object is designed primarily so that there is a clear path to follow throughout implementation.

A Five-Step Design Method

The five design steps alongside the database system explain a lot about Access and also offer a solid foundation for the creation of database applications which include tables, queries, forms, data pages, reports, macros, and simple VBA modules. The amount of time required for each stage entirely depends on the kind of database being constructed. Sometimes, for example, users may provide you with examples of reports they would like to print from their Access database, and the data sources are so clear that you will only need a few minutes to finish the design. In some cases, however, particularly if the user's requirements are extremely complicated or the business processes the program supports are likely to require extensive investigation, you may find yourself devoting several hours or even days to only the initial phase. Ensure you take adequate time to look at the design based on inputs and outputs as you are reading through each of the steps.

First Step: The total design from thoughts to completion

Determining how to best meet the end user's needs overall is the first of several connected issues that almost all software developers face. Before focusing only on the details, it is crucial to have a thorough understanding of the overall demand.

For example, you might have some users who request a database that supports the following tasks;

- Including and keeping of customers such as names, addresses, and also the financial history.
- Inputting and maintaining sales information like a method of payment, date of sales, total amount, the identity of the customer, and some other related fields.
- Inputting and maintaining sales line-item information especially details of the items purchased.
- Checking the information from all of the tables such as sales, customers, payments, and sales line items.
- Asking various types of questions about the information that exists in a database.
- Creating a monthly invoice report.
- Designing a customer sales history.
- Designing mailing labels and mail-merge reports.

It may be necessary for you to take into account additional ancillary jobs that the user has not identified in addition to the tasks stated above. Make sure you take a seat and examine the present workflow before starting to design. To do this, you need to perform a comprehensive needs analysis of the current system and look into automating it. One novel way to accomplish this is to create a series of inquiries that provide insight into the client's business and data usage practices.

For instance, when you want to automate any type of business you might need to ask the following questions;

- How are billings being processed?
- What specific reports and forms are being used at the moment?
- How are sales, customers, and some other records stored at the moment?

The customer may think of other details about his company that he feels you should be aware of while you ask these and other pertinent questions. Gaining insight into the current state of the firm can also be facilitated by closely examining every procedure that is being used. You may need to go back and record more observations regarding the procedure being used as well as how the staff members carry out their duties. As you finalize the preparations to finish the remaining steps, make sure you inform the client of everything you plan to do, give the users a preview of what you are doing, and solicit their feedback on what needs to be done to make sure the users are actually in need of it.

Second Step: Designing reports

It may seem strange to start with a report, but this is because users are typically more interested in the printed output from a database than in any other area of the application. Nearly all of the data in a report is typically maintained by an application. Reports are considered to be the most effective means of compiling data regarding database requirements because they are invariably thorough. You might be puzzled about which should come first when you see the reports that will be created in this part. Will it be the report layout coming first or is there a need to determine the data items and text that make you the report first? These items are considered concurrently. Keep in mind that the strategy used to arrange the fields in a report is also very important. The report's construction will be simpler the more time you invest in this. Occasionally, individuals even go so far as to include gridlines on the report so they can precisely see where each piece of data belongs.

Third Step: Getting data designed

Obtaining an inventory of all the information required by the report is the next stage in the design phase. Including data items in each of the above reports is one of the greatest strategies for this. When doing this, pay close attention to different items that are included in many reports. Since a data item is essentially the same entity, make sure it has the same name throughout all of your reports.

To get a sense of the Customer-Related Data Items that are included in reports, look at the table below.

Customers Report	Invoice Report
Customer Name	Customer Name
Street	Street
City	City
State	State
Zip code	Zip code
Phone Numbers	Phone Numbers
Email Address	
Web Address	
Discount Rate	
Customer Since	
Last Sales Date	

Sales Tax Rate	
Credit Information (four fields)	

As demonstrated above, there are many common fields when comparing the kinds of client data required for each report. In both reports, nearly every field related to client data is present. Only a portion of the fields—those about client information—that are used in each report are displayed in the above table. Because the connected rows' field names and other characteristics are identical, you can easily make sure you have access to all the data. Even though having to find items with ease is not important for this very small database, it will be very important when there is a need for you to deal with bigger tables that have various fields. Upon the extraction of the data from customers, you can then proceed to the sales data. In cases such as this, there is a need for the analysis of only the Invoice report for data items that are pertinent to sales.

Fourth Step: Designing tables

Selecting the fields required for the tables that will ultimately comprise the reports may appear to be the most challenging part of the process. You begin to see the fields that correspond to the different tables in the database when you examine the many fields and computations that comprise the documents that are available to you. Add all of the fields that you have to have extracted as of right now. Even if some fields won't show up in the table, you should still add the others much later. It is crucial to understand that not every piece of information needs to be added to the database table. To make it much easier to identify which specific employees are accessible on any given day, users may need to put bank holidays and other out-of-office days in the database. However, adding too many concepts during the early stages of development can easily lead to an application's basic design being overly complicated. It could perhaps be wise to put all of the less crucial items on hold until the initial design is finished since Access tables are relatively simple to modify afterward. In general, it is not so difficult to accept user requests after the database development project is underway.

Customer Data	Invoice Data	Line Items	Payment Information
Customer Company Name	Invoice Number	Product Purchased	Payment Type

Street	Sales Date	Quantity Purchased	Payment Date
City	Invoice Date	Description of Item Purchased	Payment Amount
State	Discount (overall for this sale)	Price of Item	Credit Card Number
Zipcode	Tax Rate	Discount for Each Item	Expiration Date
Phone Numbers (two fields)	Taxable?		
Email Address			
Web Address			
Discount Rate			
Customer Since			
Last Sales Date			
Sales Tax Rate			

Credit Information (four fields)			

You must start compiling the data by purpose and then look to compare it with the data that can be found across those functions once you've used each report to display all of the data. To accomplish this, you must first examine the customer data and then merge it with all the other fields to create a single collection of data items. After that, carry out the same procedure for the line-item and sales information. Data comparison of data items from information groups is aided by the table. When goods and data are compared, it can be a very good way to begin to design individual tables but you still have a lot of tasks ahead of you. The client data should be divided into two separate groups, as you will discover as you get more expertise in creating data designs. While some of these things are used just once for each consumer, others may be used multiple times. The Sales column serves as a good illustration of this, as the payment information can contain multiple lines of data. To further differentiate all related sorts of items in their columns, you must further break down each of these information categories. This may be thought of as an example of the normalization phase of the design process. For example, a client may be under multiple contracts with the business or get multiple payments for a single transaction. In this manner, the information has to have previously been divided into three groups: line-item details, invoice data, and customer data.

Remember that a customer may have multiple bills and that each invoice may contain multiple line items. Information about individual sales can be found in the invoice-data category, and details about individual invoices can be found in the line-items category. Be aware that there is a relationship between these three columns. For example, a client may receive multiple invoices, and each invoice may need to have a different set of line items. There may be variations in the relationships between tables. For example, a sales invoice may have a single customer, but each customer may have multiple sales. The sales invoice's line items and the invoice itself have numerous comparable relationships. Tables engaged in a database table relationship must have a substantially different field. For the database engine to join and retrieve relevant data, each table needs to have a unique identification. As the invoice number is the unique identifier found in the sales table, each other table must have at least one field included to act as a link to the other tables. To link customers and their invoices, database engines leverage the relationship that exists between customers and invoices. Relationships between tables are facilitated by the usage of key fields.

Fifth Step: Designing forms

You can start creating your forms once the data has been produced and the table relation has been established. Fields on forms are designed to be either editable or viewable in the edit mode. Access screens should generally resemble the forms used in a manual system far more closely. **In** the creation of forms, there is a need for you to place three different types of objects on the screen;

- **Labels and text-box data-entry fields**: The fields that are located on the Access forms and reports are known as controls.
- Special controls (command buttons, multiple-line text boxes, options buttons, list boxes, checkboxes, business graphs, and pictures).
- Graphical objects to enhance the forms (colors, lines, rectangles, and three-dimensional effects).

Generally speaking, the Access-data entry form should resemble the printed form if it is being built from an existing printed form. The fields on the screen should be positioned in the same relative manner as they are in the printed version. Labels display captions, titles, or messages. You can enter text or numbers from your database into text boxes and see them displayed. Checkboxes can be either checked or unchecked to indicate a condition. Access also includes command buttons, list boxes, combo boxes, option buttons, toggle buttons, and other option groups as control types.

Activity

1. Mention 5 vocabularies used in Microsoft Access.
2. What are the objects in the access database?
3. Highlight the various planning steps for database objects.

CHAPTER 2
GETTING STARTED

This chapter will bring to your understanding all of the major components of the Microsoft Access user interface.

The Access Welcome Screen

Upon the opening of Access, you will see the default welcome screen. The welcome screen offers various options for opening an Access database that is already in existence or you might have to create a new database. The most recent pick will appear in the upper left corner of the welcome screen. The databases that are shown here are ones that you have already opened using Access. To open any of the database files, simply click on them. It should be noted that when the Recent area is filled in, Microsoft Access does not distinguish between databases that are there and databases that have been destroyed. This merely indicates that a database that you are certain has been erased is visible in the most recent list. An error message stating that Access cannot locate the database will appear when you click on a deleted database in the recent list.

Underneath the Recent section option, you will see a hyperlink named Open Other Files.

- Click on **this link (hyperlink)** to search for and also open a database on your computer or your network.

At the very top of the welcome screen, you can search for Access database templates online. These templates are starter databases that have different purposes. Microsoft ensures that they are made available free of charge. Several pre-made templates will appear in the center of the welcome screen; all you have to do is click on them to download and utilize them. Microsoft created the online template library to provide users with the option to download or build Access apps from scratch. The template databases address a range of corporate needs, including sales management and inventory control. You can choose to spend some time browsing through the online templates to get the precise one you need before downloading it. Also at the center of the welcome screen, there will be an option for Blank Database. With this option, you can design a new database.

Creating an Empty Database

Upon initializing Access or quitting a database without exiting Access, the Microsoft Office Backstage view appears. You can use the backstage view as a starting point from which to create a new database, access an existing database, examine content from office.com, or do whatever else you can get Access to do with a database file or outside of a database instead of inside one.

When you open Access, the backstage view shows the New tab option. **The new tab offers various ways that you can use to design a new database;**

- **A blank database**: You have the option to start over from scratch if you'd like. This can be considered a very good alternative if you need to accommodate or include data that already exists or if you have certain design needs.
- **A template that is installed with Access**: for this one, you can decide to start a fresh project and you might also want an early advantage. Many templates are pre-installed in Access by default.
- **A template from office.com**: There is a ton more templates available on office.com in addition to the ones that come with Access. You can accomplish this without even opening a browser because it's so easy; the templates are available on the New tab.

There are several templates included with Microsoft Access that you can use as a starting point. Ready-to-use databases with all the tables, queries, forms, macros, and reports required to carry out some extremely specific activities are called templates. For example, some templates may be used to manage contacts, track difficulties, or maintain tabs on everyday costs. To aid in the illustration of how to utilize them, several templates additionally provide sample records. The quickest method to build a database is to use one of these templates if it suits your needs. However, you may decide that it is preferable to create a database from scratch rather than using a template if you have data in another application that you want to import into Access. The structure of templates is predefined, and it may take a lot of work to modify your current data to fit the template's structure.

- Click the **close button after selecting the file tab** if the database has already been opened. The new tab will then show the backstage perspective.
- The new tab has a variety of template kinds, some of which are pre-installed in Access. Additional templates are available for download on office.com.
- Select **the template that you would want to use.**

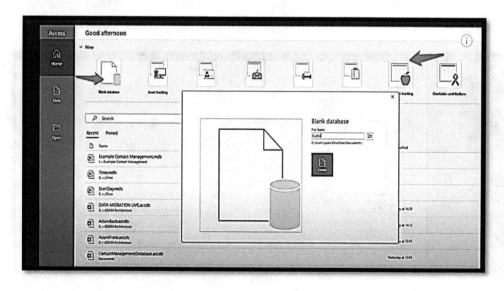

26

- The file name that Access suggests for your database will then appear in the File Name field; you have the option to modify it. Navigate to the location you want to save the database in and select the **OK option** if you want it saved in a different folder from the one that appears beneath the file name box. It is also an option for you to make your database and connect it to a SharePoint site.
- Select the **"Create" option**. Access launches the database after creating one using the selected template. You will see a form for almost all templates, allowing you to start inserting data. If your template has a variety of sample data, you can select to remove each record by using the record selector, after which you can take any of the following actions:
  - On the Home tab, in the Record group option, click on the **Delete button**.
- Once you have chosen the first blank cell on the form, you may begin designing data. Search for more forms or reports that you may need to employ by using the navigation pane. You may switch between the several databases that are available using some templates' navigation form.

If you are not interested in making use of a template you can choose to create your database by simply building your tables, forms, reports, and some other database objects.

In most cases, this might involve either one or both of the following;

- When designing a new database, inserting, pasting, or importing data into the table and then repeating the procedure with other tables that you have to build using the Table command on the build tab.
- Generating new tables concurrently with the import of data from many different sources.

To create a blank database;

- Locate the **file tab**, click on the **new button** then click on **Blank Database**.

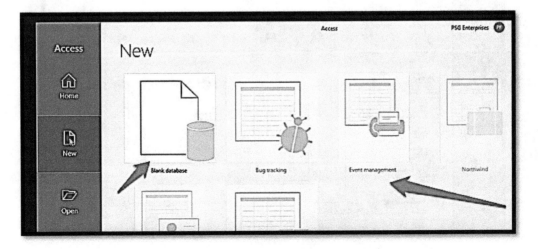

27

- Insert a name in the File Name box. If you would like to change the location of the file from the default, choose **Browse** to get a location to put the database, browse to the location then click on the **OK button**.
- Click on the **Create option**.

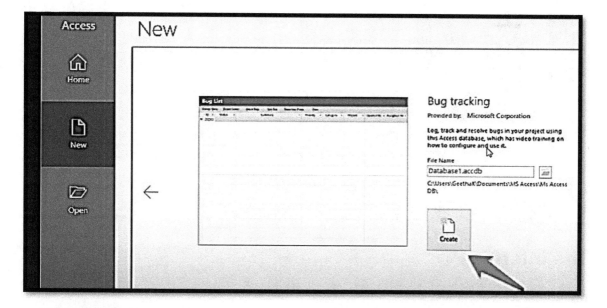

Table1 is an empty table that Access creates while designing the database. Table1 is then opened in the Datasheet view. The click to **Add column's** empty cell is where the pointer is positioned.

- You can then begin to include data or you can choose to have the data pasted from another source.

Working in an Excel worksheet is designed to be extremely similar to inserting data in a Datasheet view. Next, as you enter data, the table structure is generated. A new field is defined in the table after a new column is added to the datasheet. The data type of each field will then be automatically determined by Access based on the information you have to enter.

If you don't need to insert data in Table1;

- Simply click on the **close button**. If you have made changes to the table, Access will then prompt you to **save the changes**.
- Click on the **yes button** to save the changes, click on the **no button** if you want to discard them, or click on the **cancel button** to leave the table open.

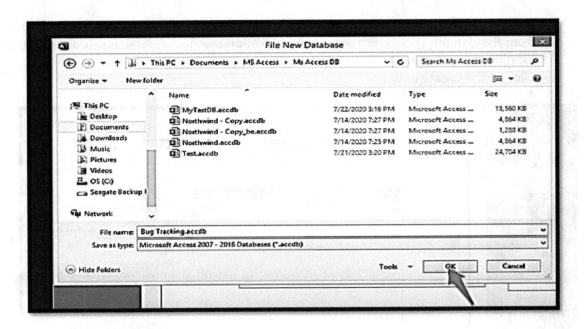

The Interface

The Access screen will fully open once you have created or opened a new database. The Access Ribbon is located at the top of the screen. You'll find the navigation pane on the left. The majority of the Access interface is composed of these two essential elements. Additionally, you have the Quick Access toolbar at your disposal, which you may personalize with the commands that you use most frequently.

The panel for Navigation

The primary way to view and access all of your database objects is through the navigation pane, which by default appears on the left side of the Access window. Access object types including forms, reports, tables, queries, and more are displayed in the left-hand navigation pane. It can also be used to display a combination of several kinds of things.

The navigation options are divided into two categories:

- Navigate **To Category and Filter By Group**.
- Before selecting an option under Filter By Group, you must first select an option under Navigate to Category. The Navigate to Category option you have chosen will determine the Filter By Group options that are displayed to you.

Custom

The Custom option designs a new grouping in the navigation pane. It has objects that can be moved and placed in the tab area. Items that are added to a custom group still show in their various object-type views.

- All of the previously created client groups are included in the Filter By Group category when you select **Custom**. Any of the defined custom groups can be filtered by using the Filter By Group category.

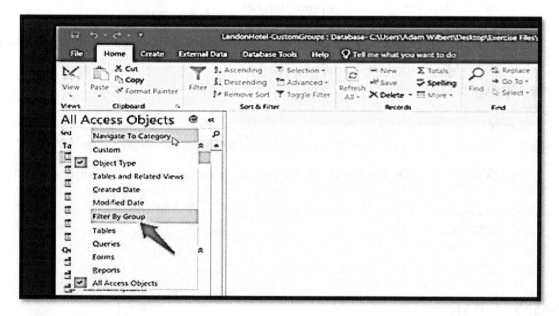

Object Type

The Object Type option is very similar to the previous versions of Access. **When you choose the Object Type, the following options are under Filter By Group:**

- Tables
- Queries
- Forms
- Reports
- All Access Objects

By default, the navigation pane displays all of the objects in the database in use.

- Choose **All Access Objects** when you must have been working with any one of the filtered views and wish to see all of the objects in the database.

Tables and Related Views

Here is where a little clarification is required. Access makes sure that the developer is always aware of the connections that are concealed between items in the database. For example, a certain table may appear in several queries or be referred to from a report or form. By choosing Tables and Related Views, you may determine which objects each table must have had an impact on.

- When you choose **Tables and Related Views**, the **Filter By Group category** will then be populated by the Tables in your database.
- Choosing each object that is in the **Filter By Group category** will also filter the list to that specific object and the other entire dependent and precedent objects that are related to it.

Date Designed

The created date option helps with the grouping of database objects by the date in which it was created. This setting is quite useful when you need to know just when an object was created.

- When you choose the **Created Date option**, some or all of the options below will be made available under the Filter By Group:
- Today
- Yesterday
- Last Week
- Two Weeks Ago
- Older

Tweaked Date

Using this option, objects can be grouped according to the date they were modified. This option resembles the generated date option slightly more. **Likewise, selecting this option will enable you to access some or all of the following options under the Filter By Group:**

- Today
- Yesterday
- Last Week
- Two Weeks Ago
- Older

The Ribbon

The Ribbon serves as Access's primary command interface and may be considered the main replacement for toolbars and menus. One of the ribbon's primary benefits is that it is supposed to combine, into one location, all the many jobs or points of entry that previously needed menus, task windows, toolbars, and other UI elements to appear. Instead of having to look in many locations, you now have a single location to look for commands. The ribbon, which displays the commands in the active command tab, appears at the top of the main Access window when a database is accessed. There are numerous command tabs on the ribbon with embedded commands. The File, Home, Create, External Data, and Database Tools tabs are the primary command tabs in Access. The instructions in each of these command tabs are grouped in relatively relevant ways, and these groups exhibit some of the recently added user interfaces, such as the gallery, which is just a new control type that presents options visually.

- **File**: Upon clicking on **the File tab**, the **Office Backstage view** will be opened. The backstage view has several different options for the creation of **databases, opening databases, saving, and configuring databases**.

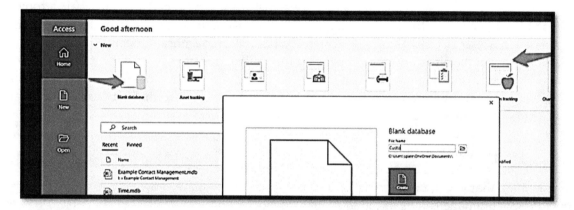

- **Home**: The Home tab's theme is frequently utilized. All of the unconnected commands that you frequently use when dealing with Access can be found here. For example, there are instructions for filtering, sorting, formatting, and copying and pasting.
- **Create**: Access contains commands on this tab that help with object design. You will undoubtedly spend a lot of time on this tab since this is where the majority of the work is done. The construction of tables, forms, queries, reports, and macros can begin here.

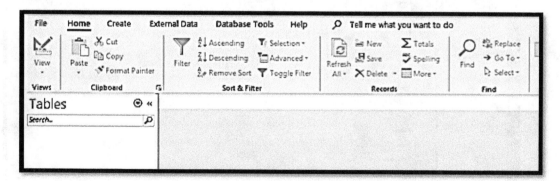

- **External Data**: The integration of Access with several different data sources is the specific focus of this page. You will find commands on this tab that allow you to deal with

SharePoint or other platforms, import and export data, and make connections to external databases.

- **Database Tools**: This category contains instructions that are especially related to your database's internal operations. Tools for building associations between tables, documenting your database, analyzing database performance, and compacting and fixing your database can all be found here.
- **Help**: There is a help tab in Access 2024 that doesn't have database functionality though it helps with the provision of various links that support training.

The toolbar for Quick Access

One-click access to a variety of actions is made possible via the Quick Access Toolbar, a toolbar that sits directly next to the ribbon. In addition to the saved, undo, and redo buttons that come pre-installed, you may tailor the Quick Access Toolbar to include more frequently used functions. Additionally, you have the option to reposition the toolbar and change its default small size to a much larger one. The command tabs on the ribbon will have a little toolbar next to it. The toolbar will then be shown beneath the ribbon with its entire width expanded when it becomes necessary to adjust to the greater size.

- When you click on the **drop-down arrow** close to the Quick Access toolbar, you will discover that there are more commands available. If you would like to add any of these commands to the Quick Access toolbar, simply **fix a checkmark** close to it.

Keep in mind that you are not restricted to the instructions that are shown in the drop-down list. Any form of command can be included at your discretion.

Follow the steps below to add a command to the Quick Access toolbar;

- Select the More Commands option by clicking on the drop-down arrow next to the Quick Access toolbar. The Quick Access toolbar dialog box will then appear as a result.
- Select **All Commands** from the drop-down list located on the left side of the screen.

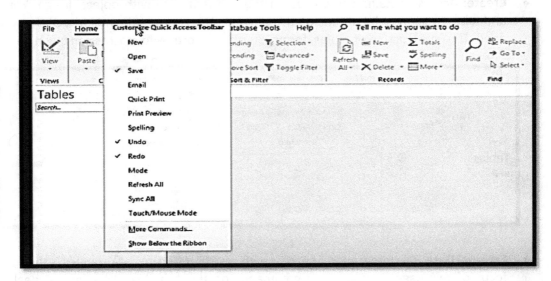

- From the alphabetical list of commands, choose **the one** you have the most interest in and then select **the Add button**.
- When all is set and done, select **the OK button**.

The aforementioned chapter provides a comprehensive description of the Quick Access toolbar, tables, and other relevant views in addition to the Access welcome page. I would assume that by this point you are familiar with table design, database design, and inserting and deleting rows.

Activity

1. Create an empty database.
2. Mention 3 features that can be found in the interface of Microsoft Access.

PART II

UNDERSTANDING ACCESS TABLES

The chapters in this aspect throw more light on the various techniques that can be used to create and also manage Access database tables, the main part of any application that is being built into Access. These chapters are way beyond merely describing how tables can be built. You will learn the basic concepts that are very important in the use of capabilities that have been documented in the other parts of this book.

CHAPTER 3

DESIGNING ACCESS TABLES

This chapter is all about the creation of tables and all that has to do with tables. Here you get to establish the database containers to get hold of tables, forms, queries, reports, and also code that you build even as you learn more about Access.

Diverse Types of Tables

A table in Microsoft Access is the same as a table containing data, although different tables have distinct functions in Access applications. A database table can be stored as one of roughly three types: an object table, a transaction table, or a join table. It will be easier for you to know how to design a table if you know exactly what kind to make.

Object tables

This type of table is the most common. All of the rows in this type of table contain information about real items. Real-world objects are those records in a table, usually called tblCustomers, that have details about a particular customer. The fields in an object table show the attributes of the object they also represent. A City field provides more information about a single customer attribute, which is the particular city in which the client resides. When creating something, it is best to consider the qualities that make that specific thing special or that are also highly significant.

Transaction tables

After the object table, the next very common table is the transaction table. Each record of a transaction table contains information about a particular event. When you place an order for a pen that can be said to be an example of an event. If you would like to have the details of all of the orders, there might be a need for you to name a **table tbl PenOrders.** Since the precise moment an event occurs is a crucial piece of information to record, transaction tables typically have a Date/Time field. Another extremely popular kind of column is one that refers to an object table, such as a customer reference in tblCustomers that placed the order. As you prepare to establish a transaction table, remember to include the information that the event has created as well as the individuals that were involved.

Join tables

Join tables are extremely important to a well-designed database and are quite simple to construct. The method of linking two tables is usually quite straightforward, although occasionally there are ambiguities in the relationship. Using a book as an example, a buyer ordering a book may request multiple writers, and an author may have multiple books as well. When this kind of relationship occurs, it is known as a many-to-many relationship, a join table will be in the middle of both tables. A join table most times has a name that shows the association like a tblAuthorBook. A join table has just three fields: a reference to one side of the association, a unique field to identify each record, and a reference to the other side of the association.

Designing a New Table

Making a new database table is a lot of fun and can include a lot of science because it also calls for some knowledge of art. You must be aware of the user's requirements before you can create a database. This will guarantee that the table you create directly satisfies the demands of the user. Planning tables is always a very smart place to start before using Access tools to add tables to the database. Many tables, particularly those that are rather small, don't require any thought before being added to the database. For example, if your goal is simply to create a table with names of states and nations, you won't need to plan as much. However, there are more intricate entities that will want additional planning. They need a significant amount of time and energy to be invested. It should be noted that failing to thoroughly plan before creating a table does not necessarily indicate that everything went wrong because you can always make changes to the table you ultimately generated, but doing so will cost you a great deal of time that might have been saved with meticulous planning.

Designing tables

There are lots of steps involved in designing tables. When you follow the steps in the order below, your table design can be created with so much ease requiring little or no effort:

- Create **the new table**.
- Insert **the field names, data types, properties, and descriptions**.

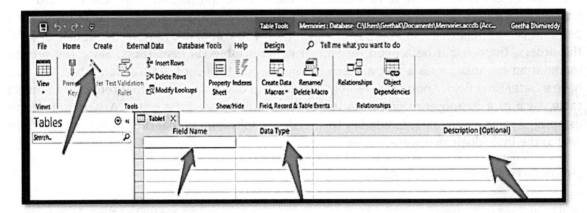

- Fix the **table's primary key**.

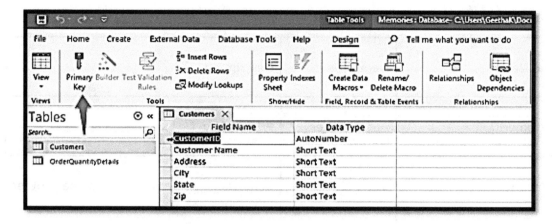

- Create **various indexes for appropriate fields**.
- Finally, ensure you **save the table's design**.

Rarely, you can truly finish "building" a table; this is because changes in the needs of users or the scope of the business may require modifications to the table, which are often made in the design view. In essence, the objects that are already there in the database handle the majority of the actions that are performed in the database on an application. Either an item you added directly or an object that another developer added later. Essentially, it is nearly the same as constructing a database component from scratch when it comes to maintaining an existing one.

There are two different ways tables can be added to the Access database and both methods are through the Tables group on the Create tab;

- **Clicking the Table button**: This technique adds a new table with a single Auto number field called ID to the Datasheet view of the database.
  Here, you will notice an option named Click **to Add column**, this option is intended to allow users to quickly include fields to a table. All that is left of you to do is to just insert data in the new column. **This is done by;**
  - Right-clicking **the heading of the field.**
  - Clicking **on the rename field.**
  - Insert **a name for the field.**
  Following the addition of the new column, you may adjust the field's formatting, validation rules, and other characteristics using the tools found on the Fields tab of the Ribbon.
- **Clicking the Table Design button**: Using this procedure, a table in the database's Design view is added. The table designer is considerably simpler to use, and each column has clear labeling. The Field Name column, located farthest to the left, is where field names are inserted into the table. Every field in the table has the data type added to it, and a description field is always available.

Study the basic design of the table below;

Field Name	Data Type	Description
CustomerID	AutoNumber	Primary key
Company	Short Text	Contacts; employer or some other affiliations.
Address	Short Text	Contact's address
City	Short Text	Contact's city
State	Short Text	Contact's state
zip code	Short Text	Contact's zip code
Phone	Short Text	Contact's phone
Fax	Short Text	Contact's fax
Email	Short Text	Contact's email address
Website	Short Text	Contact's web address
OrigCustomerDate	DateTime	Date the contact first bought something

		from SimAde Limited
CreditLimit	Currency	The customer's credit limit is Euro
CreditBalance	Currency	The customer's current balance in Euro
Credit Status	Short Text	General description of the customer's credit status
LastSalesDate	DateTime	Most recent or the last date the customer bought something from SimAde Limited
TaxRate	Number (Double)	Sales tax that applies to the customer.
DiscountPercent	Number (Double)	Customary discount provided to the customer
Notes	Long Text	Notes and observations as it pertain to this customer
Active	Yes/No	If the customer will still be buying things from SimAde Limited

Take note that the 255-character Field Size is the default setting for the fields above that contain ShortText. Even though it is unlikely that a person's name will require 255 characters, it is still free to allow for rather lengthy names.

Let me quickly add that the Table Design window consists of two major areas;

- **The field entry area**: This option is always located at the top of the window and is used to insert the name of the field and also the type of data. You can also choose to **add an optional description**.
- **The field properties area**: This is where the field's characteristics are specified, and it's often located at the bottom of the window. Among other things, some of these properties are the input mask, format, default value, and field size. The data type field determines which primary properties are displayed in the properties box.

Making use of the Design tab

The design tab of Access has a lot of controls that help with the creation of a new table definition. The controls on the Design tab affect the important table design considerations.

Primary Key

Access will automatically generate a primary key for a database table whenever you create one, but you can additionally designate a particular field to serve as the main key for your database table. In Access, a field—or sometimes a group of fields—that has unique values across all tables serves as the main key. Numerous features are offered by the primary key, such as unique identification if every database row has a value that is never changed and the row is never empty. Traditionally you will always find the primary key at the top of the list of fields in the table although it can be found anywhere right within the table's design.

Insert Rows

When you click on this option, a blank row will be inserted above the position that the mouse cursor is occupying.

- For example, when you click the Insert Rows button in the Table Designer when the cursor is in the second row, an empty row will be put in the second position, moving the second row to the third position.

Delete Rows

When you click on this option it takes off a row from the table's design.

- Note that **clicking on this row** activates the deletion immediately; there is no prompt to confirm the deletion before the row is removed.

Property Sheet

When this button is clicked, the Property Sheet for the entire table is displayed. Certain properties enable the specification of crucial table features, such as the ability to apply validation rules across the entire database or provide a different sort order for the data in the table.

Indexes

Access finds and sorts records much more quickly when it uses an index. Records' locations are stored in an index according to the field—or fields, as the case may be—that you have selected for indexing. Access can access data by merely relocating it to the appropriate area once it has determined its location through the index.

Dealing with fields

To create a field, just enter the field name and data type in the upper section of the Table Design window's field entry area. The function of the field can be inferred from the Description attribute. When data is being inserted, a description appears in the status bar at the bottom of the screen. This description can be very helpful to users of the application. You may specify how each field will be used by adding the properties in the field properties area after you have inserted the name and data type of each field.

Giving a field a name

You as a developer should make sure that the name you choose for a field adequately describes it to Access, the system user, and you. They shouldn't be excessively long, but they should be sufficiently long to enable the field's function to be immediately defined.

If you want to insert a name for a field, place the pointer in the first row of the Table Design window beneath the Field Name column then insert a valid name ensuring that the rules below are observed;

- Field names can include spaces. The spaces should be avoided in field names for the same reasons they are avoided in table names.
- You cannot make use of low-order ASCII characters, for instance, Ctrl+J or Ctrl+L.
- You cannot start with a blank space.
- Field names can be from 1 to 64 characters in length.
- Field names can include letters, numbers, and special characters except for period (.), exclamation point (**!**), accent grave (**'**), and brackets (**[]**).

You can enter field names in mixed case, lowercase, or uppercase. If you type the field name incorrectly for any reason, just move the cursor to the appropriate location and make the necessary repair. Even when the table contains data, you can always modify the name of a field. The database itself doesn't care if you name a table tblCustomers or TblCustomers because Access is not case-sensitive. It is completely up to you whether you choose to use uppercase, lowercase, or mixed-case characters, but none of your selections should be made to make the table names easy to read and descriptive. Additionally, you must have saved the table. If you alter the field name used in reports, forms, or queries for any reason, you must also update the objects. A primary source of mistakes in Access applications is renaming fundamental database objects, like tables and fields, and then not propagating those changes throughout the database.

Identifying a type of data

It isn't just enough to insert a field; you must also indicate the type of data that will be found in each of the fields. In Access, you can decide to make any choice out of the several data types.

The data types that are available are shown below;

Data Type	Type of Data Stored	Storage Size
Short Text	Alphanumeric characters	255 characters or lesser
Long Text	Alphanumeric characters	1GB of characters or lesser
Number	Numeric values	1,2,4, or 8 bytes; 16 bytes for Replication ID (GUID)
Large Number	Numeric values	8 bytes
Date/Time	Date and time data	8 bytes
Currency	Monetary data	8 bytes
Auto Number	Automatic number increments	4 bytes; 16 bytes for Replication ID (GUID)
Yes/No	Logical values: Yes/No, True/False	1 bit (0 or -1)

OLE Object	Pictures, graphs, sound, video	Up to 1GB (disk space limitation)
Hyperlink	link to an Internet resource	1GB of characters or much less
Attachment	A special field that allows you to attach external files to an Access database.	Varies by attachment
Calculated	A field that saves a calculation based on all the other fields that are in the table	Determined by setting the Result Type Property
Lookup Wizard	Shows data from another table	Generally 4 bytes

There are certain questions you need to have answers to before you make your choice of data type for the new fields in your tables;

- **What is the data type?** Verify that the data type displays the information that is kept in the field. To save numbers such as quantities and prices, select one of the numeric data types. Though your applications won't be able to apply mathematical operations like addition or multiplication on phone numbers, make sure you don't store information like social security numbers or phone numbers in numeric fields. Instead, it will use fields meant for common data, such as phone numbers and Social Security numbers.
- **What are the possible storage requirements of the data type you have chosen?** The storage requirements of a long integer (four bytes) are essentially double that of an integer, even though you can use the Numeric data type with a field size or a long integer in place of an integer or byte. This indicates that twice as much memory is required to utilize and manipulate the number, and twice as much disk space is required to store its value. Make sure you choose the smallest field size or data type that can hold the largest value you will ever have in that field in the end.

- **Will there be a need for you to sort or have the field indexed?** Since they have a binary nature, Long Text, and OLE object fields cannot be sorted nor can they be indexed. Make use of Long Text sparingly. The overhead needed to save and work with Long Text fields is quite considerable.
- **What is the impact of the data type on sorting requirements?** Numeric data is sorted in a much different manner from text data. With the use of numeric data type, a sequence of numbers will sort as expected: 1,2,3,4,5,10,100. The very same sequence saved as text data will be sorted as 1,10,100,2,3,4,5. If it is necessary to sort text data in a numeric sequence, there will be a need for you to apply a conversion function to the data first before you can begin sorting.
- **Is the data text or date?** Whenever you are working with dates, it is almost always better for you to have the data stored in a Date/Time field than as a Short Text field. Text Values sort quite differently from dates which can cause upsets to reports and other output that depend on a chronological order. Resist the urge to save dates in one Date/Time field and time in a separate Date/Time field. The Date/Time field is designed specifically to deal with both dates and times and also it is very easy to show just the date or time portion of a Date/Time value. A Date/Time field is also expected to save discrete date and time, and not a time interval. If you need to keep track of durations you can make use of two Date/Time fields- one to record the start time and the other to record the end or probably a Long Integer field to save the number of elapsed seconds, minutes, hours, and so on.
- **What reports will be needed?** You will be unable to sort or group Long Text OLE data on a report. If it is important to prepare a report based on Long Text or OLE data, simply include a Tag field such as a date or sequence number which can be used to offer a sorting key to the table.

Inserting description for a field

Inserting a description for a field is not compulsory, it is used only to help you remember what the field is about or to let another developer know what the field is about. Most times, the description column is not used at all, or you make use of it for fields that do not have a very obvious purpose. If you insert a field description, it will be displayed on the status bar anytime you make use of that field in Access within the datasheet or form. Field description helps to state specifically a field that has an ambiguous purpose or offers the user a more complete explanation of the appropriate values for the field when the data is being entered.

Specifying data validation rules

Data can be vetted or validated in Access desktop databases immediately after it is inserted with the use of validation rules. The expression builder can be used to help you format the rule rather quickly and without any form of delay. You can choose to set validation rules in either table design or table datasheet View.

There are three types of validation rules in access;

- **Field Validation Rule**: Field validation rule can be used and the specification of a criterion that all field values must meet is not compulsory for you to indicate the current field as part of the rules. You should only do that if you're using the field in a function. With the use of an input mask, it is much easier to insert restrictions on any type of character in a field. For example, you can have a date field that has a validation rule that disallows values and the past.
- **Record Validation Rule:** You can use a record validation rule to indicate a condition that all records must ensure they are satisfied. You can compare values across different fields with the use of a record validation rule. For example, if you have a record with two date fields there might be a need for the value of a field to always go before the value of the other field.
- **Validation on a form:** You can make use of the Validation Rule property of a control on a form to indicate a particular criterion that all values need to add to that control. The validation rule control property works similarly to a field validation rule. Typically you use a validation form rule rather than a field validation rule if the rule was indicated only to that form and not to the table no matter where it has been used.

The last major design is of major concern to data validation which of course becomes very necessary as users insert data. You will need to ensure that only data that is good finds its way into your system. There is a need to deal with various types of data validation. you can test for individual items that you know, and ensure you stipulate the gender field which of course can only accept male and female values or unknown ones.

Creating TBL Customers

When working with different types of data, you should be prepared to create the final working copy of TBL customers.

Making use of AutoNumber fields

Access ensures that it provides important considerations to Autonumber Fields. You will not be able to alter a field that has been defined before from another type to AutoNumber if any data has been included in the table. If you attempt to alter a field that is already in existence to an AutoNumber, there will be an error prompt saying;
- **Once you enter data in a table, you can't change**

There will be a need for you to include a new AutoNumber field and then you can begin working with it rather than changing a field that is already existing AutoNumber.

Completing TBL customers

When viewing TBL customers' design view, you are then ready to finalize all that has to do with its design. All you have to do is insert the field names and data into the table. On the next page, I'll be explaining how to alter fields that already exist which also includes organizing the field order, altering a field name, and also deleting a field. **Below are the steps for adding a field to a table structure;**

- Place **the cursor** in the field name column in the room where you want the field to appear.
- Insert **the field name** and press **enter** or you can also choose to press the **tab button** to move the data type column.
- Choose **the field data** type from the list that drops down in the data type column.
- If you need to, you can add a **description** for the field in the description column.

Go through each of the steps again to design each of the data entry fields for tbl customers. You can choose to press down the arrow key to move between rows and you can also make use of the mouse and click on any of the desired rows. For a shorter method, you can choose to tap the F6 button to switch the focus from the top to the bottom of the table design window.

Altering a Table Design

No matter how well you have designed your table, every table will require a change from time to time. You might discover that you need to include another field, remove an existing one, change the name of a field or the data type, or simply have to reorganize the order of the names of the fields. Although the design of a table can be changed at any point in time you must act every time and also ensure that you give special consideration to the table that has data in them. Ensure that you are very careful with the changes you make to avoid damaging the data in the table like making text Fields smaller or having to change the field size property of number fields. Whenever you wish, you can always include a new field to a table without having any issues but you might experience a little bit of difficulty if you attempt to change Fields that already exist. it is not advanced to change the name of the field after you have used the table in an application however there are exceptions to this.

Inserting a new field

At one point you might need to insert a new field. Follow the steps below to have a new field inserted.

- Locate **the table design window.**
- Put **your cursor** on a field that already exists.
- Right-click **on a field** in the table design surface.
- Choose to **insert rows** or you can also choose to click **the insert rows button** on the Design tab on the ribbon.
- Once this has been done a new row will be added to the table after which you can then insert a new field definition.

When you insert a field, this does not in any way disturb other fields or data contained in other fields that already exist. If you have queries, forms, or reports that you're making use of in the table there might be a need for you to add the field to those objects as well.

Deleting a field

You can make a mistake when you are creating a table. No one is perfect. There are three ways to delete a field.

- Choose **the field by selecting the role selector** and then press the select button.
- Right-click **on the field** you have chosen and click on **delete rows** from the shortcut menu.
- Choose **the field** and click on the **delete rows** button from the tools group on the Design tab on the ribbon.

There will always be a notice indicating that data in the selected field will be lost if you delete a field that contains data. Make sure you truly want to remove the data for that field if the data involves tables. Keep in mind that removing the same field from queries, forms, reports, macros, and VBA code that utilizes the field name will also be necessary. You must also update any references to a deleted field throughout all of Access if that field is removed for whatever reason. Because a field name can be used in forms, queries, reports, and even table data validation, you must thoroughly review your system to find any situations when using the particular field name could be necessary.

Modifying the location of a field

A field is not supposed to be static; rather, the sequence in which you entered them in the table's design dictates which columns appear from left to right in the datasheet view of the table. If you decide that your field has to be restructured for any reason,
- Click on **the field selector** and with the use of the mouse move the field to your preferred location.

Altering a field name

If desired, you have the option to modify the field's name by selecting it in the table design window and adding a new one. Access always makes sure that the table design is updated automatically. This may be a rather simple process as long as you are creating a new table. However, as was previously mentioned, there may be some minor issues if the name of an existing field is changed.

Changing a field size

Have you erred in your flute design, as enlarging a flute a few times is a straightforward process in a design table? All you have to do is set a whole new field size for a specific number of fields or raise the field size property for the text field. To make sure you don't select a new size that allows fewer decimal places than you already have, be sure to pay attention to the decimal places attribute in the number field. Whenever there is a need to make a field size smaller ensures that none of the data in the table is larger than the new field width. When you choose a smaller field size you might lose data in the process.

Dealing with issues regarding data conversion

If, despite your best efforts, you find yourself in a situation where you need to alter the data type of a field that holds data, you may have to lose some data while the conversion occurs.

You should also be aware of the effects of a data type conversion on data that is existing;

- **Any data type to AutoNumber**: cannot be done. The Auto Number field type must be created from scratch in a new field.
- **Short Text to Number, Currency, Date/Time, or Yes/No**: In most cases, there may be no data loss throughout the converting process. Any values entered that turn out to be improper will be instantly removed.
- **Long Text to Short Text**: a simple conversion that doesn't require data corruption. Text that exceeds the field size specified in the Short Text field will be truncated and lost.
- **Number or Large Number to Short Text**: There will be no loss of information. the number value will be converted to text with the use of the general number format.
- **Number or Large Number to Currency**: Since the currency data type makes use of a fixed decimal point some precision might be lost even as the number is truncated.
- **Date/Time to Short Text**: There will be no loss of information. The date and time will also be converted to text with the general date format.
- **Currency to Short Text**: There will also be a lot of information. as a currency value will be converted to text without the use of the currency symbol.
- **Currency to Number**: This conversion is easy to understand and uncomplicated. As the currency value is converted to feet and entered into the new number field, some data may be lost. For instance, the decimal part will be removed when converting money to a long integer.
- **AutoNumber to Short Text**: Here, there is no data loss throughout the translation process—that is unless the remaining text field cannot contain the entire Auto number value. The number will then be truncated in this scenario.
- **AutoNumber to Number**: This is equally easy to understand and simple, but since the Autonumber value is adjusted to match the new number field, some data may also be lost. For instance, when the auto number is converted to an integer field, it will be truncated if it exceeds 32,767.
- **Yes/No to Short Text**: Simple conversion of Yes/No value to the text. No loss of data.

Allocating field properties

All tables in access are made up of Fields. The properties of a field describe the features and behavior of data that will be added to that field. A field's data type is the most important property since it also helps with the determination of the kind of data the field can store. You may handle the data in your tables with the help of the extremely potent field properties that are integrated into the Access table. The database engine typically provides information for the field property, which means that the property is applied everywhere the field value is used. For instance, if you set the default value property in the design table, the default value will be visible in the table's datasheet view as well as on forms and in queries. Field properties are also among the differences that exist between access tables and Excel worksheets. Having a proper understanding of field properties is just one of the numerous skills that are needed to start using an access table to store data as opposed to using an Excel worksheet. Each form of field data has a unique set of characteristics. For instance, Short Text fields have a Text Align property and Number fields have a decimal place attribute. There are quite a few distinct field characteristics, even if many data types share a number of them, which can easily lead to confusion or improper usage of the properties.

Common properties

Below is a list of all the general properties that you might need and it is based on the data type you must have chosen.

- **Field Size**: This option when applied to Short Text fields, limits the size of the field to the indicated number of characters. Always note that the default number is 255.
- **New Values**: This option applies to the auto number field. It also allows for the specification of random type or increment.
- **Format**: This option allows you to alter the data's appearance, including the date, capital letters, and other formatting, after it has been entered. There exist multiple forms in which data can be accessed. Many of these distinctions will be discussed at a later time.
- **Input Mask**: Data entry into a specified format, such as phone numbers, zip codes, social security numbers, and dates, is done using this option. Both text and numeric data formats can use this option.
- **Caption**: This is an optional label that is used instead of the name of the field. Microsoft Access makes use of caption property when it has to display control in a datasheet on a form or a report.
- **Decimal Places**: This option also helps with the specification of the number of decimal places for the currency number and large number data types.
- **Default Value**: When fresh data is entered into the field, this is the value that is automatically supplied. As long as it fits the field data type, any value can be used for this parameter. A default value is just an initial value that can be modified during the data input process. You only need to add the desired value to the default value property set to

indicate a value. Remember that a default value can be a text string or an expression expressed in a number.

- **Validation Rule**: This option helps ensure that the data inserted into the field conforms to some business rule like greater than zero.
- **Validation Text**: This is a message displayed when data fails validation.
- **Required**: This option helps to specify if there is any need for you to enter a value into a field.
- **Allow Zero Length**: To identify an empty string from a null value, this option aids in determining whether to insert one into a Short Text or Long Text field.
- **Indexed**: This option helps to speed up data access and also reduces data to unique values. Much later in this chapter, indexing is explained better.
- **Unicode Compression**: Applications that support many languages use this option. Regardless of the language or symbol used, office documents—including Microsoft Access reports—can be shown correctly with this requirement for twice as much data storage. In general, Unicode only matters if the program is going to be used in an unfamiliar setting.
- **IME Mode**: This is also known as the kanji conversion mode property and it is used to display if the Kanji mode is kept in use when the control has been lost. The setting of this option is of no relevance in English or European language applications.
- **IME Sentence Mode:** This option is used to determine the sequence mode of different table fields or form controls that shift in response to the attention entering or leaving a field. Additionally, this option's settings are meaningless in programs that are in the English or European languages.

Format

Numbers, dates, timings, and text can all be customized for how they appear and print using the format attribute. The format will be applied across the application if it is set at the table level. For any type of data, there are multiple format alternatives. For practically every kind of field data, Microsoft Access has built-in format options. The region and language settings in Windows settings can have an impact on the precise format that is utilized to display field values. Keep in mind that a value's format attribute only affects how it is shown; it has no bearing on the value itself or how it is stored in a database. Any of the pre-established formats can be used at any time, or you can utilize formatting symbols to build your unique format. In the controls property sheet, you have the option to set this property for control. For a field, you can additionally select whether to set this property in the query window's design view or the table design view. Using macros or Visual Basic for Applications (VBA) code is another alternative available to you. If you decide to build a custom format you should then construct a string in the field format property box. There are various symbols that you can use for each data type.

Microsoft Access provides a global format specification that is to be used in any custom format.

- **Space**: this helps to show space as characters.

- **SomeText**: this helps to show the texts that are in between quotes as literal text.
- **! Exclamation point**: this helps to have the display Left-aligned.
  - **Asterisk**: this helps to fill all space for the next character.
- **\ Backslash**: this helps to show the following character as a literal text. it uses the backslash to show characters that have no special meaning to Microsoft Access.
- **Color**: this helps to show the outputs in the color either black blue green red magenta yellow or white or will be shown between the brackets.

It is worth noting that the format property will always take precedence if perhaps both a format and an input mask have been defined.

Let us consider some types of formats below;

Field formats for number and currency

There are various field formats for number and currency fields. You can make use of one of the built-in formats or you can also choose to construct a custom format for yourself.

- **General number**: this is the number that is shown in the formats in which it was inserted.
- **Currency**: This aids in adding a thousand commas and places a decimal point two digits to the right of the decimal, enclosing negative values in parenthesis after that. The currency symbol, which is determined by the region and language settings in Windows settings, is displayed in a currency field and can be either a dollar sign or a euro sign.
- **Fixed**: this always shows at least a digit to the left and two digits to the right side of the decimal point.
- **Percent**: here the number value is usually multiplied by 100 and a percent sign will then be added to the right side.
- **Scientific**: scientific notation is usually used to show the number.
- **Euro**: helps to add the Euro currency as a prefix to the number.

Custom numeric format

Customers are designed when there is a combination of several symbols to create a format. The symbols that are used with number and currency fields are listed here;

- **. Period**: helps with specifying the exact place where the decimal point should be displayed.
- **, comma**: helps with separating values.
- **0 zero**: this is a placeholder for a digit.
- **# Pound sign**: this is a placeholder for nothing or a digit.
- **$ dollar sign**: this shows the dollar character sign.

- **% percent sign**: this helps with the multiplication of the value given by 100 and includes a percent sign on the right side.
- **E - OR e**: makes use of scientific notation to show the number. It makes use of a minus sign to show a negative exponent and displays no sign at all to show a positive exponent.
- **E+ OR+e**: makes use of scientific notation to show the number. It also uses a plus sign to show a positive exponent.

Built-in Date/Time formats

Built-in timings and dates for the months are shown below. Always keep in mind that the English United States region and language settings in Windows settings are the basis for all of the examples provided.

- **General Date**: You are not required to display a time value if the value, for whatever reason, only contains a date, nor are you required to display a date if the value contains a time. Time data is shown in the long-time format, and dates are displayed in the built-in short-date format (m/d/yyyy).
- **Long Date**: Friday, May 20, 2022.
- **Medium Date**: 20-MAY-15
- **Short Date**: 20/05/2022
- **Medium Time**: 8:32 pm
- **Short Time**: 20:32

Always note that date and time formats are influenced by the region and language settings in Windows settings.

Custom dates and time formats

Custom formats are designed by the construction of a very specific string that contains the symbols below;

- **: Colon**: this helps to separate time elements such as hours, minutes, and seconds.
- **/ Forward flash**: this is in The Separation of date elements like days, months, or years.
- **C**: this helps to instruct Microsoft Access to make use of the built-in general date format.
- **d**: this helps to show the day of the month as either one or two digits. (1-31)
- **dd**: this helps to show the date of the month with the use of two digits. (01-31)
- **ddd**: this helps to show the day of the week as a three-character abbreviation(Sun, Mon, Tue, Wed, Thu, Fri, Sat)
- **dddd**: this option makes use of the full names of the days of the week (Sunday Monday Tuesday Wednesday Thursday Friday Saturday)
- **ddddd**; makes use of the built-in Short Date format.
- **dddddd**; makes use of the built-in Long Date format.

- **w**: makes use of numbers to show the day of the week
- **ww**: this helps in showing the week of the year.
- **m**: shows the month of the year with the use of one or two digits.
- **mm**: shows the month of the year with the use of two digits adding zero as a prefix where need be.
- **mmm**: shows the month of the year as a three-character abbreviation such as Jan, Feb, Mar, Apr, May, Jun, Jul, Aug, Sep, Oct, Nov, Dec.
- **mmmm:** shows the full name of the months of the year e.g. January, February, March, etc.
- **q:** shows the date as the quarter of the year.
- **y:** shows the day of the year (1 through 366).
- **yy:** shows the year as two digits (for example, 15).
- **yyyy:** shows the year as four digits (2015).
- **h:** shows the hour using one or two digits (0–23).
- **hh:** shows the hour using two digits (00–23).
- **n:** shows the minutes using one or two digits (0–59).
- **nn:** shows the minutes using two digits (00–59).
- **s:** shows the seconds using one or two digits (0–59).
- **ss:** shows the seconds using two digits (00–59).
- **ttttt:** makes use of the built-in Long Time format.
- **AM/PM:** makes use of a 12-hour format with uppercase AM or PM.
- **am/pm:** makes use of a 12-hour format with lowercase am or pm.
- **A/P:** makes use of a 12-hour format with uppercase A or P.
- **a/p:** makes use of a 12-hour format with a lowercase a or p.

Long and Short Texts Formats

Anytime format is given to the Short text box, it facilitates the understanding of the information contained therein. Consumers utilize a variety of formats. To display the data entry in uppercase, the state text feud's former property has a greater than sign. Additionally, the weeds lookup display control property for the yes/no format is set to Text Box in the active field. Fields with short and long texts are typically shown as plain text by default. Use the following symbols when creating the format if a certain format is to be applied to either long text or short text field data;

- **@**: A character or space is needed.
- **&:** a character is not compulsory.
- **<:** forces all the characters used to their lowercase equivalent.
- **>:** forces all characters used to their uppercase equivalents.

Input Mask

A characteristic of Access is also the input mask. The pattern for data entry into a database can be restricted with the use of this tool. Furthermore, it can greatly facilitate data entry. One option is to limit access solely to employee IDs, phone numbers, and social security numbers. It also prevents characters and spaces from being entered into any of the spaces when this mask is used.

- A field input mask can be applied anywhere the Feud is shown such as query forms or reports.
- The input mask property value is a string that has about three semicolons separated sections.

The mask and its associated symbols are contained in the first area. If Microsoft Access is to store the actual characters found in the mosque alongside other data, this information is communicated to it in the second section. The third section defines the place order character, which tells the user how many characters to expect in the input area. When you use a zero, Microsoft Access is told to analyze small characters as part of the data, whereas when you use a one, Microsoft Access is told to store only the data itself.

Below are the characters that are used to compose the input mask string;

- **L:** A letter from A to Z is needed.
- **?:** A letter from A to Z is not compulsory.
- **A:** A character or digit is needed.
- **a:** A character or digit is not compulsory.
- **&:** Permits any character or space (needed).
- **C:** Permits any character or space (not compulsory).
- **. (period):** Decimal placeholder.
- **, (comma):** Thousands separator.
- **: (colon):** Date and time separator.
- **; (semicolon):** Separator character.
    - **(Dash):** Separator character.
- **/ (forward slash):** Separator character.
- **< (less-than sign):** changes all characters to lowercase.
    - **(greater-than sign):** changes all characters to uppercase.
- **! (exclamation point):** shows the input mask from right to left. Characters fill the mask from right to left.
- **\ (backslash):** shows the next character as a literal.
- **0:** A digit is required, and (+) and minus (−) signs are not permitted.
- **9:** A digit is optional, and (+) and minus (−) signs are not permitted.
- **#:** Optional digit or space. Spaces are taken off once the data has been saved in the table. Plus, and minus signs are allowed.

Take note that a query or form's field attribute typically uses the same masking characters. When using an action query to import or add data to a table, an input mask is disregarded. The Format attribute that a field is assigned can override an input mask. In this type of situation, the input mask only applies while the data is imputed and reformatted according to the format after the entry is finished. The input mask wizard makes it simple to construct an input mask for short text or Data/Time type fields, even though input masks can be manually insulted. In addition to listing the names of all the predefined input masks, the input mask wizard provides an example for each name. You have the option to select one of the predefined masks from the drop-down list.

- Click in the **Try It text box** and then insert **a test value** to see just how the data entry will be displayed.
- The following wizard screen will let you select the placeholder and modify the input mask when you have to.
- You can choose whether or not to store special characters, such as dashes, in your social security number on another wizard screen.
- Microsoft Access will automatically include the input mask characters in the field's property sheet when you have finished the wizard.

Not that you can insert any amount of custom mask that you might need. You can also decide on international settings so that you can work with various country masks. a custom input mask that you create in one database is always available in other databases.

Caption

The name that appears in the report's title bar at the top is called the caption. When a field is dragged from the field list to create a report, the control's default label is attached, and the caption property specifies what should be shown in that label. In the datasheet view, the caption can also be shown as the column headings for any tables or queries that contain the field. It is important to use considerable caution while working with the caption property. This is because, in the data view, the caption text appears as the column heads. In a query datasheet view, the column title can deceive you if you're not attentive. You should be aware that the column is mostly defined by the caption property and may not display the field name whenever the field is displayed in a query. This is because there isn't instant access to the field properties. If a field's property sheet in the query design view has a caption applied to it that has different text and different characteristics from the caption assigned in the table design view, things might get even more complicated. It should be noted that captions are allowed to include up to 2048 characters, which is more than plenty for all except the most in-depth descriptions.

Validation Rule and Validation Text

Bad data is kept out of your table with the use of validation rules. They primarily resemble query criteria. Using the properties box in the table design, you may make a rule for the table or a field. In Table Design, the validation rule attribute of a field you select appears in the bottom pane. Establishing requirements for inputs into the field is made easier with the help of the validation rule attribute. The validation rule ensures that data entered into the table complies with the fundamental specifications of the application; it is often applied by the ACE database engine. Validation properties are quite a good way to enforce business rules like making sure that a certain product is not sold for zero dollars or ensuring that an employee review date comes after the hire date. When a user's input does not match the specifications of the validation rule property, a message box with a string displayed in it is displayed via the Validation Text property. The Validation Text property value has a maximum length of 255 characters. You must specify a Validation Text value when using the validation rule property to prevent Microsoft Access from automatically displaying a generic message box when the rule is broken. It then describes allowed values for the field when you utilize the Validation Text attribute to provide users with a useful message.

It should be noted that toggle buttons and check box option buttons contained in an option group on a form are not covered by the validation rule property. A validation rule attribute that applies to every control in the option group is also present in the option group itself. Validation attributes are typically used to ensure that certain dates follow one another that values such as inventory quantities are entered with non-negative numbers, and that entries are limited to specific ranges of text or numbers. The validation rule property of the new control is not instantly passed to the validation rule of the field when you change a field to a form. To accomplish this, you must add a new validation rule value to the controls property sheet. After that, Microsoft Access will apply the table-level rule that has been established. When the emphasis must have departed from the table field or form control, attributes of the validation rules for fields and controls are also enforced. Both entities will be subject to the enforcement of any validation rule property that has been applied to a field and the bound control.

Required

Microsoft Access is always instructed to demand input into the field by the required property. If this option is enabled, input is required in the field, either through a table or a form control tied to the field. Keep in mind that a mandatory field's value can never be NULL. The necessary property is often enforced by the Microsoft Access database engine. Whenever a user tries to unbind a textbox control from a field that has the needed property set to yes, an error message is often displayed. The AllowZeroLength property can be used in conjunction with the required property. In figuring out whether a conflict exists or has an uncertain value.

Allow Zero Length

The Allow Zero Length Property indicates if you want a zero-length string to be a valid entry for either a short text or a long text field.

AllowZeroLength takes up the following values;

- **Yes:** this option is used when a zero-length string is a valid entry.
- **No:** with this, the table does not accept the zero-length strings but rather brings in a null value into the field when no valid text data has been supplied.

Combining the needed and AllowZeroLength attributes enables you to distinguish between data that is completely unknown and data that doesn't exist. You may need to store the correct value in the long text or short text box at some stage. Consider a customer without a phone number as an example of data that does not exist. To inform the user that they do not have a phone number, the phone number field should be left empty. It is anticipated that the phone number field for another client who is brand-new to the business will include a null value. You can make it easier for users of your application to determine when a field contains a null value by using an input mask. While the AllowZeroLength property permits zero-length strings in the field, the required property state controls whether a null value is accepted by the field. These two properties provide different ways to determine whether a value is present in the field or not.

Indexed

Microsoft Access is informed that you wish to utilize a field as an index in the table by the indexed property. Indexed To expedite the sorting and ordering of queries, fields are internally ordered. You should set a field's index attribute to yes if you plan to add it to queries regularly, sort or group it frequently, or use it in reports. Examples of such uses include adding the social security number to queries.

The valid settings for the indexed property are as follows;

- **No**: This means the field is not indexed period this is usually set by default
- **Yes (Duplicates OK)**: this means the field is indexed and Microsoft Access also offers duplicate values in a column. This is said to be the appropriate setting for values like names where it is likely that names like John will appear more than once in the table.
- **Yes (No Duplicates)**: This field is indexed but duplicates are not allowed in the column. You can use this setting for data that should stand out within the table like social security numbers and customers.

Note that the indexed property is set in the field properties sheet or on the table's property sheet. it is expected for you to use the tables property sheet to set multi-field indexes.

Having an Understanding of TBL Customers' Field Properties

It might be necessary for you to go back and make some changes to some of the fields after you've entered the field names, data types, and descriptions. Every field has characteristics, and every data type has a unique set of these characteristics. You will need to insert properties for the different sorts of data in tblCustomers.

- The field properties pane and the field entry grid can be switched between by using the F6 button. You can also select which pane to move between by clicking on it. Certain attributes allow you to drag the pointer into a field and see a list of possible values along with a downward-pointing arrow. A drop-down list displaying the values will appear when you select the arrow.

The field properties pane of the table design window has a second tab which is known as the lookup tab. When you click this tab you might see a single property which is the display control property. This property can be used for Short Text, number, and Yes/No fields.

Configuring the Primary Key

When building a Microsoft Access database, the values that are unique throughout a table serve as the primary keys for field forms. Primary keys have distinct values for each record and can be used to refer to a complete record. There can only be one primary key per table. When you construct a table in Microsoft Access, you have the option to specify what you want to use as the main key, or you can choose to design the primary key field automatically. When creating databases in Microsoft Access, the primary key's main purpose is to facilitate the establishment of associations between the tables in a relational database. Before you create the primary key in table Q, you cannot declare a foreign key in table Q to refer to table R. It is essential because it facilitates the usage of primary keys as links to connect your table to order tables. When building a Microsoft Access database, the primary key also provides a way to precisely and uniquely define the function of the data in a table. For instance, the employee number, which identifies each employee, would be the primary key in an employee table. There are certain procedures you must take when creating an Access database to add primary keys. Remember that each row must be uniquely identified by the field for a primary key to work. The CustomID field is the primary key in tblCustomers. To enable the database engine to discern between records, each customer has a distinct CustomerID number. Within the contacts table, CustomerID15 pertains to a single client.

Selecting a primary key

You will have to rely on another field, or a combination of fields, for it to be unique if the CustomerID field is absent. Since several customers may have the same company name, you will not be able to use the company field. Additionally, since multiple customers may have the same company name and city name, you cannot utilize the company and city fields interchangeably. Therefore, you must create a field, or a set of fields, that guarantees each record's uniqueness. You can solve this problem with ease when you add an AutoNumber field to play the role of the table's primary key. The primary key in tblCustomers is CustomerID, an AutoNumber field. Microsoft Access can add an Auto number field and use it as the primary key for the table if you are unable to select a field to serve as the primary key. Keep in mind that auto number fields make excellent main keys since Microsoft Access creates value for you. The value of an auto number field cannot be changed, and the number will never appear twice in the table.

Below are the properties of a good primary key;

- A good primary key identifies each record uniquely.
- A good primary key can never be null.
- A good primary key must be in existence when the record is created.

- A good primary key must be stable; it should never be changed once it has been established.
- A good primary key should be simple and straightforward and it should also have as few attributes as possible.

In conclusion, an ideal primary key is one that is a single field that is immutable and is guaranteed to be distinct within the table.

Designing the Primary Key

You can create a primary key with any of the three methods below. you have to start with opening a table in a design view then;

- Choose **the fields** that should be used as the primary key and click on the **primary key button** in the **Tools group** on the **Design tab of the ribbon**.

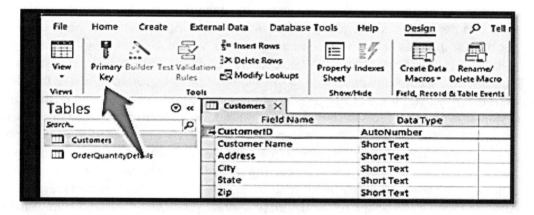

- Right-click the **field** and choose the **primary key** from the shortcut menu.
- Save the table without having to create a primary key and Microsoft Access will automatically create an Auto number field.

After you must have designated the primary key a key icon will be displayed in the gray selector area on the left of the name of the field to show that you have created a primary key.

Creating Composite Primary Keys

Stable characteristics that employ two distinct columns as the primary key are called composite keys. Keep in mind that a primary key in a table needs to have a unique value. You have the option to create your composite key if the table does not have any unique columns available. To create a unique value in your database, a composite key combines values. Primary keys improve query performance and are an important component of well-designed tables. In Microsoft Access, composite keys are completed in the design view. **To create the composite key simply;**
- Choose **the fields** you would want to add the **composite primary key**.

- Click on **the primary key button** on the tools tab of the ribbon. If you want to create a primary key from fields that are close to each other make sure you press the ctrl button when choosing the fields.

Composite primary keys are typically utilized when a developer strongly feels that data from naturally occurring databases should make up a primary key. Because developers are now aware that data can be quite unexpected, composite main keys have been increasingly popular in recent times. You will find that things sometimes go differently than expected if your users have ever promised that a certain field combination won't ever appear twice in the table. Maintaining relationships between tables is also crucial when using composite keys, as this might get more problematic because related data must be duplicated in all the databases where the primary key fields are present. By using composite keys, you are merely increasing the database's complexity without enhancing its integrity, stability, or other desirable properties.

Indexing Access Tables

Data is randomly entered into tables. However, the record in the orders table is always in chronological order which is often not helpful when compiling reports that have to do with customer orders. In cases like this, you would prefer to have data entered in the customerID order. The process of adding records to a Microsoft Access table is comparable to that of a fixed card. Typically, new records are appended to the middle of the table, which is where they should logically reside. However, it could be necessary to insert new data near existing records on the same customer in an order entry system. Sadly, this is not how Microsoft Access tables operate. A table's natural order is typically the order in which the entries were added to it; this order is also known as entry order or physical order to highlight the fact that the records are displayed in the table in the order that they were inserted. The utilization of natural order is not inherently harmful. In reality, if the table is tiny or not regularly queried, natural order makes more sense. In other cases, the data being added to the database is already in a well-organized state. Similar to how we use an index in a book, Access uses the index in a table to find data by searching for the specific spot in the index. Your table will typically contain one or more basic indexes. An index with just one field in the table is called a basic index. The table's records can be arranged in ascending or descending order using a basic index. In scenarios when natural order isn't possible, Microsoft Access provides indexing, which can expedite the process of finding and organizing records. By constructing and indexing a table, you can decide on a logical order for the records in that specific table. The index is used by Microsoft Access to maintain one or more internal sort orders for the table's contents. Access fields are not indexed by default, but it's difficult to imagine a table that doesn't require indexing of any kind. In the part that follows, I'll go over the reasons why indexing is crucial for Microsoft Access tables.

The need for indexes

Over half of the tables in Microsoft Access databases do not have indexes, according to data from Microsoft. The tables that have no index at all are included in these figures; tables that have improper indexes are not included. This indicates that a large number of people do not understand how crucial it is to index the tables in a Microsoft Access database. You can see why an index typically improves query performance. An index indicates that Microsoft Access maintains an internal sort of data on the data that are in the indexed column. As a result, practically any food that is frequently sorted on reports or forms or included in searches should be indexed. Microsoft Access has to go through every record in the database in search of matches if there isn't an index. This method is commonly referred to as "table scan." Before you can be certain you have located every pertinent card in the file, make sure you have searched every inch of the deck until you reach the end.

Multiple-field indexes

Multiple indexes also known as composite indexes are very easy to create.
- Locate **the design view** option
- Choose **the index indexes button** on the **Design tab of Ribbon**.

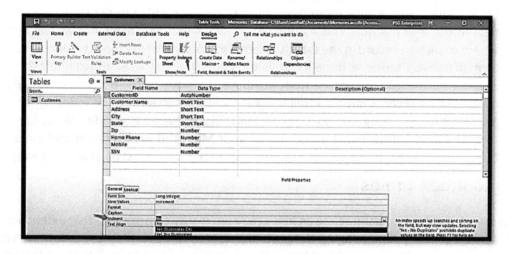

- The indexes dialogue box will then be displayed which will allow you to indicate the fields that you should include in the index.

Use the field name column to enter a name for the index. To select the fields you would want to have in the index, utilize the drop-down list. It is not a component of the composite index if any row that comes just below the row you have produced is missing the index name. To ensure that queries and sorting operations in both fields are completed quickly, Microsoft Access takes these two fields into account when determining the sort order on this table. Be aware that a composite index can have up to ten fields added to it. The only requirement is that none of the fields in the composite index be left empty and that it not be utilized as the table's primary key. The index properties are very easy to comprehend.

These properties are often applied to sing-field and composite indexes also:

- **Primary**: Microsoft Access will utilize the index as the table's main key when this option is set to yes. You have the option to designate multiple fields as the primary key, but you must make sure that you follow the rules that govern the primary keys. In particular, you must follow the rules that require the values of each primary key to be unique and that no field in the composite primary key should be left empty. As a result, NO is the default value for the Primary property.
- **Unique**: If the unique option is selected, the index needs to be unique in the table as well. Since the application's business rule may require that a Social Security number appears in the table just once, the Social Security number field can make a strong case for a unique index. On the other hand, be careful not to index the last name field because names like John and Alan are rather common, and it can only lead to more issues if a unique is indexed on last names like that. Anytime it is added to composite keys, the combination of field values must also be unique with each of the fields within the composite key duplicating fields that can be found within the table.
- **Ignore Nulls**: The records index may not contribute anything to the overall indexing if a field in the index is null. This essentially indicates that Microsoft Access will not know where to place a record in the table's internal index sort list if a record index contains any form of value. Therefore, if the index value is null, you may need to tell Microsoft Access to ignore a record. The Ignore Nulls attribute is always set by default to No, what this means is that records having a Null index value are inserted into the indexing scheme by Microsoft Access along with all other entries that also have a Null index value. Ensure you test the impact of the index properties on your Microsoft Access tables and make use of the properties that perfectly suit the data that is being handled by your database.

When to index tables

The extra work involved in maintaining an index may not justify creating one that extends beyond the table's primary key, depending on the potential number of records in the database. When a record is added or modified in a table, Microsoft Access needs to make sure that the information is updated, even if it may be considerably quicker to get data without an index. On the other hand, no additional file activity is required for modifications made to non-indexed fields. It is possible to retrieve data from fields without an index at the same speed as from fields with one. When dealing with very big tables, it is generally accepted as best practice to incorporate secondary indexes. Additionally, indexing fields other than primary keys can assist speed up searches. Indexing can reduce speed even if you have larger tables. It is almost inevitable that records in a table will be added or modified regularly. Every time you update or add a record to the table, Microsoft Access needs to update all of the indexes as well.

You might be thinking that since indexing is important why not just index everything contained in a table;

The first thing you should be aware of is that indexes make Microsoft Access databases larger. It is not necessary to have an index taking up space for every record in the table if you index a table that you shouldn't. More significantly, each time a record is added to the table, indexes cause a performance hit for every index in the table. Internal indexing has to be updated for every new record since Microsoft Access automatically changes the index whenever a record is added or withdrawn from the table. Every time a new record is added or an old record is removed from Microsoft Access, the indexes are adjusted by around ten times. This can lead to a noticeable delay on large tables, especially if your machine is running slowly. When working with Microsoft Access tables, you will probably start with the simplest one-field indexes and work your way up to more complicated ones as you gain experience with the program. Make sure you consider the trade-offs between increased search efficiency and the maintenance overhead associated with having a high number of indexes on your database.

Printing a Table Design

To print a table design simply;
- Click on the **Database Documenter button** that can be found in the Analyze group on the Database Tools tab of the Ribbon.

The tools provided by the analysis group make it simple to document your database items. Every time you click the Database Documenter button, the Documenter dialog box with the option to select which objects to print will appear. Additionally, you have the opportunity to adjust several printing choices.

Simply:
- Click on the **Options buttons**, and the Print Table Definition dialog box will be displayed which will allow you to choose the information needed from the Table Design to print. You can choose to print the different field names, all of their properties, the indexes, and also their network permissions.

Access will then produce a report once you've selected all of the desired settings. You have the option to send this report to the printer or examine it in a Print Preview window. As part of the documentation for the application, you can alternatively decide to save the report directly in the database.

Saving the Completed Table

Run through the properly to ensure that it is void of any form of mistakes. Once you have done this, you can then choose to save the table design by
- Clicking on the **file** then choosing the **save option** or you click on the **save button option** on the Quick Access toolbar in the upper left part of the Microsoft Access environment.

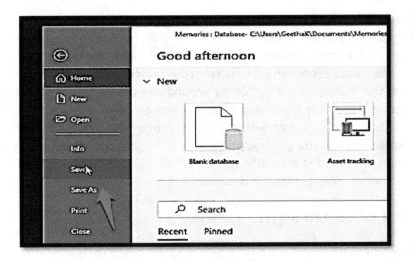

Microsoft Access needs you to give the table a name if this is the first time you're saving it. Table names are allowed to be up to 64 characters long, and they should always adhere to the standard Microsoft Access object naming conventions, which state that punctuation and numbers are allowed but not numbers at the start of the name. Microsoft Access will remind you to save a table if you are tempted to close one without first saving it, ensuring that no data is lost. **If the table has been previously saved and you only want to change the name it has been saved with;**

- Click **on file** then **save as then save Object as**. Then click on the **Save As button** and insert a **different table name**.

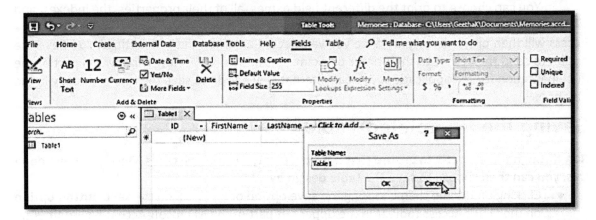

This will result in the creation of a new table and the retention of the previous table with its original name. Simply find the old table in the Navigation pane and click the **delete button** if it is necessary for you to remove it.

Adjusting Tables

There might be a need for you to make copies of the tables you have added to the database as backups. In most cases, there might be a need for you to copy only the design of the table and not necessarily have to insert all the data in the table. **Below are the table operations you can perform in the Navigation pane;**

- Changing **the names of tables**.
- Deleting **tables**.
- Copying **tables in a database**.
- Copying a **table to another database**.

Renaming tables

From time to time there might be a need for you to change the name of a table all you have to do is

- Right-click on **the name of the table** in the navigation pane and choose **the name** from the drop-down list or you can choose **the table** in the navigation pane and press the **F2 button**. When you must have changed the name of the table it's being shown in the table list and it will reorganize the tables that are in the list in alphabetical order.

Deleting tables

You created and should also be able to delete. Tables can be deleted once they have served their purpose and you are sure you will not need them again moving forward. **To delete a table,**

- You can either choose the table in the navigation pane or then hit the delete button, or you can right-click on its name to get the shortcut menu and select "**Delete.**" The table will be erased when you click the delete button, just like in practically all traditional programs. You will be prompted to confirm the deletion by clicking the **Yes button.**

It is important to remember that deleting the tables without asking for permission occurs when you simultaneously depress the shift and delete buttons. The combination of these two keys can be used to remove a table if you are certain about it; however, if you are unsure, it is best to utilize the previously described approach.

Transferring tables in a database

Alternatively, you can duplicate the table you wish to reproduce and have it put exactly where you want it, saving you the trouble of creating another table of a similar design somewhere else in the database.

- When you copy the table and then click on the **paste option**, the Paste Table As dialog box will then be displayed, which will also **ask you to choose from the three options below;**

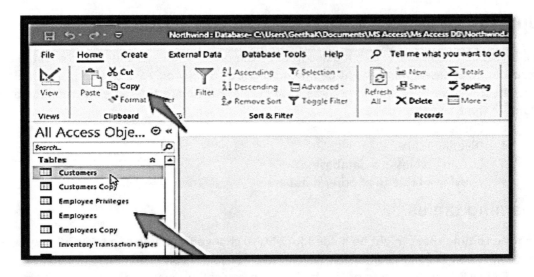

- **Structure only**: An empty table with the same design as the one you need to copy will appear when you select the structure only option. This is the ideal choice to utilize if you want an already-made framework that you can copy tables to.
- **Structure and Data**: When you click on this option, a complete table with the data in it will be displayed.
- **Append Data to Existing Table:** Adding data from the table you need to copy to the bottom of another table is made easier with the help of this option. This feature comes in handy when you need to merge tables, such as when you need to add information from a monthly transaction to a history table that spans a year.

To have a table copied, follow the steps below;

- Right-click on **the name** of the table in the navigation pane and choose the copy option from the shortcut menu or you can choose to click the **copy button** in the clipboard group on the home tab.
- Right-click **anywhere** in the navigation pane and choose the **paste option** from the shortcut menu or you can choose to click the **paste button** and the clipboard group on the home tab
- Upon completion, insert the **name** of the new table.
- Select either of the **paste options** as described above that use structure only, structure and data, or append data to an existing table.
- Finally, click on the **ok button** to complete the operation.

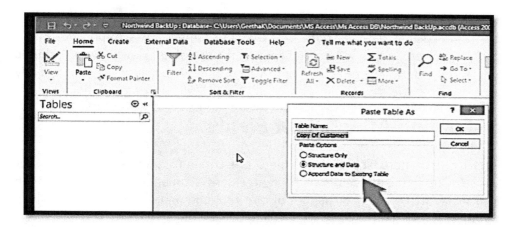

Moving a table to a different database

You can choose to copy tables between databases in the same way that you can transfer tables inside databases. It is possible that you will need to generate a backup on a different database or that you will need to share a common table across many systems. The relationship that exists between these tables will not be copied when you copy them to another database. Only the table layout and data will be duplicated to the other database using Microsoft Access. Transferring a table from one database to another is nearly identical to transferring a table inside the same database.

- Right-click **on the name** of the table in the Navigation pane and choose **Copy** from the shortcut menu or you can just click the copy button in the clipboard group on the home tab.
- Open the other **Microsoft Access database** and right-click **anywhere** in the navigation pane. Click on the **paste option** from the shortcut menu or you can choose the **paste button** in the clipboard group on the home tab.
- Insert the **name** of the new table.
- Choose one of the following **paste options; structure only, structure and data, or append data** to an existing table.
- Finally click on the **ok button** to have this operation completed.

Including Records to a Database Table

To add records to a database table is quite very simple. All you have to do is

- Double-click on **the name** of the table in the navigation pane to have the table opened.
- Once you have opened the table inserts the **values** for each of the fields.
- Once that has been done you will then proceed with adding records in the datasheet view to the table.

It should be noted that everything save the Customer ID field in the table is open to additional data. You will immediately receive a number in the AutoNumber areas. As previously mentioned, records can be inserted directly into the table using the datasheet view; however, this approach isn't generally advised. Adding records via forms is preferable because the logic underlying the form can interact with users during data entry and dynamically provide default values.

Understanding Attachment Fields

You can attach one or more files, such as papers, presentations, photos, and so on, to records in your database by using the attachment field in Access. Attachment can be used to store multiple file types in the same field as well as files of one kind and another. Additionally, attachments facilitate more effective data storage. Images and documents are stored in previous versions of Access using a technology called Object Linking and Embedding (OLE). These bitmap files have the potential to be ten times larger than the original file. Viewing an image from your database causes OLE to display the bitmap image rather than the original file. When you use attachments, you can locate and edit documents and other non-image files directly from within Access by opening them in their parent program. You need to add an attachment field to one or more of your database's tables to use attachments in Microsoft Access. There are three ways to add an attachment field to a table in Microsoft Access.

Adding an attachment field in the Datasheet view

- Make sure the table is displayed in the datasheet view by clicking on the **first available blank column**. Look for a new field in the column header to find a blank column.
- Click **the down arrow** next to the data type in the data type and formatting group on the data sheet tab, and then select the attachment option. After this is completed, Access will set the field's data type to attachment and add an icon to the field's header row.

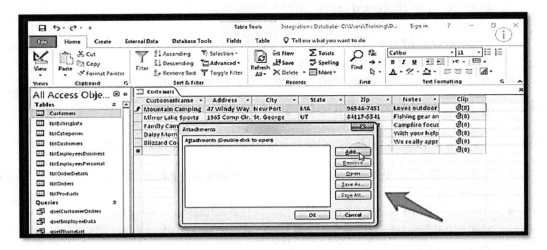

- Finally save your changes. Remember that you cannot change the new field to another data type but you can always delete the field if you think you might have made an error.

Adding an attachment field in the Design view

- Locate the **navigation pane**, right-click **the table** that you want to change, and choose the Design view option on the shortcut menu.
- When in the field name column choose a blank row and insert **a name** for your attachment field.
- Select **the attachment option** under data type in the same row.
- Save the modifications you made. Similar to the option above, you should always keep in mind that while you can select to erase the field if you believe you must have made a mistake, you are unable to convert the new field to another data type.
- To open the table for use, click t**he arrow beneath the fuel button** on the design tab in the Views group, then select the datasheet view.

Activity

1. Mention the various types of tables.
2. Design a new table.
3. Employ the use of the design tab in making some designs.
4. Create a field and give it a name.
5. Indicate data validation rules.
6. Create tbl customers.
7. Make some alterations to the table design you made.
8. Allocate field properties.
9. Configure a primary key.
10. Index tables in Microsoft Access.
11. Print the table design you made.
12. Move a table to another database.
13. Include records in a database table.
14. Add an attachment field in the datasheet view.
15. Add an attachment field in the design view.

CHAPTER 4

KNOWING THE RELATIONSHIPS BETWEEN TABLES

Eliminating any kind of data redundancy or duplicate data, is one goal of a good database architecture. You should have segregated your data into multiple subject-based tables if this is your desired outcome. In this manner, every fact in the table will only be shown once. After doing this, you may provide Microsoft Access with a way to retrieve the dividend data for themselves. This can be achieved by grouping tables with closely similar fields together that share common fields. You then need to indicate these associations within your database to complete this step correctly. Even the most complex situation is reduced to several relationships that exist between pairs of tables; even though databases are meant to be a model for ideal conditions in the real world or at the very least have data maintained in ideal situations. You may need to include additional tables in the architecture the more complicated the data that a table manages. However, you should always focus on the link between two tables at a particular point in time when working with real data.

Building Bulletproof Databases

One-to-many relationships are the most often utilized kind of relationship and can be found in nearly all Access databases. Every record in one table is directly associated with one or more records in another table in this kind of relationship. Instead of having these records spread across two or more tables, merely picture having a mix of these records in one. This implies that all you would need to do to modify the records would be to add new rows to make room for the updated information. The above-described scenario is what is obtained with Excel if it is used for a database. Since Excel is all about spreadsheets, there is no provision to have data broken into different tables, it just encourages users to have all their records kept in one large spreadsheet. **Arrangements like this can develop quite several problems;**

- **The table becomes too large to be properly managed**: Assuming that a single table contains all of the information, the table's purpose would be to represent customers and the arrangement of different things. A table like this will quickly grow to be far too big for you to handle comfortably because practically all of the customers will continue to place orders, and every time one is placed, a record needs to be updated in the table. This does not include all of the records, such as the customer's name, phone number, and address, which must have been added to the table from the beginning.
- **Data becomes extremely difficult to update and maintain**: You are likely to make a lot of mistakes while trying to make certain changes to a table with a lot of data, especially if the table needs to be updated often. A table is preferable for the user when there are fewer records to modify.

- **A monolithic table design is wasteful of disk space and other resources**: If you have a combined table, it will take up more space than necessary. When this happens, it can ultimately lead to having a slow computer if the memory of the computer is not large and it can also lead to other resources on the system being badly utilized.

The redundant data can be moved into a different database using a much superior architecture, such as the relational design. This leaves a field and the first table acting as reference points for the data in the second table. The relational model requires an extra field, which is necessary to achieve the efficiency that would have resulted from removing unnecessary information from the table. Another advantage of having data normalized and including strict database rules for Microsoft Access applications is the fact that data will become virtually bulletproofed. When a database is correctly designed and maintained, users are certain that the data they see on forms and reports is an accurate representation of the data held in underlying tables. A badly constructed database runs the danger of having data damaged, which implies that even though the user must have entered the data into the program, some records may occasionally be lost and may never be seen on forms and reports. Users frequently learn to trust what is printed on paper and what they can see on screens. Keep in mind that a poorly constructed database can never yield positive results. However, by adhering to data normalization guidelines, you can create a meticulously planned and well-organized database.

Data Normalization and Denormalization

One way to define normalization is the process of organizing data in a database. To preserve the data, this can involve constructing tables and establishing the fundamental linkages between them. It can also involve making the database very adaptable by getting rid of any redundancy and dependencies that seem incongruous. In addition to wasting disk space, redundant data causes maintenance issues. If data that is present in multiple locations needs to be modified, it must be done so using the same procedure in each location. If the data is only kept in the customer table and not somewhere else in the table, it is relatively simple to make any changes about that customer.

There are just about a few rules for database normalization with each rule known as a normal form. The database can be said to be in its first normal form if the first rule is followed and in its third normal form if the first three conditions are adhered to. Even though there may be different normalization levels, the third normal form is generally accepted as the greatest level required for nearly all applications to operate at their best. Perfect compliance is not possible in real-world settings, just as it is not possible with formal rules and their definition. Normalization typically requires the installation of additional tables, which may be difficult for certain clients to accomplish. If you have chosen to deviate from any of the first three normalization guidelines, make sure your application is prepared for potential issues such as redundant data and inconsistent dependencies.

First normal form

The first stage of the normalization is known as the first normal form and it needs the table to follow the following rule;

"Each field that is in a table must have only one value, and the table must not have repeating groups of data". Although tables are designed to be two-dimensional storage objects, allowing repeated groups or requiring multiple values to be stored in a field would add a third dimension to the data in the table. What occurs when a third dimension is added to the table? A program and some table updates are all that are required; adding a field is not the solution because this does not natively support a dynamic number of fields.

Second normal form

- Create **different tables** for sets of values that can be applied to more than one record.
- Relate **the table** that must have been created with a foreign key.

The record should only be dependent on the main key of a table, according to the second standard form. Consider an accounting system where a customer's address is involved. The customer's table, as well as the tables for orders, shipping, invoicing, accounts receivable, and collections, all require the address. Record the customer's address once, either in the customer's table or a separate address table, as opposed to having to record it as a distinct entity in each of these tables.

Identifying entities

Sometimes it seems impossible to tell one entity from another. You may mistakenly remove certain entities from the table because you believe they are not essential to the other. For instance, if you have a table that lists customers' names and the orders they place regularly, changing the customer's name won't have any impact on the order. It is recommended that you make separate tables for each customer and their orders to fix this issue.

Follow the steps below to get this done;

- Click on the **Table design** that can be found on the **Create tab** of the ribbon.
- Insert an **AutoNumber field** and give it your **preferred name**.
- Choose the **Primary key** option on the **Table Tools Design tab** of the ribbon.
- Include a **Short Text field** and **name it**.
- Make sure you set the field size of the above name to 50.
- Finally, **save the table.**

After that, you might decide to include other details about the client, such as their phone number and mailing address. Since you will be transferring data that is not essential to its table, the data will be moved into 2NF as a result.

Less obvious entities

It is easy to distinguish between customers and the real goods they order. I will now have to consider separating the other's details from the order. Simply placing the information integral to the order as a whole in a separate table from the information for each line on the order will allow the details of the order to be entered into the second normal form. To successfully segregate the order from the order details, build a new database and transfer all the order data into it. Decomposition is the process of dividing a table into separate tables, each of which describes a different feature of the data. Keep in mind that the normalization procedure includes the crucial step of deconstruction. Even though the newly formed tables can seem smaller than the original table, the information they hold is identical to that of the original table.

Breaking the rules

You might not be able to follow the rules at all times, and there are times when you might find it necessary to break the rules, but this is somewhat normal. For example, let us assume that bookstores are entitled to certain discounts which are dependent on the volume of purchases over the last year. Since the discount is based on the client rather than the order, it is expected that the discount percentage will be reflected in the bookstore's general table when all regulations are rigorously followed. However, the discount is likely applied to each order, which may appear random but may occur if the wholesaler permits the sales staff to offer exclusive discounts to specific clients. Due to this, you might need to add a discount column—even if it means creating duplicate records—to the table that holds information about book orders. You would only have broken the second normal form if this were to occur. While the real discount is based directly on the order, the default discount is applied to the consumer immediately.

Third normal form

- **Eliminate fields that do not in any way depend on any key.**

Values in a record that are not a part of that record key do not belong in the table in any way. Generally speaking, anytime the contents of a group of fields are to be applied to more than one record in the table, there might be a need for you to consider placing those fields in a different table. For example, a candidate's name and university address might not be put on an employment recruitment table. However, a comprehensive list of universities is required in case group mailings are required. There will be no possibility to compile a list of universities without any active candidates if the university's related data is saved in the candidate's table. All you need to do to solve this issue is make a separate table specifically for universities and link it to the Candidate's database using the university code key. Although it may be desirable theoretically, it is not always feasible in practice to strictly adhere to the third normal form. You must make separate tables for cities, Zip Codes, sales reps, customer classes, and other variables that could happen to be duplicated in multiple records if you have a customer table and you need to eliminate all potential inter-field dependencies. Theoretically, pursuing normalization makes sense. Many smaller tables, however, cause performance issues or exceed memory and open file limits. It can be more feasible for you to apply the third normal form to data that changes often alone. If some dependent fields remain, design your application so it needs the user alone to make some verification for all the related fields when anyone has been altered. Depending on the applications you choose to develop, you may find that saving calculated data in tables makes sense, particularly if the calculation itself can take some time to complete or if you need to use the saved value as a backup in case the calculated value printed on reports has to be verified. Calculations made during data entry may be far more effective than those made during report printing. Though you can always have higher levels of normalization, which can be found in most database applications, the third normal form is way more adequate. If you cannot attain the third normal form at the very least you should strive to get the first normal form in your tables by taking off redundant data that might be repeated to another table.

Denormalization

Denormalization is the process of adding precomputed redundant data to a relational database that has otherwise been normalized to enhance the database's read performance. Keep in mind that there are situations in which you might have to denormalize databases on your own. Essentially, the purpose of normalizing data is to enhance the efficiency of your database. For instance, even if you must have correctly indexed and normalized the data, having to search for something can still be very stressful, regardless of how much time and effort you invest in meticulously building a table. Similarly, it may take a long time to calculate some values that have already been determined. Saving a value that has previously been computed may be far simpler than computing such values while on the go, particularly if the computer you are using is slow or doesn't have a lot of memory. The capacity to retrieve a document in its previous form is another reason why the denormalization of data is typically carried out. Note that greater programming time is required for nearly every step required to denormalize data to protect both the data and the user from the various issues that could come from an unnormalized design. Make sure everything you've done to denormalize a design has been recorded. It is quite likely that you or someone else will be contacted to offer upkeep or to add a new feature to the program. Whatever you have done and all of your hard work and effort invested in optimizing the design could be undone if you have left design components that appear to be going against the normalization standards. Always bear in mind that the main purpose of denormalization is for the sake of reporting or for performance-related purposes such as just maintaining the table.

Table Relationships

The majority of the time, people starts developing databases by using spreadsheet programs like Excel. Since spreadsheets only store data as a two-dimensional worksheet (rows and columns) without any provision of an easy means to aid the linking of multiple worksheets together, it may be claimed that this is extremely bad since it does not introduce users to the complexity of a database structure. It can be very taxing to manually connect each cell in one worksheet to the corresponding cells in the other worksheet. Worksheets and other two-dimensional storage objects lack the three-dimensionality of relational databases and are referred to as flat-file databases. However, it is both feasible and simple to link the data in one worksheet to the data in another worksheet using astute programming in the Excel VBA language. Individual row data can also be changed; though using a relational database like Microsoft Access ideally avoids the necessity for this kind of work.

Connecting the data

A table's primary key facilitates the unique identification of each record within the database. Additionally, this can essentially assist in linking the data in one table to the data in another. For instance, if you have a table with employee data, the person's security number may be their ID or a mix of their first and last names used as the primary key. Let's now assume that the employee ID is utilized to select the primary key for the employee's table. The employee ID field is then employed to link or connect the tables whenever a relationship to the payroll table is built. In books such as this and almost every other book that is about relational databases like Microsoft Access, there are three types of relationships that can be found **between tables they are;**

- One-to-one
- One-to-many
- Many-to-many

One-to-one

In a one-to-one relationship each record in the first table ought to have only one matching record in the second table, and each record in the second table should also have only one matching record in the first table. This type of relationship is uncommon since the data associated with it is frequently stored in a single table. One-to-one relationships can be used to divide a table into many fields, or you can use them to isolate specific sections of a table for security purposes, or you can store information that is relevant to only a portion of the main table. Make sure that both tables have a similar field if you observe a relationship of this kind. One way to characterize another example of a one-to-one relationship is called subtyping. For example, your database may include separate tables for customers and vendors. Many of the details for your vendors and consumers may end up being the same if they are both businesses. Then, your customers and when does table would include a reference to the companies table and also include some additional fields that are specific to customers and vendors, respectively. In such a scenario, you might want to have a company's table that has all the similar data, such as the name of the company, the address, and the tax identification number. The customer and vendor entities will be regarded as subtypes of the companies and related one to one.

One-to-many

As an example, let's look at an order tracking database that has two tables: orders and customers. A client is free to place any number of orders. This means that there may be multiple orders for the same customer included in the orders table for every customer that is reflected on the customer's table. There is a one-to-many relationship between the Orders table and the Customers table. Use the primary key on one side of the connection as an additional field or fields to the table on the many sides of the relationship to express a one-to-many relationship in your database architecture. For example, in this scenario, you create a new column called customer ID and add it to the Orders database. It is the ID field from the Customers table. The customer number in the Orders table can then be used by Microsoft Access to identify the correct customer for each order in the Orders table. Beyond a reasonable doubt, one-to-many relationships are the most common type of relationship encountered in relational database systems. **Below are examples of one-to-many situations;**

- **Customers and orders**: In this type of scenario, the principal party, the customer, has placed many orders; nonetheless, all of the orders will still be sent to the same customer.
- **Teacher and student**: Each teacher has a lot of students but each student has just one teacher. This is in the concept of a particular class or a particular course of study or subject.
- **Employees and paychecks**: Every worker receives multiple paychecks, yet only one payment is presented to each worker.
- **Patients and appointments**: which patient houses none or multiple doctor appointments but which appointment is for just one patient.

Many-to-many

In this relationship let's take a look at the relationship between a product's table and an Orders table. a single order can contain more than one product. On the other hand, a single product can be displayed on many orders. Therefore, for each of the records that are in the order table, there can be many records in the product table. Moreover, there may be several records in the Orders database for every record in the product table. A many-to-many relationship is the name given to this type of relationship. It should be noted that it is crucial to take into account both aspects of a relationship to determine whether many-many linkages between tables exist. It is required to establish a third table, also known as a junction table, that divides the many-to-many relationship into two one-to-many relationships to display a many-to-many relationship. The primary key from each of the two tables can be inserted into the third table. Because of this, every instance or occurrence of the relationship will be documented in the third table. For instance, two one-to-many linkages to the orders details table define the many-to-many relationship between the orders table and the product table. One order can have many products and each of these products can be displayed on many orders. The many-to-many link is generally seen as challenging to establish and maintain because of the extra complexity associated with the junction table. Thankfully, Microsoft Access guarantees that establishing a relationship of this kind is simple if certain guidelines are observed. This book has several explanations of these rules. For instance, the junction table needs to have the main keys of both tables that the connection joins if you wish to update either side of a many-to-many relationship.

Below are examples of many relationships that are commonly used in the business environment;

- **Lawyers to clients**: each lawyer might be involved in several cases and each client might be represented by more than one lawyer in each case.
- **Patients and insurance coverage**: The majority of people only have one insurance coverage. For instance, you have various coverages if your employers provide health insurance to you and your spouse.
- **Video rentals and customers**: over some time for example a year, each video is rented by various people while every customer would have rented more than one video over a year.
- **Magazine subscriptions**: The majority of magazines have millions or thousands of readers. When it comes to publications, the majority of individuals subscribe to many ones at once.

Integrity Rules

Referential integrity can be described as a system of Rules that Microsoft Access makes use of to ensure that relationships that exist between records in tables that are related are valid and that you also do not mistakenly delete or alter data that are said to be related to one another. Referential integrity operates exclusively using the table's primary fields. When a main or foreign key field is added, modified, or removed, the database engine performs a referential integrity check. Referential integrity is violated when a change to a value in a key field results in the relationship becoming invalid. Referential integrity can be automatically enforced when tables are configured in this way. Anywhere data is shown in the database—in tables, queries, or forms—data integrity is guaranteed because the Microsoft Access database engine upholds the referential integrity principles. You don't need to worry about associated table data being destroyed or dispersed once your application's integrity needs have been determined. It is impossible to overstate the importance of referential integrity in database applications. Many developers believe that they may prevent orphaned records—which are always extremely terrible in database applications—by using VBA code or user interface design. The truth is that the information stored in a given table in practically every database may be utilized in other parts of the program or even in another application that uses the same information. It might be difficult to recall how data should be protected because many database projects take years to complete and include multiple developers. Ultimately, the most effective method for guaranteeing the accuracy of data stored in any database system is to leverage the database engine's capabilities to enforce referential integrity.

You can set referential integrity when the conditions below are true;

- The matching field from the primary table is the primary key or has a unique index.
- Except for two instances, related fields share nearly identical data: auto fields can be related to number fields with field size property settings of long integers and

replication ID for auto-number fields. Both types of fields can be related to each other.

- The Microsoft Access database that contains both tables is the same. To ensure referential integrity, if the tables are linked, they must also be in Microsoft Access format and the database containing them needs to be accessed. When linked tables are extracted from databases in different formats, referential integrity cannot be guaranteed.

The following rules apply whenever you make use of referential integrity;

- You cannot insert a single value in the foreign key field of the table that is related but does not exist in the primary key of the primary table. However, you can add a Null value to the foreign key. It is made clear by this that the records are unrelated. An order allocated to a nonexistent customer, for instance, is not possible. However, by entering a Null value in the Customer ID box, it is possible to create an order that is issued to no one.
- If adjacent tables have matching records, the entry cannot be removed from the primary table. For example, if an employee has orders allocated to them in the orders database, you cannot remove that employee record from the employee's table.
- If a record has additional linked records, the main key in the primary table cannot be modified. For example, if an employee has orders assigned to them in the Orders table, their ID cannot be modified.

No primary key can contain a null value

A field in your table that provides Microsoft Access with a distinct identifier for each row inside a table is known as a primary key. Information can be separated into many subject-based tables in a relational database like the Access database. After that, you can use the table relationships, and the primary keys in Microsoft Access will indicate how to reunite the information. Primary key fields are used by Access to quickly associate data from different tables and bring the data together in a highly useful way. Most times a primary key can be an ID number or a serial code. An example of a bad choice for a primary key can be a name or an address since both information can change with time. A Null value is known as a value that can be inserted into a field or can be used in expressions or queries to specify data that is missing or data that is unknown. In Microsoft Visual Basic, the Null keyword shows a Null value. Certain fields like the primary key fields cannot contain Null. According to the first referential integrity rule, there shouldn't be a null value in any primary key. A field that has never had a value given to it is thought to be null. No record in the database table can contain a null in its primary key since the primary key's principal function is to guarantee the row's uniqueness. If primary keys are nullable, then null values cannot be unique and the relational model will not function. You cannot make a field that already has null values as the primary key in Microsoft Access.

Furthermore, Microsoft Access is unable to analyze a null value. It cannot be compared to any other value because there isn't a null value. It just doesn't exist; it is neither larger nor smaller when compared to any other value. As a result, a null value can be used to establish a relationship between two tables or to look for a record in one. Every field in a composite primary key including several fields must have a value whenever the composite key is utilized. Any of the fields being empty is not allowed. The composite primary key's value combination needs to be distinct.

All foreign key values must be matched by a corresponding primary key

A primary key-foreign key relationship describes a one-to-many relationship between two tables in a relational database. A foreign key can be described as a column or a set of columns that are in one table and reference the primary key columns in a different table. The primary key is known as a column and can be a set of columns where each value is simply unique and also identifies a single row of the table. According to the second referential integrity criterion, matching primary keys must match all of the values of the foreign keys. This could also imply that each record on the many sides of a one-to-many relationship's table should have a corresponding record on the relationship's one side. Any record that appears on many sides of a relationship but does not have a matching record on one side is considered orphaned and will be removed from the database schema. Having to identify orphaned records in a database can be very difficult. It is much better to then avoid the situation in the first place.

The second rule simply means the following;

- You cannot have rows added to a many side table if there is no corresponding record on the one side of the other table.
- The primary key value in a one-side table cannot be changed if the change will bring about the creation of an orphaned record.
- Deleting a row on one side must not create an orphaned record on the corresponding many sides.

One extremely interesting outcome of the differential integrity criteria is that it is very conceivable to have a parent record for which there isn't a corresponding child record. This implies that there might be workers at a company who haven't received their paychecks yet. Although one or more comparable child records will eventually match the majority of existing records, a relational database is not required to meet this criterion.

Keys

It is imperative that every database table be assigned a primary key upon creation. You can be certain that the table records will only have one unique value once this key is assigned. A primary key's only function is to provide each record in a database with a unique identity. Make sure that no two records have the same number at all times.

Below are reasons why this should be avoided;

- It can make updating the record of the customer almost impossible.
- You want to be sure and certain that all of the records that are in a table are accurate to be sure the information that is gotten from the table is accurate.
- You don't want to make the table any larger than it already is. When you add redundancies or have fields or records duplicated, it will just complicate the database and add no value.

Entity integrity, often known as adding a single unique value to every record in a table, is a technique that makes tables dependable and tidy. Even if all other fields in two records are identical, you can distinguish between them if each record has a unique primary key value. This is extremely important since you can easily have two individual customers with a common name on your table. If you indicate a primary key when you're creating a Microsoft Access table Microsoft Access will ask if you want one. If you reply by saying yes, Microsoft Access will use the auto-number data type to create the primary key for the table. Every time a record is added to the database, an auto number field is automatically created. Once the value has been formed, it can be modified. Furthermore, even if the record containing the value has been deleted and the value is no longer shown in the database, once any other numerical value has been displayed in a table, it will never be used again.

Making a Decision on a Primary Key

The entity that gives a record in a table its unique identity is the primary key, as was previously established. It is an identification that is frequently a data type that is text, numeric, or AutoNumber. You have two options when it comes to creating a unique value: either utilizes the AutoNumber value to have Microsoft Access generate the main key automatically for you, or select a method of your own. However, since the primary key value's primary purpose is to ensure that each row is distinct and to serve as an anchor for table relationships, there is no compelling reason why it needs to mean anything to the application. Auto-number fields are used as primary keys by the majority of Microsoft Access developers primarily because they fulfill all the requirements of a primary key without increasing the complexity of an application. The easiest way is to utilize auto-number fields for the primary keys in your table, even though using logic to generate unique numbers for a primary key field might be very challenging. The author number field is special since it cannot be altered, which makes it perfect for usage as a primary key. It should be noted that while extreme uniqueness is always guaranteed, sequentiality is not. There are a few reasons why AutoNumbers may have gaps, such as when entries are deleted. You should never rely solely on AutoNumbers being sequential. Although sequence numbers may seem to make information searching more challenging, it's important to keep in mind that you often search for information based on the table's purpose rather than using an ID field.

Looking at the benefits of a primary key

Primary key is of utmost importance in any database as it does the job of linking records together working hand in hand with the foreign key. Aside from the primary key serving as a link between tables in a database, the **primary key field in Microsoft Access has the following benefits;**

- Fields that pertain to the primary key field are typically indexed, which helps to quickly speed up query searches and sorting.
- Every time you add a record, Microsoft Access ensures that you include a value. You can be certain that your database tables adhere to the referential integrity guidelines to the letter with this.
- When new records are added to a table, Microsoft Access looks for duplicate values in the primary key. It also assists in preventing duplicate entries and guarantees data integrity.
- By default, Microsoft Access will show your data in primary key order.

Designating a primary key

As was previously mentioned, you should be aware that selecting a primary key is crucial to the security of a database architecture. The primary key can aid in stabilizing and safeguarding the data that has to be stored in Microsoft Access databases when used appropriately. Remember that a primary key field in a table needs to have extremely unique values, and this is the fundamental rule that determines those values. It's also important to remember that a stable primary key is essential.

Single-field versus composite primary key

When the perfect primary key cannot be located in a database as a single value, you may be able to combine Fields to make a composite primary key. For instance, you might not be able to build a main key with just the first name, but you might be able to create a unique combination of values that can be used as the primary key if you combine the last name with your likely birthdate. This section demonstrates how simple it is to combine Fields as composite primary keys in Microsoft Access.

Below are things you should consider when using composite keys;

- None of the fields in a composite key should be null
- There are times when building a composite key from naturally occurring data within the table proves to be extremely difficult.
- Each of the fields can be duplicated within the table but it is impossible to duplicate the combination of composite key fields.

Natural versus surrogate primary keys

Data that already exists in the database, such as an employee's number or social security number, can be used to obtain a natural primary key. It is advisable to combine fields to create a composite primary key if no single field can uniquely identify the records that are in a table. One of the biggest problems is that, after a record is committed to the database, it becomes impossible to add it to a table if the primary key value is unknown. It is also possible to take into account the amount of fixing that will be done in associated tables, even if temporary values are entered until the permanent value is determined.

Creating primary keys

To create a primary key,

- Open **a table** in the **Design View**.
- Choose **the fields** that you would prefer to use as a primary then click on **the primary key button** on the **Table Tools Design tab of Ribbon**. If you need to indicate more than just a single field in the creation of a composite key, **press down the ctrl key** then choose the fields before you go ahead to click on **the primary button**.

Creating relationships and enforcing referential integrity

You can establish relationships and referential integrity rules that need to be implemented to the tables contained inside a relationship by using the Relationship pane. **The steps listed below can be used to easily create a managed relationship that is permanent and ensures referential integrity between Microsoft Access;**

- Choose the **Database Tools Relationships**; this will then display the relationship window.
- Select the **Show Table button** option on the Ribbon or you can choose to Right-click the **Relationships window** and choose the **select Show Table option** from the shortcut menu. The Show Table dialog box will then be displayed.
- Double-clicking on each table in the show table dialog box will add your desired table name to the relationship pane. Alternatively, you can pick each table individually and click the **Add button.**
- Move the primary key field from one table to the foreign key in many tables, and then drop it there to establish a relationship. Alternatively, you might drag and drop the foreign key field onto the primary key field. After doing this, Access will launch the Edit Relationships dialog box right away, allowing you to specify the specifics of the relationship you want to establish between the tables.
- Select the option to "**Enforce Referential Integrity**." Microsoft Access will not permit you to have records erased from the table of your choice if this checkbox is left unchecked. With this item checked, the deletions will automatically cascade

throughout the relationship. Since the deletions in the many tables occur without confirmation, cascading deletes can be extremely delicate operations.

- Lastly, press **the "create" button**. The sort of relationship that exists will then be indicated by a line drawn by Microsoft Access between the tables displayed in the relationships window.

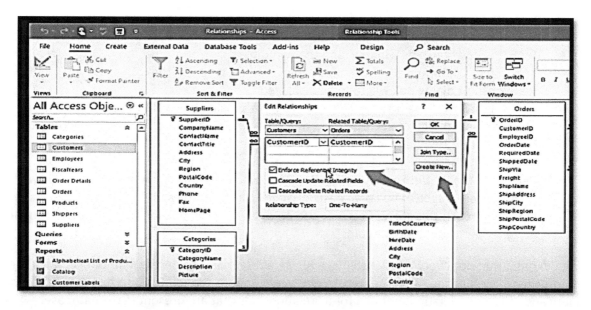

Specifying the join type between tables

There are about four buttons on the right-hand side of the Edit Relationships dialog box.

They are;

- **Create**: This button takes you back to the Relationships window with the changes outrightly indicated.
- **Cancel**: This button takes off the current changes and also takes you back to the Relationships window.
- **Join Type**: The join type button when clicked opens up the Join Properties dialog box.
- **Create New**: The create new option enables you to indicate an entirely new relationship between the two tables and fields.

When processing a query on connected tables, Microsoft Access by default delivers only those records that are visible in both tables. When this occurs, the relationship is commonly referred to as an inner join as only records that are present on both sides of the relationship are seen. Still, Microsoft Access does not support the inner join as its exclusive join type.

To find out the join types that is supported by Microsoft Access;

- To open the Join Properties dialog box, select the **Join Type button**. The Join Properties dialog box has alternative settings that allow you to specify whether you want to see records from the parent table or the child table, regardless of whether they match against each other. The Outer join is a type of join that is particularly useful since it accurately displays the state of the data in the application.

To indicate an outer join that will connect customers to another table follow the steps below;

- From the relationships window, add the two tables.
- Move the **Customer ID** from one table and drop it on the other table. The Edit Relationships dialog box will then be displayed.
- Click on the **Join Type button**. The Join Properties dialog box will then be displayed.
- Choose the **Include All Records** from one table and Only Those Records from the other table Where the Joined Fields Are Equal option button.
- Tap **the OK button**. You will then be taken back to the Edit Relationships dialog box.
- Select the **Create button**. You will return to the Relationships pane by doing this as well. By now there ought to be an arrow connecting the two tables in the Relationships pane. Once you reach this stage, you may use an outer join relationship to set the referential integrity between the two tables.

Keep in mind that not every relationship in your database needs to have a joint type created for it. To achieve the desired outcome, most developers update the joint properties data on each query and utilize the default inner join for all relationships that are present in the database.

Enforcing referential integrity

Referential integrity between the tables should be indicated after using the Edit Relationships dialog box to establish the relationship, validate the table and any associated Fields, and specify the kind of join that exists between the tables.

- Choose the **Enforce Referential Integrity checkbox** that can be found in the lower portion of the Edit relationship dialogue box to specify that you want Microsoft Access to enforce the referential integrity rules on the relationships that exist between the tables

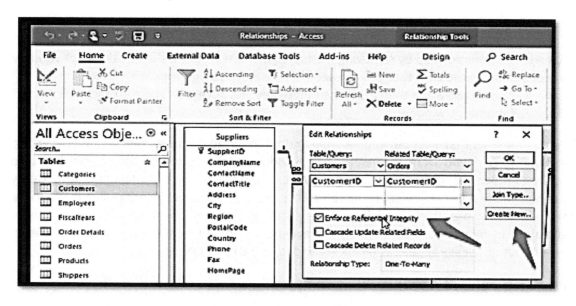

You will not receive a notice regarding a referential integrity breach if you elect not to enforce referential integrity. Instead, you can choose to add a new record, modify important Fields, or have linked records destroyed. This gives you the ability to alter important fields and corrupt the application's data. It is possible to create tables with orphans when there is no active integrity. Referential integrity rules should be enforced during routine operations such as data entry or information changes. There are two other options that referential integrity also enables and can be of extreme importance to you they are; cascading updates and cascading deletes. These two options can be found close to the bottom of the Edit Relationships dialog box. Keep in mind that occasionally you may notice Microsoft Access will not let you construct a relationship and enforce referential integrity if you choose to do so and click the create button (if you have reopened the Edit relationship dialogue box to edit a relationship). The most likely explanation for this is that you are asking Microsoft Access to establish a relationship—such as a child table containing orphans—that is against referential integrity rules. When this occurs With Microsoft Access, you get alerted with a message. Because the data in the tables already breaks the rule, Microsoft Access is unable to maintain referential integrity between the tables. Either way, you can fix this by going back to the relationship box, selecting referential integrity between the two tables, and deleting the offending records. Whether or not it is customary to purge records to tidy up data depends entirely on the application's business rules. Deleting orders just because referential integrity cannot be enforced might be considered a very bad idea in most environments

Viewing all relationships

If you would like to view all relationships;

- Open the **Relationships window**.

- Click on the **All Relationships** option on the Relationships Tools Design tab of the Ribbon to view all of the relationships in the database.

You can hide a relationship by removing the tables that are visible in the Relationships window if you need to make the view that you can see in there more straightforward.

- Click on **a table** and then press the **delete key** and Access will take off the table from the Relationships window.

Any relationships that exist between a table and other database tables remain intact even after the table is removed from the relationship window. Make sure that the foreign key field's Required Property is set to Yes whenever you create database tables. By doing this, the user will be compelled to enter the relationship route between the tables and insert a value in the foreign key field. Be aware that the relationships listed in the Relationships window are usually maintained by Microsoft Access and are permanent. When permanent relationships are created, they will automatically appear as tables are added in the Query Design box.

Deleting relationships

Sometimes a change is necessary, and it may involve ending and re-establishing some connections. All that exists in the Relationships pane is an image of the relationships that exist within tables. The photo will be erased but the relationship will remain intact if all you do is open the relationship window and click the delete button. To completely remove the relationship, you must first click on the line that joins the tables, and then select the **Delete option** to erase the relationship and all of the table images.

Following application-specific integrity rules

You can establish several business rules that are enforced by the Microsoft Access applications you design, in addition to the referential integrity rules that the ACE database engine enforces.

Business rules include the following items;

- The order-entry clerk must insert his ID number on the entry form.
- Quantities can never be less than zero.
- The unit selling price can also never be less than the unit cost price.
- The order ship data must always come after the order date.

Usually, when a table is designed, it has rules in it. The value of the data that the database manages is greatly preserved when such a regulation is enforced. To guarantee that the data in the table is somewhat protected, you may also decide to build a validation rule that applies to the entire table by using the validation rule attribute on the table's property sheet. This means that only one rule can be made for the entire table, which makes it very challenging to provide a specific validation text for every scenario in which a violation could occur. The rule property valuation has several restrictions. For instance, it is not possible to employ user-defined functions within rules. Moreover, tables, data in other records, and other fields cannot be referenced in your rules. By displaying alerts that the user can ignore, validation rules aid in preventing user entry. You should not utilize the validation rules if you must issue a warning while allowing the user to proceed.

Activity

1. Build a bulletproof database.
2. Normalize and denormalize data in Microsoft Access.
3. What are table relationships?
4. Mention some integrity rules.
5. Create primary keys.
6. Decide on a primary key.
7. What are the benefits of a primary key?
8. Create relationships and enforce referential integrity.
9. Make use of application-specific integrity rules.

CHAPTER 5
WORKING WITH ACCESS TABLES

This chapter will cover dealing with a datasheet and how to use it to exhibit data in a variety of ways after inserting it into a Microsoft Access table. You can view multiple records at once in the familiar spreadsheet format by using the Datasheet. Additionally, you will learn how to add, edit, and remove records from a table in this chapter.

Comprehending Datasheets

Microsoft Access displays tables and query results in the Datasheet view when a table is accessed or a query is examined. A datasheet is most typically used to refer to table data or query results that are shown in the Datasheet view. A datasheet's appearance can be altered to display extremely particular information for usage as a straightforward report. A datasheet can be thought of as a visual depiction of the information contained in a table or the outcomes of a query. It displays each record's fields in a tabular style from a table, form, or query result. Tables and queries are always opened in the Datasheet view by default.

- **In the Navigation Pane, right-click on a table or query > click on the Open button on the shortcut menu to open the table or the query as a datasheet.**

A datasheet can also be used as a basic report by applying specific formatting to rows and columns or adding a Total row. You can see the rows (records) that don't fit on the screen by scrolling up or down, and you can also see the columns (fields) that don't fit by scrolling left or right. Keep in mind that this chapter will mostly cover behaviors related to access forms. One record at a time is displayed on the majority of Access forms, and interacting with the data on such a form is equivalent to working with a single row of data on a datasheet. You can alter datasheets so that you can see the data in different ways. For example, you can adjust the font size's height, the width of the columns, and the row heights to fit more or less of the data on the screen at once. To ensure that the rows and/or columns are arranged correctly, you can also decide to rearrange their order. It is also possible to have columns locked in this manner; in this case, they will stay in place even if you scroll to another section of the datasheet, or you can select to conceal them so they vanish. To have records hidden, all you have to do is filter the data that does not match the specified criteria. The best approach to view multiple records in a table at once is with a datasheet. A single record will show up in the datasheet as a row, with unique information specific to that record appearing in each row. In the datasheet, the fields will be shown as columns, each containing a unique field's content. This style of rows and columns will allow you to view all of the data at once.

Looking at the Datasheet Window

The primary key in a datasheet is essentially used to assist organize records; fields are also arranged according to their order in a table design. The Quick Access toolbar, the Ribbon, and the title bar, which displays the database filename, are all positioned at the top of the Access window. The Access window's status bar, which displays datasheet information, is located at the bottom. For example, this may have a progress meter, a warning, or field description information. Error and warning messages are typically displayed in dialog boxes that are positioned in the center of the screen, opposite the status bar. Some of the items in the status bar will display a brief message explaining what they are and occasionally what they perform when you move the mouse pointer over them. There is a scroll bar on the right side of the datasheet window that allows you to view a different subset of entries. A scroll hint will always inform you of the record that will be shown first as you proceed upward. You can get an idea of the overall number of records displayed by looking at the size of the scroll box. Additionally, a scroll bar that displays several fields is located at the bottom of the Datasheet window. The Datasheet window's bottom-left corner will also show the navigation button, which is used to navigate between records.

Moving within a datasheet

All that's required to navigate around the datasheet and indicate where changes should be made or where additional data might be needed is a mouse click. Additionally, it can be rather simple to navigate between fields and records by using the navigation button, scroll bars, and ribbon tabs. Consider the datasheet as a spreadsheet sans the row numbers and column letters to make things easy for yourself. Instead, rows are highly distinct records with easily identifiable values in each cell, and columns have field names.

Below are the keys that are used for navigation within the datasheet;

Navigational Direction	Keystrokes
Next field	Tab
Previous field	Shift + Tab
The first field of the current record	Home
The last field of the current record	End

Next record	Downward pointing arrow
Previous record	Upward pointing arrow
The first field of the first record	Ctrl+Home
The last field of the last record	Ctrl + End
Scroll down one page	PgDn
Scroll up one page	PgUp
Scroll right one page	Ctrl + PgDn
Scroll left one page	Ctrl + PgUp

Using the Navigation buttons

The six controls that are located at the bottom of the Datasheet window and are used to navigate to a different record inside the datasheet are called navigation buttons. You can access the first or previous entry in the datasheet by using the two controls on the farthest left of the screen. You can navigate to the rightmost controls on the following record, the last record, or the most recent record in the datasheet using the three controls on the right.

- Make use of the record-number box if you know the record number or the row number by clicking on the **record-number box, inserting** a **record number,** and then pressing the **Enter button**.

Checking Out the Datasheet Ribbon

A method to make the most of the datasheet is provided by the Datasheet Ribbon. There are some familiar items on the Home page, but there are also some new ones.

Views

With the Views group, you can change between the Datasheet view and the Design view. **Both choices can be seen when you;**
- Click on the d**ownward pointing arrow** of the view command.

You can alter the object's design, including the table, query, and other elements, by clicking the **Design View button**. You will be returned to the datasheet upon selecting the **Datasheet View option.**

Clipboard

There are options for copying and pasting items onto the clipboard. You can also use the undo drawing tool with it. These choices operate similarly to those found in Microsoft Excel or Word. Paste, Paste Special, and Paste Append are the three options available when using the paste command. Pasting contents from the clipboard in many formats, including text and CSV, is possible with the Paste Special option. The clipboard's contents are appended as a new record by the paste. It only takes a row on the clipboard with a comparable structure.

Sort & Filter

This allows you to make changes to the order of the rows and also limit the rows being shown depending on the criteria you prefer.

Records

You can add, remove, or save a record to the datasheet using the record group. Additionally, this group contains instructions to show totals, check for spelling mistakes, hide columns, adjust row height, and widen the field.

Find

This group allows you to find and replace data and also locate specific records in the datasheet. You can make use of the Select command to choose a particular record or all of the records.

Window

There are two buttons in the Windows group with which you can control the items like reports, table's forms and so on that are opened in the main Access window;

- **Size to fit form**: When this button is pressed, the form's size can be adjusted to match the dimensions specified during its original creation. Because the borders of Access forms are large, all the user needs to do is resize the forms.
- **Switch windows**: You can select which open windows you want to work with by using the switch window button. A report that a user wants may be hidden behind another report

or form, but the switch windows button also provides a very easy way to select the objects in the Access main window that are at the top of other objects.

Text formatting

The datasheet's text fields can have their appearance altered by using the text formatting group. These instructions allow you to adjust the font, size, bold, italic, color, and other settings. For example, when you select a specific font, it will be used for every field in the datasheet. Utilize the center, align left, and align right commands to align the data with the selected column.

- Click on the **gridlines command** to toggle the gridlines either on or off. Make use of the alternate Row color command to alter the colors of alternating rows to ensure that they are all the same.

Take note that the Text Formatting group will act very differently if the selected field in the datasheet happens to be a long text field. If the Text Format property is set to Rich Text, you can alter the font properties of the individual letters and words within the Long Text field, such as making them bold, underlined, italicized, etc.

Launching a Datasheet

Below are the steps to follow if you want to open a datasheet from the window of a Database;

- Locate **tables** in the navigation pane.
- Click **twice** on the name of the table you want to open.

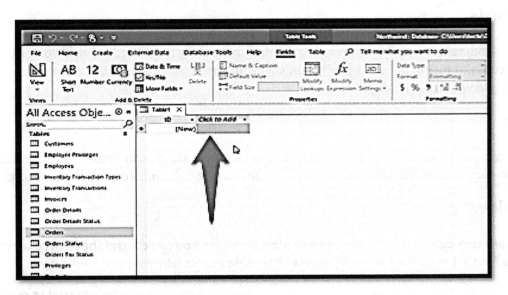

If probably you are in any of the design windows;

- Choose the **Datasheet View command** in the View group of the Ribbon to view your data in a datasheet.

Entering a New Data

Once you have the Datasheet view open, you can see every record in your table. The new datasheet will be blank if the table is brand-new. In this scenario, the record selector's first row will have an asterisk to indicate that it is a new record for you. You have practically everything you need to make a complete table in the Table Tools tab group in the Ribbon. From the controls in the Table Tools tab group, you may select to specify the data type, default formatting, indexing, field and table validation, and other activities related to table development.

The new row will be displayed at the bottom of the datasheet when the datasheet already has the records.

- To transfer the pointer to the new row, click the **New Record button** below the datasheet, the **New command button** in the Records group of the ribbon, or, even better, click **the last row** where the asterisk button is located.

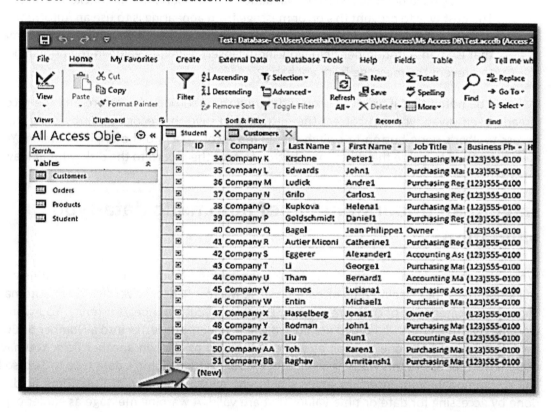

When you are about to start typing the data, the asterisk sign will turn into a pencil which is an indication that the record is being edited or a new record is being added to the datasheet.

Follow the steps below if you would like to add a new record to the opened datasheet view;

- Select the New button option located in the records group on the Ribbon's Home tab.
- Enter the values in each field of the table. You can also use the Tab key to navigate between fields instead of using the Enter button.

Three options are often displayed whenever you are adding or editing records in the datasheet.

- **The record being edited**: this option displays a pencil icon.
- **Record is locked**: This option displays a padlock icon.
- **New record**: this option displays an asterisk icon.

Saving the record

When you move to another record, the record that has been edited will be saved automatically. When you tab through all the various fields, click on the navigation buttons, and

- Click on the **Save button** in the records group of the ribbon, all of these will write the edited record to the database. When the pencil icon leaves the record selector, it is a sign that the record has been saved.

To get a record saved, all you have to do is

- Enter the appropriate values in each field. Data type, uniqueness, and any validation rules that may have been added to the validation rule property are all checked for in the fields. The best way to prevent this error message from appearing is to use an AutoNumber field while the data is being inserted as the table's primary key. If your table has a primary key that isn't an Autonumber field, you should insert a unique value in the primary key field to prevent the message from appearing.

It should be noted that if an error occurred during the insertion of a record and the record has already been saved, you can correct the mistake and save the record again by using the Quick Access toolbar's undo button to switch the edited record back to the original version. You also have the option to utilize the shift+enter button to save the record to the disk without leaving the record itself.

Having an understanding of automatic data-type validation

When the characteristics of the table have been specified, you don't need to enter any data validation rules for certain types of data because Microsoft Access verifies them automatically. These three categories of data are Yes/No, Date/Time, and Number/Currency. You won't get a warning that the letters you typed are invalid when you enter a letter into a Number or Currency field; but, you will see one as soon as you exit the field or click on another field. You have two options in response to this warning sign: either modifies the column's data type to Text so that it will accommodate your insert, or enter a different value. Validation of Date/Time fields is also done by accessing for date or time values that are valid. A warning message as earlier explained will also be displayed when you try to insert a date like 12/27/02 or a time like 45:16:87.

For the Yes/No fields you must insert any of the defined values below;

- **Yes:** Yes, True, On, -1, or a number other than 0.
- **No**: No, false, off, or 0.

You also have the freedom to define your values in the Format property for the field and these values will generally become the acceptable values.

Understanding how properties affect data entry

Different data-entry technique types have to be used because field types are not all the same.

Below are the various types of data entry formats that we have;

Standard text data entry

Assume that the first field in this data entry is an AutoNumber Contact ID and that the remaining elements in the table are Short Text fields. Once the contact ID has been omitted, fill in the other fields with a value and continue. After that, the data entry for the zip code will employ an input mask (0000\ -9999;0; _). Take note that an optional number entry is indicated by 9 in an input mask. The first five digits of the zip code input mask are required; the remaining four are essentially optional. The characters that can be entered in the Short Text field are unlimited unless they are restricted by an input mask.

Date/Time/data entry

The ideal date entry format for this choice is to have the short date given as 3/17/2022, the medium date as 17-Mar-2022, or the long date format as Thursday, March 17, 2022. Therefore, as soon as you exit the field, Microsoft Access will display the data in the designated format if you enter the date as 3/17/22 or 17 Mar 22. Dates are frequently recorded in the database without requiring any kind of preparation. In this approach, the format you select for a field won't have an impact on how the data is kept. It is important to remember that formats have no bearing on how the data is stored in the table; instead, they only impact how the data is shown. In general, adding an input mask to Date/Time data is not a smart idea. Access makes sure that it accepts responsibility for verifying date and time information. Undoubtedly, using an input mask on a date that contains control increases the likelihood of running into issues with data entering more than it does the likelihood of avoiding issues.

Number/Currency Data entry with data validation

Using the help of the validation rule, you can enter any credit limit you choose using this option. The validation text for the field will be added to a dialog box that appears whenever the rule is broken. You must modify the validation rule in the table design if you wish to change the credit limit that you have already established. The regional settings options that have been selected in the Region and Language settings in the Windows settings determine the currency character that Microsoft Access will use.

OLE object data entry

The OLE (Object Linking and Embedding) object is essentially inserted into the database using this option. Keep in mind that you can still choose this option even if you cannot see the thing. An OLE field can store a variety of items, such as Word or Excel documents, sound files, business graphs, and bitmap images. Typically, objects that are compatible with an OLE server are stored in the Access OLE object field. Since these things are entered into a form, the value can be seen, heard, or even used. When OLE objects appear in the datasheets, a description of the object can be seen. **OLE objects can be inserted in two different ways, they are;**

- Pasting from **the clipboard**
- Right-clicking on the **OLE Object field**, and then choosing the insert Object option from the shortcut menu.

Long Text field data entry

This feature aids in the storing of substantial volumes of alphanumeric data, with each field holding up to around 1GB of text in phrases and paragraphs. Only a few characters will be shown at a time when you introduce a long text field; the remainder of the string will then scroll out of view. You can view more characters at once by using the scroll bar in the zoom window that appears when you hit the Shift+F2 button. All of the text will be selected the first time it appears in the Zoom window. To deselect the text, simply click anywhere within the window.

If by mistake you happen to delete all the text or you change a particular thing you never wanted to change all you have to do is;

- Click on the **cancel button** to go back to the datasheet with the original data of the field.

Moving between Records in a Datasheet

You may need to make adjustments at any time to the records you have previously entered into the table. This could be the result of an error you made when you first entered the data or because you wanted to add additional information.

When you want to make changes to the record in a table, begin by

- Opening **the table** if it is not opened already.
- Click **twice** on the table you want to make changes to and this will open the table in the datasheet view.

If on the other hand, you are in the design view, click on the **datasheet View button** to change views.

A column with the plus symbol appears when a datasheet containing related tables is accessed in Microsoft Access; this facilitates the identification of related entries or sub-datasheets.

- Click on a **plus sign** of a row to open the sub datasheet for the row.

Moving between records

It's really simple to navigate through the records; just use the mouse to scroll through them and point the arrow at the one you want. It could be challenging to navigate through every record in a very large table by just scrolling through; you might need to utilize different strategies to find the desired record more quickly. To navigate between records fast, utilize the five Navigation buttons. To get to your favorite records, simply click on these buttons. Utilizing the record number box is possible if you are aware of the specific record number.

- Insert the record number and then press the **Enter button**.

You can also choose to make use of the Go-To command button in the Find group of the Ribbon to move to the First, Previous, Next, Last, and of course the New records.

Looking for a certain value

If the record number is unknown, it might be extremely difficult to locate a certain value in a table. To proceed, simply enter the number in the record number box and hit the **Enter button** if you possess it. **Alternatively, you can also choose to make use of any of the methods below for finding a value in a field;**

- Choose the **Find command** option from the Find group of the Ribbon.

- Click on the **Ctrl+F buttons**.

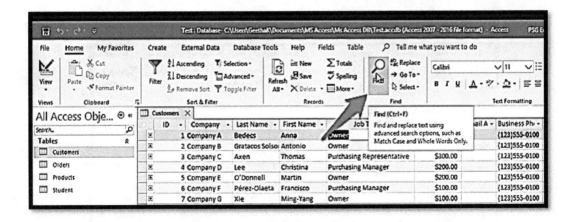

- **Make use of the Search box located at the lower part of the Datasheet window.**

The Find and Replace dialog box will appear when you utilize the first two of the above methods. Before launching the dialog box, point the cursor in the field you wish to search to restrict the search to that field. Next, change the dialog box's options to find all searches. You can customize every part of searches with complete control using the Find and Replace box. To search for a value, simply enter it in the Find What combo box, which contains a list of recently performed searches. Additionally, you have the option of inserting a specific value or utilizing a wildcard character.

Below is a table that contains wildcard characters;

Character	Description
* Asterisk	This matches any number of characters.
? Question mark	This matches any single character
[] brackets	This matches at least one of a list of characters.
! exclamation point	When this has brackets with it, it excludes a list of characters.
-hyphen	When it has brackets it matches a range of characters

#hash	This matches only one number

Getting Values in Datasheet Altered

If there are no values in the field that you are in, you can choose to insert new values into the field. When you insert new values into a field, all you have to do is make use of the same rules as for a new record entry.

Manually replacing an existing value

In essence, you introduce a field whose characters are either not selected at all or not selected in its entirety. It is preferable to select the entire value when inserting a field using the keyboard. The value you have already selected will be effortlessly and automatically replaced when you begin inputting fresh text. The value is not selected when you select a field.

If you want to choose the whole value with the use of the mouse, make use of any of the methods below;

- After making a click inside the field, hit **F2.**
- To select the entire value, choose **the left portion of the value**, depress the mouse's left button, and then move the mouse.
- When you see a big plus sign with the cursor, select only the left portion of the data.

There might be a need for you to change a value that already exists with the default value of the field.

All you have to do is to

- Choose **the specific value** then press the **Ctrl+Alt+Spacebar.** If you would like to change the value already existing with the one from the same field for the record that precedes it, Press the **Ctrl +; (semi-colon)** to add the current date in the field.

Altering a value that exists

If you would like to change a value that exists rather than having to replace the whole value, make use of the mouse and;

- Click at **the front** of any character in the field to activate the insert mode; the value that exists will then move to the right even as you are typing the new value.

Your entry will switch to Overtype mode if you hit the insert key, allowing you to replace characters one at a time while typing. To switch between characters without disturbing the others, use the arrow keys.

You can also choose to erase the characters by simply

- Pressing the **backspace key** will erase to the left-hand side or you can choose to press the **delete button** and this will erase to the right-hand side.

Below is a table that displays some of the various editing techniques;

Editing Operations	Keystrokes
Insert a value within the field	Choose the point of insertion with your mouse then type the new data.
Toggle the whole field and the insertion point	Press the F2 button.
Move the insertion point to the end of the field	Press the end button.
Select the next character	Press the Shift + right arrow key
Choose from the point of insertion to the place where the word begins	Press the Ctrl Shift + left arrow key
Pick from the insertion point to the beginning of the field.	Press the Ctrl+Shift+Home buttons
Choose from the insertion point to the end of the field	Press the Ctrl + Shift +End buttons
Replace a value that already exists with a new value	Choose the whole value and then insert a new value.

Replace a value with the value of the former field	Press Ctrl + the apostrophe sign
Replace the current value with the default value.	Press Ctrl + Alt + Spacebar
Insert a line break in a Short Text or Long Text field.	Press the Ctrl + Enter buttons.
Include the current date.	Press the Ctrl +; semi-colon
Insert the current time.	Press the Ctrl +: colon
Add a new record	Press the Ctrl + plus sign
Undo a change to the current field	Press the Esc button or choose the Undo button.

Note that not all fields can be edited; the following are fields that cannot be edited: Auto number fields, Calculated Fields, and Fields in multi-user locked records.

Using the Undo Feature

When there is nothing at all to undo, the Quick Access toolbar's undo button is typically not illuminated. However, you can utilize the button to reverse the typing you've done in the field as soon as you start editing a record.

You can also undo a change with the use of the Esc key;

- If you are not currently changing any fields, pressing the **ESC key** will undo any changes you have made to the field you are currently editing as well as any changes you have made to the previous field you modified.
- You can reverse any modifications you must have made to the entire current record by pressing the **Esc key twice.**

When you must have typed a value into a field,

Selecting the **Undo button** will reverse any modifications made to that specific value. By simply clicking on the undo button, you can choose to reverse the modification made to the field that comes before the value when you absolutely must have moved to another field.
You can also undo all the changes that have been made to the current record that has not been saved all you have to do is to
- Click on the **undo button** after you undo the field.

After you must have saved a record you can still choose to undo the changes by
- Clicking on the **undo button**.

Nevertheless, after the next record has been edited, changes that have been made to the record will then become permanent.

Copying and Pasting Values

Depending on the kind of data being copied, Microsoft Office or Microsoft handles the task of copying or cutting data to the clipboard. Note that practically all of the Microsoft Office suite products can perform this, so it's not primarily an Access feature. Using the paste command in the Ribbon's clipboard group, you can paste data into another field after copying or cutting it.

Data can be cut, copied, or pasted between tasks in Microsoft Access or between any Windows application. Using this method allows you to copy entire records between tables or databases as well as datasheet values to and from any Microsoft Office suite. The paste command has three different options: paste, paste special (which allows you to paste in multiple formats), and paste append (which pastes the contents of the clipboard as a new record and also gives you a row with nearly the same structure).

Replacing Values

The Find Replace dialog box facilitates the process of easily finding an existing value to replace. **Show the Find and Replace dialog box with the use of any of the following methods;**

- Press the **Ctrl +H buttons**.

- Choose the **Replace command** from the Find group of the Ribbon.

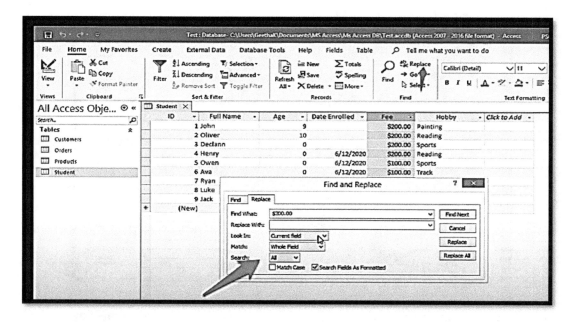

You can replace a value in the current field or throughout the table by using the Find and Replace dialog box. It can also be used to find a certain value and then substitute it with a different value anywhere that value appears in the table or field. After the Find and Replace dialog box has opened, select the **Replace tab**, type the desired value into the Find What box, and then

- Click on the **Find Next button** to locate the next occurrence of the inserted value.

You can choose your search options on the Find tab and then

- Choose the **Replace tab** option to ensure continuity of the process.

Nevertheless, it is much easier to do the whole process by making use of the Replace tab. Insert the value that you want to locate and the value that you would like to replace it with. After completing the dialog box and making sure all the information is correct, select any of the following commands: replace, which replaces the value in the current field alone; find next, which looks for the next field with the same value that has been inserted; cancel, which closes the form without completing the find and replace operation; and finally replace all, which locates all the fields with the value that has been inserted using the Replace With Value command. If you are certain that you want to alter every value in the box, then this is the option to choose.

Adding New Records

There are different ways in which you can add a record to a datasheet and they are;

- Choose the **last line** of the datasheet where the record pointer is an asterisk.
- Right-click on any **record selector** then clicks on the **New Record option** from the shortcut menu. The new record will still then be appended to the bottom not minding the record selector that was chosen.
- Press the **Ctrl + the + sign**.

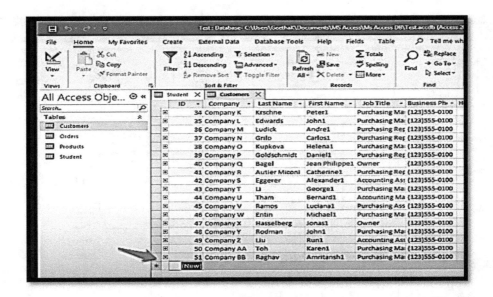

- Move to the **last record** and then click on the **downward pointing arrow key**.

Once you get to another record, insert data into the preferred fields then finally save the record.

Deleting Records

If you would like to delete any record in the table, follow the steps below;
- Choose **one or more records** with the use of the record selectors.
- Click on the **Delete key** then choose the **Delete commands** on the Record group of the Ribbon or you can choose to **right-click a records selector**.

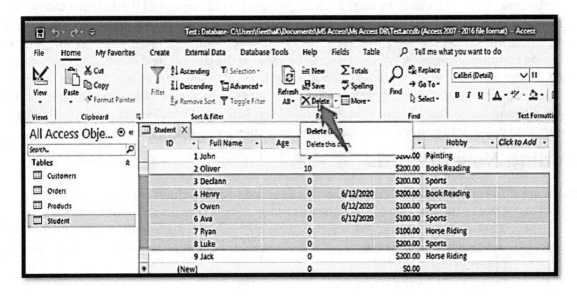

The Delete Record command, which is available in the Delete commands drop-down list, aids in deleting the current record even if it is not selected. A dialog window asking for confirmation will appear after you delete a record.

- If you choose **the yes button**, the records will be deleted and if you choose **the No or press the Esc button**, no changes will be made.

If you want to choose various consecutive records with the use of the keyboard,

- To select records nearby, press the **Shift + Spacebar key** to choose the current record and then the **Shift + downward or upward arrow keys** to expand the selection.

Displaying Records

When records are added or modified, there are a few strategies that can aid in the productivity increase. You can choose to alter column width or row height, display typefaces, field order, hide and freeze columns, and remove gridlines to make data entry simpler.

Changing the field order

Access displays datasheet fields in a way that mirrors how the table design displays them by default. Sometimes, to properly examine the data, you will need to see some fields that are adjacent to one another. Should you wish to reorganize the fields?

- Select **the column** by just clicking on **the heading of the column** then move the column to your desired location.

With the use of this method, you can choose to move a single field or multiple fields. If you want to move multiple fields,

- Select the **multiple fields** by dragging the mouse across the heading of the diverse fields. You can then move the fields to the left or the right or past the right or left boundary of the window.

Changing the field display width

It is possible to modify the field display's width by dragging the column border or specifying the precise width to be altered in the dialog box. The cursor will change to a double arrow sign when you move the mouse over a column border. **If you would like to make certain adjustments to the width of a field simply follow the steps below;**

- Position the **mouse arrow** between two column names on the field separator line.
- Drag **the column border** to the left side to make the column smaller or the right side to make the column bigger.

It should be noted that any modifications you make to the columns will not impact the maximum character count permitted in the table's field size. All that's happening is that the value of the column's data viewing space is being altered.

You can also choose to resize a column by

- Right-clicking on **the header** of the column and then choosing **Field Width** from the shortcut menu to show the Column Width dialog box.

Ensure you set the number of characters you would like to fit into the column or you can choose to;

- Click on the **Standard Width check box** to configure the column to its default size.
- Click on **Best Fit to Size** the column to the widest visible value.

Changing the record display height

It may be necessary for you to increase the row height to accommodate text with several lines or larger fonts. By adjusting a row's border to vary the height of the row, you may modify the record (row) height of every row.

If you would like to either increase or decrease the height of a row, follow the steps below;

- Place **the mouse arrow** between the record selectors of the two rows.
- To increase all of the row heights, move the row border lower; to decrease all of the row heights, move it higher.
- By selecting **more > Row height** in the Records group of the Ribbon, you can also opt to change the size of the rows. When you insert the row height in point size, the Row Height dialog box will appear. To restore the rows to their original size, make sure the Standard Height checkbox is selected.

Changing the display fonts

All of the data in the datasheet will be displayed in Microsoft Access by default in the Calibri 11-point typeface. To alter the appearance of the datasheet text, utilize the drop-down list and actions found in the Text formatting group of the Ribbon.

The entire datasheet will change as you adjust the font display. Use a typeface that is relatively small if you need to view more information on the screen. You have two options if you need to see a much larger character: either click the **bold button or increase the font size.**

Showing all cell gridlines and different row colors

Gridlines are shown by default between records and between fields. The Gridlines command in the Text Formatting group of the Ribbon allows you to choose how the gridlines should be presented.

Make your choice from the options below in the Gridlines drop-down list:

- **Gridlines**: Horizontal
- **Gridlines**: Both
- **Gridlines**: None
- **Gridlines**: Vertical

The datasheet's background color can be altered, and you can also use the background and alternate colors found under the Text formatting group. The background color palette will vary the color of every row in the datasheet, while the alternate row color palette will alter the color of the even-numbered rows. Microsoft Access will then prompt you to save the modifications you have made to the Datasheet layout once you have adjusted the Gridlines settings or the alternate row colors.

- If you want the changes made to be permanent, then click on the **Yes button**.

With the Datasheet formatting dialog box, you will have total control over the way the datasheet looks.

You can open this dialog box by;

- Clicking on the **Datasheet Formatting** launcher in the bottom right corner of the Text formatting group of the ribbon. Make use of the flat, sunken, And Raised option button beneath the Cell Effect to have the grid changed to a 3-D look.

You can alter the appearance of the grid lines by using the border and lines style drop-down list. Both the Datasheet Border and the Column Header Underline can have their styles altered. Select an alternative line style for every option in the first drop-down menu.

The different line styles that you can choose from are;

- Transparent Border
- Solid
- Dots
- Double Solid
- Dash Dot
- Sparse Dots
- Dash-Dots-Dots

Arranging data in columns

The alignment option allows you to have data-oriented to the left, right, or center. Select alignments that differ from the ones that are set as default. Access decides based on the field's type of data. **Follow the steps below to make changes to the alignment of the data in a column;**

- Place the **cursor anywhere** within the column whose alignment you want to change.
- Choose the **Align Left, center, or Align Right commands** in the Text formatting group of the ribbon.

Concealing and Revealing columns

You can choose to hide columns by configuring the column width to 0 or by moving the column gridlines to the preceding fields:

- Place **the cursor anywhere** within the column you want to hide.
- Click **on more,** and then hide fields in the records group of the ribbon.

When you must have hidden a column, you can choose to display the column again by simply choosing;

- **More > Unhide Fields** in the Record groups of the Ribbon. You will be able to choose which columns are visible next to each field by using the dialog box that appears. By unchecking the checkbox next to the field you want to conceal, you can also utilize this dialog box to hide multiple columns.

Freezing columns

Columns can scroll out of the view when you are scrolling either left or right. To stop this from happening you can simply;

- Choose the **More option** then choose **Freeze Fields** in the Records group of the Ribbon.

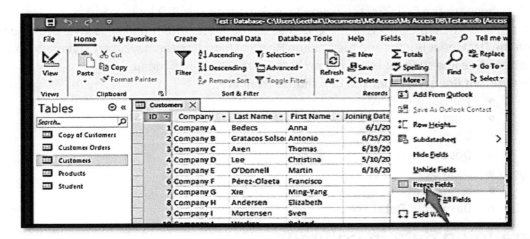

The remaining fields will scroll out of view horizontally, leaving only the previously frozen columns visible on the far left of the datasheet. Make sure the fields are arranged so they are close to one another if you would like to freeze multiple fields at once. **When you are done scrolling and you want to unfreeze the fields all you have to do is;**
- Choose the **More option** then click on the **Unfreeze All Fields option**.

Saving the changed layout

Although it's highly likely that you'll lose your layout adjustments, saving data changes is fairly simple: once you exit the datasheet, all of your modifications are preserved. Ideally, you should make the necessary modifications to the datasheet only once. Microsoft Access will automatically remind you to save any layout changes you make when you close the datasheet if you make one.
- Click on the **Yes option** to have the changes saved. The layout can also be saved manually by clicking on the Save button in the Quick Access toolbar.

Saving a record

Saving a record with Access is done instantly when you leave the record.

If you are still in the record and you want to save it immediately simply;

- Either select the **Save option** from the Ribbon's Records group or press **Shift + Enter**. It also aids in saving the records when you close the data sheet as a whole.

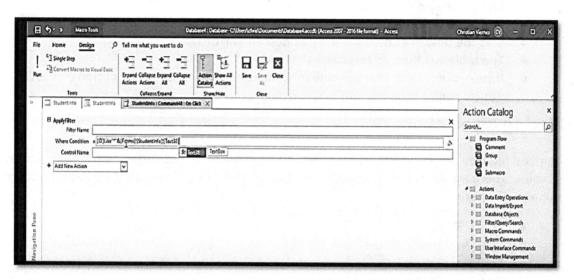

Filtering and Arranging Records in a Datasheet

A group on the Ribbon called the Sort and Filter group can assist you in both reducing and rearranging the number of rows. The records will be shown exactly as you would like them to when you use the command in this group. You may personalize your data and make it easier to deal with by using tools like sorting and filtering.

Sorting records

Sorting records entails grouping related data in a logical sequence and organizing the information accordingly. This means that sorted data is frequently simpler to read and comprehend than unsorted data. Microsoft Access automatically sorts records based on their ID codes. However, there are numerous more methods for organizing records.

Let's take the data belonging to a bakery as an example and see how we can sort such data;

- Orders can be sorted by order date or by the last name of the customer who must have placed the order.
- Customers can be sorted by their names, the city, or the zip code where they live.
- Products the bakery offers can also be sorted by name, price, or category.

Text and numbers can be arranged in two different ways: either ascending or descending. In ascending order, the data is arranged from the smallest to the largest, whereas in descending order, the data is arranged from the largest to the smallest.

Follow the steps below to have records sorted;

- Choose **the field** you want to sort by.
- Click on **the Home tab** on the Ribbon and find the Sort and Filter group.
- Sort **the field** in either ascending or descending order.
- The table will then be **sorted** by the field.
- If you would like to save the new sort, click on the **Save command option** on the Quick Access Toolbar.

Filtering a selection

When you filter by the selection, you will be able to choose your records based on the current field value. **There are four choices provided by Microsoft Access when you choose the Selection command; they are**

- Equal "Trucks"
- Does Not Equal "Trucks"
- Contains "Trucks"
- Does Not Contain "Trucks"

You can see if the data sheet is filtered or not by looking at the area to the right of the Navigation buttons in the lower section of the Datasheet window. Additionally, if the Toggle Filter command on the Ribbon is highlighted, it means that the filter is being used. Adding values is all that is needed to filter by selection. Every time you click on the **Selection command,** you can always keep selecting values.

When you are making use of the Selection command on numeric or date fields,

- You can insert a range of values by selecting one of the available commands. To limit the records to values within the required range, enter the smallest and greatest numbers of the oldest and newest dates.

When a datasheet has been filtered, each column will have an indicator in the heading of the column which simply lets you know that a filter has been applied to that column. When you move the mouse over the indicator you will see a screen tip that displays the filter.

- When you **click on the indicator,** more requirements to utilize the shortcut menu will be indicated. Alternatively, you can select an unfiltered column with a comparable menu by clicking on the downward arrow next to the column title.

The menu includes actions that assist with clearing the filter from the field, selecting a specific filter, checking the values you want to display in the datasheet, and sorting the column either ascending or descending. Depending on the column's data type, different instructions will be accessible. When a situation like this arises, you may use the Text Filter to provide criteria that will filter the data according to its kind. Data that is shown in the column is likewise presented in the checkboxes included in this menu. The options in this instance are Select All, Blanks, and an entry for each of these options. Identify in the table. If you wish to filter data but are unable to locate the value you wish to utilize even though you are aware of its value,

- Click on the **text filters** which can be either number filter, date filters, etc.

111

- Choose **one of the available commands** which will then display a dialog box wherein you can insert the desired value.

Filtering a form

You can add criteria to your filter by form that will let you enter a single row on the data sheet. The data sheet will change into a single row with a drop-down list in each column when you click the Filter by Form button. All of the column's distinct values are also included in the drop-down list. You may also specify OR conditions for each group by using the Or tab located at the bottom of the window.

To filter by form simply go through the following steps below;
- Click on the **advanced option t**hen select **Filter By Form** in the Sort and Filter group of the Ribbon to get into the Filter by Form mode.

You can enter as many conditions as you want with the use of the Or tab. **In case you even need a more advanced tweak of your selections simply follow the steps below;**
- Click on **Advanced** then **Advanced Filter/Sort** from the **Sort & Filter group** of the Ribbon to get an actual Query by Example (QBE) screen that you can make use of in entering more complex criteria.

Aggregating Data

Support for a total row is provided at the bottom of Microsoft Access data sheets. Clicking the Totals button in the Record groups on the Ribbon's Home tab opens the total row. The total row's columns can be set up to do different aggregation computations, including counts, sums, averages, minimums, maximums, standard deviations, and variances.

If you would like to make use of the Total row, simply follow the steps below;
- Click the **Totals button** in the Records group on the **Home tab of the Ribbon** after opening a table or form in the Datasheet view. The Total row will then be added by Microsoft Access to the datasheet's lower section, directly below the New row.

A drop-down list appears in the datasheet cell when you click on a column in the Total row. The items in the drop-down list are unique to the column's data type. The selected Totals computation ought to be dynamic. After a little wait, the calculation result displayed in the Total row will automatically be updated whenever you make changes to data in the datasheet or an underlying table. You may want to hide the Total row when not in use because doing so will result in a slight performance cost when you recalculate a lot of totals. The Totals option selected for the datasheet's columns will remain unchanged. The Total row remains intact even if you close and reopen the datasheet for whatever reason!

But if for reasons best known to you, you need to remove the Total row,

- Open the **datasheet** then choose the **click Totals button** in the Records group on the Ribbon.

Printing Records

All the records in your datasheet can be printed in a simple row and column layout.

The simplest and easiest way to print a record is to;

- Click **on File**
- Print and **choose one of the print options.**

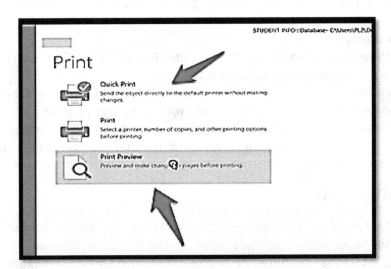

If you go straight to choosing the print option and not Quick Print or print Preview, Microsoft Access will show the print dialog box. **From this box you can choose to customize your printout by choosing from various options;**
- **Copies**: this option helps to determine the number of copies that should be printed.
- **Collate**: this helps to determine the various copies that are collated.
- **Print Range**: this helps to print the whole datasheet or just the chosen pages or records.

When printing the datasheet, the printout will display every layout option that is selected. Currently concealed columns will not print at this time. Only when the cell gridlines' attributes are enabled do gridlines print. The designated row height and column width will also be displayed on the printout.

Previewing Records

Even when the datasheet contains all the information you require and you are prepared to print, it is advisable to double-check that the columns and rows' heights and widths are appropriately set and to see if your font size needs to be changed before printing.
To preview your print simply

- To display the **Print Preview window,** select the **Print Preview command** located beneath the Print menu. The first page of my single-page preview is the default view. Utilize the Ribbon commands to select different perspectives and adjust the zoom level.
- To print the datasheet to a printer, click t**he print button.**
- To return to the Datasheet view, select the **Close Print Preview command** found on the Ribbon's right side.

Activity

1. What are Datasheets?
2. Make some movement within the datasheet.
3. Open a Datasheet.
4. Insert new data and save the record.
5. What does automatic data-type validation mean?
6. How do properties affect data entry?
7. Move between records and search for a value.
8. Copy and paste values in the datasheet.
9. Alter the display fonts.
10. Filter and arrange records in a datasheet.
11. Preview and print records in a datasheet.

CHAPTER 6

IMPORTING AND EXPORTING DATA

I'll walk you through both exporting data from the Access database and importing data from a source outside of it in this chapter. I'll also demonstrate how exporting data may be used to create external files. By importing data, you can add more information to what is already in the database, such as an XML file. Additionally, when you export data from Access, you create other data outside of Access databases, such as data contained in XML or EXCEL files.

Access and External Data

It is rather possible to exchange data between databases in the modern world. Generally speaking, data is always saved in a multitude of application applications and data formats. Access databases, like certain other databases, possess a unique file format designed to assist with rich data types such as OLE objects. To complete the task, though, you typically require more than just the Access database. The need to transfer data across Access database files or utilize data from another software with a distinct but different format arises frequently.

Types of external data

Data kept outside of the current database are referred to as external data. This data may be stored in a different Microsoft Access database or a text document, spreadsheet, ASCII, SQL, Server, Oracle, or even another file format such as ISAM (Indexed Sequential Access Method). Data can be moved across several application types using Microsoft Access, including database management systems, text files, and mainframe files, and Macintosh and Windows applications.

Different methods of dealing with external data

As was previously said, you will typically need to transfer data from one application to the Access database and the other way around. It may be necessary to obtain some data that you now own in an Excel spreadsheet. All of the data may be simply loaded automatically into the database. There are tools in Microsoft Access that can be used to transfer data between spreadsheet files and other databases. **The various ways Access does this include;**

- **Linking**: Connecting to data involves creating a link to a table located in a different Access database, or connecting to data in a different format. Data in the source file format, such as Excel or XML, is used for linking. The primary file will still be the linked data. It should be noted that moving, altering, or deleting the file containing the linked data would prevent Access from finding the data when it needs it later.

- **Importing**: Importing data from another application database or another Access database, for example, causes the imported data to be translated to the proper Access data type, saved in a table, and then handled by Access going forward.
- **Exporting**: Exporting takes data away from your Access database to another Access database or another file of an application. Unlike importing if the location of the source data is changed, this doesn't affect the exported data.

When to link to external data

Importing data and linking to external data are fundamentally very different. The linked data will remain in its original format. Once an external data link has been established, you can create queries, forms, and reports that display that data. Once you have created a link to external data, you cannot remove it on your own; the link will remain in place indefinitely. The only distinguishing feature between the connected table and any other Access table that is shown in the Navigation pane is its icon. Moreover, users of applications developed in native database formats such as FoxPro, dBase, or paradox, as well as users of the data sources themselves, may opt to make modifications to the data if the data permits multiple users. The inability to change a linked table's structure from within the Access database is the primary distinction between a linked table and a native table. Working with linked tables has one major drawback: unless the linked tables are all in the same external Access database or in another database that supports referential integrity, you will not be able to enforce referential integrity between the linked tables. There are situations when connected tables perform significantly worse than local tables. Users may notice a slight delay while opening a form or report that uses linked data, depending on the source and location of the source data.

When to import external data

Access will create a copy of the data and insert it into the Access table when you import data into it. Access will handle the data as it would any other Access table after it has imported the data. Moreover, neither you nor Access can determine the source of the data. As a result, imported data offers the same performance and versatility as data from other Access tables. You may feel compelled to remove the previous file after importing the copy into Microsoft Access since importing creates a new copy of the data. Sometimes, though, you might wish to hold onto the older albums as well. Improving the data to the point where it satisfies all of your requirements is one of the primary reasons you could import data. Despite the fact that the new table has been built inside the existing database, you can work with it once you have imported it into an Access database. However, there is a limit to how many modifications you may make using linked tables. Furthermore, linked tables might complicate the deployment of your applications since they point to external files that Access expects to find in a designated area. Keep in mind that you can use a VBA function or a macro to automate the process if you plan to export data from the same source frequently. This can be quite helpful when you need to import data from an external source frequently or when you need to perform complex transformations to the imported data.

When to export data

You may need to export data from a database for a number of reasons. You may wish to convert to a new software program, share data with another party, analyze the data, and utilize it for other purposes. When data is exported from Microsoft Access, it is first converted to an external format and then copied into a file that is easily readable by another program. You may occasionally need to work with data from a program that is not saved in an external database or file format that is supported, even though unsupported formats are somewhat uncommon. In situations like this, the programs can frequently export their data or have it translated into forms that Access can understand. Should you wish to utilize the data in these apps, export the data in a format that Access can understand and then import it into Access.

Various Choices for Importing and Exporting

We will examine the choices for importing and exporting data in this section. Because Access is easy to use and allows databases to be modified across several apps, most developers prefer to use it. For instance, you could need to gather information from an XML document or even SQL or Oracle. Microsoft Access makes this easy since it can transfer data between different application types, database engines, and platforms like Macintosh computers and mainframes. The import and link group has the following options; New Data Source, Saved Imports, and Linked Table Manager.

The drop-down menu of the New Data Source Option has about four categories which have various data formats like;
- **From File**
    - Excel
    - HTML Document
    - XML File
    - Text File
- **From Database**
    - Access
    - From SQL Server
    - From Azure Database
    - dBase File
- **From Online Service**
    - SharePoint List
    - From Dynamics 365(Online)
    - From Salesforce
    - Data Services
- **From Other Services**
    - ODBC Database
    - Outlook Folder

Importing External Data

The process of importing involved bringing in an Access database. After being imported, a copy of the external data will be stored in the Access database, but it will still be at its original location. Access will turn a copy of the data from an external source, such as SQL, into records in an Access table when you bring in a file. Importing the data does not modify the external data source. Additionally, take note that after the import procedure is finished, there won't be any link to the external source. Data can be imported into both newly created and pre-existing tables. It is possible to import any kind of data into a new table. However, some import formats—such as text files and spreadsheets—do not have a table structure that Access can use. In any situation similar to this, Access will create a table structure for you. Be sure to design the table before importing it if you would prefer to have control over it.

Importing from another Access database

Data from one database can be imported into the one you're working on right now. It is possible to import items such as tables, queries, forms, reports, macros, or modules.

To complete this process simply follow the steps below;

- Open the **destination database** you would like to import.
- Choose the **External Data tab**.
- Select **Import & Link** then choose **New Data Source> From Database> Access** then click on the **Browse button** to choose the **filename** of the source database.

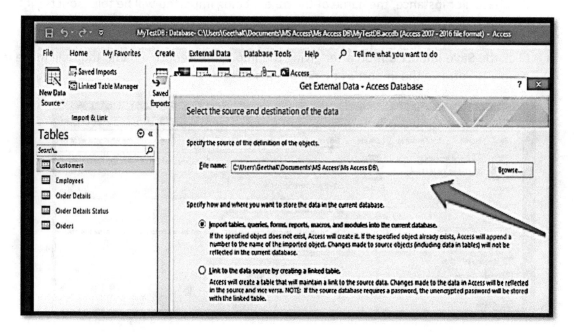

- Choose the **Import tables, Queries, Forms, Reports, Macros, and Modules** into the Current Database option button and then click on the **Ok button**.

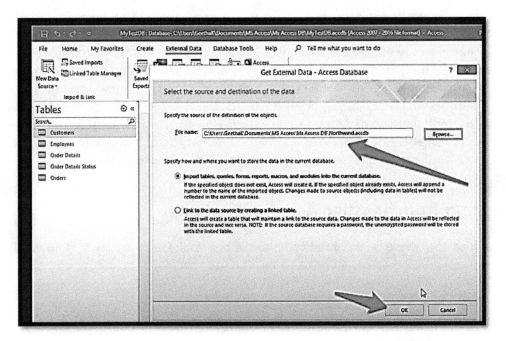

- After selecting a table, press the OK button. The name of the object you just imported will then have a sequential number appended to it if there is already an item in the destination database. For instance, the name of the object being imported will be tblproducts1 if the existing object's name is tblprodcts.
- Check the **Save import** steps checkbox.
- Click the **Save import option** after giving the import procedure a name that will make it simple to retrieve the import's original purpose.

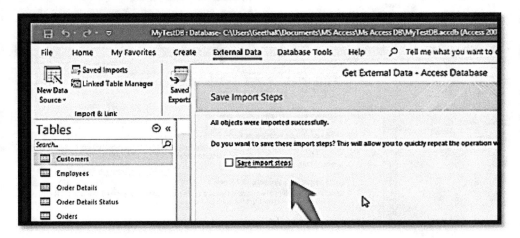

You can choose to run the saved import option much later all you need to do is to click on the Saved Imports button in the Import & Link group of the External Data tab of the Ribbon.

Importing from an Excel spreadsheet

If you want to import data from an Excel spreadsheet, just make sure you abide by the fundamental requirement that all of the data in a column be of the same type. When you are going to import data into a new table, Access will automatically determine what kind of data is there so that it can correctly allocate the data to the relevant field. You have the option of importing only the data from the designated range of cells or the entire contents of an Excel spreadsheet. Microsoft Access can make the importing process simpler when the cell range is named.

Follow the steps below to import from an Excel sheet;

- Start by **opening the database**.
- Click on the **Import & Link option>New>Data Source> From File> Excel on the External Data tab**.

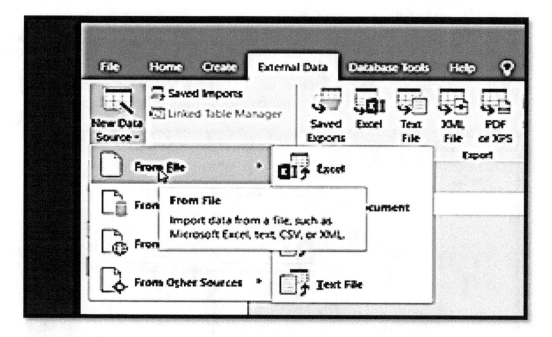

- Navigate through till you get to the Excel file
- Pick **Import Source Data** into a New Table in the Current Database then Click on the **OK button.**
- Select a **worksheet** or named range then click on the **Next button**.

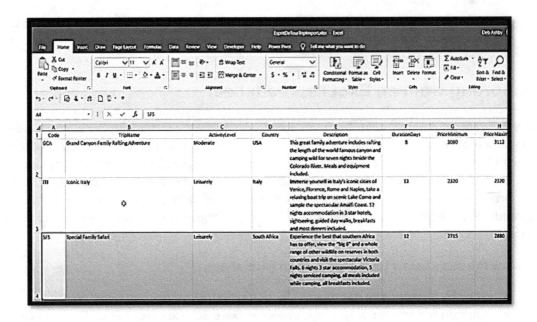

- On the next screen, choose the **First Row** that Contains Column Headings checkbox and then click **Next**.
- You can modify the default field name and data type, delete fields from the import, and create an index on a field on the screen that appears next. After finishing, press the **Next button**.
- On the next screen, configure **a primary key** for the new table and then click **Next**.
- Indicate **the name** of the new table and then click on the **finish button**.

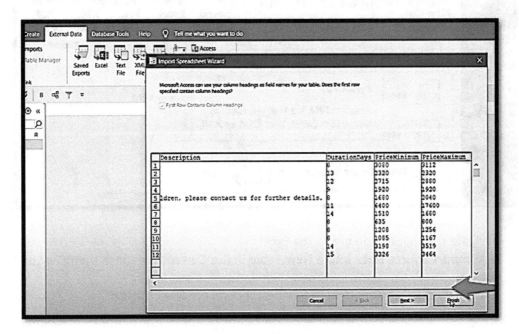

- If you would like to, save the import process for later execution.

Importing a SharePoint list

A SharePoint list is essentially a group of items arranged in rows and columns that resemble Microsoft Excel tables. It can be used to hold data to which you can attach files, such as papers or pictures. SharePoint lists are hosted on web servers, so users can access their data from any network that is suitable for them. This allows Access to share data almost anywhere in the world. Given the widespread deployment of SharePoint on business intranets, Microsoft Access may very well remain a component of enterprise setups.

Importing data from text files

There are two methods available for importing data into Access from a text file. If you would like a duplicate of the data, you can use the Import Text Wizard to edit the text in Access and import the file into a new or existing table. You may easily utilize the Link Text Wizard to link to the text file in your database if all you want to do is access the most recent source data that Access has to offer for improved querying and reporting. A text file has unformatted readable characters like letters and numbers and also special characters like tabs, line feeds, and carriage returns. Microsoft Access offers support for the following file name extensions- .txt, .csv, .asc, and .tab. A text file must have its contents well-organized for the linking and importing wizards to be able to divide it into a set of records (rows) and each record into collection fields (columns) if you would like to use it as a course file for importing and linking. Well-organized text files can be classified as Fixed-width files or Delimited files.

Delimited text files

Every record in a delimited file will be shown on a different line, and the fields will be divided by a single character called a delimiter. Any character that is not displayed in the field values, such as a tab, semicolon, comma, space, and so on, can be used as the delimiter.
Below is an example of comma-delimited text;
- , Company A, Anna, Bedecs, Owner
- , Company C,   Thomas, Axen, Purchasing Rep
- , Company D, Christina, Lee, Purchasing Mgr.

If you would like to import a delimited text file, take the following steps below;
- Start with **opening the database**.
- Choose the **External Data tab**.
- Select **Import & Link > New Data Source>From File>Text File**.
- Browse to the file, choose the **import option button** then select the **ok button**.
- Select the **Delimited button** on the ensuing screen, then press the Next button. The Text Wizard will subsequently appear as a result. You can select the separator that was used in the delimited file on this screen. (A separator is a character that I insert in between

fields in a text file that has been delimited; it can also be any other character. Usually, a comma or semicolon is used.

- Choose the **delimiter** that separates your fields; if the delimiter used is not a common one, click on **Other** and insert the **delimiter in the other box.**
- To proceed, simply select the First Row Contains Field Names checkbox and then click the **Next option** if the field names for the imported table are present in the first row. the screen that displays further actions that are comparable to those that need to be taken while importing Excel worksheets. Additionally, you have the opportunity to store the import option for later use and modify certain fields, such as names, to indicate a primary key.

It should be noted that no field in the text file that contains the separator character as data has ever used the separator that should be used. For instance, make sure that you do not use a comma in any of the fields if you have chosen to use one as a separator; otherwise, Access will encounter issues when importing the file. However, there is a workaround for this issue: use double quotes. As a result, the comma that is utilized in the fields won't be misinterpreted as a separator. Oftentimes single or double quote marks are used for this purpose and bring a solution to the issues of special characters contained within data fields.

Fixed-width text files

Every record in a fixed-width file is shown on a single line, and every field's width is the same from record to record. For example, every record will always have a first field that is seven characters long, a second field that is twelve characters long, etc. Values in fields that don't meet the specified width must be padded with space characters if the field's real length varies from record to record.

Here's an illustration of fixed-width text.

- Company   A   Anna   Bedecs   Owner
- Company   C   Thomas   Axen   Purchasing Rep.
- Company   D   Christina   Lee   Purchasing Mgr.

Below are the steps to follow if you want to import a fixed-width text file;

- Open the **database**.
- Choose the **External Data tab**.
- Select **Import & Link**, then **New Data Source>From File>Text File**. Browse to the text file you wish to import, then click the Import button, then click OK. This will display the Import Text Wizard's first screen, which will display the data in the text file and give you the option to choose between delimited and fixed-width fields. Select Fixed Width, then click Next. Modify the field widths as necessary. Keep in mind that Access will always estimate the best field breaks to use, and its estimations are based on the most consistent spacing between rows, so you can rely on the field breaks to be very consistent.
- Select the Advanced option located in the wizard's lower section. This will cause the Import Specification dialog box to appear, allowing you to modify the data types, dates,

times, and indexing default formats. Additionally, it will provide you with the option to exclude fields that you do not want to import.

- Ensure that the Four-Digit Years check box is selected and that the DATE Order is fixed at MDY.
- Select the **Leading Zeros** check box under the Dates section.
- To close the Import dialog box and Specification dialog box, click the **OK button.**
- You can proceed with the renaming of Import Text Wizard Screens.

Make sure there is a separator between the months, days, and years whenever you import text files with Data-type. If you specify a date/time type in any field without using a delimiter, Microsoft Access will indicate an error. Generally, the separator is not required for exporting day fields. You can designate a different separator to be used between the sections of times values in a text file by using the Time Delimiter option. Simply place a new separator in the Time Delimiter box if you would like to switch out the current one.

- Choose the **Four-Digit Years checkbox** to indicate that the year portion of a date field is formatted with about four digits. When you check this box, dates that include a century like 1981 or 2002 can be imported. Note that the default setting here is four-digit years.

Importing and exporting XML documents

This is a really simple Microsoft Access process. In essence, XML is used to move data between platforms, including businesses, operating systems, and apps. XML is used for data processing, metadata, and raw data. It may be said that nearly all Access developers will need to import or export data in XML format at some point.

Below are the steps to follow when you want to export data from Access to an XML file:

- Open the **database.**
- Open **the field** you would like to export in the Datasheet view.
- Click on the **External Data tab** and choose **XML File** in the Export section.

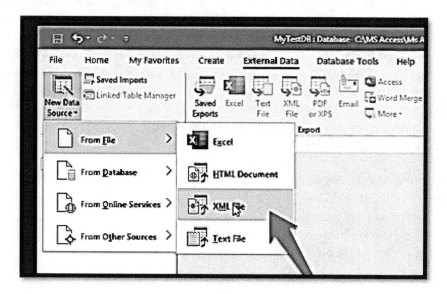

- Give the file a name that terminates with the customary XML, after which press the **OK button**. The export dialog box will appear as a result of this process, and it has several choices that can be used to specify advanced settings for the XML export procedure. A new dialog box with several crucial XML settings will open when you select the More options button. Schema files are frequently required for some other apps to fully comprehend sophisticated XML. Because Access opens the schema file automatically for data exported in XML format, it is recommended to use it.
- Click on the **OK button** to have the process exported.

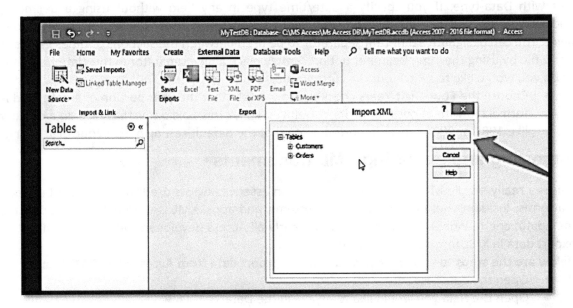

The primary key of the source table and the data types of each field are included in XML schema files. As the XML export is improved, it will specify exactly how the exported data should be shown in an application to display the XML data. Since the program created to use the XML file presents the data as needed by its users, there is typically never a requirement for the XML file to be shown. Keep in mind that XML uses a variety of tags to give the data context. The beginning of a tag indicates the beginning of a structure. Text is located between a greater-than symbol (>) and a less-than symbol (<). The structure comes to an end when the tags are closed.

Follow the steps below to have Access import XML files;
- Click on the **Import & Link > New Data Source>From File>XML File** on the External Data tab.
- Locate the **XML file** which usually ends with.xml then click on the **Open option** then click on the **OK button**. This will also display the Import XML dialog which tells how Access will interpret the XML data.
- Click on the **OK button**.
- Click on the **Close button.**

After completing the aforementioned procedures, Access would have successfully imported the XML file as a table, and you would have the option to rename the file at that point. Keep in mind that the data included within the field tags will also form the new table, and the tags that define the fields are those that are located within the file tag and its closing tag.

Importing and exporting HTML documents

With Microsoft Access you can also import HTML tables with ease as with any other database, text file, or Excel spreadsheet.
All you have to do is;
- Choose an **HTML file** to import and also make use of the HTML import Wizard.

To initiate this procedure, you must first export a table to create an HTML file, which can then be imported back into Microsoft Access to build a new table;
- Open the **database** and choose the **specific table** you would like to export from the Navigation pane.
- Select the External Data tab, and then select **HTML Document** by clicking the More drop-down menu next to the Export drop-down menu.
- Make sure the Export -HTML Document dialog box is displayed with an HTML file selected as the export destination.
- Select the HTML output options that you want and press the **OK button.** Clicking the **OK button** will cause the HTML export to start immediately.

Additional export options are displayed by selecting Export Data with Formatting and Layout, another option in the Export-HTML Document dialog box. Among these possibilities, the most significant one is the ability to specify an HTML template for your export. Importing HTML is similar to importing a text file; the Import HTML Wizard shares nearly all of the Import Text Wizard's screen settings, such as requiring the primary key to be identified and defining data types for fields.

Importing Access objects other than tables

You can import other objects into Access, such as queries and forms. The simplest method is to copy the object and then paste it, although there are other options available when using the import option. **Objects are imported basically when there is a need for you to do one of the following;**
- Copy the **design and layout of a form**, a report, or some other object.
- Make a copy of a form, report, or other object in its most recent version. One way to accomplish this is to import the object the first time and then use the import specification to repeat the import process later.

Be aware that there is not much of a difference between starting a second database and exporting the object from the original one established when you import an object into an Access database.

The two main differences that exist between importing and exporting objects are;

- Multiple objects can be imported in a single action; however, multiple objects cannot be exported in a single operation. It is recommended that you open the destination where the object should be and then import it if you need to export more than one item.
- You can import relationships between tables as well as any other import or export specification, which includes menu bars and toolbars, in addition to database objects. The query can also be imported as a table. Be aware that exporting does not provide these choices.

Follow the steps below to complete this import process;
- Open **the database**.
- Selecting **Import & Link >New Data Source> From Database>Access** will allow you to import data from an additional Access database. You will be presented with a screen where you can specify whether you want to link to tables in an external Access database or import database objects.
- Find the file, select it, and then click **OK after selecting the Open option.**

Anytime you are adding tables, forms, queries, modules, or macros all in the same import, you can choose objects from each of the tables and then have all of the objects imported at once.

Importing an Outlook folder

Microsoft automatically saves messages, contacts, appointments, tasks, notes, and journal entries in one of the following locations;
- On your computer in a personal storage folder, commonly referred to as a.pst file.
- Within a mailbox located on the server. If you use the Microsoft Exchange Server, your mailbox is often located on the server.

In the event of a hardware malfunction, unexpected data loss, the need to move data from one machine to another or the need to move data from one hard drive to another, you can create a backup copy of your Outlook file and use it to restore or migrate your data. You can specify the data type, add a primary key, import outlook data into a new or existing table, and schedule the import procedure for far later execution.

Exporting to External Formats

An export helps with the copying of data from an Access table to another application or data source like an XML document. The expected result makes use of the format of the destination data source and not the format of an Access database. You can choose to copy data from an Access table or query into a separate external file. You can also export tables to various other sources.

Exporting objects to other Access databases

You have the option to export any kind of Access object (tables, queries, forms, reports, etc.) to an Access database. You can only export one object at a time when exporting, unlike when importing, which often allows you to import multiple objects at once.
If you would like to export other objects simply follow the steps below;

- Open the **source database** and choose **an object** that you would like to export.
- Choose the **Access button** in the Export group of the External Data tab. This will then display the **Export -Access Database dialog box**.
- Employ the use of the **Browse button** to find the destination Access database. Make sure that the database is not opened at the time you want to export it. If it happens to be open, there might be a conflict.
- After selecting the Save option, select the OK button. You will be prompted to replace the item in the target database if the object you are exporting is already present in the database you wish to export to. You won't be able to make the object into anything else in the database if you don't.
- After choosing Definition and Data, press the OK button.
- You can store the export configuration for later use during the wizard's final step. This is a really useful option if you anticipate doing exports regularly.

Exporting through ODBC drivers

You can export files or objects with Microsoft by using ODBC (Open Database Connectivity). An ODBC driver is included with databases that are compliant with ODBC, and it serves as a bridge between Access and the database. The majority of widely used databases, including Access, are ODBC-compliant.

Follow the steps below to export files or objects through ODBC;

- Open **Access** and choose **the object** you would like to export.

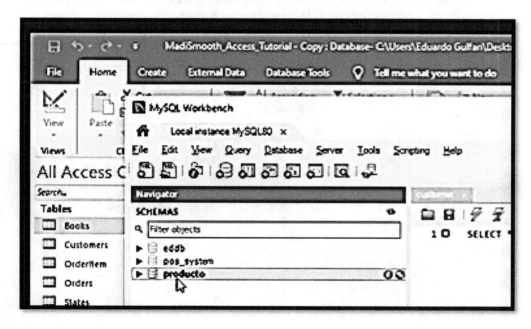

- Click on the **More button** then click on **ODBC Database** in the Export group of the External Data tab. This will display the Export dialog box.

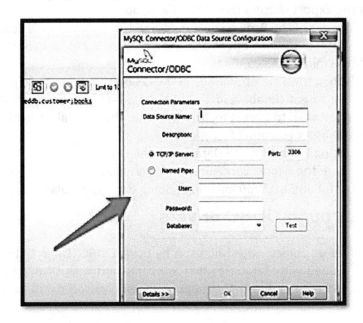

- If you want to use the default name, you can enter a name for the table or just click the **OK button.**
- From the **Select Data Source dialog box,** select **the driver that is right for your database.**
- Finally, save the export steps if necessary (especially if you export frequently).

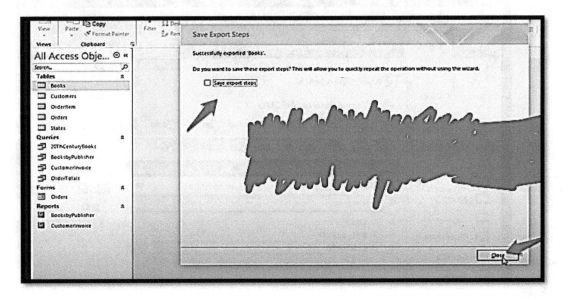

It should be noted that certain ODBC drivers may inquire for additional details, such as the database or table name. You can utilize the table in the other database once the export has finished.

Exporting to Word

There are two main ways to move data from Access to Word: export to Rich Text Format (RTF) or merge Word. Rich Text Format is a type of plain text file that has special characters that aid in formatting definition. A document with an RTF extension rather than a standard Word document will be created if you select the export to RTF option.

Merging data into Word

This is the most effective way to export Word. You can finally decide where you want your data to be used in a Word document with Word Merge. If you happen to be working on projects like creating file folder labels, addressing envelopes, or producing reports, this can be quite helpful.

If you would like to create file folder labels for departments in a table, go through the following steps;

- Open the **desired table in the Datasheet view**.
- Select the **Word Merge button** in the Export group located on the **External Data tab**.

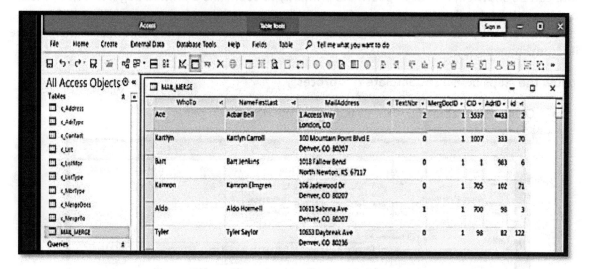

- Select **Create a New Document** from the Microsoft Word Mail Merge wizard's first screen. Link the data to the document and click the **OK button.**
- Follow the instructions provided by the Words Mail Merge Wizard. Select the label style after selecting the labels as the document type.

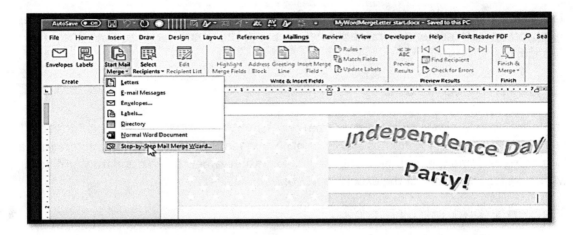

- Arrange **the names and characters** on the label and template then complete the merge process.

Access can be easily imported from Microsoft Word by first turning the Word document into a text file. Alternatively, Word and Excel can be combined to create a delimited text file.

Publishing to PDF or XPS

Data can be shown in PDF or XPS formats primarily to seem like a printed page. It is not possible to change the dates that appear in this format. When you publish to either the PDF or XPS format, you have very little file, but this method is quite helpful if you want to prevent the recipient of the file from changing it.

Follow the steps below to complete this process;

- Choose **the table** you want to publish in the navigation pane.

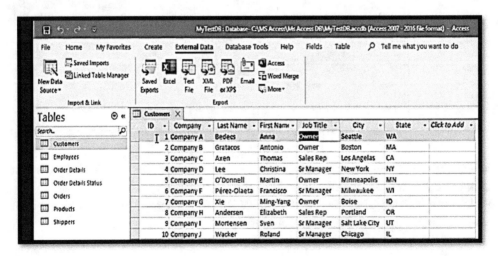

- Select either **PDF or XPS** from the Export group on the External Data tab of the Ribbon. They will then display the Publish as PDF or XPS dialog box is displayed.

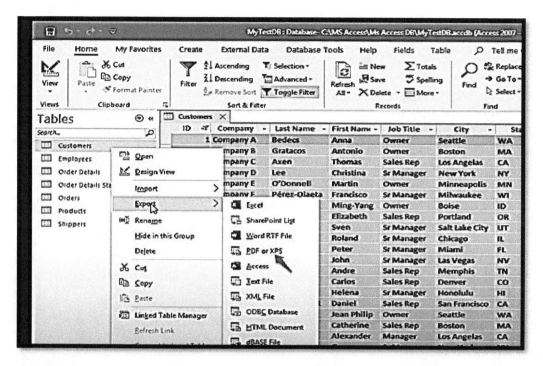

- Pick the **PDF** from the **Save As Type drop-down list**.
- Choose the **Publish button**.

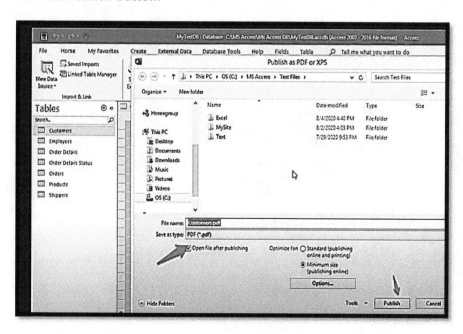

Once all of the above has been completed, you will then have a PDF file that can be opened by various PDF reader programs.

Activity

1. How does Access work with external data?
2. Mention the various types of external data.
3. When do you import external data?
4. When do you link external data?
5. Import external data either from Excel or from Sharepoint.
6. Import an outlook folder.
7. Export to external fonts.
8. Export objects to other Access databases.
9. Export objects to Microsoft Word.

CHAPTER 7
EXTERNAL DATA LINKING

The utilization of external data and how to link data to Access are covered in detail in this chapter. Additionally, you will discover that because Access is unable to function with relative paths, it must employ a specific component for every file. This implies that until you link the various external files, copying some files cannot work. This chapter also highlights many of the issues that may come up when you decide to link to external data; it is intended to act as a reference when you perform these link actions in your different Access applications.

Linking External Data

Working with a variety of information from multiple sources will become more necessary as the database market expands. The hassle of having to enter data again into Microsoft Access from an Excel spreadsheet or an SQL server will not be something you want to endure. You won't want to take the chance to prevent data duplication, given all the restrictions around external files. You would like to be able to access the Access table containing the necessary information without having to build a translation program or duplicate it. When copying or translating data between applications, using code can be very expensive and time-consuming. As a result, an intermediary between the many data sources in your environment may be necessary. With Microsoft Access, you can choose to link to various tables that are in the same database systems at the same time. Upon the linkage of an external file, Access saves the link specification and makes use of the external data as though it were contained in a local table.

Locating linked tables

Access provides links to specific database tables and various file formats when it comes to working with external data. In addition to using a unique icon to indicate that a table has been connected rather than local, Access will show the names of the linked tables in the object list. The table name displays a linked data source when it is indicated by an arrow pointing to an icon. You will utilize an external data table in your Access database just like any other table once you have linked it to your database. Users of Microsoft Access who use connected data genuinely have no idea where the data will end up or where it will go. All they need is the information in the format of their choice. The person who knows every obstacle in the process of integrating the data into the user interface will be the developer. Aside from the restrictions, users might be unable to distinguish between linked and native data.

Limitations of linked data

The crucial repute of connected data in Microsoft Access should always be kept in mind when working with it. Since the processes in many apps cannot be fully completed without the usage of data that I already have in Microsoft Access, you may need to integrate external data with Microsoft Access while using it in your organization. You will be able to use the data in its original format when you use Microsoft Access to utilize external data, but first, you must link the external data with the application. This essentially means that you will be able to use data in Microsoft Access that comes from another application. Nevertheless, there may be restrictions if you decide to link data from outside sources to Microsoft Access. Microsoft Access does not allow users to change the original data that uses Access, even if it allows users to utilize data from another application within Access.

Below are some other limitations;

- **Excel Data**: whenever you are making use of a Microsoft Excel worksheet in the Microsoft Access database, changes cannot be made to worksheets that already exist. Furthermore, adding and deleting more rows will not be possible in cases where data is linked. When data is linked, Excel Data can be used in Microsoft Access basically in a read mode.
- **Text Files**: Although you will have a little more access than only the read mode when using text files in Access as linked data, not much access will still be available. You can add rows to the data that already exists with this option, but you are still unable to modify, remove, or update any existing rows. This is mostly done for you to prevent any form of interruptions to the processes that you are now carrying out using the provided text files.
- **HTML**: The access that is granted in this option is read-only, almost the same as the access granted when making use of Excel Data as linked data. HTML cannot be changed by any known means. You cannot also update, delete, or include any more information to what has been created already in the HTML table.
- **dBase**: You can alter this file format just as much as you would regular Access databases because it is easily accessible in Microsoft Access. It is still necessary for you to have access to each database table's primary key. Your actions may be restricted once more if you lose the key.
- **ODBC**: One way to describe this technology is as a data access method that uses the driver that sits between Access files and the files from the associated data or application. Database software such as SQL Server and Oracle are included in this as well. Because the linked data source is also a database table, you have complete control over what can be added, deleted, or edited. Keep in mind that the linked database needs to have a uniquely specified index before this can happen. Therefore, you will need to have a unique index for each linked data set if you want to access linked data from another database application as freely as though it were a native Access database there will be a need for you to have a custom index for all of the databases that are linked. It is always prudent to have a professional tool at hand so as to be able to recover files that become corrupted before the initiation of a drastic change.

Linking to other Access database tables

You can bring in data from one Access database into another in different ways. Copying and pasting is a very simple way but the use of importing and linking provides you with a much better opportunity and also gives you better control over the data that you bring, and also over how you bring the data into the destination base. You may want to think about linking data if your company uses many databases, but keep in mind that some table data, such as Employees, must be shared throughout databases. The data in your database should be accessible to another department or workgroup, but the table structure should remain your property.

Below are steps you should follow to link to a particular table in the database.

- Open **the table** you want to link.
- Click on the **External Data tab** of the Ribbon, and then click on **Import & Link > New Data> From Database>Access**. This will then display the Get External Data -Access Database dialog box.

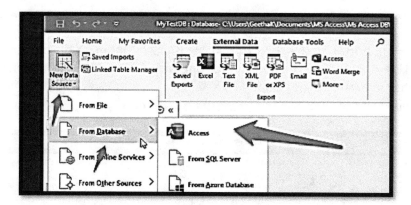

- Click on the **Browse option**.

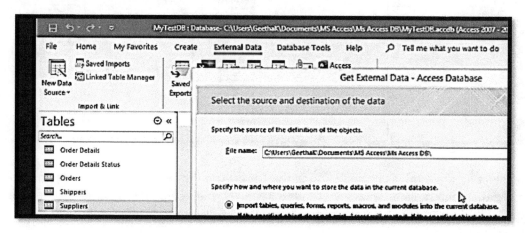

- Find the data you want to link then click on **open**.

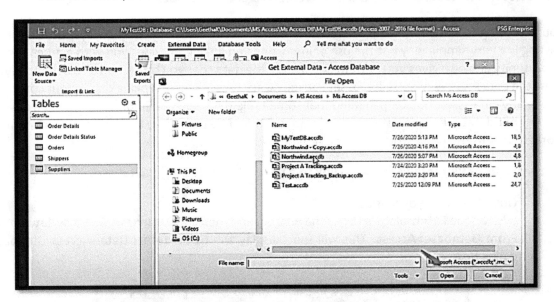

- Click the **OK button** in the Get External Data-Access Database dialog box after selecting the linking option button. You can pick one or more tables from the chosen database using the Link Tables dialog box.
- In the end, click the table and choose the **OK option.**

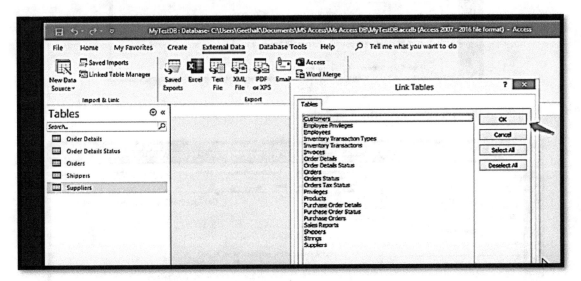

If you select multiple tables before clicking the **OK button** in the Link Tables dialog box, you can link more than one table at once. All of the tables will be selected when you select the Select **All buttons.** If it is necessary to deselect any of the tables, you can choose specific areas of the table after selecting every table.

Linking to ODBC data sources

Microsoft and a few other companies established the Open Database Connectivity (ODBC) standard, which is a significant advancement in data exchange. Software companies use the ODBC specification extensively while developing different database products. This specification enables Access programs to interact with data consistently across various database platforms. Any application that complies with ODBC specifications will undoubtedly be able to utilize any back end that complies with ODBC. Using the SQL Server ODBC driver is the method most frequently employed to fulfill this requirement. You must have constructed the program when you discover that an organization with whom you are affiliated would like to use it as well, but Oracle is their database host. You should be able to utilize the same program with Oracle by just obtaining an Oracle ODBC driver if your application has closely adhered to ODBC syntax. In addition to providing drivers for their goods, companies today increasingly develop and provide ODBC drivers for software.

Linking to non-database data

There is also a need for you to link non-databases like Excel, HTML, and text files. Whenever you choose these types of data sources, **Microsoft Access will run a Link Wizard that will prompt you through the entire process;**

Linking to Excel

Below are the main things you must bear in mind to link with Excel data;

- An Excel workbook file might java various worksheets. There is a need for you to make a choice of the particular worksheet within the workbook file you would like to link except in terms of you making use of named ranges.
- One option is to link to certain ranges within the Excel spreadsheet. In Microsoft Access, each range will then appear as its own linked table.
- Excel columns can include almost any kind of information. Your application may not be able to utilize all of the data in the Excel worksheet even though you were able to link it properly. There is no restriction on the kinds of data that can be included in an Excel worksheet, so it's highly likely that your application will come across many data types in a single column of a linked worksheet.

This simply means that there is a need to include a code or get some other strategies for working around the different types of data that are in an Excel worksheet.

Follow the steps below to link to an Excel spreadsheet;

- In the database, click **on Import & Link > New Data Source>From File>Excel** on the External Data tab of the Ribbon.

- After making a linked table, select the **Link to the Data Source option** and then select **Browse**. Be aware that the Get External Data dialog box is identical for both link and import procedures; make sure you select the appropriate action before moving further.
- Find and open **the Excel file**.
- Click on **OK** when you get to the **Get External Data- Excel Spreadsheet dialog box**.
- Choose the **Products worksheet**.
- With the help of the Link Spreadsheet Wizard, you can specify information such as the type of data to be applied to each Excel spreadsheet and whether the first row has column headings. The name of the table that was recently linked will then be requested on the Link Spreadsheet's final screen.
- Finally, click on the **Finish button**. The linked table is then created and you will be taken back to the Access environment.

Linking to HTML files

When it comes to linking to HTML files, Access imposes a lot of restrictions. For example, Access cannot import data from an arbitrary HTML file unless the data is clean and presented in an HTML table with rows and columns. If the data is presented in a hierarchical fashion or if multiple HTML tables are displayed on the website, extra issues could occur. Rather than trying to interact with random HTML files, it is far easier to link with an HTML document that has been specially prepared as a data source for your Access application.

Follow the steps below to link HTML data, and note that the process is quite similar to that of Microsoft Excel;

- Choose the **Import & Link > New Data Source > From File > HTML Document** on the External Data tab of the Ribbon.

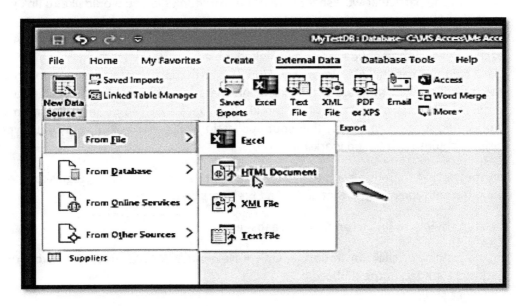

- Choose the **Link to the Data Source** by establishing a Linked Table option, and also click on the **Browse option**.

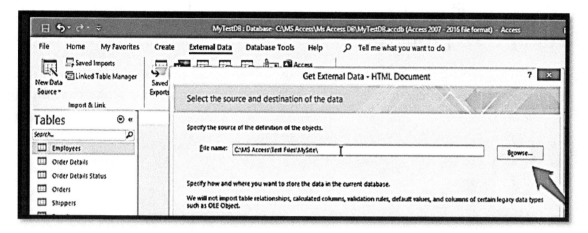

Once you have completed the steps above, the remaining steps are similar to linking to other types of files. **If you will need to provide the field names,**
- Click on the **Advanced button** to get to the Link Specification dialog box.

Linking to text files

The need to link to data contained in plain text files is a more frequent occurrence. The majority of programs, including Word and Excel, include the ability to publish data in many text forms.

The most common formats you might come across are;

- **Fixed Width**: A single row of a database table appears on each line in a text file with a specified width. The character count of every field included within a line is equal to that of the comparable fields located in the lines above and below the current line. To fill the field's designated width, spaces are padded to the right of each data field.
- **Comma-separated values (CSV)**: Compared to the fixed width, these are a little more complicated and technical to understand. In addition to taking up the space required to be able to absolve the data, each field is separated by the comma character (,). In a CSV file, there is essentially never any blank space between fields. Because each field in a CSV file only contains the space required for the data, more data can be stored in a much smaller file.

Using Linked Tables

Use an external table from another database just like you would an Access table once you have linked to it. When using an external table, you can change the majority of its features at any time. It is possible to modify features like changing the view attributes, renaming the tables, and creating linkages between the tables. It should be noted that changing the name of the table within Access does not alter the name of the file that is connected to that program. The linked table that will continue to be maintained with the application is called Acres; the name Acres has no bearing on the associated physical table.

Setting view properties

As earlier explained above, you can change the view properties of the table linked with Access but you cannot change the structure of the table. **Below are the various properties you can choose to set for the field:**

- Decimal places
- Format
- Caption
- Display control
- IME sequence mode

To have these properties changed simply;

- Launch the Design view of the associated table. Access will alert you that it cannot be changed when you do this. Just choose to disregard the alert and carry out the changes.

Configuring relationships

Using the Relationship pane in Access, you can establish permanent links between linked non-Access tables and native Access tables at the table level. Nevertheless, you won't be able to establish referential integrity across internal tables or connected tables. The association that may already exist between the external tables is preserved when you link to an external Access table. Therefore, when you link to a backend database, the front-end database is aware of the relationships that have been established in the backend as well as any validation and default values. This is great news since it means that the established rules will be followed regardless of how many front ends are made to utilize the tables.

Optimizing linked tables

When having to work with linked tables, Access will have to get records from an external file. This process can take quite a while and might even be a much longer process if the table is on a network or in an SQL database.
Whenever you are working with external data ensure you optimize performance by taking into consideration the rules below;
- **If records are added to externally linked tables, design a form and have the Data entry property configured to true**: When you select this option, the form becomes an entry form that always starts with a blank record. Typically, data from the bound table is not pre-populated on data entry forms. You can be certain that using a much more specialized

data entry form will be more efficient than creating a standard form, filling it with information from the linked source, and then having to go to the end of the data to add a new record.

- **Avoid multiple movements in datasheets**: Here, all you should do is look at the necessary data on its own in a datasheet. Please make sure that you do not navigate up and down the page or move from the start to the last record in any of the large tables.
- **Reduce the number of external records that should be viewed**: build a query with the use of a criterion that reduces the number of records from an external table. You can then make use of the same query with other queries, forms, or reports.
- Avoid the use of functions in query criteria: This is especially true for aggregate methods, such as DTotal or DCount, which frequently retrieve records from the connected table before starting the query.

Deleting a linked reference

There are three steps involved with deleting a table from a database.

Below are the steps;
- Locate the **navigation pane** then choose the **linked table** you would like to delete.
- Click the **Delete key**, or you can also choose to right-click and choose the **Delete option** from the shortcut menu.
- Click on the **OK button** in the Access dialog box in order to delete the file.

Viewing or altering information for linked tables

Whenever you rename, or modify tables, or relationships associated with linked tables, make use of the Linked Table Manager to update the links. To do this simply;
- Choose the **External Data tab** of the Ribbon and then choose the **Linked Table Manager** option.
- Select the **check box** close to a linked table and then click on the **OK button**.
- Locate the **missing file** and link it again to Access. Note that if all of the files happen to be linked already when you click on the **OK button**, Access will ensure it verifies all the links that are associated with all the tables that were chosen.
- Click the **OK button** after selecting the **Always Prompt for New Location checkbox** if you are aware of every linked data source that needs to be transferred. After that, Access will ask you for the new location and link every table in a batch operation. Compared to linking the tables one at a time, the batch process is much faster. The Linked Table Manager will still require you to select each source individually even if your tables are all from separate sources.

Refreshing a data source and its linked tables

Refresh a data source and also its linked tables so as to ensure that the data source is accessible and the linked tables are working normally.

Follow the steps below to refresh linked tables;

- Choose **External Data** then click on **Linked Table Manager**.

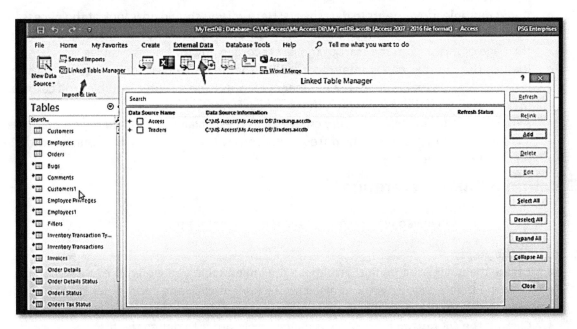

- Select a data source or specific linked tables while in the Linked Table Manager dialog box. All of the tables that are related to a data source will be automatically selected when you choose it. Click on the **Data Source** items to select specific related tables.
- Choose the **Refresh option**.

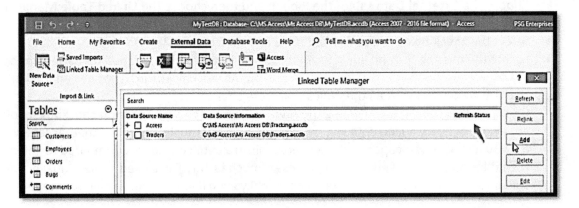

- If there happens to be any problem with the data source location, insert **the location** that is correct if you are prompted to or you can also choose to edit the data source as an alternative.
- **Ensure that the status column is visible and then check properly to view the results;**

- Success: this will be displayed when the linked tables have been refreshed successfully.
- Failed: If there is an issue with one or more linked tables, this will be shown. The two most frequent causes of a failed status are: when the table name is changed or new credentials are used. Relink the connected table or the data source to resolve this issue.
- Click on the **Refresh option** again until you are sure you have fixed all of the failed linked tables and the Status column shows "success".

Splitting a Database

Tables can be split in the same manner that they can be linked to a database. When a database is split, two distinct ACCDB files must be created, one titled "backend" and the other "front-end." Tables and relationships are the only things found in the backend; macros, code, queries, and user interface components like reports and forms are found at the front end. Links to every table on the back end are also available from the front end.

The benefits of splitting a database

You will undoubtedly need to partition your Access database for at least one valid reason. A database that has been split into two files—a front-end database and a back-end database—will be rearranged. A local copy of the front-end database will be used by each user to interact with the data. You must utilize the Database Splitter Wizard in order to separate a database. Make sure you share the front-end database with each and every one of your users once you have completed separating the database.

The benefit of a split database includes;

- **Improved performance**: Since just the data is transferred over the network, the database's performance always increases. When a database is not split, more than just the data is transferred over the network—queries, tables, forms, reports, macros, and modules are among the database objects.
- **Greater availability**: Since it is just the data that is sent across the network, database transactions like record edits will be completed faster leaving the data more available to edit.
- **Enhanced security**: If the back-end database is kept on a machine that uses the NTFS file system, you can use the security capabilities of NTFS to help safeguard your data. It is less likely that some hackers will obtain illegal access to the data by stealing the front-end database or by pretending to be an unauthorized user because users access the back-end database through linked tables. Ask the system administrator if you are unsure about the file system your server is using. Alternatively, if you have administrator capabilities on the file server, you can use the msinfo32 command to find the file system on your own.

- **Improved reliability**: Any database file corruption is always restricted to the copy of the front-end database that the user has to have opened in the event that a user encounters an issue and the database closes unexpectedly. The back-end database file may not be corrupted since linked tables are the sole way for the user to access the data in the back-end database.
- **Flexible development environment:** Each user can create queries, forms, reports, and some other database items separately without negatively affecting other users because they are all working with a local copy of the front-end database. Furthermore, updating the front-end database doesn't have to interfere with users' ability to access data stored in the back-end database.

Knowing where to put which objects

All of the UI objects, such as forms, reports, macros, queries, and modules, are present in the local ACCDB. The performance of the UI components can be enhanced by keeping them locally installed. It will not be necessary for you to transfer forms, queries, or reports across the network because you can manage these items more easily locally than when they are accessible remotely. All of the shared tables ought to be placed in the back-end database and also kept on the server with all the relationships that exist between those tables. The tables in the server database are linked to the front-end ACCDB on each user's desktop. When many users access a table, it is possible for the same record to be modified by the same users. To prevent this from happening, Access database engines lock the record while it is being edited by a user. In the event that many users attempt to update the same record, a lock contention will also occur. The record will only be accessible to one person at a time; all other users' edits will be delayed or locked until the record holder has finished making all required changes.

Making use of the Database Splitter add-in

An application can be divided into front-end and back-end databases with the use of the database splitter. By using this Wizard, you will be able to create and test your database, which will relieve you of the strain of getting everything ready for the multi-user access application.

Follow the steps below to make use of the Database Splitter;

- Begin the **Database Splitter** by choosing the **Database Tools tab** of the Ribbon then select the **Access Database button** in the Move Data group.
- Following this operation, a wizard screen will appear, informing you of the Database Splitter's actions and suggesting that you make a backup of the database before continuing.

The only information that Database Splitter needs is where you would like to have your back-end database.

Using the Edge Browser Control on a form

To display web pages on a form and specify a URL, use the Edge Browser Control. For every form record, you can generate a dynamic web page by mapping Access fields to URL parameters. By entering a file URL, you can also browse files and directories.

Add an Edge Browser Control to a form

With the exception of the control source being a URL, adding an Edge Browser Control to a form is comparable to adding other controls.

- In the Navigation Pane, right-click the form to which you would like to include an Edge Browser Control, and then choose Layout View.
- In the Controls group on the Form Design tab, choose Edge Browser Control.
- Place the pointer where you would like to have the control, and then choose to place it. Access will then launch the Insert Hyperlink dialog box.
- Get any of the following done;

Include a simple URL

You want every record in the form to lead to the same webpage. For instance, the webpage serves as the user's resource for additional information or assistance.

- Choose **Browse the Web** to the right side of the Address box.
- Once the preferred page is shown in your browser, copy the **URL** from the address bar, and then get the browser closed.
- Select **OK** in the Insert Hyperlink dialog box.

Add a URL with a query string

Every record in the form should have a different webpage shown for it. A query string that sets values for parameters is one option.

The Web page, for instance, is a map that changes according to the address fields in every record.

- Next to the Address box, select Browse the Web.
- Open your web browser and go to the page you want the control to appear on.
- Paste the URL into the Address box of the Insert Hyperlink dialog box, then hit the Tab key.

After clearing the Address field, Access divides (or parses) the URL into the Base URL, Paths, and Parameters boxes. Below the lists of Paths and Parameters, a box displaying the entire URL is shown.

- Replace the relevant URL components with phrases that refer to the relevant form controls if you want to configure the Edge Browser Control to alter its URL in response to the data presented on your form. For every part that has to be changed:
  - After selecting the path or parameter to be changed, click the Build button to see the button image.
  - If the element lists are not visible in the Expression Builder dialog box, click More >> to make them visible.
  - Locate the control that has the data you wish to replace for that path or parameter in the element lists, and then double-click it to add it to the expression box.
  - To end the Expression Builder, click OK after adding the required operators and expression components if there are any more calculations that need to be done with the value.
  - Choose OK in the Insert Hyperlink dialog box.

Navigating to Local Files

The https://msaccess prefix needs to be used before the file path in the address if you wish to open a local file rather than a webpage. As an illustration, consider this: https://msaccess/C:\Users\user\Documents\test.html

Trusted Domains Property

Links that take users away from the page their browser is currently showing and automatic redirection is by default disabled. You can designate a table name or query name in the Trusted Domains field of the field Sheet to permit these navigations. In this scenario, the URLs you want the browser to link to and automatically redirect to must be in the first output column of the table or query. Pages that automatically reroute to a login page that doesn't exist on the same domain would particularly benefit from this.

Alter the position and size of the Edge Browser Control

The Edge Browser Control may initially take up a relatively small cell in a layout when you first place it on a form. Generally, you will have to change the layout such that the majority of the Web page is visible.

Starting off by combining the control cell with nearby empty cells is a smart idea:

- To access the Edge Browser Control, choose the cell containing it.
- To make the control occupy any vacant neighboring cell, hold down the CTRL key when choosing that cell.
- Click Merge in the Merge / Split group on the Arrange tab.
- To adjust the size of the resultant cell, pick it and drag its edges to the desired size.

Modify the control source of an Edge Browser Control

You may need to adjust the Edge Browser Control's control source (URL) after adding it to a form. To make modifications, enter the Insert Hyperlink dialog box by following the steps below.

- Right-click the form that has the **Edge Browser Control** in the Navigation Pane, then select **Layout View.**
- In the Tools group, select the **Edge Browser Control** and then click Form Layout **Design > Property Sheet.**
- Click the **Build button picture** after selecting the **Control Source property** on the All or Data tab of the property sheet.
- Make the required adjustments to the URL components in the Insert Hyperlink dialog box, and then click **OK.**

Activity

1. Link external data together.
2. What are the limitations of linked data?
3. Link objects to Excel.
4. Work with linked tables.
5. Configure relationships.
6. Optimize linked tables.
7. Refresh a data source and its linked tables.
8. Split a database.
9. Make use of the edge browser control on a form.

PART III
WORKING WITH ACCESS QUERIES

You will learn more about the fundamental analytical tools and methods that you can use with Access from the chapters in this section. It will also provide you with more information on handling queries. Queries gather information from multiple data sources and display it in a way that is highly helpful. Access tables' raw data can be combined with queries to provide a very insightful analysis.

CHAPTER 8

SELECTING DATA WITH QUERIES

Queries cannot be overlooked in any database application. They are used to get data from various tables, combine the data, and then present the data in a meaningful way to the user(s) as a form, datasheet, or printed report. Queries are basically used to bring data sources together and also present the combined information in a manner that users will be able to work with the data with ease.

Introducing Queries

A well-designed database will typically include multiple tables containing the data you need to convey through a form or report. To display data in a form or report, you can retrieve data from multiple tables using a query and then combine them together. A query can function both ways: it can be used to take action on the data or as a request for data results from your database. A query can be used to add, modify, or remove data from a database, get the answers to basic questions, and carry out basic calculations and data aggregation from several tables.

What Queries can do

With queries you can combine data and also analyze them effectively. Below is a list of things you can do with queries;

- **Make changes to data in tables:** You can change several rows in the underlying tables as a single operation by using queries. Action queries are typically used to maintain data, for example by adding new data, updating particular fields, or removing obsolete information.
- **Show query data on forms and reports**: It's possible that the record set produced by a query has the fields you require for a report or form. Simply put, when you create a report or form that depends on queries, you can be sure that the tables include the most recent data whenever you need to print the report or access the form.
- **Create tables**: You can create an entirely new table based on the data that the query returns.
- **Perform some calculations**: You can use queries to perform some simple calculations like averages, totals, or simply counting of data that are in a record.
- Sort records: Queries are a tool for sorting records. You might need to view a customer's contacts, for example, if they have been arranged either by last name or by first name.
- **Choose tables**: Data can be obtained from a single table or from multiple tables that are connected to one another. In case you're curious about a customer's name and the products they purchased. Microsoft Access may aggregate the data into a single record set by using multiple tables.

What Queries return

After a query is executed, Microsoft Access combines a report with the query and displays it in the Datasheet view. A record set is the collection of records that a query returns. The records in a database or the results of running a query are displayed by a Recordset object. Data manipulation at the record level frequently involves the use of record-set objects. When DAO objects are used, you end up having to manipulate data while almost making use of the whole Recordset objects. All Recordset objects are created with the use of records (rows) and fields (columns).

There are basically five types of Recordset objects.

Note that the record set returned by a query is not usually stored in the database except if you have instructed Access to build a table from those records. The read makes sure that a query reads the underlying tables and then recreates the record set every time it is executed. Even in a real-time multi-user system, a query will automatically reveal any changes made to the underlying tables since you last ran the query because recordsets themselves are typically not saved. The record set of a query can be viewed as a datasheet, report, or form, depending on what format works best for you. Every time you access a form or report that you have chosen to base on a query, the query's record set will be recreated and bound to the form or report.

Designing a Query

Once you have created a query, you are then set to begin work. To create a query follow the steps below;

- Click on the **Create tab on the Ribbon**.
- Click on the **Query Design button** in the Queries group. This will then open the query designer. In the dialog box that is then displayed afterward, ensure that you add the tables needed for the query.

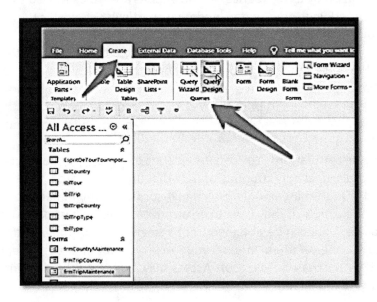

If you would like to include tables to the query simply;

- Right click on **anywhere** in the upper part of the **Query Designer** and choose **Show Table** from the shortcut menu that is being displayed.
- With the Show Table option opening, you will then be able to choose **all the table**s and query objects you might be in need of to successfully build your table.

Dragging the tables or queries from the navigation pane to the top of the Query Designer is another quick and simple way. If you have already closed the Show Table dialog box and you need to add a table or object to your query quickly, you can use it with great efficiency.

The query design window has about three primary views which are;
- **Datasheet view**: which shows all of the records that are returned by the query?
- **SQL view**: which shows all of the SQL statements behind the query?
- **Design view**: this is the very location where you build a query.

There are also about two different sections in the Query Designer, they are;
- **The table/query pane (top):** This is the exact location where the fields and tables that make up the query are integrated with the query design. There will be distinct fields presented for each list of objects that need to be added. The names of every field in the different tables or queries are also included in each of the field lists. **You can also choose to change the size of the field list by**
  - Clicking on **its edges** and then moving the edges to your preferred size.
- **The Query by Design (QBD) grid**: The names of the fields included in the query and any other criteria used to select the records are kept organized in the QBD grid. Information about a single field from a table or query in the upper lane is contained in each of the columns.

The QBD grid has about six rows that are labeled, they are;
- **Field**: This is where the names of the field are either labeled or inserted.
- **Table**: This row displays the table the field is from. This is also quite useful in queries that have various tables.
- **Sort:** This row allows the sorting of instructions for the query or queries.
- **Criteria**: This row has the criteria that filter the records that are returned.
- **Or**: this is the first of the number of rows in which you include various query criteria.
- **Run**: This facilitates the query's execution. The datasheet for a selected query is displayed, which performs the same purpose as selecting the Datasheet view from the view button. Keep in mind that the run button executes the actions specified by the query when you are working with action queries.
- **Selec**t: When you choose this option the opened query will be changed into a select query.
- The buttons labeled MakeTable, Append, Update, Crosstab, and Delete denote the many types of queries that can be created. Most of the time, clicking one of these buttons turns a select query into an action question.
- Show table: this button opens the Show Table dialog box.

Adding fields to your Queries

There are various ways in which fields can be added to a query. You can choose to add fields one at a time or you can also choose to add more than one field or choose all the fields in the field list at once.

Including a single field

You can add a single field in various ways.
- You can choose to click **twice** on the name of the field in the table that can be found in the top pane of the Query Designer.
- You can also choose to **move a field** from a table in the top pane of the Query Designer and then drop it on a column in the QBD grid. This action will have the other fields pushed to the right side.

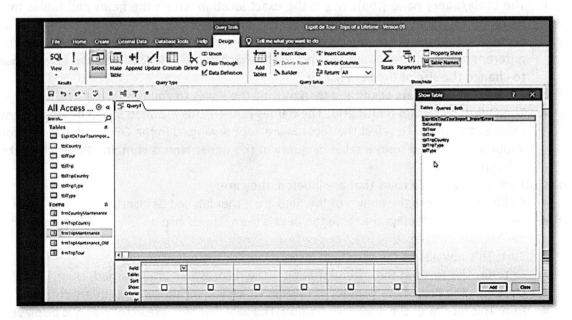

Adding multiple fields

You can include more than one field by simply;

- Choosing the **preferred files** from the field list window and then moving them to the QBD grid. It is not compulsory that the fields are in sequence, you can hold down the Ctrl key and choose the various fields as you wish.
- Alternatively, you can click and drag the asterisk (*) to include it in the QBD grid or click twice on the asterisk to move it from the field list to the QBD grid. The asterisk makes

sure that Access is directed to add all of the fields in the table in the query, even though this action does not include all of the fields in the QBD grid.

Using an asterisk to indicate every column in a table has the drawback that the query will retrieve every field in the table without taking into account whether the field is utilized on a report or a form. Retrieving data that is not needed might be a very ineffective procedure. Performance issues are typically caused by the asterisk removing more fields from a form or report than are necessary. Additionally, you won't be able to change the datasheet's field display order.

Running your query

Once you have finished choosing your preferred fields, you will then need to execute the query by;

- Clicking on the **Run button** located on the **Query Tools Design Ribbon.**

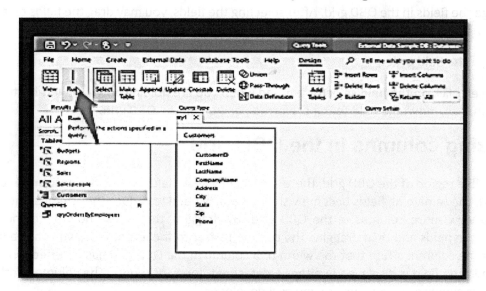

If you would like to go back to the QBD grid, simply;
- Locate the **Home tab** and then click on the **View option > Design view**.
As an alternative, you can also choose to;
- Right-click on the **tab header** for the query then chooses the **Design view option**.

Working with Query Fields

It is occasionally necessary to modify the fields you have previously selected, rearrange their order, add a new field, or even remove an existing item while working with the query fields.

You can choose to utilize the hidden field as a criterion or sort based on the hidden fields when you add one without necessarily needing to make it visible.

Choosing a field in the QBD grid

A field must be selected before its location may be changed, and the field selector must be used to do this. The narrow gray box at the top of each column in the QBD grid at the bottom of the Query Designer is the field selector. Every column represents a field.

If you would like to choose the category, simply;

- Move **the pointer** until a little selection arrow is displayed in the field selector then **select and drag the column**.

Altering field order

The QBD grid's field display order dictates the order in which the fields appear in the Datasheet view as well. To obtain a different set of fields in the query result, it could be necessary to rearrange the fields in the QBD grid. After selecting the fields, you may drag the fields on the QBD design by just dragging them to a different location.

To change the field order,

- Left click on the **field selector bar** and when you are holding down the left button of the mouse, move the field to the preferred position on the QBD grid.

Resizing columns in the QBD grid

In the visible region of the QBD grid, there are roughly 8–10 fields. When the horizontal scroll bar is moved, the remaining fields become visible. You may need to reduce the size of some fields in order to view more columns in the QBD grid. By dragging the mouse pointer to the margin between the fields and then dragging the column resizer to the left or right, you can reduce the width of the columns. Note that the width of a column in the QBD grid has no effect on the way the data in the field is displayed in either a datasheet, form, or report. The column width in the QBD grid is simply a convenience to you as a developer.

Taking off a field

To take a field off the QBD grid simply;

- Select the desired field to be deleted, and then click the **delete button**. Another approach is to right-click on the field's selector bar and selects the "cut" option from the shortcut menu.

Inserting a field

To insert new fields into a QBD grid simply;

- To add a field to a column in the QBD grid, drag it from the list of fields inside the grid. After that, the field you dropped will be on the left side of the new column. The new column will be added to the right side of the QBD grid when you double-click on a field in the field list.

Hiding a field

There might be a need for you to sometimes hide a field when a query is being performed.
To hide a field all you have to do is to;
- Uncheck the **specific field** you want to hide in the Show Check box in the State column. One other common reason why a field is usually hidden is if the field is used either for sorting or as criteria but the value of the field is not needed in the results of the query.

Changing the sort order of a field

To make data analysis considerably easier, you may frequently need to display the data when you are viewing a record set in sorted order. Records are arranged in either numerical or alphabetical order when they are sorted. You have the option of sorting using several fields or just one field. Additionally, the order of sorting can be either ascending or downward.

To have a sort order specified, take the steps below;

- Place **the cursor** in the Sort cell in the specific field you want to sort.
- Click on the **drop-down list** that is displayed in the cell and then choose **the sort order** option you would like to apply.

Take note that the fields are sorted in the same order as they appear in the datasheet, which is not the only reason for this. The Sort order precedence refers to this arrangement. The sort criteria is located farthest left in the field; typically, the left is sorted first, followed by the right.

Adding Criteria to Your Queries

Almost every user prefers to work with records that conform to some criteria. If this isn't done lots of records might have to be returned by a query which can lead to very serious problems as regards performance. With Microsoft Access, it is very easy to have your data specified.

Understanding selection criteria

The rules that are applied to data as it is retrieved from the database are known as selection criteria. Access will be able to determine which records in the record set you wish to view thanks to the selection criteria. You can also set a limit on how many records a query will return using the selection criteria. Understanding how to use query criteria is essential since they play a major role in the Microsoft Access database's ability to function properly. Users frequently take what is shown on a form or report as an accurate representation of the database without knowing what data is kept in a database's tables. A badly selected criterion has an impact on the data since it may conceal information from the application's users, which may cause them to make poor business decisions.

Entering simple string criteria

The Text-type field is frequently the foundation for the criteria that are applied to a field. You will type the desired character extraction from the text into this field. Keep in mind that Access does not always enforce case sensitivity when inputting characters; you are free to enter the character however you see fit. In general, you should insert equalities, inequalities, or at the very least, a list of acceptable values, when working with character data.

If you have a reason to remove the criteria that you have inserted into the cell, all you have to do is;

- Choose **the contents** and press **the delete button** or you can choose **the contents** and then **right-click** on the cut option from the shortcut menu that is displayed.

Entering other simple criteria

Additionally, you have the option to define criteria for Date, Numeric, and Yes/No. To complete the task, simply enter the value in the criteria area using the same format as the text. Most of the time, Access recognizes the criteria you enter right away and makes the necessary adjustments to apply them accurately to the query fields.

Printing a Query's Recordset

Once your query has been created, you may easily print every record on the recordset. It is not possible to specify a specific report type; however, you can select to generate a basic matrix-style report of the record set that your query produced. There is some versatility in the way a record set can be printed.

Follow the steps below to indicate some of the options you might prefer;

- Execute **the query** you have just created.
- Click on the **file option** then choose the **print** option. Following that, you will be given three options: print without specifying any parameters, print using certain print settings, or select print preview to see how the printing will look before you actually print it.
- Make **a choice** of the print options you want in the dialog box that is displayed and click on the **OK button**.

Saving a Query

You can always save your query so you can get back to it anytime you need to.

To save a query simply;

- Click on the **Save button** on the **Quick Access Toolba**r located at the top of the screen. Access will ask for the name of the query if it is the first time you are saving the query.

Once you have saved the query, Access will take you back to the mode in which you were working before.

Creating Multi-Table Queries

Using a query to extract data from a table is now quite common, but frequently you will need to pull data from several tables that are connected in some way. You can create more than one table query to retrieve data from different connected tables once you have built a table and defined how the tables should be associated with each other.

In creating a multi-table, the first step to take is the addition of tables to the query design window;

- Create a **new query** by clicking on the **Query Design button** on the **Create tab of the Ribbon**.
- Add the tables you want to obtain information from by double-clicking on **each of the names of the tabl**e in the Show Table dialog box.
- Finally, click on the **close button**.

Just follow the same steps as you would with a single table to add fields from several tables. When a field with a shared name across many tables is selected, Access appends the table name, followed by the period, and finally the field name.

Viewing table names

The field names in the QBD grid might be particularly confusing when you are working with multiple tables in a query. Access maintains the table name automatically for every field that is shown in the QBD grid.

Adding multiple fields

A single-table query's method of adding multiple fields and a multi-table query's method of adding multiple fields are fairly comparable. One table at a time must be added fields when adding fields from multiple tables. The easiest way to achieve this is to select many fields and then drag them all in the direction of the QBD grid.

To choose multiple sequential fields simply;

- Click on **the first field** that is in the field list then hold down **the shift key** and run through to the last field. You can also choose to select **non-sequential fields** by **pressing down the ctrl key** and then choose **the individual fields** you prefer.

Getting to Know the Limitations of Multi-table Queries

There are restrictions on how much each field can be modified when constructing a query that includes many tables. Generally speaking, anything you make to the data in a query's record set will also be automatically preserved in the underlying tables. The primary key of the table is the one exception to all of this; if referential integrity is in place and the field is part of a connection, its value cannot be changed. Sometimes it may be necessary to manually alter the records that a query has returned. You might not always be able to update the records in your table when using Microsoft Access.

Below are rules for updating queries;

Type of Query or Field	Update able	Comments
One table	Yes	
One-to-one relationship	Yes	
Results contain Long Text field	Yes`	Long Text field is updateable if the underlying query is not based on a many-to-many relationship
Results contain a hyperlink	Yes	Hyperlink is updateable if the underlying query is not based on a many-to-many relationship
Results contain an OLE object	Yes	Ole object will be an updateable if the underlying query is not based on a many-to-many relationship.
One-to-many relationship	Usually	Restrictions based on design methodology
Many-to-many relationship	No	Can update data in a form or data access page if

159

		Record Type = Recordset
Crosstab	No	Creates a snapshot of the data.
Two or more tables without join line	No	Must have a join in order to determine update ability
Unique Value property is Yes	No	Shows unique records only in a snapshot.
Totals query (Sum, Avg, and so on)	No	Works with grouped data creating a snapshot
Calculated fields	No	They will be calculated automatically.
SQL-specific queries	No	Union and pass-through work with ODBC data
Read-only fields	No	If opened read-only or on read-only drive(CD-ROM)
Permissions denied	No	Insert, replace, or delete not
Locked by another user	No	Cannot be updated when a field has been locked by another field.
ODBC tables with no unique identifier	No	Unique Identifier must exist

Paradox table without a primary key	No	Primary key file must be in existence.

Overcoming query limitations

The table above illustrates that there are situations in which certain table fields and queries will not be updated. Some columns in a query that contain several tables and some of those tables have a one-to-many relationship may not be updateable; this also depends on how the query is designed.

Updating a unique index (primary key)

The primary key from the "one" table must be included in the query if it uses a table that is part of a one-to-many relationship. It is required. Because Access has the primary key value, it can find related records in the two tables.

Replacing existing data in a query with a one-many relationship

Primarily all the fields that are in a "many" table can be updated in a one-to-many query. Furthermore, all the fields in the "one" table can also be updated with the exception of the primary key. This can be used for most database application purposes.

Updating fields in queries

Make sure you add the foreign key from the "many" table and then display the field in the datasheet if you need to add entries to two tables that have a one-to-many relationship. Start with the "one" or "many" table to determine when you have to have completed this task. The "many" tables that join the field will automatically copy the principal field of the "one" table. If you need to incorporate records from more than one table in your form, make sure you include all the fields from both tables; otherwise, your form won't include the whole set of records.

Working with the Table pane

The table pane of the Query Designer has information that is of great importance to your query. When you have a perfect understanding of the table pane and how you can work with the field list you will be able to build complex queries with ease.

Looking at the join line

A join line in the Query Designer is the line that joins tables. Additionally, it links a foreign key in one table to the primary key in another. The relationship between two tables in the Access database is represented more easily with the help of the join line. Microsoft Access will utilize a thicker line for the join in the Query Designer that joins the table if the referential integrity of the set on the relationship is compromised. On the "many" table end of the join line, an infinity symbol (∞) indicates a one-to-many relationship. **Anytime the conditions below are met, Access will join two tables automatically;**

- The two tables have fields at the same time.
- The fields that have the same data type also have the same data type (text, numeric, and so on). Note that the AutoNumber data type is basically the same as the Numeric (Long Integer).
- One of the fields is a primary key in its table.

These join lines can be particularly confusing because they can overlap when working with numerous tables. The line will eventually become visible as you navigate through the table, and it will also become quite clear the field it was linked to.

Moving a table

You can drag and drop the field list within the Query Designer by using the mouse to adjust the field list window's title bar. Alternatively, you can opt to modify a field's width and height by just clicking on the field's border and making the necessary changes. Additionally, when you save and close a query in Access, it usually saves the configuration. In essence, the next time the query is opened, the field list will appear in the same arrangement.

Removing a table

There might be a need for you to remove tables from a query. With the use of the mouse,

- Choose **the table** you want to remove at the top pane of the query design window
- Press the **Delete key**.

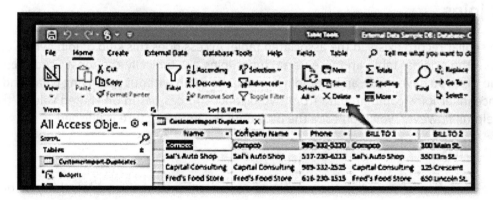

As an alternative, you can also choose to right-click on the field list window and then select the **Remove Table option** from the shortcut menu.

Including more tables

While working you might delete a table by mistake and seek to add the table again.

To add a table simply follows the options below;
- Click on the **Show Table button** located on the **Query Setup group in the Design Ribbon** option. When this is done the Show Table dialog box will then be displayed.

Creating and Working with Query Joins

Microsoft Access creates joins that depend on established relationships between tables when you add tables to a query. Even though they don't reflect relationships that have previously been established, you still have the option to manually create joins in queries. When a query uses another query as a data source, joins can be made between the queries and any table that is utilized as a data source, as well as between the source queries. In that they establish rules that the data must adhere to in order for the query operations to be performed, joins function very similarly to query criteria. Unlike criteria, joins guarantee that every pair of rows that satisfy the join conditions is brought together in the record set and that the joins are created correctly. Joins are to what queries what relationships are to tables: and an indication of how data in both sources can be combined depending on the values they both have in common.

Getting to Know Joins

There are basically four different types of joins they are; inner joins, outer joins, cross joins, and unequal joins. Cross joins and unequal joins are both advanced join types and they are not commonly used but you ought to know about them to have a complete understanding of how joins work.

Inner joins

When a similar record exists in the associated table, Access does this kind of join, which contains data from the original table and vice versa. Inner joins are typically the most used. Access will presume that you have made an inner join if you make a join without specifying what kind of join it is. Since inner joins combine data from two distinct sources based on shared values, they are quite helpful; however, you won't see the data until the entire picture is finished.

Outer joins

With the exception of including the remaining rows from one of the tables, this sort of join is nearly identical to an inner join. The records from the left table, which is the first table in the join, are all included in a left outer join, and the records from the right table, which is the second table in the join, are all included in a right outer join.

Full outer join

In some systems, an outer join can have all the rows from both tables, with rows being combined when they respond. This is known as a full outer join, and Access does not totally offer support for them. Nevertheless, you can make use of a cross-join and criteria to get the same effect.

Cross joins

A cross join is frequently an unintentional consequence of adding two tables to a query without joining them. This will be interpreted by Microsoft Access as meaning that you must view every record from one table in addition to every record from the other table. Although there are certain very rare situations where you would need a cross-join, this type of join typically does not yield any results because there can be no combination of data.

Unequal join

When comparing values and deciding whether and how to combine the data, unequal uses an operator instead of the equality sign. Although cross-join criteria can be used to achieve the same result, unequal joins are not officially supported.

Leveraging ad hoc table joins

When more tables are added to the query, an ad hoc table is created. If a table has never been joined at the table level, if it lacks a common named field for a primary key, or if the Enable Auto join option is off, it may not always join tables automatically in a query.

Identifying the type of join

The main problem encountered with the specification of joins is the fact that they show inner join behavior as the query is being executed.

To specify a join all you have to do is to;

- Right-click **on the line** that joins the two tables together then chooses the Join properties to command from the shortcut menu.

Once this is done, it will **open the Join Properties dialog box** which will enable you to indicate an alternate join between the tables.

Deleting joins

If you want to delete a join that is between two tables;
- Choose **the join line** and click on **the Delete key**.

Activity

1. What are queries and what can they do?
2. What do queries return?
3. Create a query.
4. Add fields to your query.
5. Execute the query you created.
6. Resize columns in the QBD grid.
7. Remove, conceal, and insert a field.
8. Add criteria to your queries.
9. What are the selection criteria?
10. Create multi-table queries.
11. What are the limitations of multi-table queries?
12. Move, remove, and add more tables to your query.
13. What are joins?
14. Create and work with Query joins.
15. Delete joins that are not needed.

CHAPTER 9

USING OPERATIONS AND EXPRESSIONS IN ACCESS

This chapter deals solely with the use of operators and expressions in calculating information, having values compared and displaying data in a much different format- making use of queries to build examples.

Unveiling Operators

Operators are useful for comparing values, joining strings, formatting data, and performing a variety of other tasks. You can instruct Access to take a specific action against one or more operands by using operators. An expression is the result of combining operators and operands. You will utilize the operator in Access each time you need to generate an equation. For example, operators can be used to create computed fields in forms and reports, provide criteria in queries, and express data validation rules in table attributes.

Types of operators

Operators can be divided into the following types as seen below;

- Mathematical
- Comparison
- String
- Boolean(Logical)
- Miscellaneous

Mathematical operators

Numerical computations are carried out using mathematical operators, sometimes referred to as arithmetic operators. They are accustomed to dealing with numbers as operands by definition. Any numeric data type can be used as a number when working with mathematical operations. The number may represent a field's contents, a constant value, or the value of a variable. These numbers can be used singly or in combination to create some rather intricate phrases.

There are basically seven basic mathematical operators;
- **Addition**

If there is a need for you to create a calculated field in a query for the adding of a value, you will make use of this operator.
- **Subtraction**

The subtraction operator (-) does the work of very basic subtractions.
- **The multiplication operator**

You can use the multiplication operator when there is a need to calculate several items. All you have to do is create a query to show the number of items purchased and then the price for each of the items.

- **The division operator**

This operator is used in dividing two numbers.

- **The integer division operator**

Any two numbers can be divided into integers by rounding them up or down, dividing the first by the second, and then removing the decimal part to leave only the integer value. Take note that Access uses the rounding half or banker's rounding method to even. Every time, rounding is done to the closest even value.

- **The exponentiation operator**

This operator raises a number to the power of an exponent. This simply means multiplying a number by itself. For example, **3^3** means **3x3x3.**

- **The modulo division operator**

Any two numbers can be used with the modulo operator; it rounds them both up and down to integers, divides the first by the second, and returns the residual. The highly unpredictable part of modulo division is that the value that is obtained is often the remainder obtained from the operands' integer division. By using modulo division with 2 as the divisor, the mod is frequently used to determine if an integer is even or odd.

Comparison operators

These operators help with comparing two different values or expressions in an equation.

There are basically six comparison operators;

- Equal =: which returns true if both expressions are the same.
- Not equal <>: simply the opposite of the equal operator.
- Less than <: returns a logical True value if the left side of the equation is less than the right side.
- Less than or equal to < =: this returns true only if the operand on the left side of the equation is either less than or equal to the right side operand.
- Greater than >: it is also the opposite of the less-than operator. It returns True when the left side operand is greater than the operand on the right side.
- Greater than or equal to >=: this returns true if the left side is greater than or equal to the right side.

String Operators

There are basically three-string operators for working with strings in Access.

The string operator is designed basically to work with string data:

- & Concatenates operands
- Like Operands are similar
- Not Like Operands are dissimilar

Boolean (logical) operators

Consider Boolean logic as a very basic means of comparing distinct expressions and inputs. It uses what are known as logical operators to perform such comparisons. Be aware that one type of reasoning that aids in reducing all values to either True or False is Boolean logic.

Boolean operators include the following;

- And returns True when the two expressions are True.
- Or returns True when any one of the two expressions is true.
- Not returns True when the Expression is not true.
- Xor returns True when either of the two expressions is true but not the two of them.
- Eqv returns True when both of the expressions are true or both are false.
- Imp This does the bitwise comparisons of bits that are identically positioned in two different numerical expressions.

Miscellaneous operators

Microsoft Access has about three useful miscellaneous operators which are;

- Between..... And Range
- In List comparison
- Is Reversed word

The Between......And operator

Consider Boolean logic as a very basic means of comparing distinct expressions and inputs. It uses what are known as logical operators to perform such comparisons. Be aware that one type of reasoning that aids in reducing all values to either True or False is Boolean logic.

The In operator

This operator helps to determine if the value of an expression is the same as any value that can be found within the list. The general syntax of In is

    Expression In (value 1, value 2, value 3)

If the value of the expression is found right within the list, the result then is True; otherwise, the result is false.

The Is operator

This operator is generally used with the keyword Null in order to determine if the value of an object is null:

- **Expression Is Null**

The Is operator in the VBA operator can be used to compare various objects to determine whether or not they represent the same entity. It is crucial to remember that this operator only works with objects and object variables. This operator cannot be applied to simple variables, such as strings or numbers.

Operator Precedence

Access will make sure to identify which operator will be evaluated first and which operator will be assessed after if you need to work with complicated expressions that contain a number of operators. Operator precedence refers to the predefined order that Access has built-in for logical, Boolean, and mathematical operators. This is the order that Microsoft Access will always adhere to until you use parentheses to change the default behavior. Parenthetical operations are frequently carried out before non-parenthetical operations. Microsoft Access makes sure that it follows the default operator precedence when enclosed in parenthesis.

The operator ranked by order of precedence is:

- Mathematical
- Comparison
- Boolean

The mathematical precedence

The order of precedence mathematical operators follow is;

- Exponentiation
- Negation
- Multiplication and /or division (left to right)
- Integer division
- Modulus division
- Addition and/or subtraction (left to right)
- String concatenation

The comparison precedence

The order of precedence comparison operators follows include;

- Equal

- Not Equal
- Less than
- Greater than
- Less than or equal to
- Greater than or equal to
- Like

The Boolean precedence

The Boolean operators go after this order of precedence;

- Not
- And
- Or
- Xor
- Eqv
- Imp

Using Operators and Expressions in Queries

One of the most popular uses of operators and expressions is the construction of sophisticated query criteria. Having a comprehensive comprehension of all of this can make it easier to construct very beneficial queries. It is crucial that you understand how to formulate questions correctly and how to specify criteria. While a single query can be used to retrieve data from a single table based on a single criterion, multiple queries use more complicated criteria to retrieve data from multiple tables. Your queries can only retrieve the data you require and in the exact order that you require it because of this intricacy. With the use of operators and expressions, you will be able to create complex select queries in order to limit.

Dealing with query comparison operators

In order to restrict the amount of information that is presented, you may be required to specify one or more criteria whenever you deal with queries. Using comparison operators in equations and computations is all that is required to specify criteria. There are four different types of operators: string, logical, mathematical, and relational. Operators in select queries can be used in the Query by Design (QBD) grid's field cell or criteria cell.

With the use of these operators, you can sort out groups of records such as;

- A range of products like all the sales made between March and April.
- Product records that have a picture.
- All records that do match a value.

Knowing complex criteria

You can use any combination of the operators to create complex query criteria. Complex criteria are typically composed of a sequence of Ands and Ors for the majority of queries that are constructed. They can also frequently be formed by putting sample data into various QBD pane fields. You should be aware, though, that selecting data based on more than one criterion is not limited to the application of Boolean operators. When working with complex criteria, one of the operators that is most frequently utilized is the And/Or operator. After considering two alternative expressions, the operator decides whether or not each expression is true. After doing this, the operators will check the outcomes of the two expressions to see if there is a logical true or false response. The query additionally displays the records that satisfy the true condition whenever the outcome of an And/Or operation is True, indicating that the overall condition is also true. Keep in mind that an OR operation can produce a true result when any of the expression's sides are true, but an AND operation can only produce a true result when both of the expression's sides are true. Actually, even if one side is null, the operation's outcome will still be true if the other side is true. The fundamental distinction between the And/Or operators is this.

Making use of functions in select queries

A mathematical expression that is evaluated against each item returned by a query and whose outcome is also kept in a dynamic, temporary field created at query time is what is known as a query function. You may need to use the built-in Access functions to display information whenever you deal with queries. For sales dates, for example, you may wish to provide details like the day of the week. When you create calculated fields for the query, this data may be shown.

Referencing fields in select queries

It is best to have referenced field names in an enclosed bracket ([]). Microsoft Access needs brackets around any field names that have spaces or punctuation marks. If by mistake you fail to add the brackets around a field name in the QBD grid. Access might have a quote placed around the field name and then treat it as literal text rather than treating it as a field name.

Inserting Single-Value Field Criteria

You will undoubtedly reach a point in your job where you may need to restrict the query records that are returned based on a single field requirement. A single value condition, or simply the entry of a single phrase in the QBD grid, will be required for the queries. Keep in mind that you can provide your criteria expressions for almost any type of data, including text, numeric, date/time, and more. The criterion for calculated field types and OLE objects can also be set.

Inserting character (Text or Memo) criteria

Character criteria are used basically for Text or for Memo data-type fields. They are neither examples nor patterns of the contents of the field.

If you would like to create a query that returns customers that live in California for instance, take the steps below:

- Open a **new query** in Design view based on the customer's table and include the company, phone, and state fields to the QBD pane.
- Click on the **Criteria cell** for the State field.
- Enter **CA in the cell**. Once you have done this, click on the **Datasheet View button** in the Home Ribbon's view group in order to check the result of the query.

There is no need for you to type quotes around CA. Access usually assumes that you are using a literal string CA and will automatically include quotes for you.

The Like operator and wildcards

The Like operator can be used to find values in a field that correspond to the provided pattern. When it comes to patterns, you have the option of displaying the entire value or using wildcard characters to find a range of values. The Like operator in an expression can be used to compare a field value to a string expression. An SQL query that contains the expression "C*" will, for example, return all field values that begin with the letter C. You can ask the user to find a pattern in a parameter query. Use the Like operator to do wildcard searches against the field's contents in the Criteria cell of a field. Microsoft Access searches the field for patterns; you may use the asterisk (*) to display multiple characters or the question mark (?) to display a single character. Any single character that appears in the same location as the question mark in the sample phrase is shown by the question mark (?). Any number of characters in the same position as the asterisk (*) also denotes something. Wildcards can be used alone and they can also be used in conjunction with one another. They can be used various times within the same expression.

Indicating non-matching values

If you would like to indicate a non-matching value, you can simply make use of either the Not or the <> operator at the front of the expression that there is no need to match.

Follow the steps below to specify non-matching values;

- Open a **new query** in **Design view** and include the customer table.
- Include **Company and State** from the customer table.
- Click **anywhere** in the Criteria cell of State.

- Enter **<> CA** in the cell. With this Microsoft, Access will automatically add quotation marks around CA if you do not add it yourself before leaving the field. The query will choose all of the records except for customers who live in the state of California.

Entering numeric criteria

Utilize numerical criteria in fields that have either a numeric or monetary data type. If necessary, you can just enter the decimal symbol and the numbers, followed by the comparison or mathematical operation. Just be careful not to use commas. More frequently than not, comparison operators like less than \, more than >, or equal to = are applied as criteria to numerical fields. You must put the operator along with the value if you need to indicate a comparison that is not equal. Keep in mind that when you run the selected query in Access, the default will be set to equal.

Entering true or false criteria

True and False criteria are used basically with Yes/No type fields. There is no use of the Not and the <> operators to show the opposite, but the Yes/No data also has a null state that might be worthy of consideration. Microsoft Access understands lots of forms of true and false.

Hence, rather than typing yes, you can insert any of the following in the Criteria;

Indeed, on Not -1, Not, <>, No, or \No. Keep in mind that a Yes/No field might be in one of three states: null, yes, or no. When a table's default value was left unfixed and the value was not yet put, the result is null. Only the record with the Null in the field is displayed when testing for Is Null, whereas usually checking for Is Not Null displays all records with either Yes or No in the field. A Yes/No box that has been checked can never be unchecked. Either Yes or No (-1 or 0) must be selected.

Entering OLE object criteria

You can choose to indicate criteria for OLE objects: Is Null or Is Not Null. Note that the Is Not Null option is the right syntax, you can also make use of the Not Null option in the QBD grid, Access will then provide the Is operator for you.

Employing the use of Multiple Criteria in a Query

In this section, you will need to deal with many criteria based on a single field. In this situation, the QBD can be useful to you. In a select query, it can be useful to specify criteria for different fields. For example, using numerous queries allows you to find the products that have been sold during the last sixty days.

Understanding an OR operation

When a field must satisfy one of two requirements, the OR operator is employed. For example, you may be required to view all the records in which the customer's address is in San Francisco or California. Simply put, this indicates that you would like to find out whether a customer has addresses in S.F., CA, or most likely both. The answer will also be true if either of these expressions turns out to be true.

Consider the points below to help clarify the point;

- Customer 1 has an address in CA: the expression is true.
- Customer 2 has an address in S.F.: the expression is true.
- Customer 3 has an address in both CA and S.F.: the expression is also true.
- Customer 4 has an address in LA: the expression is false.

Specifying multiple values with the Or operator

The Or operator can be used in the specification of various values for a field.

To perform this operation, follow the steps below;

- Open a **new query** in the Design view and then add for example tables for customers and tables for sales.
- Add **the company** and state from the customer's table and the date of the sales from the sales table.
- Select the **criteria cell** of the state.
- Insert either **CA or S.F.** in the cell.

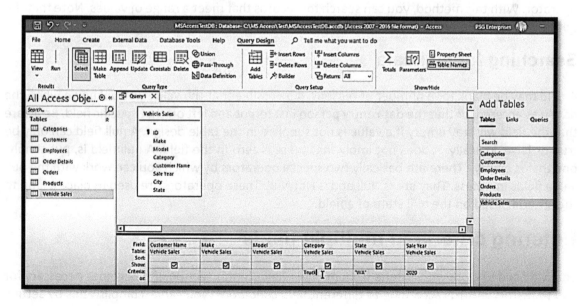

Using the or cell or the QBD pane

In addition to providing distinct criteria for each field vertically on separate rows of the QBD pane, you may also use the literal or operator as a single expression on the Criteria row beneath the State field. When Microsoft Access builds a query using "vertical" or criteria, it optimizes the SQL statement underlying the query by condensing all of the criteria into a single expression.

Using a list of values with the In operator

An alternative method you can make use of in indicating various values of just one field is the use of the In operator. The In operator searches for a value from a list of values. The list of values that are embedded in the parentheses will then become an example criterion.

Using And to specify a range

The And operator is frequently employed in fields containing date/time or numeric data types. It can be this way in some circumstances, although it is rarely utilized with text data types. When a field needs to satisfy two or more requirements, the AND operator is employed. The And operation is only true when both sides of the expression are true, in contrast to the Or operation, which can be true under a variety of circumstances. A range of allowable values in the field is established when an And operator with a single field is employed. Thus, setting a range of records that will be examined is the primary goal of an Ad operator in a single field.

Using the Between… and And operator

You can ask for a range of records with the use of another method which is the Between….And operator. With this method, you can search for records that meet a range of values. Note that the operands for the Between….And operators are inclusive.

Searching for null data

A field may be blank for a number of reasons. It's possible that the value was unknown when the data was entered, or that the data entry person just forgot and left off that specific field. Be aware that the field will stay empty if a value is not supplied in the table design. A null field can only be true or false, logically. It does not imply that there is zero in the field. A null field is, put simply, one that is empty. There are basically two special operators by which you can work with the null value fields in Access. They are Is Null and Is Not Null. These operators are used to place a limit to the criteria based on the null state of a field.

Entering criteria in multiple fields

You will need to work with criteria from multiple fields in this section. If it becomes necessary for you to restrict records according to different field conditions, you can accomplish this by setting criteria in every field you plan to utilize for the scope. Keep in mind that the queries will also require the criteria to be entered on different lines and in different fields.

Using And and Or across fields in a query

In order to make use of the And operator and the Or operator across various fields, ensure you place the example or pattern data in the Criteria cells for the And operator and also for the Or cells of one field that is relative to the placement in a different field. Place the example or pattern data you wish to work with across the same row in the QBD pane whenever you need to utilize the And operator between two or more fields. Additionally, the criteria should be positioned on different rows in the QBD window whenever you need to utilize the Or operator between fields.

Specifying Or criteria across fields in a query

While the And operator is utilized more frequently in all domains, the Or operator is also very helpful in rare cases. For example, regardless of the customer's place of residence, you may be required to view certain customer records.

To create this kind of query, follow the steps below;

- **Add the customer's table, sales table, and also products table to a query that has just** been created.
- Include **the Company and State** from the customer's table and also the Description and the Category from the products table.
- Insert **CA** as the criteria for states.
- Insert **the produc**t in the or cell under Category.

Note that when a criterion is placed on a different row in the QBD grid, Microsoft Access will interpret this as an Or between fields. This query will also return customers who either live in California or happen to have purchased a product.

Utilizing And & Or together in different fields

You should now be prepared to construct a query using And & Or in several fields after working with them separately. All that has to be done in this section is to combine the two operators in the same field. When you do this, make sure that the query makes sense.

A complex query on different lines

It is possible to refer to the application of And and Or operators in many fields as a sophisticated query. Keep in mind that dates were always interpreted by Access using the language and region settings found in the Windows Control Panel. Access can be configured to interpret short dates as either dd/mm/yyyy or mm/dd/yyyy. When working with dates, make sure you take all of these regional variations into consideration. Additionally, keep in mind that Access reads two-digit years from 00 to 40 as 2000 to 2040. For this reason, it's usually a good idea to input data using four-digit years.

Activity

1. What are operators?
2. Mention 2 types of operators.
3. What does operator precedence mean?
4. How can operators and expressions be used in queries?
5. Insert single-value field criteria.
6. Employ the use of multiple criteria in a query.
7. Insert criteria in various fields.
8. Use And to specify a range.
9. Specify the OR criteria across fields in a query.
10. Use And and Or together in different fields.

CHAPTER 10

GOING BEYOND SELECT QUERIES

One of the main components of Microsoft Access data analysis is using a select query to show and retrieve records. Data analysis has a wide range of applications, such as gathering and comparing data, updating and removing data, structuring and reporting data, and more. Access comes with a number of built-in tools with unique features that are essentially meant to handle this task. This chapter contains various in-depth knowledge on tools that are available for use in Access and how they can help you go past just select queries.

Aggregate Queries

An investigation of a set of individual data items can yield group and subgroup data; this is known as an aggregate query. Both database developers and administrators frequently use this word. An aggregate query allows you to receive a summary overview of all your data, including counts, averages, totals, and much more. A select query only retrieves records as they are displayed in the data source.

Creating an aggregate query

An aggregate function in a query is a kind of function that can be used to sum a column of numbers. Aggregate functions compute a single value based on a single column of data. Sum and count are only two of the many aggregation procedures available in Microsoft Access. Max, Min, and Average. You can use the count function, etc., to count data and you can add the sum function to your query to total up data. Furthermore, there are numerous ways to include sum and other aggregate functions in a query using Microsoft Access.

You can simply;

- Open **your query** in the datasheet view and add **a Total row**. With the help of Access's Total Row functionality, you can utilize an aggregate function in one or more query set columns without requiring altering the query's structure.
- **Create a totals query**: A total row computes the grand total for one or more data columns, while a totals query computes subtotals for a collection of Records. For example, you can use a total query to group your records by the required category and then sum the sales figures if you want to subtotal all sales by City or by quarter.
- **Create a crosstab query**: A crosstab query Is a unique type of query that shows its results in a grid that looks like an Excel sheet. Crosstab queries help to summarize your values and then drop them by two sets of facts - one set down the side and the other set of facts across the top.

About aggregate functions

There are various aggregate functions and it is expedient for you to know a particular function that best fits your data analysis.

Group By

One aggregate function in Access that helps combine entries that are identical in the specified field into a single record is Group By. In the event that you include a SQL aggregate function, such as Sum or Count, in the SELECT statement, a summary result will be generated for each entry.

There are a couple of things that you should have in mind when you are making use of the Group by aggregate function;

- Before doing any other type of aggregation, Access executes the Group By function in your aggregate query. When utilizing a Group by function in conjunction with another aggregate function, the Group By function will be executed initially.
- Each group is arranged by field in either ascending or descending order by Access. In the event that your query contains multiple group-by-fields, the leftmost field will be the starting point for each field's ascending sorting order.
- Access treats various group-by-fields as one unique item.

Sum, Avg, Count, StDev, Var

All of these aggregate functions perform mathematical calculations on the records in the field you have chosen.

Bear in mind that these functions do not include any records that are configured to null.

- **Sum**: this function helps to calculate the total value of all of the records in the designated field or grouping. This function works only with data types such as; Currency, AutoNumber, Date/Time, and Number.
- **Avg**: This function aids in figuring out the average of every record within the selected field or grouping. Data types including AutoNumber, Currency, Date/Time, and Number can be used with this function.
- **Count**: This function simply helps in counting the number of entries within the chosen field or grouping. This function is very unique too as it works with all types of data.
- **StDev**: This function aids in determining the standard deviation for each record inside the chosen field or grouping. The following data types will also function nicely with this method: AutoNumber, Currency, Date/Time, and Number.
- **Var**: This function calculates the difference between the average value of the group and all of the values in the selected field or grouping. Additionally, this method operates independently on data types including AutoNumber, Currency, Date/Time, and Number.

Min, Max, First, Last

These functions in this section help to evaluate all of the records in the designated field or grouping and then return just one value from the group.

- **Min**: This helps to return the value of the record with the lowest value in the chosen field or grouping. This function works with data types like; AutoNumber, Currency, and Date/Time. Number and Text.
- **Max**: The value of the record with the greatest value in the selected field or grouping is returned by this option. With data types like AutoNumber, Currency, Date/Time, Number, and Text, this method can also operate on its own.
- **First:** The value of the first record in the selected field or grouping is returned by this function. The fact that this function operates on all data types makes it special as well.
- **Last**: This function helps to return the value of the last record in the chosen field or grouping. It is also a unique one as it works with all of the data types.

Expression, Where

Expressions can be used for a number of tasks in Microsoft Access like performing mathematical calculations, combining or extracting text, or validating data.

Expressions can be used in the following ways;

- **Calculate values**: Expressions can be used to calculate numbers that aren't necessarily present in your data. In addition to choosing to calculate in controls on forms and reports, you can also select to calculate in fields in tables and queries. A calculated field is a column in a table or queries that result from a calculation. A calculated field that combines two or more table fields can be created.
- **Defining a default value**: expressions can be used to define a default value for a table field or for a control on a form or report. These default values are displayed anywhere you open a table, report, or form.
- **Create a validation rule**: with the use of an expression, you can create a validation rule that can help to control what values users can insert in a field or control.
- **Define query criteria**: Expressions can be used to limit the results to a desired subset. If you want to specify a skate range, you can insert criteria, in which case Access will only return the rows that meet the criteria. When you add criteria to a query and execute it, it will only return results that correspond to the specified dates.

A where clause allows you to apply a filter to your analysis by allowing you to apply a criterion to a specific field that is not present in your aggregate query. Lastly, take note that fields that have the where clause tagged cannot be shown in an aggregate query. If you accidentally check the Show checkbox of a field that has the where clause tagged, you will receive an error message stating that the field for which you inserted the where clause in the Total row cannot be shown.

Action Queries

Queries in database management systems such as Microsoft Access and others are capable of much more than merely displaying data; they can also be used to carry out different operations on the data within your database. Action queries are those that can add, modify, or remove many records at once. By completing all of your analytical tasks inside of Access, you can use action queries to both boost productivity and lower the likelihood of errors. Just as you would with a select query, consider an action query. An active query, like a select query, aids in the extraction of a data set from a data source in accordance with the parameters and criteria that are supplied to the query. The primary distinction is that an action query does an action on the returned results instead of displaying a data collection. Its type frequently determines the action it takes. You will learn about the four main categories of action questions in this section.

Make-table queries

A make-table query creates a new table that has data from an already existing table. The table that is created has records that must have met some definitions and criteria of the make-table query. This essentially means that you can use the make-table query to create a hard table containing the results of your query when you have to create a query and then need to have the results of your query captured in a separate table. After doing this, you can utilize your table for more analytical procedures. Take note that there is absolutely no relationship between the data in a table created by a make-table query and its source data. This implies that when data in the original table is modified, the data in your new table won't be updated.

To create a make-table query simply follow the steps below;
- Have a **query created** in the Query Design view.
- Choose **the Design tab** of the Ribbon then select the **Make Table button**. The Make Table dialog box will then be displayed.

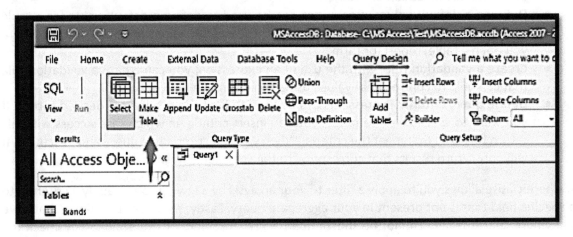

- Enter the name you want to give your new table in the Table Name field. Make careful not to enter the name of a table that already exists in your database since that will cause it to be overwritten.
- After selecting the **OK button** to exit the dialog box, you can run your query by selecting the **Run command option.**

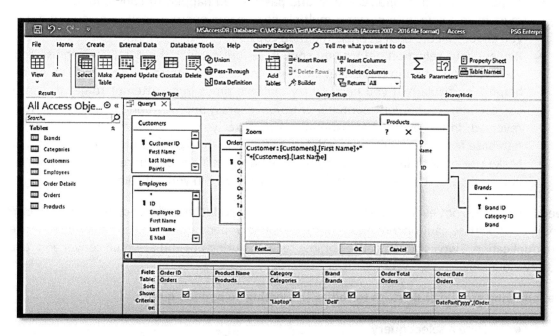

- Click on the **Yes button** in order to confirm and then create **your new table**. Once your query has been executed, you will find a new query in your Table objects.

Delete queries

A delete query is one that pulls data from a table using the specified criteria and definitions. This implies that a set of records that satisfy a specific criterion may be impacted by a delete query. While it is possible to remove records by hand, using a delete query is far more effective. If records in a table need to be removed based on a comparison with another table, delete queries are also the best option. Note that queries that have been deleted can in no way be recovered hence it is best for you; to make a backup of your database before you execute the delete query.

Append queries

Using an append query, records are selected from one or more data sources and then copied into an already-existing table. Assume, for instance, that you have a database with a table of prospective new clients and that you presently have a table in your database that contains the same information. The choice to replicate the data from the new database to the current table was made since it will be necessary to have it kept in a single location. In order to avoid inserting the new data manually, you can simply make use of an append query in copying the records.

When you make use of an append query, you can;

- **Append more than one record in one pass**: if you happen to copy data manually, you must have a course to perform multiple copy/paste operations. When you use a query, you choose all the data at once and then copy it.
- **Review your selection before you copy it**: Before copying the data, you can use add to view your selection in Datasheet view and make any necessary edits. This can be quite helpful, particularly if you need to try multiple times in an attempt to get the answer correct and your query contains criterion expressions. An append query cannot be reversed; in the event that you make a mistake, you will need to either restore your database from a backup or use a delete query or manual correction to fix your mistake.
- **Make use of criteria in refining your selection**: For instance, there might be a need for you to append the records of the customers who live in your city alone.

Keep in mind that not every record you believe is being added actually ends up in the table. You should also exercise caution when executing the same append query more than once to prevent data duplication. Two common causes of lost records during append are type conversion failure and key violation.

The following are the basic steps to follow in creating an append query;

- Create a **select query**.
- Change the **select query** to an append query.
- Make a choice of the destination fields for each column in the append query.
- Preview and then **execute** the query in order to append the records.

Update queries

Using an update query is mostly recommended to ensure time savings. Using an update query is the only way to edit a lot of data at once more easily than any other method. You should always exercise caution to make sure that you are not in a scenario where you are unable to reverse the consequences of an update query, just like you would with practically any other action query. Make sure you always build a backup before running your query. Alternatively, you can run a select query to display data and then modify it into a make-table query; run the make-table query to generate a backup of the data you're about to update, then run the query again as an update to overwrite the records.

Note that your update query will not be successful if any of the following applies;

- A join to another query is being used by your query. Create a temporary table that you can use in place of the combined query to address this problem.

- Your query is built upon a subquery with aggregate functions, a union query, or a crosstab query. Instead of using the query to provide answers to this problem, create a temporary table that you may use.
- Your query has a many-to-one-to-many relationship and is based on three or more tables. Provide a workaround for this issue by creating a makeshift table that you may utilize independently of the relationship.
- A SQL pass-through query is the foundation of your query. Create a temporary table that you can use in place of the query if you would prefer to get around this.
- You have your query based on a table in a database that is already opened as read-only or can be found on a read-only drive. To have your way around this problem, all you have to do is obtain written access to the database or drive.

Crosstab Queries

Similar to a spreadsheet, a Microsoft Access crosstab query presents summary data in a condensed style. Instead of needing to view the information in a database form, these kinds of queries can display a significant quantity of summary data in a manner that is much easier to analyze. A crosstab's anatomy is rather straightforward.

The matrix structure that will eventually become your crosstab can only be created with a minimum of three fields. The row headers are composed of the first field, the column headings are composed of the second field, and the aggregated data, which is always found in the middle of the matrix, is composed of the third field. In general, there are two approaches available for building a crosstab query. The query design grid can be used to manually generate a query, or you can use the Crosstab Query Wizard.

Designing a crosstab query using the Crosstab Query Wizard

Follow the steps below to make use of the Crosstab Query Wizard in the creation of a crosstab query;

- Choose the **Create tab** of the Ribbon then click on **the Query Wizard button**. This will then open the New Query dialog box.
- Choose the **Crosstab Query Wizard** from the selection list then choose the **OK button**.

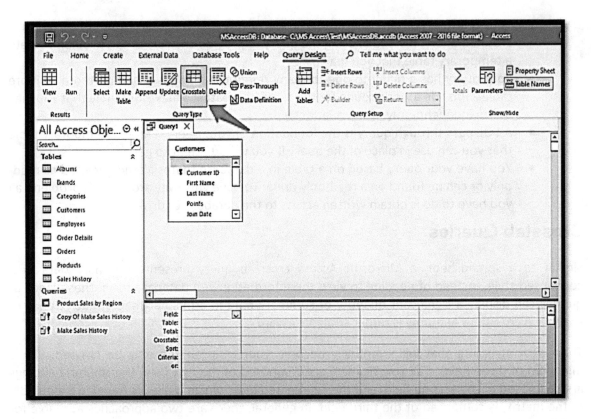

- Choose the **Dim_ Transactions** option then choose the Next button. The next step then is to identify the fields that you would like to make use of the row headings.
- Choose the **ProductID field** and then choose the **button** with the >symbol on it to move it to the Selected Fields list. It should be noted that you can select up to three fields to use as row headings in your crosstab query. Remember that Access handles every combination of headings as if it were a unique object. This essentially indicates that the combination is grouped before the records are combined from each group.
- Click on **the Next button**. The only thing left to do is choose which field to utilize as the column heading for your crosstab query in the following step. Remember that your crosstab can only have one column header.
- Choose the **OrderDate field** from the field list.

If your Column Heading is a date field, as the OrderDate you will then see a step in which you will have the option of specifying an interval to group your dates by.

- Choose **Quarter** and notice that the sample diagram at the lower part of the dialog box updates as it should.
- Choose **the LineTotal field** from the Fields list and then choose Sum from the Functions list.
- Give your **query a name** you can also view **your query** or modify the design.
- Lastly, you can view your query results by simply clicking on the **Finish button**.

185

Creating a crosstab query manually

Though the Crosstab Query Wizard makes it much easier to build a crosstab in just a few clicks, it does have its own limitations that might inhibit your effort on data analysis:

- Your cross tab will be based on a single data source that you can select. This means that in addition to building a temporary query to serve as your own data source, you will also need to crosstab data that is spread over multiple tables.
- Using criteria from the Crosstab Query Wizard, you are unable to filter or limit your crosstab query.
- You are limited to just three-row headings.
- You will not be able to explicitly define the order of your column heading from the Crosstab Query Wizard.

Utilizing the query design grid to design your crosstab query

Below are steps used in creating a crosstab query with the use of the query design grid:

- Create an **aggregate query**
- Choose **the Design tab** of the Ribbon and then click **on the crosstab button** with this a row called Crosstab has been added to your own query grid.
- Under each field in the Crosstab row, choose if the field will be a row heading, a value, or a column heading.
- Run **the query** in order to see your crosstab in action.

Customizing your crosstab queries

The crosstab has to be adjusted somewhat even if it is a very helpful tool by itself. Some methods by which we can tailor your crosstab inquiries to your requirements are described in the section below.

Defining criteria in a crosstab query

To have your filter defined for your crosstab query simply;

- Insert **the criteria** as you normally would for just any other aggregate query.

Changing the sort order of your crosstab query column headings

Crosstab queries frequently arrange their column headings alphabetically by default. A crosstab query's column order can be altered by modifying the Column Headings property in the Query Properties.

To locate the Column Headings attribute:

- Open **the query** in the Design view

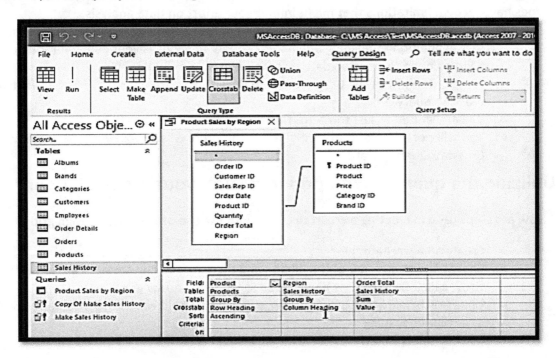

- Right-click **in the gray area** above the white query grid and then choose the Properties option.
- Enter **the order** in which you would like to see the column heading by changing the Column Headings attribute.

Optimizing Query Performance

All should function easily while processing a sizable amount of data, but performance can become a real problem when thousands of entries are being analyzed. You may minimize the time it takes to run your extensive analytical procedures and maximize query performance by taking specific actions. There's an integrated query optimizer in Access. The responsibility of developing a query execution strategy falls to this optimizer. A set of instructions provided to the Access database engine (ACE) that tells it how to execute the query as quickly and economically as feasible is known as the query execution strategy.

Access query optimizer bases its query execution on the factors below:

- Whether indexes exist in the tables used in the query.
- The number of tables and joins used in the query.
- The presence and also the scope of any criteria or expression used in the query.

Due to the fact that the Access query optimizer's functionality is mostly dependent on the content and usefulness of your tables and queries, the terms garbage-in and garbage-out also apply to it. Poorly built tables can also reduce the effectiveness of the Access query optimizer.

Normalizing your database design

When they first start using Access, most users create simply one very big table and call it a database. Because you only need to reference one table when building your queries and joins are not required, this structure can be a very smart choice. Your data will eventually be divided into numerous smaller tables if you decide to normalize your database such that it has a relational structure.

Using indexes on appropriate fields

Access must first scan the entire data set before it can produce any results when you perform a query that requires you to sort and filter on a column that hasn't been indexed. In contrast, since Access uses the index to validate locations and limitations, queries that sort and filter on indexed fields execute significantly more quickly. All it takes to create an index on a field in a table is to open it in the Design view and make some changes to the Indexed attribute.

Optimizing by improving query design

Take a look at the steps below to help speed up your queries and also optimize your analytical processes;

- Be sure to **avoid** sorting or filtering fields that are not indexed.
- Avoid **creating queries** that select from a table.
- There might be a need for you to add more fields in your query design only in order to set the criteria against them.
- Do not use **open-ended ranges like > or<** rather you can make use of the Between...And statement.
- Avoid **making use of calculated fields** in subqueries or domain aggregate functions. When you make use of calculated fields in them it compounds the query's performance loss to some extent.

Compacting and repairing the database regularly

Your database may have undergone long-term changes, such as an increase or decrease in the number of tables, temporary additions or deletions of various tables and queries, or an unusual closure of the database. Anytime you perform database repairs, Access will automatically build table statistics and optimize your queries, ensuring that they are recompiled the next time the query is run.

To repair your database simply;

- Choose **the Database Tools tab on the Ribbon**.
- Click on **the Compact and Repair Database command**.

You can choose to set your database to repair automatically anytime you close it by doing the following;

- Locate **the Ribbon** and then choose **the File option**.

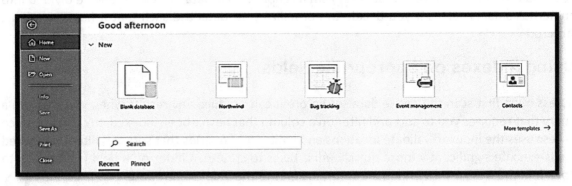

- Click on **Options** then the **Access Options dialog box** will then be displayed.
- Choose the **Current Database** to show the configuration settings for the current database.

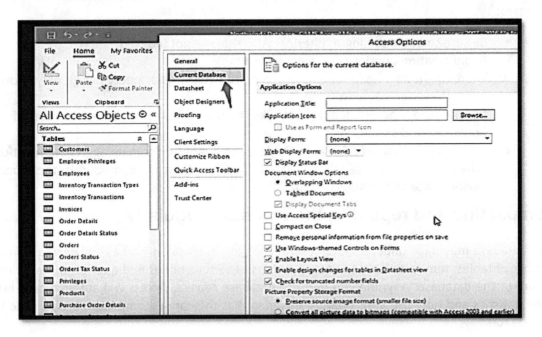

- Place a **checkmark** close to **Compact** on Close and then click on the **OK button** in order to confirm the change.

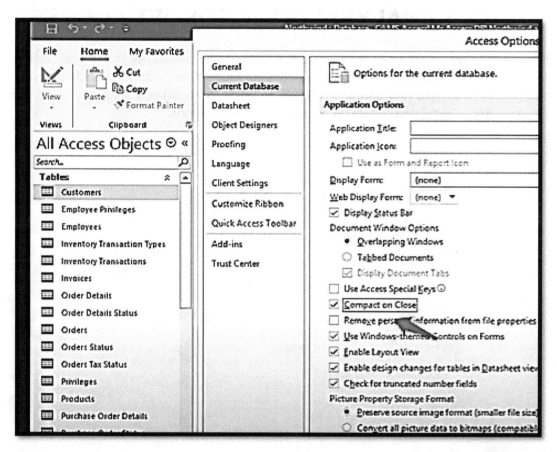

Activity

1. Create an aggregate query.
2. What are aggregate functions?
3. Mention 4 action queries.
4. Make table queries.
5. Create a crosstab query.
6. Customize your crosstab query.
7. Optimize query performance.

PART IV

DATA ANALYSIS IN MICROSOFT ACCESS

This section covers chapters 11 through 16 and teaches you how to use the several features and tools in Access 2024 that can help you analyze data more meaningfully. It should be noted that using Access to analyze your data can help you examine much larger quantities of data, improve your own productivity, and streamline your analytical operations.

CHAPTER 11

TRANSFORMING DATA IN ACCESS

The process of transforming data typically involves a number of steps that should assist in cleaning up specific tasks, such as organizing data fields into tables, removing duplicates, cleaning text, and so forth. There will undoubtedly be occasions when you receive data that is completely raw, in which case you will need to undertake some sort of data transformation in order to conduct a meaningful analysis of the data. This chapter will teach you how to use several Access techniques that will make cleaning and transforming your data—without using Excel—quite simple.

Locating and Removing Duplicate Records

When you have duplicate records it can be really detrimental as it can kill any form of data analysis. Hence, there is a need for you to take off duplicate records each time you receive a new set of data.

Stating duplicate records

It is crucial that you understand that two records in a column with identical values do not necessarily indicate that the records are duplicates. When you must have configured them as either a primary or combination key, you may test your table for duplicates with great ease if you know exactly which field in your table produces a unique record. Otherwise, you will not be able to correctly have duplicate records.

Finding duplicate records

Prior to needing to delete duplicate records, you must find and review any duplicates in your data if you have thoroughly examined your records and are confident that your data contains them. By doing this, you may ensure that you won't make any mistakes by removing duplicate records from your study.

The easiest way to locate duplicate records in your data is to execute the Find Duplicates Query Wizard:

- Select **the Create tab** option of the Ribbon and then pick the **Query Wizard button**.
- Select **Find Duplicates** Query Wizard and then select the **OK button**.
- Choose the **specific data set** you would like to make use of in Your Find Duplicate query then click on the **Next option**.
- Locate **the field or combinations of fields** that best define a unique record in your data set then choose the **Next option**.
- Indicate any **additional fields** that you would like to see in your query.

- Give your **query a name** then click on the **finish button.**

Removing duplicate records

When working with a small set of data, removing duplicates can be fairly simple. However, when working with a large set of data, you may find it more challenging to handle your Find Duplicates query in terms of deleting records.

To remove lots of data at once, follow the steps below;

- Right-click on the **LeadList table** and then choose the **Copy option.**
- Right-click **one more time** and choose **the paste option** which will then display the paste As dialog box.
- Give your new table **a name** and choose **Structure only** from the paste option that is displayed in the dialog box.
- Open your **new leadlist_NoDups table** in the Design view and choose the **appropriate field or combination of fields as the primary key.**
- Design **an append query** that will append all of the records from the LeadList table to the LeadList_NoDups table.

It should be noted that Access makes no attempt to ascertain whether records are duplicates logically. It will immediately process the outcome. For instance, if you type in the wrong address or phone number, duplicate rows will be accepted because there is already a mistake in one of the rows.

Common Transformation Tasks

This section deals with the types of common transformation tasks that might be needed by unpolished sets of data;

Filling in blank fields

It's common to encounter fields with null values, in which case you'll need to enter some form of logical code to indicate the missing value in the blank spaces. All you need to do is run an update query to fill in the null fields in your data set. It is crucial to remember that there are two different kinds of blank values in a text field: null and empty strings. You can be certain that no field will be left out by including the empty strings as a condition in your update query whenever you need to fill in the blanks.

Concatenating

There is no need for you to export data out of Access to Excel simply because you want to concatenate. Concatenation can be done in Access by simply updating the query.

Concatenating fields

Concatenation in Access is all about modifying the query, as was previously stated. Keep in mind that you need to make sure the column you are trying to update is large enough to accommodate the concatenated string before running an update query that performs the concatenation. For example, if the field size of the field you wish to change is 25 characters and your concatenated string is approximately 50 characters long, your concatenated text will be trimmed short without informing you.

Augmenting field values with your own text

You have the option to add your own text to your fields to enhance the values already present. To get this to function properly, all you have to do is make sure the text is enclosed in quotes. Nevertheless, numbers can be joined together without the need for quotation marks.

Changing case

Is it capitalized or lowercase? Make sure that the text in your database is capitalized correctly at all times. Access comes with a few built-in features that can make switching situations simple. For example, you can use the StrConv function, which helps to convert a string to a special case, if you have values in the Address field. The field you are working with will be the string that is transformed. In a query environment, you can use the field name to specify that you are converting every row value in that specific field. The type of conversion chosen will let Access know if you want to convert the specified text to all uppercase, all lowercase, or a proper case.

Take a look at the explanation below;

- **Conversion type 1**: this option helps to convert the text indicated to uppercase characters.
- **Conversion type 2**: this choice aids the conversion of the indicated text to lowercase characters.
- **Conversion type 3:** this option helps to convert the text indicated to a proper case (the first letter of every word is an uppercase) character.

It should be noted that if you wish to change your text to uppercase or lowercase, respectively, you may also use the Ucase and Lcase functions.

Removing leading and trailing spaces from a string

Data with leading and trailing spaces may exhibit some irregularities, particularly when values containing these gaps must be appended to clean values. The Trim function can be used to remove the leading and trailing spaces. Leading spaces are eliminated by the Ltrim function while trailing spaces are eliminated by the RTrim function.

Finding and replacing specific text

Imagine that you have added a specific text to every customer's address on your table, and later on, it is determined to be offensive, therefore you have to remove it. It might be quite time-consuming and stressful to visit each address one after the other; in this situation, the replace feature can be quite helpful.

Note that there are basically three arguments that are deemed required and three that are deemed optional in a Replace function:

- **Expression (required)**: This is the entire string that you are going to assess. In a query context, you can utilize a field's name to signal that you are analyzing every row value in that specific field.
- **Find (required):** this is the very substring that you need to find and replace.
- **Replace (required):** this is the substring that is used as a replacement.
- **Start (Optional)**: this is the position that is within a substring from which the search can be started.
- **Count (optional):** this is the number of occurrences that should be replaced.
- **Compare (optional)**: This is the appropriate comparison to make. You have three options: the default comparison process, textual comparison, or binary comparison.

Adding your own text in key positions within a string

In the course of transforming data, there might be a reason for you to include your own text in key positions with a string. This editing can be done with the use of the Right function, Left function, and the Mid function and they can also be used with each other.

For instance, the Right, Left, and Mid functions enable you to retrieve portions of a string beginning from different positions:

- The Left function assists in returning a certain amount of characters starting with the string's leftmost character. The text that you are evaluating and the number of characters that should be returned are the only arguments needed for the Left function.
- The Right function, starting from the string's rightmost character, returns a certain number of characters. The text to be evaluated and the number of characters to be returned are mandatory inputs for the Right function.
- The Mid function returns a specified number of characters beginning from the specified character position. The required arguments for the Mid function are the text that is being evaluated beginning with the position, and the number of characters that should be returned.

Parsing strings using character markers

When data is contained in a field and is separated by commas, the parsing string is frequently utilized. For instance, entering a contact's three names in the field as their middle, first, and last names. Three distinct fields will need to be created by parsing this string of data. Adding spaces is not enough to complete parsing; you also need to utilize the Instr function. This function will look through another string for a given string, find it, and return its location.

Query 1

The ContactName field's last name will be extracted by the first query, which will also update the Conatct_LastName column. The remaining strings will then be updated in the Contact_FirstName field. You may see the result of your first update query when the LeadList table opens.

Query 2

The Contact_FirstNmae and Contact_MI fields will be updated by the second query. You can open your table and see the results after your second query runs successfully.

Activity

1. What are duplicate records
2. Locate and remove duplicate records.
3. Concatenate fields.
4. Augment field values with your text.
5. Remove leading and trailing spaces from a string.
6. Find and replace specific text.
7. Add a text of yours in important positions within a string.
8. Parse strings with the use of character markers.

CHAPTER 12

WORKING WITH CALCULATIONS AND DATES

Organizations frequently need to perform some computations before presenting the data analysis's overall image. This chapter will cover the tools that Access offers as well as the built-in functions that it employs to calculate and potentially operate with dates.

Employing the Use of Calculations in Your Analyses

When having to work with Access or any database environment, it is best you keep data separate from the analysis. **With this, you will be able to store a calculation in your data set although the use of tables to store data can be somewhat problematic for a number of reasons;**

- Stored calculations have a need for constant maintenance as the data in the table might change from time to time.
- Stored calculations have the data configured to a particular analytical path.
- Stored calculations take up valuable storage space.

It is preferable to carry out the calculation when needed rather than to keep the findings as data. This will free you from being restricted to a single analytical path and ensure that your result is current and precise.

Common calculation scenarios

Expressions are utilized for calculations in Microsoft Access. To put it simply, an expression is a set of variables, operators, or functions that are evaluated and return a new value that can be utilized in another procedure. For instance, the result of 3+3 is a single number, 6, which you can utilize for further analysis. Expressions are widely used in Microsoft Access to do a variety of tasks in reports, forms, data, and even tables to a particular degree.

Using constants in calculations

A constant can be said to be a value that is static. I.e. it doesn't change. In almost all calculations, you will have a need to make use of constants or hard-coded numbers.

Utilizing fields in calculations

The majority of the computations you may need to do on data are already included in fields in your data set, so you won't always need to declare the constant you're using. You can execute any kind of computation using fields; it doesn't matter if it's structured as a number or as currency. Working with fields frequently means that your computation will rely on values from each record dataset, which are more akin to the cell values that a Microsoft Excel formula references.

Using the results of aggregation in calculations

By using the results of aggregation you would be able to perform various analytical steps in a single query.

Note that the query will be executed in the order;

- The query will start by grouping records.
- The query will calculate the count of orders if the table has to do with purchasing of items
- The query will then assign the aliases that you must have defined respectively.
- The query will then use the aggregation results for each of the tables as expressions.

Employing the use of the results of one calculation as an expression in another

Bear in mind that you can always have more than one calculation in a query. Furthermore, you can choose to make use of the result of a particular calculation as an expression in another calculation.

Using a calculation as an argument in a function

If a particular query's calculation yields a number with a fractional portion, this can simply mean that it will return a number with many trailing digits after the decimal point. To make the data easier to read and comprehend, it is preferable to return a round number rather than a decimal. You can convert the output of your calculation into an integer by using the Int function. A mathematical function called the Int function can be used to remove a number's fractional portion and return an integer instead. Note that you can use any function that takes a number as a parameter; any calculation that returns a number can do so.

Constructing calculations with the Expression Builder

Another tool in Access that can assist with creating an expression with a few mouse clicks is the expression builder. This is quite simple; all you need to do is select the relevant functions and data fields to form an expression.

Before using the expression builder, there is a need for it to be activated. To do this;

- Make a click **inside the query** grid cell that has the expression then right-click and choose Build.

- You can right-click **anywhere** (control properties form, control properties reports, etc.) you would like to write an expression to activate the Expression Builder.

The Expression builder consists of roughly four panes: the upper pane is where you insert the expression, and the lower pane displays the different objects that you can work with. Additionally, you can use the plus icons here to enlarge the database objects.

- To make use of any function in Access all you have to do is to click **twice** on the function and Access will insert the function automatically in the upper pane of the Expression builder.

Frequent calculation errors

No matter how flawless you are or how reliable the platform you are using is, mistakes will nevertheless inevitably happen to you. There are some basic steps you can take to avoid some of the most common math errors, but Microsoft has not yet created a feature in Access that can assist you in preventing errors during analysis.

Understanding the order of operator precedence

There are fundamental guidelines to adhere to in order to make sure you avoid common mistakes, much like BODMAS in mathematics. When using expressions and calculations involving numerous operations, each operation will be evaluated first, followed by its resolution in a predefined sequence. It is imperative that you understand the concept of operator precedence in Access as improper expression construction can result in issues.

Below are the orders of operations for Access:

- Evaluate the items in parentheses first.
- Perform exponentiation.
- Perform negation.
- Perform multiplication and division.
- Perform addition and subtraction at equal precedence.
- Evaluate string concatenation.
- Evaluate comparison and pattern-matching operators.
- Evaluate logical operators in the order; Not, And, Or.

If you do not follow the above precedence in any given calculation, you might be getting the wrong answer. Ensure you follow this precedence at all times.

Looking out for the null values

A null value only indicates that no value was provided. When a table entry is empty, it is referred to as null.

Access just returns a null value whenever it encounters a null value rather than assuming it to be zero. By using the Nz function, which lets you replace any null value you come across to a predefined value, you may prevent errors in null calculations.

The Nz function takes up two arguments;

- **ValueIfNull**: this simply means the value that should be returned if the variant is null.
- **Variant**: this is the data you are working with at the moment.

Watching the syntax in your expressions

Making some basic mistakes with syntax in your calculation expressions can also lead to errors.

Below are guidelines to follow in order to avoid any form of slip-ups;

- Avoid the use of illegal characters like period (.), square brackets (**[]**), etc in your aliases.
- When you are adding an alias to a calculated field, ensure you don't inadvertently make use of a field name from any of the tables that are queried.
- Ensure the names of the fields are well spelled.

Using Dates in Your Analyses

With Microsoft Access, all the possible dates that begin from December 31, 1899, are stored as a positive serial number. The system of storing dates as serial numbers is commonly referred to as the 1900 system which is also the default for all office applications like Excel, Word, and PowerPoint.

Simple date calculations

Dates must be in a field that is formatted as a Date/Time field in order for calculations to be done correctly. When you enter a date into a Short Text field, Access will interpret it as a string even if it appears to be a date. As a result, any calculations involving dates in this format will fail. Verify that every date is entered into fields with the Date/Time format.

Advanced analysis using functions

Access 2024 has about 25 in-built date/time functions. Though you might not make use of all of the functions, it is necessary for you to know how to make use of the very important ones.

Below are a few of the functions that you might need to use on a daily basis.

The Date function

Access comes with a built-in function that can be used to retrieve the current system date or today's date. You won't have to utilize a constant for today's date when calculating thanks to this function. When you add a criteria expression, you can use this function to filter out records. You can also round the number of years using the Round function. Additionally, make sure that the Int function is used for all of your computations. This will guarantee that your results are precise and free of fractions.

The Year, Month, Day, and Weekday functions

The Year, Month, Day, and weekday functions are usually used basically to return an integer that shows their respective parts of a date. All of these functions need a valid date as an argument. Be aware that the weekday function retrieves the current week's day from a given date. In Microsoft Access, the weekdays are always numbered from 1 to 7, with Sunday serving as the start of the week. Thus, Wednesday is simply shown if the weekday function returns 4, which denotes the fourth day of the week starting on Sunday. With the FirstDayOfWeek argument, you can always modify the first day of the week to suit your schedule. The day you wish to recognize as the first day of the week can be specified with the help of the argument.

The Date add function

The majority of organizations employ analysis to assist adds a deadline for when the benchmark will be met. For instance, the majority of firms establish a benchmark date for paying salaries.

There are about three required arguments in the DateAdd function;

- Interval (required): this is simply the interval of time that should be used.

The intervals are:

- "yyyy": Year
- "q": Quarter
- "m": Month
- "y": Day of year
- "d": Day
- "w": Weekday
- "w": Week
- "h": Hour
- "n": Minute
- "s": Second
- **Date (required)**: this is simply the value of the date you are working with.

- **Number (required):** this is simply the number of intervals that should be added. A positive number brings back dates in the future while a negative number brings back dates in the past

Grouping dates into quarters

If you need to turn dates into quarters in order to evaluate your data on a quarter-over-quarter basis, you must always group your dates. You have the Format function in Access, even though there isn't a single feature that lets you divide dates into quarters. You can turn a variation into a string based on formatting instructions by using the Format function, which is a part of the Text category of functions. **There are basic valid instructions you can pass to a format function to ensure it is able to group to quarter:**

- Format (#01/31/2019#, "yyyy") which returns 2019.
- Format (#01/31/2019#, "yy") returns 19
- Format (#01/31/2019#, "q") returns 1

Note that the value that is returned when a date is passed through a Format function is a string that you shouldn't make use of in subsequent calculations.

The DateSerial function

By mixing the provided year, month, and day components, you can create the date of your choosing using the DateSerial method. The best application for this function is to turn two different strings that each represents a date into an actual date.

There are basically three arguments with the DateSerial function:

- **Year (required):** this is simply any number from 100 to 9999.
- **Month (required):** simply any number.
- **Day (required):** any number or expression.

Activity

1. What are common calculation scenarios?
2. Make use of fields in calculations.
3. Make use of the results of aggregation in calculations.
4. Make use of the result of one calculation as an expression in another calculation.
5. Construct calculations with the use of Expression Builder.
6. Make use of dates in your calculations.
7. Group dates into quarters.

CHAPTER 13

PERFORMING CONDITIONAL ANALYSES

A conditional analysis is one that is contingent upon a predetermined list of parameters. It differs significantly from the typical easy approach of merely creating a query, adding some criteria and calculations, and then running the query. The creation of conditional analyses is made possible by a few tools, including parameter queries, the Iif function, and the Switch function. This chapter will provide you with information on how to utilize these tools and functions to improve your analysis, streamline your workflow, and save time.

Making use of Parameter Queries

You can know the criteria before you run the query by using parameter queries. When performing an operation and you need to query different queries using different criteria, a parameter query might be very helpful. You can create conditional analysis—an analysis that is dependent on different variables you specify for each query execution—by utilizing parameter queries.

To build a parameter query all you have to do is;
- Replace **the hard-coded** criteria with text that you must have enclosed in square brackets. A parameter query will forcefully open the Enter Parameter Value dialog box and ask for a variable when it is executed. At this point, the dialog box will display the text that you have to write inside the square brackets.

How parameter queries work

When you run a parameter query, Microsoft Access attempts to change any text to a literal string by enclosing the text on quotes. Note that if you place squares in brackets around the text, Microsoft Access will assume it is a variable and will attempt to bind some variable to the variable with **the use of the following series of tests:**

- If a name is entered into the variable field, Microsoft Access will verify it. In the event that it is recognized as a field name, the field will be utilized within the phrase.
- Access will verify that the variable is a calculated field if it is not a field name. Access will perform the mathematical operation if it determines that the expression is a calculated field.
- Access will check to determine if the variable is referring to an object, such as the control on an open form or an open report if it is not a calculated field.
- If all of the above options fail, the option left will then be to ask the user what the variable is, with this, Access will display the Enter Parameter Value dialog box, displaying the text you inserted in the Criteria row.

Ground rules of parameter query

Parameter queries also have their own ground rules that should be followed so you can make use of them properly;

- A field's name cannot be utilized as a parameter. If you do this, Access will substitute the field's current value for your argument.
- The parameters must be surrounded by square brackets. Access will automatically convert text into a literal string if this isn't done.
- Your parameter's character count must be restricted. If you enter a parameter prompt in the Enter Parameter Value dialog box and it is too long, it may be terminated.

Dealing with parameter queries

Learning how to work with your parameter queries and get the most out of them is actually extremely creative; it will be highly helpful and improve the way your data analysis is solved. Further information about the several ways you can utilize the parameters in your queries is provided in this section.

Working with multiple parameter conditions

You are free to work with as many Parameters as needed in a query. When you execute a query you will be prompted to insert some information that will enable you to filter on two different data points without the need to rewrite your query.

Bringing together parameters with operators

Combining parameter prompts can be done with any operator you would normally use in a query. You can modify the size of the filters in your analysis without rewriting the query by utilizing parameters with standard operators.

Combining parameters with wildcards

When using a parameter query, one of the main issues that frequently arise is that the query will never return any records if the parameter is left blank throughout execution. The usage of wildcards is a tried-and-true solution to this problem; in this way, all entries will be returned even if the parameter is blank. It should be noted that users can enter an initial parameter and still receive results when the *wildcard is used in conjunction with a parameter.

Utilizing parameters as calculation variables

Parameters can be used at any point where a variable is used and not only used as criteria for a query. Parameters can also be of great importance when it has to do with calculations.

Using parameters as function arguments

Functions for arguments can be utilized with parameters. You are promoted to a start date and an end date when the query with the parameter is being executed. The DateDiff function will then take those two dates as inputs. Additionally, you do not need to rewrite the query if you decide to specify new dates whenever you execute it. Keep in mind that the values you enter in your parameters need to exactly match the data type required for the function's argument.

Using Conditional Functions

Data validation, conditional evaluation, and value comparisons are made possible by Microsoft Access's built-in features. The switch function and the IIf function are two examples of such functions. These functions, which are often referred to as program flow functions, are made to test different scenarios and provide results that are contingent on the tests' outcomes. You'll learn more about how to utilize the IIf and Switch functions to manage the flow of your analysis in the sections that follow.

The IIf function

Anywhere those expressions may be used, so can the IIf function. You can use this method to find out whether an expression is true or false. IIf will return a single value if the expression is true and a different value if it is false. Its return value, whether true or false, is entirely up to you. Despite returning only one value out of the two, IIf will always analyze both the true and false parts. It is therefore best that you keep an eye out for any potentially unwanted side effects. The IIf function can be used in queries, complex expressions, reports, and forms.

Using IIf to avoid mathematical errors

The IIf function can help you avoid some errors, all you have to do is perform a conditional analysis on your data set with the IIf function and then evaluate the field that should be calculated just before you calculate.

Saving time with IIf

The IIf function can help you save steps and save a significant amount of time. The IIf function can help expedite such procedures and yet yield accurate results, saving you from having to execute two or more queries.

Meeting IIf functions for multiple conditions

Nested IIf functions which means IIf functions in another IIf function can come in very handy whenever you have to test for conditions that are too complex to be handled by a basic IF ... .THEN....ELSE structure. It should be noted that the condition utilized can be expanded anytime an IIf function returns a true or false result by setting the false expression to another IIf function instead of a hard-coded value. No restrictions whatsoever apply to the number of nested IIf functions you can utilize.

Using IIf functions to create crosstab analysis

The IIf function is used by most data analysts to create unique crosstab analysis. The option to include many calculations in the crosstab report is one benefit of creating a crosstab analysis without using a crosstab query.

The switch function

There are pairs of expressions and values in the switch function argument. The value corresponding to the first expression to evaluate to True is returned when the expressions are evaluated from left to right. A run-time error will arise if the pieces are not paired correctly.

The switch returns a null if value:

- None of the expressions is True.
- The first True expression has a value corresponding to Null.

Although it will only return one of the expressions, the switch makes sure it evaluates each one. It is crucial that you keep an eye out for any unfavorable side effects. For example, there will be an error if any expression evaluated leads to a division by zero error. Additionally, it's critical to remember that the switch function can evaluate an infinite number of expressions.

Getting to Compare the IIf and Switch Functions

The IIf function has a limited amount of parameters, which restricts it to a simple IF...THEN...ELSE structure, while being a very useful tool that can handle practically any conditional analysis. Because of this restriction, evaluating complicated conditions without using nested IIf methods can be very challenging. While nesting IIf functions is perfectly acceptable, there are various analyses that should be considered in order to render the process of creating nested IIFs at most impracticable. The issue with using the IIf function is that there are some circumstances in which using substantial nesting may be appropriate. This implies that in order to handle the simple layer of likely circumstances, you will have to use the IIf expressions. Keep in mind that utilizing the switch function rather than the nested IIf function is frequently more practical.

Activity

1. What are parameter queries?
2. What are the ground rules of parameter query?
3. Combine parameters with wildcards.
4. Make use of parameters as function arguments.
5. Use the IIF condition to avoid mathematical errors.
6. Differentiate between the IIF and switch functions.

CHAPTER 14

THE FUNDAMENTALS OF USING SQL

Regarding relational database management systems such as Access, Structured Query Language (SQL) is a language that is utilized for various activities. SQL is required to convey your message to a database management system (DBMS) such as Access. In addition to learning how to work with statements created by SQL when creating queries, this chapter will provide you with a quick overview of the role that SQL plays in your use of Access. The knowledge you gain from this course will improve your performance and your ability to navigate any database management system you encounter.

Understanding Basic SQL

If you've been using Access for a long time, you may not know much about how SQL is used because Access is more user-friendly and performs the majority of its functions in an environment that makes the primary work that occurs behind the scenes visible. Because of Access's extremely user-friendly interface, you don't actually need to understand SQL to perform all of the key functions behind each query. Having said that, you must possess a thorough understanding of SQL foundations if you hope to fully utilize Access's capabilities for data analysis.

The SELECT statement

The SELECT statement is the core part of SQL which is used to collect records from a set of data. The basic syntax of a SELECT statement is;
- **SELECT column_name(s) FROM table_name**

For perfect results, the SELECT statement is often used with a FROM clause which helps with the identification of the tables that make up the source for the data.

Choosing specific columns

You can retrieve the exact columns from your data collection by using the SELECT statement and correctly describing your data set. When crafting your SQL query, keep in mind that any column in your database with a name that comprises a character or number that isn't alphanumeric needs to be enclosed in brackets.

Choosing all columns

The preceding chapter provided a brief explanation of how to use the wildcard. I should also mention that you won't need to specify each column individually when using the *wildcard to select every column from a batch of data.

The WHERE clause

The WHERE clause can be used to sieve your data set in a SELECT statement. Oftentimes, the WHERE clause is used with an operator like; equal =, greater than >, less than <, greater than equal to >=, less than equal to <=.

Knowing more about joins

Joins are often used to bring two or more tables that are related together in order to achieve the desired result. There are different types of joins available and the very type of join used will also determine what the result will be.

Inner joins

Access is directed by inner joins to select just those records from the tables whose values coincide. In the two tables that are missing from the query results, records with values in the joined column will not be shown.

Outer joins

An outer join selects every record from a given table, then selects records from the second table that match the records it selected from the first table. The right joins and the left joins are the two additional divisions of the outer join. When joins are done correctly, only records from the first table whose records match the values of the joined field are also picked, and records from the second table are chosen without taking into account whether or not the records match. The left join chooses records from the first table without also considering if the records match and it also chooses records whose values match the joined field from the second table.

Getting Fancy with Advanced SQL Statements

With the SQL statement you can do more than just the basics such as SELECT, FROM, and WHERE statements. The section below tells you more about SQL and other things you can accomplish with it.

Expanding your search with the Like operator

The equal = operator and the Like operator are fairly similar. The Like operator is most effective when used with wildcard characters; doing so will enable your search to be expanded to include any record that fits a pattern.

Below are some wildcard characters that can be used in Access;

- *: this is used in representing any number and type of characters.

- []: with the bracket, you can pass just one character or lots of characters to the Like operator. Values that are of the same match with the character values that are embedded in the brackets will also be added to the results.
- ?: this sign is a representation of any single character.

Selecting unique values and rows without grouping

You can extract only the unique values from selected fields in your set of data by using the DISTINCT predicate. In order for a specific record to be included in the results, if your SQL statement selects more than one field during this process, the values from each field must likewise be unique. The DISTINCTROW predicate can therefore be used if it's necessary for the entire row to be unique. This will allow you to obtain only the records that contribute to the row's uniqueness. This indicates that no record in the data set returned matches the set of all the values in the selected fields.

Grouping and aggregating with the GROUP BY clause

The GROUP BY clause in Microsoft Access helps with the combination of records that have identical values in the indicated field list into just one record. A summary value will also be created for each of the records if you add an SQL aggregate function like Sum or Count in the SELECT statement. Observe that GROUP BY is not required. In the event that the SELECT query lacks an aggregate function, summary values are always omitted. In GROUP BY fields, null values are frequently not omitted. However, in most SQL aggregate functions, Null values are not analyzed. A column in the GROUP BY field list can really refer to any field in any table specified in the FROM clause if it does not include Memo or OLE object data, even if the field is not included in the SELECT statement, provided that the SELECT statement contains at least one SQL aggregate function. Keep in mind that the Memo and OLE Object fields are not groupable by the Microsoft Access database engine.

Configuring the sort order with the ORDER BY Clause

Access's ORDER BY clause facilitates the sorting of a query's resultant record in either an ascending or descending order based on a specific field or fields. Moreover, ORDER BY is optional. However, you must utilize the ORDER BY if you need to display your data by order. An error will occur if you specify a field in the ORDER BY clause that contains Memo or OLE Object data. These kinds of fields are generally not sorted on by the Microsoft Access database engine. Keep in mind that a SQL statement's last item is typically ORDER Y. You have the option to expand the ORDER BY clause with more fields. Following ORDER BY, records are sorted starting with the first letter in the field. The value in the second field listed will be used to rank records that also have equal values in that field, and so on.

Creating aliases with the AS clause

You can add aliases to your tables and columns using the AS clause. Aliases are frequently used when working with many instances of the same table and require a way to quickly refer to one instance over another, or when you need to shorten and make table or column names easier to understand.

Creating a column alias

One way to think of a column alias is as a temporary replacement name. In order to name or rename columns and make the table's output more readable and understandable, aliases are frequently mentioned in the SELECT clause. Every column name in the SELECT clause may have an alias; column aliases are optional. You can utilize an alias to refer to a column in any other clause after you've assigned it to one. Note that it is advisable to avoid writing code that references column aliases in a WHERE clause, GROUP BY clause, or HAVING clause if you want the most mobility of the SQL code used outside of the Access SQL procedure.

Creating a table alias

You can refer to a table in a SELECT statement in your FROM clause by using a different name by using a table alias. When you use an expression as a data source or to make the SQL statement easier to read and type, a table alias is only a name that is allocated to a data source in a query. When numerous fields with the same name from different tables are involved, this might be especially helpful if the data source name is too long or challenging to write.

Showing only the SELECT TOP or SELECT TOP PERCENT

All records that satisfy the specified definitions and criteria will be retrieved upon execution of a SELECT query. When you run a top values query or the SELECT TOP statement, you are essentially telling Access to assist in filtering the returned data set so that it displays just a predetermined number of records.

Top values queries explained

The Top value query might be useful in situations when you need to establish tables and prioritize the records within them. When creating a Top Value query in Microsoft Access, you can choose to display a percentage or a value that represents a portion of the total number of records in the record set. This query type is very easy to use.

The SELECT TOP statement

When using the SELECT TOP statement, it is very important for you to indicate the sort direction very accurately since it can make all the difference between choosing the biggest ten results or the smallest ten results. Bear in mind that you can choose to sort on a field without having to show that field.

The SELECT TOP PERCENT Statement

With one exception—the records produced by the SELECT TOP PERCENT statement display the nth percent of all records rather than the nth number of records—this statement functions exactly like the SELECT TOP command. Keep in mind that the SELECT TOP PERCENT instructions do not provide you with the percentage of the overall value in your records; rather, they only provide you the top or bottom percent of all the records that are returned in the collection of data.

Performing action queries via SQL statements

Creating an action query is equivalent to creating an SQL statement with the same goal in mind. You will be able to do more with the SQL statement than merely select records.

Make-table queries translated

Make-table queries make use of the SELECT …. INTO statement in order to make a hard-coded table that have the results of your query.

Append Queries translated

You can use the INSERT INTO statement with the append query to add new rows to a designated table.

Update queries translated

Update queries make use of the UPDATE statement and SET in order to change the data in a data set.

Delete queries translated

Delete queries make use of the DELETE statement to delete rows in a set of data.

Creating Crosstabs with the TRANSFORM statement

With the TRANSFORM statement you can create a crosstab set of data that shows data in a more compact view.

For you to get the best of the TRANSFORM statement it needs basically three components which are;

- The field to be aggregated.
- The SELECT statement that determines the row content for the crosstab.
- The field that will make up the column of the crosstab.

Using SQL-specific queries

In essence, SQL-specific inquiries are action queries that you are unable to run through the Access query grid. These specific queries need to be run via code (VBA or macro) or via SQL view. SQL-specific queries come in several varieties, and each one has a unique function.

Merging data sets with the UNION operator

As the name UNION suggests, this operator is used to combine two compatible SQL queries into a single read-only data set. The UNION operator is the most effective tool to employ whenever you need to combine two distinct sets of data to produce an analysis that will show the details and totals in a single table. Keep in mind that Access will match the column from the two sets of data according to their respective locations in the SELECT statement when you run a union query. This essentially indicates that the precise number of columns in your SELECT statement is required and that the column order in both SELECT statements is crucial. Once the columns have matching data types, Access will produce a union of the two tables making use of the position of each of the columns.

Creating a table with the CREATE TABLE statement

It will occasionally be necessary for you to make temporary tables so that you may store, organize, and work with data. The CREATE TABLE statement is useful in this situation since it enables you to accomplish it with only one SQL-specific query. The CREATE TABLE statement only permits the establishment of a table's structure and schema; records are not returned.

If you would like to make use of the CREATE TABLE, simply;

- Begin a new query.
- Change to SQL view
- Define the structure or schema for the table.

Manipulating columns with the ALTER TABLE statement

Using the ALTER TABLE statement, you might decide to make some changes to a table's structure. The ALTER TABLE statement can be used with a number of clauses, some of which are quite helpful for analyzing data in Microsoft Access. The ADD, ALTER COLUMN, ADD CONSTRAINT, and ADD CONSTRAINT classes are these ones. Keep in mind that once an action is carried out using the ALTER TABLE statement, it cannot be undone.

Adding a column with the ADD clause

The ADD clause allows you to include columns in tables that already exist.

To use the ADD statement simply

- Start **a new query** in SQL view then define the structure for your new column.

Altering a column with the ALTER COLUMN clause

With the ALTER COLUMN, you can specify an already existing column in an existing table. With this clause, you can change the data type and field size of a specific column.

To make use of the ALTER COLUMN statement simply;

- Begin **a new query** in the SQL view and then **define changes** for the particular column.

Deleting a column with the DROP COLUMN clause

With the use of the DROP COLUMN, you can delete a particular column from a table that exists.

To make use of the DROP COLUMN simply;

- Begin **a new query** in the SQL view and then **specify** the structure for your new column.

Dynamically adding primary keys with the ADD constraints clause

The majority of analysts utilize Access as a user-friendly extract, transform, and load (ETL) tool. This essentially means that Access provides space for you to rearrange the data into consolidated tables after extracting the data from sources. Using macros to help launch some queries, analysts also automate the ETL process. Having said that, there are instances in which an ETL procedure requires the inclusion of primary keys in temporary tables in order to standardize the data while it is being processed. Most people try to use other options, but you can construct primary keys dynamically by using the ADD CONSTRAINT clause.

To use the ADD CONSTRAINT clause simply;

- Start **a new query** then define the primary key you would like to implement.

Creating pass-through queries

A query that assists in sending SQL commands straight to a database server is known as a pass-through query. These database servers are typically referred to as the system's back end, with

Access serving as the front end or client tool. The main benefit of using pass-through queries is that they frequently eliminate the need for Access processing and parsing and instead handle it on the back-end server. Because of this, they are significantly faster than queries originating from connected tables, particularly when the linked table is sizable.

Follow the steps below to create a pass-through query;

- Locate **the Create tab** of the Ribbon then click on **the Query Design Command**.
- Close the **Show Table dialog box**.
- Click on the **Pass-Through** command on the **Query Tools Design tab**. This will then display the **SQL design window**.

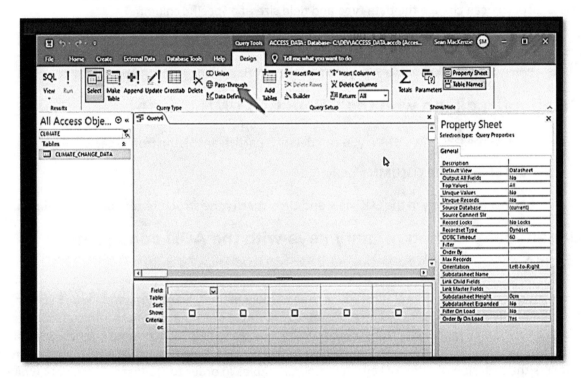

- Insert an **SQL statement** that suits the target database system.
- Locate **the Query Tools Design tab** and click on the **Property Sheet command**. This will also display the Property sheet.

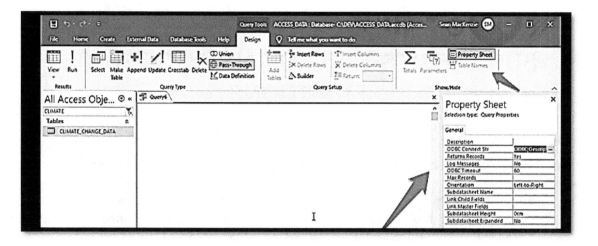

- Insert the **appropriate connection** string for your server
- Finally click **on the Run button**.

Activity

1. What is SQL?
2. What are joins?
3. Expand your search with the use of the Like operator.
4. Select unique values and rows without grouping.
5. Configure the sort order with the ORDER BY Clause.
6. Create a column alias.
7. Create a table alias.
8. Perform action queries with the use of the SQL statements.
9. Add a column with the use of the ADD clause.
10. Alter a column with the use of the ALTER Column clause.
11. Create a pass-through query.

CHAPTER 15

SUBQUERIES AND DOMAIN AGGREGATE FUNCTIONS

One of the things you will do in Access is to carry out analyses in layers with each layer of analysis being built on the previously existing layer.

When it has to do with layering analyses, there are basically two things in common and they are;

- In order to layer studies, temporary tables or transition queries must be created. This overload of table and query objects could result in an extremely complicated analytical procedure and an easily expanding database.
- Your analytical procedures can benefit from an additional phase when you layer analyses. Keep in mind that each query must be run in order to feed another query or all of the produced temporary tables, allowing you to progress with your investigation.

With Subqueries and domain aggregate functions, you will be able to build multiple layers into your analyses within just one query while removing any need for temporary tables or transition queries.

Making sure your Analyses with Subqueries are Enhanced

One way to think of a subquery is as a SELECT query statement enclosed in another query. In the query design, Microsoft Access will generate a statement that explains what you are requesting when you drag and drop fields and type expressions. This statement is going to be written in SQL, the most widely used language for relational databases. If SQL is not your first language, you can create a mockup of a query, such as a subquery, convert it to SQL view, and then paste it into your main query. This is the simplest method for creating a subquery, albeit there will be some cleanup involved. You can use subquery to specify new fields to be used in your data analysis or to indicate criteria for additional selection. Subquery allows you to answer different portions of a question. The basic notion of a subquery is to run it first and then utilize the result in the outer query as a criterion, an expression, a parameter, etc. This is because a subquery is a query embedded in another query.

Why use Subqueries?

As you may already be aware, subqueries frequently operate more slowly than typical join-based queries, particularly when handling huge amounts of data. Then, are you asking why you ought to utilize them? The ideal way to have a simplified process and an enhanced analytical process is to use subqueries. They work best when combined with in-the-moment queries to maximize efficiency and minimize downtime.

Subquery ground rules

There are quite a few rules that you need to adhere to when making use of subqueries. They are;

- Subqueries must be enclosed in parentheses.
- They must have a SELECT statement and a FROM clause in their SQL string.
- If a subquery returns a single value, it can be utilized as an expression.
- Only subqueries that are SELECT TOP or SELECT TOP PERCENT statements are eligible to use the ORDER BY clause.
- In a subquery with a GROUP BY clause, the DISTINCT keyword can be used.
- In queries where a table is used in both the outer query and the subquery, you have to set up table aliases.

Creating Subqueries without typing SQL statements

Writing an SQL statement can be an extremely difficult undertaking. As a matter of fact, very few Access users write their SQL statements from scratch. The majority of them utilize the built-in features of Access to save a ton of time and worry.

To create these Subqueries without having to type SQL statements, follow the steps below;

- Create **a query**.
- Change over to the **SQL view** and then copy the **SQL statement**.
- Create **a query** that will specify basic criteria.
  - To zoom in, right-click on the criterion row and select Zoom. Basically, the Zoom dialog box's purpose is to make the text easier for you to see quickly and clearly.
  - You can then paste the previously copied SQL statement into the white input area once the Zoom dialog box has started.
  - Put a greater than > symbol in front of the subquery to finish the query, and then change the GROUP BY of your chosen criteria to a WHERE clause. To preserve the modifications that have been made, click the **OK button.**

The more you make use of SQL; you will discover that you can create Subqueries manually without encountering any problems at all.

Using IN and NOT IN with Subqueries

You can effectively run two different queries in one with the use of the IN and NOT IN operators. The basic idea behind this is that the subquery will be executed first and then the resulting sets of data will be used by the outer query in sieving out the final output.

Using Subqueries with comparison operators

As the name implies, a comparison operator like (=, <,>,<=,>=,<>) does the comparison of two different items and returns True or False. Whenever a subquery is used with a comparison operator this implies that you are telling Access to compare the resulting data set of the outer query to that of the subquery. The subquery will be executed first, giving a single value which Access will use to compare the resulting data of the outer query's data set. Note that for this to be done accurately a single value must be returned when a subquery is used with a comparison operator.

Using Subqueries as Expressions

You can choose to make use of a subquery instead of an expression in the field list of a SELECT statement or in a WHERE or HAVING clause. In a subquery, you make use of a SELECT statement in making a set of one or more specific values to evaluate in the WHERE or HAVING clause. To obtain records in the main query that satisfy the comparison with any record retrieved from the subquery, use the ANY or SOME predicate. Only the records in the main query that pass the comparison with every record retrieved in the subquery are to be fetched using the IN predicate. Next, retrieve only the subquery entries with equal values by using the IN predicate. Retrieving only the records in the main query for which no record in the subquery has an equal value is not possible with NOT IN. Utilize the EXIST predicate to determine whether the subquery will return any records by doing true/false comparisons. Some Subqueries can also be used in crosstab queries basically as predicates. Subqueries as outputs are not allowed in crosstab queries.

Using correlated Subqueries

A query that makes reference to a column present in the outer query is known as correlated. A correlated query is special in that it needs to be evaluated multiple times, one for each row that the outer query processes.

Uncorrelated Subqueries

You can denote an SQL statement using an uncorrelated subquery when the subquery is evaluated one time to provide you with the average for the whole set of data.

Correlated Subqueries

When a subquery refers back to the outer query, you can use it to indicate an SQL statement. This will ultimately yield a dataset that displays the average for a subset of the entire collection of data.

Making Use of a Correlated subquery as an Expression

Each row selected by an outer query only has to have a Correlated Subquery executed once. Additionally, it contains a reference to a value selected by the outer query from the row. It can also be used to find the difference between the selected criteria.

Using Subqueries with Action Queries

Action queries can fit well with Subqueries just as select queries can also fit well. Below are ways a subquery can be used in an action query.

A subquery in a make-table query

The example below shows how to make use of a subquery in a make-table to design a new table that contains data for all employees that have been hired before March 1996.

```
    SELECT E1.Employee_Number, E1.Last_Name, E1.First_Name
        INTO OldSchoolEmployees
        FROM Employee_Master as E1
        WHERE E1.Employee_Number IN
(SELECT E2.Employee_Number
FROM Employee_Master AS E2
WHERE E2.Hire_Date <#1/3/1996#)
```

A subquery in an append query

The example below makes use of a subquery in an append query to include new customers to the customer master table from the LeadList:

```
INSERT INTO CustomerMaster (Customer_Number, Customer_Name, State )
SELECT CompanyNumber, CompanyName, State
FROM LeadList
WHERE CompanyNumber Not In
    (SELECT Customer_Number from CustomerMaster)
```

A subquery in an update query

The example below makes use of a subquery in an update query to increase all the prices in the PriceMaster table by 5% for just the branches that are in the North region.

```
    UPDATE PriceMaster SET Price = [Price]*0.5
WHERE Branch_Number In
    (SELECT Branch_Number from LocationMaster WHERE Region = "North")
```

A subquery in a delete query

The example below makes use of a subquery in a delete query to delete customers from the LeadList table if they already in existence in the CustomerMaster table;

```
DELETE *
FROM LeadList
WHERE CompanyNumber In
   (SELECT Customer_Number from CustomerMaster)
```

Domain Aggregate Functions

A domain aggregate function provides a statistical value by acting conditionally on a field's record. Unlike standard SQL aggregate functions, which are always a part of the SQL, Microsoft Access domain aggregate functions are typically used to assist in finding a value depending on the requirements you have set. Each domain aggregation has a function name, which is sometimes referred to as an appropriate name. The name of the column containing the value that the function will be applied to can be used as the expression argument. An expression based on calculations may also be used. The name of a table or query that doesn't require an external value can be used as the domain argument. You can specify the condition under which a particular record is selected by using the optional condition argument. Like a WHERE condition, it will behave. **As a result, a domain aggregate function resembles a SQL statement's function formula more than anything else;**

```
SELECT expression FROM domain WHERE condition
```

Understanding the different domain Aggregate function

There are about 12 different domain aggregate functions in Access with each of them performing different operations.

DSum

This function returns the total sum value of an indicated field in the domain.

DAvg

The DAvg function returns the average value of an indicated field in the domain.

DCount

The DCount function returns the total number of records in the domain.

DLookup

The lookup function aids in returning the first value of a field that is indicated and that exactly satisfies the DLookup function's defined requirements. In the event that a criterion is either absent or insufficiently precise in identifying a unique row, the DLookup function will yield an arbitrary value inside the domain.

DMin and Dmax

The DMin and DMax function help to return the minimum as well as the maximum values in the domain respectively.

DFirst and DLast

The DFirst and DLast functions seek to return the first and the last values respectively in the domain. Note that you might just get a random value if you fail to make use of an ORDER BY clause to sort the field used in your DFirst or DLast function.

DStDev, DStDevp, DvarP

The DStDev and DStDevP functions can be used to get the standard deviation for both a population and a sample of a specified population. Additionally, you can return the variance across a population sample and a population by using the Dvar and DVarP functions.

Examining the syntax of domain aggregate functions

The syntax to make the Domain Aggregate function work is quite unique as it varies based on the scenario involved. Below are sections that can help you build your domain Aggregate function properly.

Utilizing no criteria

To sum up all the values in the specified field(s), use the no criterion option. Keep in mind that you must always enclose the names of your field and the data set in quotes. Additionally, it is normally recommended to use brackets whenever you identify a field, table, or query.

Using text criteria

With the use of the text criteria it is essential that when specifying the criteria that are textual or s string, your criteria must be wrapped in single quotes. Furthermore, the whole criteria expression must also be wrapped in double-quotes.

Making Use of Domain Aggregate Function

Domain Aggregation functions work best when applied to specialized studies involving much smaller data subsets than when applied to wide-scale data processing and handling extremely massive data sets. This function is typically seen in situations where the datasets are predictable. Here are some simple examples of common activities that can be accomplished by using domain aggregate functions; these are covered in the section below.

Calculating the percent total

Finding the percent total in any table is always a valuable analysis, and it's always possible to do it much more quickly and easily by adding a column that yields the percent total for each entry. This type of computation can also greatly benefit from the use of the DSum function.

Creating a running count

To create a running count you can make use of the DCount function which in terms of sales of a product can help to return the number of invoices that have been processed on each of the invoice days.

Using a value from the previous record

The DLookup function can help you to return a value from the previous record. It will help to search the records and return the value needed based on your specified criteria.

Activity

1. Make use of correlated subqueries.
2. Employ the use of correlated subqueries.
3. Examine the syntax of domain aggregate functions.
4. Create a running count.

CHAPTER 16

RUNNING DESCRIPTIVE STATISTICS IN ACCESS

Descriptive statistics make it simple to make complex data easily understandable by simplifying it. It is vital to remember that descriptive statistics are simply meant to provide for comparisons that can be utilized in other studies, as well as to profile a data collection. In essence, you can use descriptive statistics to provide an overview of the survey findings for each customer and to characterize the data using metrics that are simple to comprehend.

Basic Descriptive Statistics

This section will enlighten you on certain basic steps you can perform with the use of descriptive analysis.

Executive descriptive statistics with aggregate queries

You have probably run a few aggregate queries by now, as we covered in earlier chapters. Descriptive statistics creation and aggregate query execution are nearly identical processes; an aggregate query can be used to construct the most basic descriptive query.

Determining rank, mode, and median

Ranking records, and calculating mode and median are all the tasks performed by a data analyst. However, you will have to devise a means to get this data as there are no built-in functions in Access to help carry this function out.

Ranking the records in your data set

There will undoubtedly be instances where you should rank entries in your data according to certain criteria, such as revenue. Records must be ranked carefully, particularly when it comes to calculating statistics like the mean, median, percentile, and quartile. Using linked subqueries makes ranking records in a set of data simpler.

Developing the mode of a data set

The number that appears the most frequently in a piece of data is frequently referred to as the mode. The mode of (6, 3, 3, 3, 1, 6, 5, 7), for instance, is 3. Since Access lacks an internal function to assist with mode calculation, you must perform this task on your own. Using a query to count the occurrences of a specific data item and then check it for the highest count is an easy technique to determine the mode of a huge amount of data.

Getting the median of a data set

The number that is discovered to be in the middle after the numbers have to be rated is known as the median of a set of data. For instance, the middle number after the numbers have been ranked in descending order is 5, which is the median (9,8,7,6,5,4,3,2,1). Access, like mode, lacks an integrated feature for calculating the median of a data set; you will need to perform this task independently.

Follow the steps below to determine the median by building a query in two steps;

- Create **a query** that will help to sort and rank your records.
  - Determine which record in your data collection is actually in the center by counting the total number of records and dividing the result by two. You'll have a median value with this. The reasoning behind this is that the record that has the same value as the middle value will automatically be the median because it has been sorted and ranked.

Pulling a random sampling from your data set

Strictly speaking, statistical analysis is based on random sampling. Although there are other ways to create a random sampling of data in Access, using the Rnd function is the simplest. Using an initial value as a basis, this method assists in returning a random base. The basic idea here is to construct an expression to a number field that uses the Rnd function, then place a limit on the number of records that are returned, thereby establishing the query's Top Values Property. Keep in mind that if any of the fields include text or null values, the End method won't function. Even if a field is designed as a Short Text field, the Rnd function will still function with fields that contain just numerical values. If, on the other hand, all of the fields in your table include text, you can use the Rnd method with an AutoNumber field.

Advanced Descriptive Statistics

This section will describe statistics that can be used for more advanced statistical analyses.

Calculating percentile making

A score's percentile rank indicates how it compares to the typical group or standard scores. The word "percentile," as it suggests, is frequently used in reference to %, particularly when discussing scores and outcomes. When analyzing data, percentiles are frequently used to gauge a subject's performance in comparison to the group as a whole. Keep in mind that the process of determining a percentile score for a given collection of data is essentially mathematical.

For the step below to complete this operation;
- Build **your preferred query**.
- Add **a field** that will produce a count of all the records in your data set.
- Create **a calculated field** with the expression ([RCount]-[Rank])/[RCount].

- Once you have successfully completed the above steps you can then execute the query.

Getting to Know the Quartile Standing of a Record

A quartile can be described as a statistical division of a data set into four equal groups with each of the groups making up 25 percent of the data set. The first quartile is the top 25 percent of the data set and the bottom 25 percent is known to be the fourth quartile. The quartile can be found by just comparing the data; a mathematical procedure is not required. This implies that all you need to do is contrast the rank values of each record with the data set's quartile standards. Making the Rank and RCount fields in your query and using them in a switch function to tag each item with the correct quartile standing is a much quicker and simpler method to accomplish this.

Making Frequency Distribution

You can think of the frequency distribution as a type of analysis that arranges data according to the number of times a variable takes on a specific value attribute. Using the Partition function is the simplest way to accomplish this. This function helps to show where a given number appears in a carefully computed sequence of ranges by locating the range that the number falls into.

The Partition function needs the following arguments to fully function well;

- **Number (required)**: This relates to the numerical value you are assessing. In a query context, you essentially indicate that you are assessing all of the row values in a field by using its name.
- **Range Start (required)**: this is a whole number that will be the overall range of numbers. Note that this number must not be less than zero.
- **Range Stop (required)**: This full number signifies the end of the range of numbers in total. Keep in mind that this figure cannot be less than or equal to the Range Start.
- **Interval (required)**: this is a whole number that is to be the span of each range in the series of Range Start to Range Stop.

Activity

1. Execute descriptive statistics with aggregate queries.
2. Determine rank, mode, and median.
3. Rank the records that are in your data set.
4. Get the mode and median of a data set.
5. Pull a random sampling from your data set.
6. Determine the quartile standing or a record.
7. Create a frequency distribution.

PART V

MICROSOFT ACCESS FORMS AND REPORTS

Forms and reports are essential components of Access that you cannot function without. Building user interfaces on top of database tables is possible using Access forms, which offers many enterprises a reliable and quick application development platform. Access's primary goal is to seamlessly combine your database analysis with elegant PDF-style functionality reporting, which includes conditional formatting, grouping, and sorting.

CHAPTER 17

CREATING BASIC ACCESS FORMS

A form is a type of database item that can be used to create the user interface of a database application. They can also be used for system flow-regulating messages, switchboards, and dialog boxes. This chapter also covers the many types of forms in Access. Remember that one of the most important parts of the application you write is the forms you add to the Access database. Forms' built-in tools efficiently maintain the accuracy of database data. Forms using macros or VBA code allow them to check for deletions or validate data entering before it occurs.

Using Form Views

These views are ways by which users interact with forms. You can also choose to place a restriction on the views that are made available. **To have a change in the view of forms simply go through the following steps below;**

- Make use of **the View drop-down** list that is located on the Home Ribbon. Choose among the various views available;
  - **Form view**: This is the most common way that users interact with forms. The form view doesn't employ any layout or design—it merely works with the data.
  - **Datasheet view**: this view also allows users to interact with data. It looks almost the same as the Datasheet view but it is not often used as the form view.
  - **Design view:** as the name implies, this view is where most of the design is done. It has major areas such as header, footer, and detail.
  - **Layout view:** This can be considered a combination of the form and design views. The data may be viewed in this view just as it is displayed on your form. In this view, the only things you can do are move controls around and change their attributes.

If you would like to switch views at any point in time,

- Locate the **View control** on the Home Ribbon.

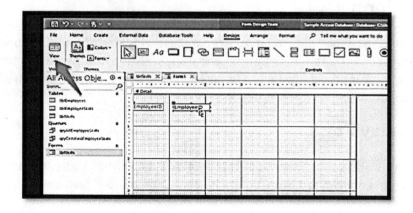

- Right-click **the form title ba**r if it is opened or you can as an alternative choice right-click **on the icon** of the form in the Navigation pane if the form is not opened.

Understanding Different Types of Forms

With Microsoft Access, you can create forms that carry out a number of tasks, like adding and changing data stored in a database. You can develop forms that satisfy the basic needs of your business. Having a solid understanding of Access's many form types can help you choose the right form for your needs. There are basically two kinds of forms in Access. For the first category, "bound form" is used. Forms that have a link between the Access database and the form are said to have data connected to them. Keep in mind that these two are dependent on one another, thus any changes made to the data in the bound form will also affect the database to which it is tied. On the other hand, unbound forms do not update or modify the database in any way, yet they are nevertheless highly helpful in other respects.

Switchboard Form

The switchboard forms can be used to construct menus for databases. Since altering data on the switchboard form has no bearing on altering data in the database, it can be considered an unbound form type. Databases can also be opened and closed with ease using switchboards. Moreover, the form may be quickly utilized to retrieve data from any other forms connected to your database.

Dialog Box form

Database menus can be created using the switchboard forms. The switchboard form can be regarded as an unbound form type as changing its data has no effect on changing data in the database. Switchboards can also be used to easily open and close databases. Additionally, the form may be used to easily retrieve data from any other form that is linked to your database.

Data Entry Form

Since it can be used to change data in an Access database, this kind of form is bound. You can use this form to request important data from your end user, such as a new name or address, and have the form and the relevant database record updated at the same time. Users are free to enter and amend the information on this form as needed.

Record Display Form

This type of form is also a bound form in that it shows data from a spreadsheet based on the criteria that have been indicated. Note that with this form you can also create forms that show various records also.

Creating new forms

There are so many ways forms can be created in Access. The easiest is to;

- Choose **a data source** like a table
- Click on **the Form command option** on the Create tab of the Ribbon.

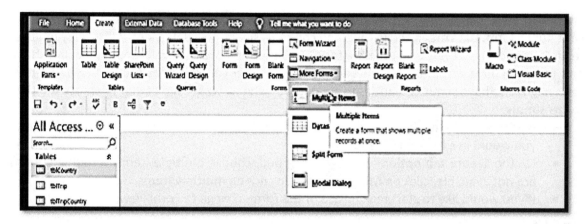

Using the Form command

Alternatively, you may use the Form command in the Ribbon's Forms group to have a new form automatically created depending on the selected table or query in the Navigation pane. By selecting this option, a new form will open in the Layout view. This form contains numerous controls, each of which is linked to a field in the data source underneath.

Using the Form Wizard

Another tool for creating forms is the form wizard. Before assisting with the form's automatic development, the form wizard will ask you a series of questions about the form you wish to create. The versatility and variety of control provided by the form wizard allow you to select the fields you want on the form as well as the layout, which includes Tabular, Datasheet, or Justified. There are two main advantages to using the form wizard: it guarantees that the new form is connected to a data source and adds controls to the specified field.

Looking at special types of forms

We'll look at the many types of special forms that Access offers in this section. Depending on the context, the word "form," especially when referring to Microsoft Access, might signify many things. The various uses of forms in Microsoft Access are covered in the following sections.

The navigation forms

Navigation contains several tabs that offer instant access to other forms in Access in either a form or subform arrangement. Subforms are simply forms that are presented in another form.

Multiple-item forms

Users can view data in numerous records at once with this form style, often known as the continuous form. Data organized in rows and columns, similar to a datasheet, will display multiple records at once. However, because it's a form, it allows for more customization than a datasheet. This form can have graphical elements, buttons, and other controls added to it. A multiple-item form might also have some similarities to a datasheet when it was first created. **To create multiple forms simply;**

- Navigate to **the navigation pane** then click **on the table or query** that has the data that you would like to see on the form.
- On the **Create tab option**, in the forms group, choose **multiple items**. If multiple items are not available, click on **More Forms** then click on **multiple items**.
- If you would like to start making use of the form, change to Form view.

Split forms

Your data is displayed simultaneously in two separate formats on a split form: a form view and a datasheet view. These views are linked to the same data source and are always in sync with one another. If a field is selected in one section of the form, it will also be selected in the other section. You can add, change, or even remove data from any area of the display. **To create a split form simply;**

- Locate **the navigation pane**, and choose the table or query that has the data you need on your form. You can also choose to **open the table or query** in the Datasheet view.
- Locate **the Create tab** in the Forms group, **choose More Forms,** and then click on the **split Forms option**.

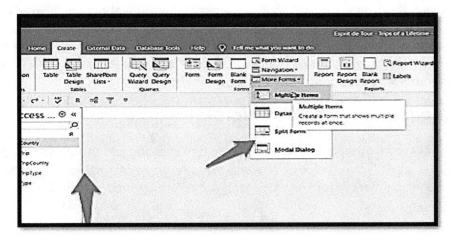

Datasheet forms

A datasheet form is a type of form that displays data from many records simultaneously. The form displays multiple records at once with the data organized in rows and columns. A datasheet can also be thought of as a visual representation of the information that can be found in a database or the results of a query. It tabulates the fields of each record from a table or query result.

To create a datasheet form simply;

- Locate the **navigation pane**, click **on the table or query** that has the data which you would like to see on the form.
- Locate **the Create tab option** in the forms group and click on the **more forms option**, and then click on **Datasheet**.

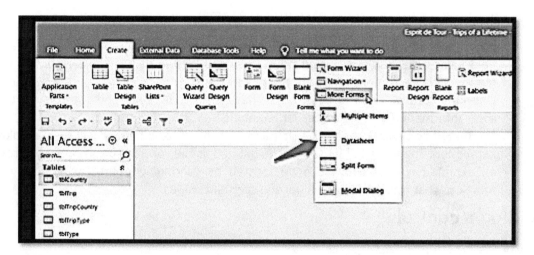

Resizing the form area

You can simply add controls to the form from the areas with gridlines that are in the design view. **You can have the size of the form adjusted by simply;**
- Placing **the cursor on any part** of the border and then **dragging the border** of the area to either enlarge or decrease it.

Saving your form

Saving forms is as easy as simply;
- Clicking on the **Save button** in the **Quick Access toolbar**.

When you select the "Save" option, you will be prompted to give the form a name, so choose something you'll find easy to remember going forward. Remember that if you work on a form and neglect to sign it, you could lose all of the records on it.

Working with Controls

Properties and Controls are the basic parts of every form or report. On a form or report, a control is just a label or text box. You can display data and accept data entry into controls. Some controls are created separately and are known as ActiveX controls; not all of these are part of Access. ActiveX controls, which extend Access's default feature set, are available from various vendors.

Grouping controls

Forms and reports have a number of embedded controls. The Controls group on the Design tab can be used to add controls to forms. The control will display a ScreenTip that explains what it performs when you move your mouse pointer over it.

There are basically three categories of control, they are;

- **Bound controls**: The data source for this control is a field in a database or query. Database field values are displayed using bound controls. These values can be shown as text, numbers, dates, options for yes or no, pictures, etc.
- **Unbound control**: this is a control that has source data. Unbound controls are used to show information, pictures, lines, or rectangles.
- **Calculated controls**: Instead of using a field as its data source, this control employs an expression. The value to be used will be defined as the control's data source by providing an expression. Expressions can be created by combining operators, control names, functions that return a single value, and constant values.

Adding a control

To add a control follows the steps below;

- After you pick any button in the Controls group on the Ribbon's Design tab, draw a new unbound control on the form. You may also drag a field from the field list to add a bound control to the form. Subsequently, Access will automatically choose and assign a control to the chosen field that is appropriate for the field's data type.

Using the Control Group

Use the buttons in the Controls group to add a control. This method allows you to choose the precise type of control you wish to apply to each field, so it's fairly versatile. The newly formed control is not unbound and comes with a default name. Once the control is established, you may select any other attribute you like, as well as which table field to connect it to and what text to put on the label.

Using the field list

The field list as the name implies shows a list of fields from the table or query the form is based upon.

You can open a field list by simply;
- Clicking on **the Add Existing field's** button in the **Tools group** which is located on the **Design tab of the Ribbon**.

Note that fields are not static; they can be moved either singly or in groups. Multiple fields can only be dragged to a form that is already bound to a data source.
- Simply **drag a field** to move it and then click on **the key** or the **shift key** to move more than one field.

When you remove the mouse button, the field list window's drag function will be your first control to release. Verify that the label controls have enough space on the left side. If there's not enough room, the labels will move behind the controls.

Selecting and deselecting controls

Before a form's size can be changed, it must be selected. Depending on its size, a selected control may have four to eight handles encircling it at the corners and halfway along the sides. The moveable handle is used to move the control, and the other handles are used to change its size.

Selecting a single control

You can select a single control by;
- Clicking **anywhere** on the control.

If a control has a label attached, the move handle for the label will also be shown in the upper-left corner of the control when you click it. The sizing handles will also be visible.

Selecting multiple controls

Multiple controls can be chosen in the following ways;

- Hold down the **shift key** and then click **each of the controls**.
- Move the **point around** the controls you would like to select.

Deselecting controls

The easiest way to deselect a control is by

- Clicking on a form field that is unselected and uncontrollable. The handles from any selected control will vanish after this is finished. Selecting a different control will also deselect the one you have already selected.

Manipulating controls

After adding controls to a form there might be a need to move them and properly size them. Controls can be manipulated in the Arrange tab of the Ribbon.

Resizing a control

The tiny handles on a control's upper, bottom and right edges can be used to simply resize the control. You may adjust the control in terms of both width and height using the handles located in the corners of the control.

- When the mouse arrow is on the corner sizing handles, it changes into a double diagonal arrow that you can use to drag the sizing handle until the controls are the size you want. Access may adjust the size of the control to precisely fit the text inside it by double-clicking any of the size handles on the control.

Sizing controls automatically

There are various commands on the Size/Space drop-down on the Sizing & Ordering group of the Arrange tab of the Ribbon.

- **To Fit**: this aids in modifying the height of the control for the font of the text that is in them.
- **To shortest**: this makes the chosen controls control the height of the shortest selected control.
- **To Tallest:** this makes the chosen controls control the height of the tallest selected control.
- **To Grid**: this drags all of the sides of the selected controls in or out to meet the closest points on the grid.
- **To Widest:** this makes the chosen controls control the height of the widest selected control.

Moving a control

Once you have clicked on a particular control, you can easily move that control by making use of any of the listed methods below;

- Click and drag **the control's upper-left corner handle**. The fact that this approach can shift the control or its label independently sets it apart from all the others.
- After selecting the control with a single click, drag **the mouse over any highlighted boundaries.**

Aligning controls

Aligning controls makes them more orderly and well organized.

The Sizing & Ordering group's Align gallery on the Arrange tab of the Ribbon has the following alignment commands;

- **To Grid**: this helps to align the top-left corners of the chosen controls to the nearest grid point.
- **Left**: this helps to align the left edge of the chosen controls with the left-most chosen control.
- **Right**: this helps to align the right edges of the chosen controls with the right-most chosen control.
- **Bottom**: this aids in the alignment of the bottom edge of the chosen controls with the bottom chosen to control.

To align any number of chosen controls all you have to do is choose the Align command button. When you do this, Microsoft Access will use the control that is the closest to the preferred selection as the model for the alignment.

Altering the appearance of control

To make some changes to the way control is displayed,
- Choose the **control** and then click on **the commands** that modify that control like the options in the Font or Controls group.

Grouping controls

If you often make changes to the properties of various controls, there might be a need for you to group such controls.

To group controls together simply;
- Choose **all the controls** by holding down the shift button and clicking on each of these controls.
- Once you have **chosen your preferred controls**, choose the **Group command** from the Size/Space gallery on the Arrange tab of the Ribbon.

Copying a control

You can copy any control to the clipboard and then paste it wherever you like. You are now able to duplicate the control in many copies. If you have entered a control with many attributes or have established a specific format for it, you can choose to duplicate the control and change only its properties to create an entirely new control.

Deleting a control

You can always delete a control by simply;
- Choosing the **particular control** in the forms **Design view** and then pressing the **Delete key**. This will make the control and any label attached disappear.

Controls don't have to be deleted one after the order; you can choose to delete more than one control at a particular time.

All you have to do is

- Choose **all of the controls** while pressing **the shift key** then click on **the delete button**.

Reattaching a label to control

To have a label reattached to control simply follow the steps below;

- Select **the Label button** located on the **Controls group**.
- Position **the mouse pointer** in the **Form Design** window the mouse will then be in the form of the capital alphabet A.
- Pick and hold down **the mouse button** where you would prefer the control to begin from; move the mouse to close up the control.
- Type **Description** and then choose **outside the control**.
- Choose the **Description label control**.
- Choose **the Cut option** from the clipboard group on the Home tab of the Ribbon.
- Select the **Description text box control**.
- Click on the **paste option** from the Clipboard group on the Home tab of the Ribbon in order to attach the label control to the text box control.

Introducing Properties

The qualities of database objects, fields, or controls that can be used to modify the characters within those elements are referred to as "properties". A few examples of these attributes are the color, appearance, or name of an object. Reports and forms often employ properties to change the attributes of controls. Each control on the form is associated with a set of attributes. The form itself has attributes, just like every one of its parts. When you customize parameters, you can do much more than just resize and move controls. You can also change the font and color scheme.

Displaying the Property Sheet

Properties are always displayed in a property window or property sheet window. **To show the Property sheet for the Description text box, follow the steps below;**

- Drag the **Description of the preferred form**.
- Click on the **Description text box** control to choose it.
- Click on the **Property Sheet command** in the Tools group located on the **Design tab of the Ribbon** or as an alternative press **the F4 button** in order to show the Property Sheet.

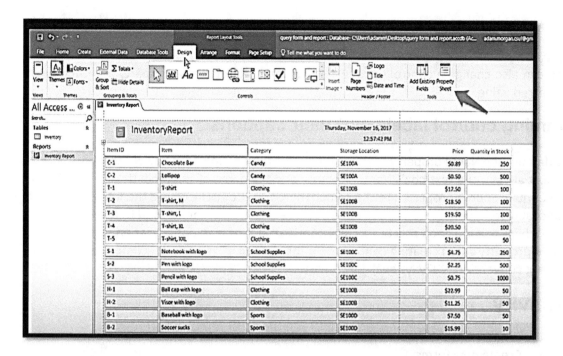

Getting acquainted with the Property Sheet

The Property sheet has an All tab with which you can see all the properties for a control. The basic tabs and groups of properties are as follows;

- **Format**: These characteristics define the appearance of a value or label. This is where you set the text size, color, scroll bars, and special effects.
- **Data**: These characteristics affect how a value is displayed and the data source it is connected to. They include input masks, validation, default value, and other attributes of data types.
- **Event**: Simply put, event properties are those events for which you might create a reaction, such as clicking the mouse, creating a record, or hitting a key.
- **Other**: Other properties display some other characteristics of the control like the name of the control or the description that is shown in the status bar.

Changing a control's property setting

There are various methods by which property settings can be adjusted and they are;

- By changing the control itself, like changing its size.
- Insert or choose the **preferred value** in a Property Sheet.
- Make use of **inherited properties** from the bound field or from the default control of the property.

- Change label text style, size, color, and also alignment with the use of the Ribbon commands.

You can also change a control's properties by simply clicking on a property and then typing the preferred value.

Naming control labels and their captions

By default, the Name property of the text box and the Caption property of the label are the same. Almost always, the text box's Name property and the name of the table field that is displayed in the Control Source property are the same. There are situations where the label's caption differs noticeably from field to field in the table because a value has been added to the Caption property for each field. It is a good practice to use standard naming conventions when setting the control's Name property when creating controls on a form. Keep in mind that a comprehensive, accepted naming convention is always available online.

Activity

1. What are the different types of forms?
2. Create new forms.
3. Categorize controls.
4. Add a control.
5. Make use of the control group.
6. Choose multiple controls.
7. Size controls instantly.
8. Move and align controls.
9. Alter a control's property configuration.

CHAPTER 18

WORKING WITH DATA ON ACCESS FORMS

Forms make up the client interface of an Access application. Forms display and modify data, recognize data that isn't being used, and link to the customer. Forms transmit a great deal of an application's identity, and a well-designed client interface significantly reduces the learning curve for new clients.

Using Form View

You can examine and modify specific data in the form view. With a minor presentational change, the data in the Form view is identical to the data seen in a table or query's Datasheet view. Form view allows you to establish a more user-friendly format in which the data is displayed.

Follow the steps below to create a new form:

- Select **your preferred table** in the Navigation pane.
- Click on the **Create tab on the Ribbon**.
- Select the **Form command** in the Forms group.
- Choose the **Form View button** in the **Views group** of the Home tab to change from **Layout view to Form view.**

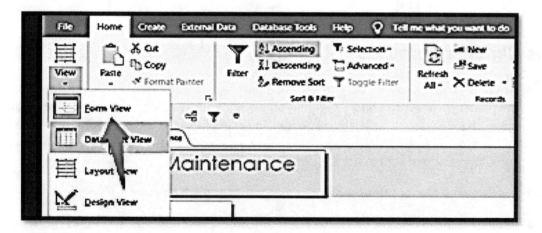

Looking at the Home tab of the Ribbon

Working with the data is possible through the Ribbon tab's Home tab. Some of the items on the Home tab are familiar to you because they are present in other Microsoft apps as well as some new ones. The Home tab is examined in this section.

240

The views group

To the far left of the Ribbon is the view group which enables you to change to any view you prefer which you can view by clicking on buttons or the drop-down arrow.

- **Form view**: gives you the freedom to make changes to data on the form
- **Datasheet view**: displays the data in the row-and-column format.
- **Layout view**: allows you to alter the form's design while also viewing data at the same time.
- **Design view**: enables you to modify the form's design only.

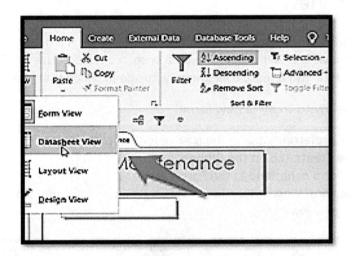

The Clipboard group

The commands for Cut, Copy, Paste, and Format Painter are in the Clipboard group. The way these commands function in Word and PowerPoint and other apps is exactly the same. Note that you cannot copy an Excel spreadsheet and paste it in an Access form using the Form view because the view is not compatible with Excel spreadsheets. However, you can cut and copy items and certain objects and have them pasted in Access.

There are three different options with the paste command which are;

- **Paste:** You can use this option to insert any object that has been copied to the Windows Clipboard into Access at the current position. The pasted item can be a text, a control, a table, a form, or any other object, depending on what you're working on.
- **Paste Special:** with this option, you can paste the contents of the Clipboard in different formats such as text, CSV, records, and so on.
- **Paste Append:** If a record with a comparable structure has already been copied to the Clipboard, you can use this option to paste the contents of the Clipboard as a new record.

The Sort & Filter group

With the Sort & Filter group, you can make changes to the order of the records and also limit the records shown on your form (based on your criteria).

The Records group

The record group allows you to add, remove, and save records to your form. In addition, it contains commands to alter the width and height of the cell when the form is in the Datasheet view, as well as commands to display totals, freeze, and conceal columns.

The find group

Finding replacing data can be done with ease with the use of the find group. Make use of the Select command option to choose a record that should be found.

The Window group

There are two controls in this group;

- **Size to Fit Form**: Sometimes, while working on a form, the user needs to make it larger so that it is easier to view. The Size to Fit Form can be used to restore the form to its initial dimensions after this is completed and the user has completed completing the form.
- **Switch Windows**: With the Switch Windows, all items are easily visible, and you have the option to switch to a different object by selecting it from the drop-down list that appears when you click Switch Windows.

The Text Formatting group

You can change the datasheet's appearance in either the Datasheet view or the Design view by using the Text Formatting group. Utilize these instructions to adjust the font's size, color, and other properties. To organize the data in the chosen column, use the Align Left, Align Right, and Center commands. Toggle grid lines on and off by selecting the Gridlines option.

Moving among fields

Navigation within forms is quite similar to moving in a datasheet. You can move around with ease by simply clicking on the controls and making the desired changes.

Navigational Direction	Keystrokes

Previous field	Shift+Tab, left-arrow (←) key or up-arrow (↑) key
Next field	Tab, right-arrow (→) key, down-arrow (↓) key
First field of current record	Home
Last field of current record	End
Next page	PgDn or Next Record
Previous page	PgUp or Previous Record

Moving among records in a form

Using the navigation buttons located in the bottom left corner of the Form window is the simplest method to navigate between records in a form. The record number displayed in the navigation controls is merely a pointer for the record's current location within the record set; it may vary depending on how the records are sorted or filtered.

Knowing which controls you can't edit

Not all the controls in a field can be edited; the controls you cannot edit in a field are;

- Controls that show AutoNumber fields.
- Fields that are locked or disabled.
- Calculated controls.
- Controls in multi-user locked records.

Using pictures and OLE objects

Another name for OLE objects is Object Linking. The items that are not a part of the Access database is called embedding objects. OLE objects are frequently images, but they can also be any kind of data, including Word documents or audio files.

Without access to the OLE server, it is not possible to view an image or other OLE object in a Datasheet view. Nevertheless, you can enlarge the OLE control area in the design view to display an image, chart, or other OLE object.

Entering data in the Long Text field

Fields that hold up to 1GB of characters are known as longtext fields. When you click on the textbox, a vertical scroll bar appears, allowing you to view every piece of data in the control. Additionally, you can adjust the form's size in the Design view to enlarge the text.

Inserting data in the Date field

The date field has been configured in such a way that it only accepts and shows date values.
Below is an instruction on how to operate in this field;
- When you click **on the inside of the text box,** a Date picker icon will be displayed next to it automatically and when you also click on the Date Picker it will show a calendar from which you can pick a date.

Using option group

You are able to select a single value from a range of options when using the option group. In an option group, there are checkboxes, toggle buttons, and option buttons.
To create an option group;
- Change to the **Design view** and choose the **Option Group button** from the Design tab's Control group.

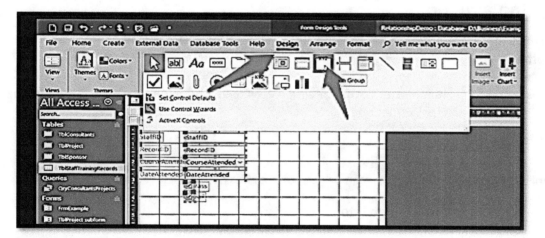

Using combo boxes and list boxes

List boxes and combo boxes are two sorts of controls in Access that are used to display lists of data that the user may select from. The combo box must be selected in order to access the list, and the list box typically displays the most of the list. One way to think about a combo box is as a

244

list box combined with a text box. A combo box's text box section is always visible, and users can enter text into it in the same manner they would any other text box. Instead of typing an item, the user can select it by using the drop-down arrow to reveal the combo box's list box.

To design a combo box;

- Change to the **Design view** and choose the **Combo Box command** from the controls group of the Design tab. Ensure that the Use Control Wizards command has been chosen.

Switching to Datasheet view

To change to a Datasheet view, ensure that a form is opened then make us of any of the options below;

- Select the **Datasheet View command** in the Home tab's Views group.
- Tap on the **Datasheet View button** in the View Shortcuts section which is located at the bottom-right of the Access window.
- Right-click the **form's title bar** or any blank area of the form and click on **Datasheet View from the shortcut menu.**

Saving a record

Records in Access are saved automatically when you leave a particular record and move to another.

Alternatively, you can also;

- Press the **Shift + Enter button** or click on the **Save option** on the **Quick Access toolbar** to save the record without having to leave.

Printing form

Printing a form is very easy; you can print a form as it is being displayed on the screen.

The easiest way to print a form is to;

- When you hit the **Ctrl + P keys,** the print dialog box will appear. From there, you can choose whether to print the entire form or just a specific page, set the number of copies to be printed, and decide whether to collate the copies or not.

Changing the title bar text with the Caption property

The form's Caption property indicates the text shown in the title bar when the form is in Form view.

Follow the steps below to change the title bar text:
- Choose **the form selector** to be sure the form itself is selected.
- Select the **Property Sheet button** in the Design tab's Tools group, or you can also **press F4 t**o open the Property Sheet.

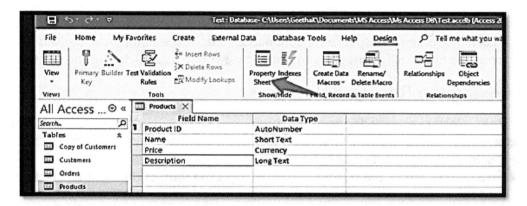

- Click on the **Caption property** in the Property Sheet and insert Products in the property's text box
- Choose any **other property** or press **Enter** to move off of the Caption property.
- Switch to **Form view** to see the form's new title bar text.

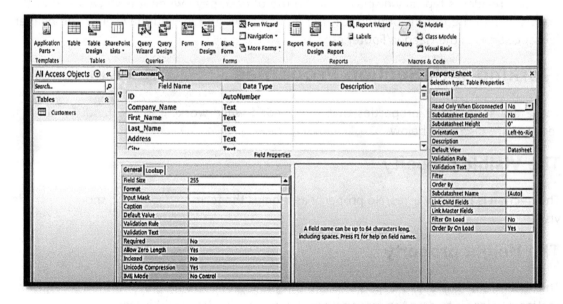

246

Creating a bound form

When a user navigates to a different record in the form, a bound form automatically updates the data in the bound source. An immediate link exists between this form and a data source, such as a table, SQL statement, or query. Keep in mind that you need to provide a data source in the form's record source before you can construct a bound form.

Specifying how to view the form

Microsoft uses a number of properties to determine the appropriate way to display a form. Forms can be seen as a datasheet, split form, continuous form, single form, or single form that shows one record at a time. Split forms also present two views of the same data at the same time.

Removing the Record Selector

The record selector property decides if the record selector should be displayed or not. The record selector is very important when it has to do with dealing with various record forms or datasheets since it points to the current record.

- To remove the record selector simply **changes the form of the Record Selector** property to No.

Adding a Form Header or Footer

Another crucial component of the form is the header or footer. Typically, the form footer appears at the bottom of each page when it is viewed and at the bottom when the form is printed, while the form header is typically displayed at the top of each page when it is viewed and at the top likewise when the form is printed. On the Ribbon's Design tab, you may select the header and footer options in the Header/Footer group.

Working with Section Properties

There are some other properties that are needed while working in the field. Some of these sections are discussed below

The Visible property

This section is basically a Yes/No property as it helps the form to decide if it should be hidden or visible.

The Height property

The section's height is also displayed using this parameter. The simplest method of adjusting the section's height is to drag the mouse up or down to make the height larger or smaller.

The Back Color property

The Back Color property determines the color of the background of the controls. You can change the BackColor property by using the drop-down control on the Property Sheet.

The Special Effect property

The Special Effect property can be configured to be Flat, Raised, or Sunken. The flat is the default value and Raised and Sunken offer a rounded effect at the edges of the section.

The Display When property

The Display When property can be configured to Always, Screen Only, or Print Only. This enables you to hide or show a section when printing.

The printing properties

Reports are more suited for the remaining section attributes, such as Auto Height, Can Grow, and Can Shrink, than forms. You can adjust a section's height using these parameters according to the data it contains. They are also rarely utilized, and they have no bearing on how your form appears on the screen.

Altering the Layout

To change the layout of a form simply follows the steps below;

- Open **a form** in the layout view.
- Pick **the Arrange tab option** in the Form Layout Tools area of the Ribbon. You can then begin to make the changes in accordance with your preference.

Changing a control's properties

You can change the properties of the control in the layout view by following the steps below;

- Choose **the Property Sheet command** in the Form Layout Tools Design tab's Tools group to show the Property Sheet for the chosen control.

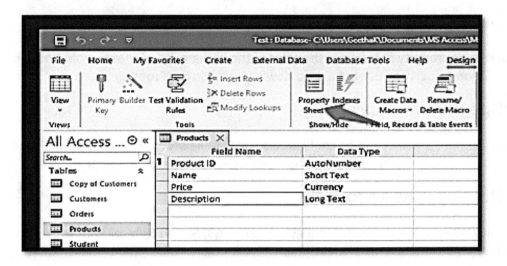

Setting the tab order

The tab order of the form is the order in which the focus moves from one control to another as you press Tab. **Moving controls around the form mean there will be a need for you to make certain changes to the tab order of the form.**

- When in the Design view, select the **Tab Order** from the Tools group on the Design tab to open the Tab Order dialog box. After that, the dialog box will show the controls in the tab order that is now visible. If the tab arrangement seems jumbled, you can rearrange it using a number of the buttons therein.

Modifying the format of text in a control

To change the formatting of text within a control;

- First select it, and then choose **a formatting style** to apply to it.

You can find some more commands for making changes to the format of control on the Format tab of the Ribbon.

Using the Field List to add controls

A list of the fields from the database or query that the form is based on is displayed in the Field List section of the form. Use the Add Existing Fields button on the Design tab to access the Field List if it isn't already visible.

- To **add bound** controls to the form, **drag fields** from the Field List to the form's surface.
- Select and **drag them** one at a time, or use **the Ctrl or Shift keys** to select several fields.

Switching a Form to a Report

To convert a Form to a Report;

- Open the **form in the Design view** and choose **File Save As** to save it as a report. The entire form is then used to construct the report. The form's headers and footers serve as the foundation for the report's header and footer sections. If the form has page headers and footers, those are used as the report's Page Header and Page Footer sections. The report may now be used in Design view, which spares you from having to start from scratch when adding groups and other features.

Activity

1. Explore the home tab of the ribbon.
2. Mention the controls you can edit.
3. Move among records in forms.
4. Make use of combo and list boxes.
5. Alter the title bar with the caption property.
6. Indicate how to view a form.
7. Remove the record selector.
8. Add a header or footer to a form.
9. Alter the control of a property.
10. Modify the format of text in a control.
11. Convert a form to a report.

CHAPTER 19

WORKING WITH FORM CONTROLS

This chapter helps you to understand forms and subforms well and all that has to do with the control of forms. You will also learn how to create forms from scratch.

Setting Control Properties

The controls group, found on the Ribbon's Design tab, contains the controls, which are the fundamental components of Access. It has a variety of controls, such as list boxes, combo boxes, option groups, checkboxes, and other elements. Every one of these controls has a set of characteristics that determine how it acts and how it is displayed. You can click on any control in the form to view its property settings after the Property sheet has appeared.

If you would like to display the properties of the form in the property sheet when you must have shown the properties of the control;

- Click on a **totally blank area** in the form design window.

Customizing the default properties

When you design a control from the Ribbon, the control will also be created by default with a set of property values.

If you would like to control defaults,

- Choose **a tool** in the Controls group of the **Design tab** and then configure the properties in the Property Sheet without adding the control to the form.

Assigning default properties to a control type is equivalent to assigning default properties to the current form that is being used.

Looking at common controls and properties

In this section, the most commonly used controls that are mostly used in the Access application and the properties that control their appearance and behavior.

The Text Box control

Text box controls can display text, numbers, dates, times, and note fields. A field in a subordinate table or query can be connected to a text box. By putting a new value in a text box attached to a field, you can change the value in a field in the underlying table or query. Calculated values can also be shown in a text box.

The Command Button control

To initiate a macro or a Visual Basic process, use command button controls. When a user hits the button, Access opens a hyperlink address that you define.

The Combo Box and List Box controls

To show an editable text box and a list of potential control values, use a combo box control. To create the list, input values for the combo box's Row Source attribute. It is also possible to have the values in the list originate from a query or table. Access displays the value that is currently selected in the text field. Clicking the arrow to the right of the combo box causes Access to display the values in the list. To reset the value in the control, select a new value from the list. If the combo box is bound to a field in the underlying table or query, you can modify the field's value by selecting a new option. Use a list box control to keep a list of potential values for the control. You can input the values for the list in the Row Source attribute of the list box. You have the option to designate a table or a query as the source of the values in the list. List boxes remain open at all times, and they highlight the value that is currently selected. You select a new value from the list to reset the control's value. Selecting a new value from the list will update the value in the field if the list box is tied to a field in the underlying table or query. Access presents the user with a list of checkboxes so they can select several values when you link the list box to a multi-value field. A column's width can be set to 0 to hide one or more of the list's columns, and you can tie multiple columns to the list.

The Checkbox and Toggle Button controls

To hold an on/off, true/false, or yes/no value, use toggle button controls. When you click a toggle button, its value changes to -1 (which stands for "on," "true," or "yes"), and the button seems to be pressed in. The value goes to 0 (which denotes off, false, or no), and the button reverts to its initial state when you click it again. You can assign a distinct numerical value to a toggle button and include it in an option group. Any previously selected option, toggle, or check box in a group of controls is cleared when a new button is selected (unless other buttons or checkboxes in the group also have the same value). Use a check box control to hold an on/off, true/false, or yes/no value. A checkmark appears in the check box and the box's value changes to -1 (which indicates "on," true or yes) when you select a checkbox. The check mark disappears from the box and the check box's value changes to 0 (off, false, or no) when you choose it again. You can add a checkbox and assign it a distinct numerical value in an option group. Any previously selected toggle, option, or check box in a group of controls is cleared when a new checkbox is selected (unless other buttons or checkboxes in the group also have the same value).

- If the checkbox is bound to a field in the underlying table or query, clicking the **checkbox** toggles the field's value.

The Options Group control

To hold an on/off, true/false, or yes/no value, use an option button control (also known as a radio button control).

- When you choose **an option button**, its value changes to -1 (which stands for on, true, or yes), and a filled circle appears in the button's center.
- The filled circle disappears and the button's value changes to 0 (which indicates off, false, or no) when you choose it again. An option button may have a distinct numerical value assigned to it and be a part of an option group.
- Any previously selected toggle button, option button, or check box in a group of controls is cleared when a new option button is selected (unless other buttons or checkboxes in the group also have the same value).

If you link the choice button to a field in the underlying table or query, you may use it to change the value of that field.

The Web Browser control

Use a web browser control to show online page content immediately within a form. An address input in a table, for instance, can be shown on a map using a web browser control. You can link the web browser control to a field in your form's record source by using the Control Source property. It is not possible to utilize a bound web browser control in a continuous form's Detail section.

Creating a Calculated Control

You can use calculated controls on forms and reports in Access databases to show the outcome of a computation. You can add a calculated text box that multiplies the number of goods sold and the price per unit, for example, to a report that displays those two data to display the total price. The Control Source attribute of the computed text box has an equation that multiplies two fields (the number of items times the unit price) to produce the result.

To create a calculated control simply follows the steps below;
- Right-click **on the form** of the report in the **Navigation pane** then clicks on **the Design View.**
- On the **Design tab**, in the **Controls group**, click on **the tool** for the type of control you would like to create.
- Place **the pointer** where you would like the control to be located on the form or the report then choose to **insert the control**.
- If a control wizard should start, choose the **Cancel option** to close it.

- Select the control then **press F4** to display the property sheet then insert an expression in the Control Source property box.
- Alter to the **Form view** or the Report **view** and then determine the calculated control should work just how you would want it to.

Working with Subforms

To display data from two different tables or queries on the same screen, subforms are necessary. When there is a one-to-many relationship between the record source of the main form and the record source of the subform—that is, when several records in the subform are linked to a single record in the main form—subforms are usually used. Access uses the LinkMasterFields and LinkChildFields attributes of the Subform control to identify which records in the subform are related to each record in the main form. Anytime the value in the link field of the main form changes, Access immediately queries the subform. You might want to display subform aggregate information in the master form while generating a subform. It's worth noting that you have to find the value of aggregate data in the subform before you can put it in the master form.

Form Design Tips

In the section below are various form design tips that might be very useful to you. Study carefully and apply to bring the best out of your form.

Using the Tab Stop property

Occasionally, a control on a form may be placed with the intention of triggering an action that will have a somewhat drastic outcome, such as printing an extremely long report or erasing it. It is advisable to use the Tab Stop property, which indicates whether you can use the Tab key to change the focus to the control, if you would like to control the effect that this type of control might have.

Tallying check boxes

This option is usually used when there is a need to count the number of True values in a Check Box control.

Setting up combo boxes and list boxes

The list box control shows a list of options or values. The list box is typically sized so that multiple rows can be shown at once and holds rows of data. Each row may have one or more columns, with or without titles. Access shows a scroll bar in the control if there are more rows in the list than it can display. There is no way to type a value into a list box; the user's selections are restricted to those available in the list box. A more condensed list of alternatives is displayed by the combo box control; the list is hidden until you click the drop-down arrow. A combo box can also be used to enter a value that is not in the list. This is how the combo box control combines the features of a list box and a text box.

To create a Listbox or a combobox with the use of the wizard, simply follow the settings below;

- Right-click **the form** in the Navigation pane and then click on the **Design View option**.
- On the **Design tab** which is located in the **Controls group**, make sure that the Use Control Wizard option is chosen.

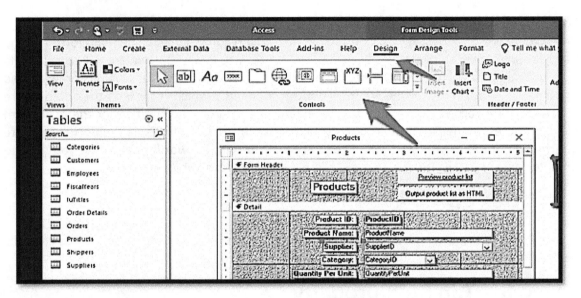

- Choose either the **List Box tool or the Combo Box too**l.
- On the form, click on **the very place** you would prefer to put the list box or the combo box.
- When **the wizard prompts** a query asking how you want to get the values for the control, choose your preferred option.

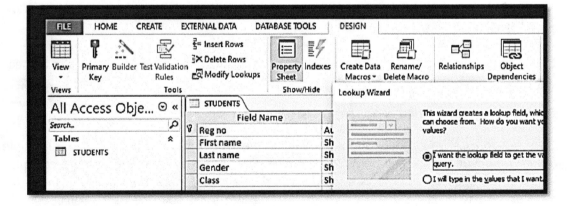

- Follow through on the instructions indicating how the values will be displayed.

- Click on the **Next button** and **type a label** you would like to use for the control. This label will be shown next to the control.
- Click on the **Finish button**.

Tackling Advanced Forms Techniques

This section discusses the various features that have been in Microsoft Access for quite a while but have not been discovered by lots of developers.

Using the Page Number and Date/Time controls

Forms usually mention the current date and time. Access facilitates this inclusion procedure using the Date and Time command in the Header/Footer group on the Design tab of the Ribbon. When the Date and Time command is selected, the Date and Time dialog box appears and asks how you want the date and time formatted. Once you make your choices and click OK, Access inserts a form header with the date and time formatted as requested. You may also add a title and a logo (nearly any image file) to the form header section using other commands in the Header/Footer group. All forms in an application will look the same if the Header/Footer controls are used.

Morphing a control

The requirement to define the control type when a control is added to a form is undoubtedly one of the most aggravating issues when creating Access forms. You can alter the type of control in Access to any other kind that works.
Simply;
- Right-click **on the control** and choose the **Change to Command option** from the shortcut menu in order to have the options displayed.

Using the Format Painter

A Format Painter in Access functions similarly to Word's Format Painter. When building a form, you first configure control's appearance before copying its properties to a dedicated internal buffer by

- Clicking the **Format Painter** button on the Font group on **the Design tab of the Ribbon**.

The aesthetic characteristics of the control that has been chosen and placed in the internal buffer will be passed to the second control whenever you click on another control of the same kind.

Offering more end-user help

ScreenTips note that appear when you hover the mouse over control or button in Microsoft Office products. You should use ScreenTips consistently across an application.

Adding background pictures

Adding visually appealing forms to Access applications is always a good idea. Access makes it easy to add a graphic to a form's backdrop, just like a watermark can appear on expensive bond paper. The form's Picture attribute defines the picture, which can be linked to an external file or embedded inside the form itself. If the picture is connected, all changes made to the external file will be reflected in the form's graphic.

If you would like to include a picture on your form,

- Open **the form** in the Design view and then display the Property Sheet. If the Property Sheet is not displaying the properties of the form already, you can choose Form from the combo box.

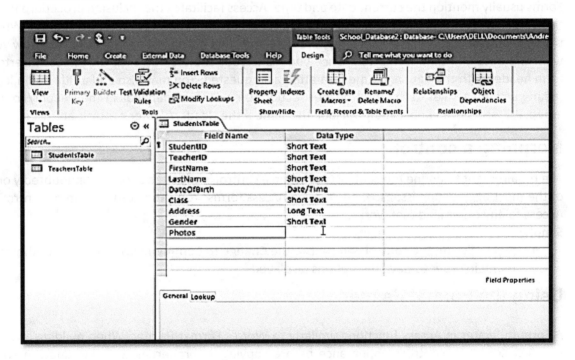

- Click on **the builder button** for the Picture property to choose **the picture** you would like to add to the form.

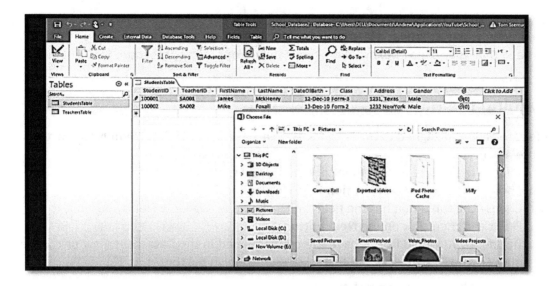

- Change **the Picture Tiling**, and **Picture Size Mode properties** to show the picture in various ways.

Limiting the records shown on a form

The Record Source property usually determines how many records a form displays, but if you want to show fewer records, simply changes the underlying query or SQL expression.

Using the Tab Control

A Tab control shows several pages, each of which can be opened by selecting a tab located at the dialog box's top, bottom, or side. Multiple tabs constitute a tab control.
- The quickest and easiest way to add or delete a page from the user interface is to right-click **the control** and selects **the relevant command** from the shortcut menu.

Controls that are found in a Tab control include text boxes, combo and list boxes, choice buttons, check boxes, and OLE objects. While a form can have several Tab controls, it is generally not a good idea to overwhelm the user with too many Tab controls.

Using Dialog Boxes to Collect Information

Dialog boxes typically record a particular type of data, such hardcopy parameters or typeface characteristics. Dialog windows are an excellent technique to prefilter or qualify user input without overcrowding the main form. As an alternative, use a dialog box to gather data for the header or footer area of a report or to allow the user to choose query criteria prior to executing a query that populates a form or report. Dialog boxes, although they are forms, seldom look or perform like other forms in the application. It is common for dialog boxes to show up over the user's work. Dialog boxes can also be used to cancel a query without harming the user's workspace if they are utilized appropriately. Keep in mind that there are a few guidelines that you may need to adhere to when creating the dialog boxes. By following these guidelines, you may be guaranteed that your dialog boxes follow the standard operating procedure for Windows dialog boxes.

Designing the query

Queries are always designed in order to focus on a specific set of data. Simply follow the steps to create a query;

- Choose the **Create option** then click on the **Query Wizard**.
- Choose the **Simple Query option** then click on the **OK button**.
- Choose **the table** that has the field then include the Available Fields you want to Selected Fields and then click on the **Next button**.
- Decide if you would like to have the query opened in the Datasheet view or change the query in the Design view and then click on the **Finish button**.

Setting up the command buttons

When a command button is added to a form, Access shows a wizard to help you specify the button's actions. On the wizard's subsequent screen, the query to execute will be selected as qryDialog, and the Execute Query action will be selected for the execute Query button. Consequently, the query will execute and the text field on the form will be used as a criterion when the button is hit.

Adding a default button

If the user clicks the Enter key while the dialog box is open, a button on the form should be immediately selected. The default button does not need to be selected by the user to be triggered; when the user taps the Enter key, Access automatically fires the default button's Click event. Note that the button that should be chosen should be one that won't cause any harm if accidentally it is pressed as the default for a form.

Setting a Cancel button

If a user presses the **Esc key** while the form is open, the Cancel button on the form is immediately selected. In most circumstances, the dialog box ought to close if the user presses the Esc key while it's open.

Removing the control menu

Once the default and cancel buttons have been set, you won't need to use the control menu button located in the upper left corner of the form. Set the Control Box property on the form to No in order to hide the control menu button. Once the control menu box is gone, the user will have to utilize the Cancel or Run Query buttons to get the form off the screen.

Designing a Form from Scratch

This section explains how a form can be created from scratch; here you will need to apply all you must have learned in previous chapters.

Creating the basic form

Any table in your database can be used to construct a form in Access. Any form you generate from a table will allow you to view existing data in the table as well as add new data.

After you've generated a form, you can customize it by adding new fields and design elements such as combo boxes.

- Navigate to the **Navigation pane** then select **the table** you would like to make use of in creating the form. There is no need for you to have the table opened.
- Choose the **Create tab option**, find the Forms group and then choose the **Form command.**
- Your form will then be launched in the Layout view.
- Save **the form** by clicking on the **Save command** on the **Quick Access toolbar**. Anytime there is a prompt, include a name for the form and then click on the OK button.

Creating a subform

A subform is a datasheet form that shows linked records in a table-like format.

To create a subform;

- Locate the **navigation pane**, right-click and then choose the **Design view option**.
- Locate the **Controls** on the **Toolbar in the Design tab** then click on the **downward arrow** to expand the control's toolbar.
- Click on the **subform.**

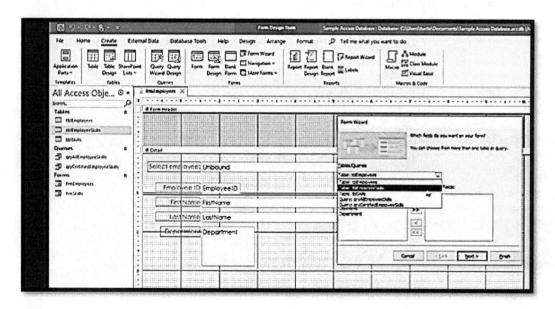

- Select the **exact location** you would like to have the subform.
- Upon the confirmation of the **location** click on the **Next option** where you will choose the field that you would like to show in your subform.
- Link the **subform** to the access form and then click on the **Next button**.
- Name your **subform** and then click on the **finish button**.

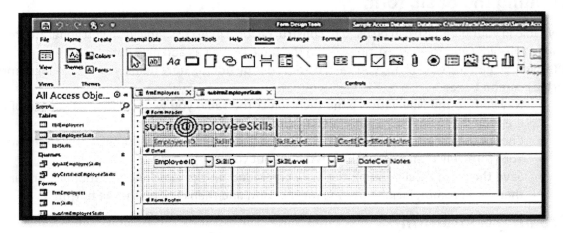

- The subform will then be saved as a separate form.

Adding the subform

To add a subform;
- Open the **form**.
- Expand the **controls Toolbar**
- Choose the **Subform option**.
- Choose the **Data Source** to use for the subform
- Choose the **fields**
- Choose the **linking fields**
- Make some modifications if need be.
- Click on the **finished button**.

Changing the form's behavior

In this section you have to change some of the properties of the form and also its controls so you can get the behavior that you want.

Setting the form's properties

Make changes to the form properties below to the values given;

- **Caption: New**: Invoice Entry
- **Allow Datasheet View**: No

- **Allow Layout View**: No
- **Record Selectors**: No
- **Navigation Buttons**: No
- **Control Box**: No
- **Data Entry**: Yes
- **Cycle**: Current Record

Looking up values during data entry

You can choose to look up values either from the subform or from the main form, where you basically have more fields.

Saving the record

To create a command button that will save the record simply follow the following steps below;
- Find the **Controls group** of the **Design tab of the Ribbon** then choose the **Button control** and put it on the form.
- Locate the **command button Wizard** first screen then choose the **Record Navigation** option and locate the **Next Record option** then click on the **Next option**.
- On the screen that follows in the wizard, check on the **Show All Pictures checkbox** and then click on the **Save Record** picture and then click on the Next option.
- On the Last screen of the wizard, include a name for the button then click on the **Finish button**.

Changing the form's appearance

Putting the form's appearance together is the last step. Modify the main form's controls' width and location, and position the command buttons in the lower right corner. This is your space to experiment and customize the form to look exactly as you want it.

CHAPTER 20

DATA PRESENTATION WITH ACCESS REPORTS

A great way to view and print data from your database is with reports. You can read or print the information in a number of formats, and it can be shown in a way that is highly summary, detailed, or somewhere in between. Multilayer totals, statistical comparisons, and pictures and graphics can all be found in a report. You will learn how to use the Report Wizard and create reports in this chapter.

Brining in Reports

Reports are ways in which data can be presented. You can either print a report or view it on the screen. Pictures and other images, as well as memo fields, can be used in reports.

Identifying the different types of reports

There are various types of reports in Microsoft Access. Some will be discussed in the section below;

Tabular reports

In these reports, data is printed in rows and columns along with categories and totals. Reports that are summary and group/total are instances of variants. These reports often include report dates, lines and boxes, or page numbers to separate content. Reports can make use of color and shading, just like images, graphs, and memo fields. All of the components of a detailed tabular report are included in a summary tabular report, but record details are absent.

Columnar reports

Columnar reports display data in the same way that a data entry form does, but they're only used to examine data, not to enter it. They usually display reports with one or more records per page and in a vertical format.

Mailing label reports

One report category for which Access offers a Label Wizard to help with report creation is mailing reports. The Label Wizard allows you to select from a wide range of label styles. Based on the label type you select, Access offers an accurate report design. After that, you may access the report in Design mode and make any necessary changes.

Distinguishing between reports and forms

One database object that can be used to create the user interface of a database application is a form. Using forms, one can view real-time data from a table. Its main purpose is to facilitate the entry and editing of data. One kind of item found in desktop databases is a report, which is used for data formatting, calculations, printing, and summarization. You may even choose to alter the report's appearance and feel. Except for data input, a report can replicate any action you may take with a form. A form can also be saved as a report so that it can be modified in the Report Design box.

Designing a Report from Beginning to End

The process involved in creating a report in Microsoft Access is quite simple. Note that the main purpose of a report is for you to transform raw data into information.

Below are the processes involved in creating a report;

- You begin with **defining** the layout of the report.
- Bring the **data that will be transformed together**.
- Create the **report with the use of the Access Report Wizard**.
- Print the report (hard copy) or you can decide to simply view it on the screen.
- Save **the report**.

Defining the report layout

When putting up a report, think about how the data should be categorized (by invoice number or by week, for example), sorted (by name or chronologically), and limited by the amount of paper needed to print the report.

Assembling the data

This is the next step after you must have concluded with the layout of the report.

Microsoft Access makes use of data from two main sources;

- A single database table
- A record set produced by a query

Building a report with the Report Wizard

It is simpler to create reports of any kind when you utilize the report wizard. You can use the report wizard to create a basic style for your report, which you can then modify to your own specifications.

Creating a new report

To create a new report begins by;

- Clicking on the **Report Wizard button** which will then display the first screen of the Report Wizard.

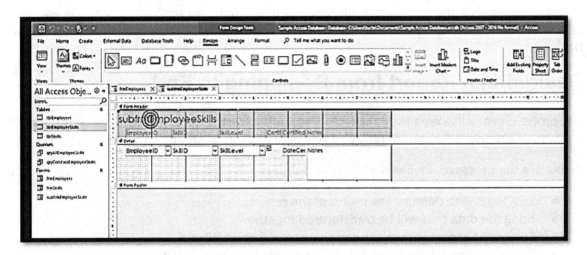

- Choose **the table** for which you would like to create a report in the navigation pane.

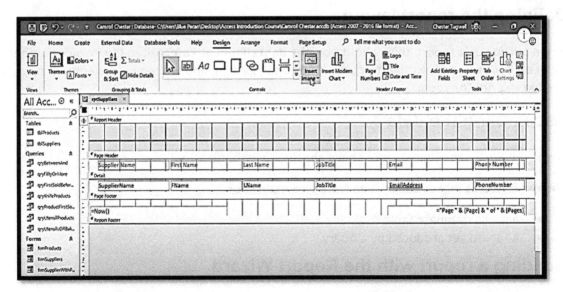

- Beneath the drop-down list of the table are fields wherein you would find the data.
- After you must have chosen your data, click on the **Next button** to move to the next step in the Wizard.

Selecting the grouping levels

The fields that you want to utilize to group data can be selected in this dialog box. The field selected for grouping will determine how the data is shown; the grouping field will also appear as group headers and footers in the report. It should be noted that you can select up to four group fields for your report when using the Report Wizard.

Stating the group data

Once you have chosen your preferred group field(s);

- Click on the **Grouping Options** button which can be found at the bottom of the dialog box in order to help show the **Grouping intervals dialog box** which will allow you to define how you would like the group to be displayed on the report.

Once you have shown the Grouping Intervals dialog box, you can then return to the wizard and then select the Next button in order to move to the sorting screen of the wizard.

Selecting the sort order

It's a good idea to give a sort within each group even though Access sorts grouped records in a meaningful order based on the grouping field(s). This is because the order of the records within a group cannot be guaranteed. Only fields that haven't been grouped yet can be selected for sorting. The fields specified in this dialog box only affect the data sorting order in the Detail portion of the report.

- Choose **either ascending or descending sort** by clicking on **the button** that can be found on the right of each of the sort fields.

Selecting summary options

A Summary Options button may be found near the bottom of the Report Wizard's sorting screen.
- The Summary Options dialog box, which provides additional display options for numeric fields, will appear when you click on the button.
- When you click the **OK button** in the dialog box after finishing this, the Report Wizard's sorting screen will reappear, and you can click the Next button to proceed to the next screen.

Choosing the layout

The Layout area enables you to determine the basic layout of the data. The Layout area provides three layout choices that tell Access whether to repeat the column headers, indent each grouping, and add lines or boxes between the detail lines.

- As you select **each option**, the picture on the left changes to show how the choice affects the report's appearance.
- You can choose between **Portrait and Landscape layout** for the report in the Orientation area. Finally, the Adjust **the Field Width So All Fields Fit** on a Page check box enables you to compress a lot of data into a little area.

Once you have done the above, you can then click on the Next button in order to move to the next wizard screen.

Opening the report design

You can assign a title to the report using a text box on the last Report Wizard screen. Rather than at the top of every page, this title shows just once, at the beginning of the report. The new report is named after the report title as well. The name of the table or query that you initially chose to use as the report's data source is what appears in the default title.

Once you have done that, select one of the option buttons at the bottom of the dialog box:

- Preview **the report**
- Make **some changes** to the design of the report.

Modifying the report's layout

If you have a need for you to make changes to the layout of the report, you can choose to do this in the Layout view wherein you can choose to work with the controls in this view which is the same as working with the Layout view for a form.

Choosing a theme

A theme establishes the color pattern, font face, font colors, and font sizes for Access forms and reports. The concept of themes is important in Access 2024. The report in the Layout view beneath the gallery changes to show you how the report would appear with the selected theme when you move your mouse over the theme icons in the gallery. There is a name for each theme, for example, Office, Facet, Organic, or Slice. Theme names are in handy when you want to make reference to a particular theme in the documentation of the program, or in an email or other correspondence.

Designing new theme color schemes

There are several pre-installed themes in Access 2024, and each one has a matching set of fonts, colors, and attributes. One great way to accomplish this is by applying a company's corporate color scheme to forms and reports within an application through the use of a custom color theme.

267

To create a new theme color scheme, have the report or form opened in the Design view then follow the steps below;

- Choose the **Colors button** in the **Themes group on the Design tab of the Ribbon**.
- Choose the **Customize colors command** at the bottom of the list of color themes.
- Once you are done with the customization choose a name for the custom color theme then click on the **Save button**.

Using the Print Preview window

If you would like to open a report in the Print Preview,
- Right-click **on the report** in the Navigation pane and click on **the Print Preview option**.

The typefaces, coloring, lines, boxes, and data in your report are displayed in this view exactly as they will appear on the default printer when printed. Using the left mouse button on the report's surface, you may switch the view between a zoomed-in view and a full page view. The Print Preview tab of the Ribbon contains controls to change the size, margins, page orientation (Portrait or Landscape), and other printing properties. Additionally, there are Print and Close Print Preview buttons on the Print Preview page that allow you to print the report or go back to the Design, Layout, or Report view, respectively.

Publishing in alternate formats

An amazing feature of the Print Preview tab in Access 2024 is its ability to print the Access report in certain formats which include; PDF, XPS, HTML, and others.

- To access the Publish as PDF or XPS dialog box, just click the **PDF or XPS button** located in the Data group on the Print Preview tab of the Ribbon. This dialog box provides a number of options for output in either a condensed or normal PDF format

Viewing the report in Design view

To view the report in Design view,

- Right-click on the **title ba**r of the report then chooses the **Design view option**.

Printing or viewing the report

Printing is the final step when it has to do with creating a report.

Printing the report

There are various by which you can print your report one of which is;

- Click on **File** then choose the **Print option** in the main Access window which will display various options for you to choose from.

- Click on the **Print button** on the **Print Preview tab of the Ribbon**.

Viewing the report

There are four methods to examine a report: print preview, layout, report, and design. The Layout view displays the margins, page headers and footers, and other report features in addition to the relative positions of the controls on the report's surface. The primary drawback of the Layout view is that it does not allow you to fine-tune a report's design until you navigate to the Design view. It is not intended to move individual controls about the report; instead, the layout view is meant to be used to change the relative positions of elements on the report.

Saving the Report

You can save the report design by;

- Choosing the **file option** then clicking **on saves** then clicking on the **save as option**. The first time you will click on the **save as option**, you will be prompted to insert a name.

Banded Report Design Concepts

The banded report design is a key concept in Access development. An Access report processes data one record at a time. On a report, individual fields can be positioned in different places and, if needed, displayed more than once. Given that Access procedures report data one record at a time, the design view is intended to allow you to choose how each row is laid up on the printed page. Features like a page's header and footer, as well as areas occupied by group headers and footers, are also visible in the design view. The print appearance of the report is affected by each control region.

The Report Header section

A Report Header section is frequently used as a cover page, a cover letter, or for information that needs to be delivered just once to the report's user.

- Set the **Force New Page** to attribute in the Report Header section to the After Section to use the Report Header section as a title page. The controls in the Report Header section will be printed on their own page as a result of this.

The Page Header section

Typically, controls are located in the Page Header section, which is printed at the top of every page. Report header information appears directly below page header information if the first page's report header isn't on a separate page. Column heads are typically used in page headers of group/total reports. Page headers usually feature the title of the report that appears on each page.

The Group Header section

Usually, the group name appears in the Group Header section. Access knows that every record in a group has been shown in a Detail section when the group name is changed. It is important to note that group footers and headers can have several levels.

The Detail section

Each value is printed in the Detail section, which processes every record in the data. Calculated fields, such as profit, are usually found in the Detail section and are the outcome of a mathematical equation.

The Group Footer section

Navigate **to the Group Footer section** to calculate summaries for each detailed entry inside a group. By adjusting the text box's Running Sum attributes, you can modify the Report Design window's calculation of summaries. When a Running Sum is set to No, the value of the current record is all that is displayed. If the value of Over Group is applied, the amounts for that control will be added up for each record in the group. The OverAll function gathers the control's values from every record in the report.

The Page Footer section

The Page Footer area is often where page numbers and control totals are displayed. It is also possible to supply the time and date the report was printed. The Page Footer section contains the text box for the page number.

The Report Footer section

The Report Footer part is printed once at the conclusion of the report, following the printing of all detail records and group footer sections. Report footers frequently include grand totals or other data (like averages or percentages) for the whole document.

Building a Report from Scratch

More information on creating tables from scratch is provided in this section. Generally, you will create a report by using the Report Wizard or another shortcut, which you can then modify to suit your requirements.

Creating a new report and binding it to a table

Follow the steps below to create a new report;
- Choose the **Create tab** option of the Ribbon.

- Select **the Blank Report** button in the Reports group.
- Right-click **on the title bars** of the report and choose **the Design View** from the shortcut menu.

Defining the report page size and Layout

As you plan your report, take into account the features of the page layout and the kind of paper and printer you want to use for the final product. As you change these options, a number of dialog boxes and settings are employed to make adjustments. Together, these prerequisites provide the desired outcome. The report's margins, paper size, and orientation (portrait or landscape) can all be altered on the Page Setup page. From the drop-down option, choose Size or Margins to bring up a gallery of commonly used values for each of these properties.

If the margins you require for your report aren't listed in the Margins options,

- Open the **Page Setup dialog box** by clicking **Page Setup** in the **Page Layout group**. The margins, orientation, and other page layout criteria can all be specified in this dialog box.

Placing controls on the report

Placing control on a report is quite easy. Follow the steps below;
- Select the **Add Existing Fields button** in the **Tools group** on the **Design tab of the Ribbon.**

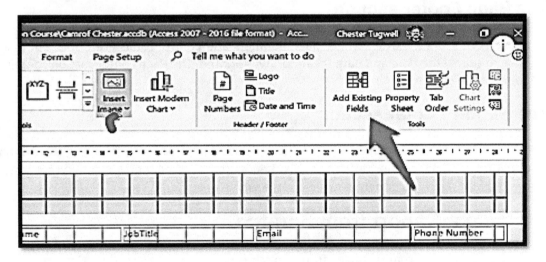

- Select **control** in the **Controls group on the Design tab** if there is a need for you to use something other than the default control types for the fields.

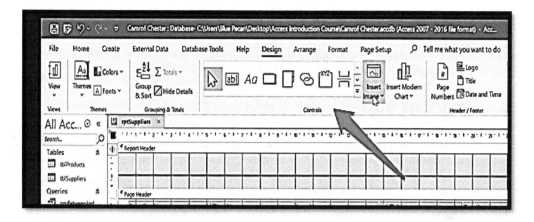

- Choose each of the **fields** that you would like to have on your report and then move them to the **appropriate part of the Report Design window**.

Controls are necessary in order for information to be presented in the page header section. To make room for them, you must first make changes to the page top.

Modifying the size of a section

If you need to make space for the title information in the page header, you will need to resize a section. To resize, just drag your mouse over the bottom of the desired piece. The mouse pointer changes into a vertical double-headed arrow when it crosses the bottom of a report section. You can drag the segment border up or down to change the size of the portion.

Modifying the appearance of a text in a control

To change the appearance of the text in a control, select it and then click the relevant option on the Format tab to apply a formatting style to the label.

Working with Text BOX controls

Unbound text boxes are another sort of Text Box control that is commonly used in reports to hold phrases such as page numbers, dates, or a computation.

Adding and using Text Box controls

In reports, TextBox controls serve two major purposes, which are;

- Enabling the display of stored data from a specific field in a query or table.
- Displaying the result of an expression.

Entering an expression in a Text box control

Expressions can be used to generate values that don't exist in a query or database. They could be as straightforward as a page number or as intricate as intricate mathematical calculations.

Sizing a Text Box control or Label control

You can choose a control by clicking on it. When the mouse pointer crosses over one of the side handles, it transforms into a double-headed arrow. Click and drag the control to resize it to the appropriate size when the pointer changes. Access adjusts the size of the control to accommodate the text within it when you double-click one of the sizing handles. This option is helpful if you increase the font size and then notice that the text no longer matches the control.

Deleting and cutting attached labels from Text Box controls

In a report, you may easily delete one or more associated controls.
- Simply **choose the controls** you want to delete and press Delete.

If you wish to move the label to the Page Header area (rather than just deleting it), you can cut it instead of deleting it.

Pasting labels into a report section

It is just as simple to cut labels from controls and paste them into the page header as it is to delete labels and add new ones there as well. The shortcut keys for cutting (Ctrl + x) and pasting (Ctrl + v) are available for use.

Moving Label and Textbox controls

When a Text Box control is joined with a compound control, an accompanying label is created automatically. In a compound control set, if one control is moved, the other control also moves. This implies that the linked control will move in tandem with the label or text box. To move both controls in a compound control, choose one of the control pairs with the mouse. If you move the mouse cursor over any of the objects, it changes into a hand. Click and drag the controls to move them to a new spot. When you drag, a composite control outline follows your pointer's movement.

Modifying the appearance of multiple controls

The instructions below will show you how to change the appearance of text in numerous Label controls:
- By selecting **each Label control** at the bottom of the Page Header section one at a time while holding down the Shift key, you can select all of them.
- On the Format tab, select the **Bold option**.

Changing Label and Textbox control properties

Open the Property Sheet for the Text Box or Label control to make changes to its properties. You can see and modify a control's properties using the Property Sheet. The Ribbon's Format tab has tools, including text formatting buttons and font dropdowns that can be used to modify the property settings of control.

Growing and shrinking Text Box controls

When you print or print preview controls with different text lengths, Access gives you the ability to let control expand or contract vertically depending on the precise contents of a record. Whether or whether a Textbox control's vertical dimension is adjusted to fit the amount of text in its bound field depends on its Can Grow and Can Shrink properties. Although these properties can be applied to any text control, Text Box controls benefit most from them.

Sorting and grouping data

By combining the data in interesting ways, you may often make the data on the report more valuable to users.

Creating a group header or footer

When you group on a field in the report's data, you get two new sections: Group Header and Group Footer. **Follow the steps below to create a group header or footer.**
- Choose **the Group & Sort button** in the Grouping Totals group on the Design tab of the Ribbon.
- Select the **Add a Group button in the Group, Sort, and Total area**.
- Choose the **Category option** from the Field List.

Sorting data within groups

Sorting lets you select which records show up in the report and in what order, depending on the values of one or more controls. This order is important if you want to view the data in your tables in a different order than the order you entered. While you can sort data by any field in a query or by the primary key in a table, there are a few benefits to sorting the data in the report first. Firstly, the report will stay in order even if the query or table is modified.

Removing a group

If you would like to remove a group,

- Simply **display the Group, Sort, and Total area**, select the **group or sort** specifier to delete, and then click on the **Delete key**. Any controls in the group header or footer will be removed.

Hiding a section

Microsoft Access also provides ways by which we can hide a section. Follow the steps below to have a section hidden;
- Select **the section** you would like to hide.
- Show **the Property Sheet of the section**.
- Choose the **Visible property option** and then click on the **No button** from the drop-down list in the text box property.

Sizing a section

Depending on what needs to be done, you may need to change controls within the section or even between sections after the group header has been created. A section needs to be the correct height before you can begin adjusting controls within it. You can adjust a part's height by dragging the top edge of the section beneath it. A section's bottom border can be moved to enlarge or reduce its size.

Moving controls between sections

You can move one or more controls across sections by dragging them from one section to another with your mouse or by cutting and pasting them from one section to another.

Adding page breaks

Depending on the groupings, you can add page breaks using Access. It is possible to insert breaks within portions, with the exception of the Page Header and Page Footer sections. Periodically, you may wish to add a page break, and not just because of a grouping. The answer is found in the Controls group of the Ribbon's Page Break control.

Improving the Report's Appearance

To make a report more visually appealing, you often include a few graphic elements like lines and rectangles, along with possibly some special effects like shadows or sunken portions. Make sure that every component has distinct sections that are divided by colors or lines. Verify that there is no contact between the controls. Make that the text is aligned with the content to the left and right, as well as with the text above and below.

Adjusting the page header

Many large labels are positioned widely apart in the page header. The little column headers have a floating appearance. One font size increase could be applied to them. The entire page header should be divided into the Detail part by a horizontal line.

To add this line simply follows the steps below;

- Choose **the Line tool** in the Controls group of the Ribbon.
- Move **the line** below the page header.
- Click **on the line and change the Border Width property** to 2 pt on the line of the Property Sheet.

Creating an expression in the group header

To create an expression in the group header simply follow the settings below;

- Choose **the Category control** in the Category Group Header section and show the Property Sheet for the control.
- Make changes to the **Control Source property to =" Category: " & [Category].**
- Then finally, change the **Name property to textCategory.**

Creating a report header

The report header should provide information such as the report title, a logo, and the print date and time. Any user of the report can easily discover what's in it and when it was printed thanks to the inclusion of this information in the report heading. When the report is in the Design view, the Ribbon has a Design tab. You can add important elements to the header and footer of the report using a number of controls on the Design tab's Header/Footer group. Examine the Design tab and experiment with the controls to determine the most appropriate option for your report heading.

Activity

1. Create a report with the use of the report wizard.
2. Choose the grouping levels.
3. Define the group data.
4. Choose the sort order.
5. Modify the layout of the report.
6. Publish in alternate formats.
7. View your report in a design view.
8. Define the report page size and layout.
9. Modify the appearance of a text in a control.
10. Create an expression in the group header.

CHAPTER 21

ADVANCED ACCESS REPORT TECHNIQUES

In the last chapter, you followed the basic processes that were emphasized and produced some very helpful reports. You will learn more about reports that you cannot create using only the Access default reports in this chapter, along with some advice on how to prevent blank reports.

Grouping and Sorting Data

Having a data group well-sorted is very important as it will make your data look well organized. Grouping data that is quite similar can make the specific data you might be looking for easier to find and will also reduce the amount of data presented.

Grouping alphabetically

The primary goal of organizing the report group alphabetically is to guarantee that the data is neatly and efficiently arranged. For instance, if you were to show sales data for a product from several clients, it may be quite awkward and challenging to grasp if the data wasn't grouped. However, if the data is grouped, you can easily interpret the data and extract the information you require. Another option is to arrange the information in a table.

To add a text box containing an alphabetic character, go through these steps;

- Right-click on **the title bar** of the report and then click on **the Design view**.
- Choose **Group &Sort** from the **Design tab of the Ribbon.**
- Include a **group name** for the desired field.
- Choose **the More option** and make sure that the With a Header Section option has been selected. Once this is done, it will add a band for a group based on the field you have chosen.
- Select the **By First Character option** rather than choosing the **By Entire Value option.**
- Expand the **group header** of the field you have chosen and include an unbound text box to the group header of your desired field.
- Configure **the Control Source property text box** to your preferred expression.
- Delete **the label** and ensure you set the other properties of the text box like font and font size properly.
- While grouping make sure that the names in the field are well sorted.
- Finally, **include a sort for the records** in the field you have chosen.

Grouping on date intervals

There are a ton of reports that may need to be categorized using dates. The Access report engine has a function that lets you group and arrange data based on dates.

To make use of this report simply;
- Open the **Group, Sort, and Total pane** again and then build **a group for the OrderDate field**.
- Choose **the with a Header Section** option from the header drop-down.
- Once the option above has been completed, you can then choose **any of the options** such as Year, Quarter, Month, Week, and so on. Note that there is still a need to sort the whole value of the OrderDate to make sure that they are in sequential order within the week option.

Hiding repeating information

When information that appears to be repeated is reduced to the barest minimum it appears to help to make the tabular report quite more efficient. **To hide reports that appears to be repeating simply:**

- Open the **report in the Design view**.
- Locate **the Detail section** and then choose **the field** that has the information that might be repeating.
- Open the **Property Sheet** for the name of the field.
- Change the **Hide Duplicates property to Yes**. Note that this step is quite important as the default is No.
- Change to **Print Preview mode** and view the new report layout.

Keep in mind that the Hide Duplicates property option is only available for records that the report displays consecutively. Once a name has been added by Access to a report, it won't appear again throughout the document.

Hiding a page header

You don't necessarily have to always show the page header in your reports.

If you would like to hide the header after the first page;
- Include **an unbound Text Box control** to the report with its Control Source property set to the expression = HideHeader ().
- **Delete the label of the text box**. The HideHeader () will then return a null string which will make the text box invisible.

Starting a new page number for each group

Reports often consist of several pages for every set of data. There may be a need for you to reset all page numberings to 1 for each group to have its numbering and print independently. You can accomplish this by using the Report Page Property. This essentially indicates that while the report is printing, you have the option to customize the page at any moment. Additionally, you have the option to use the group header format to even reset the report's page property to 1.

Formatting Data

By adding specific information to reports through formatting, you can make them much more valuable. You can choose to number the bullet points in your report and utilize lines or spaces to divide different sections if you want it to look more professional. A well-presented report should also have well-chosen data that is presented attractively and correctly. The arrangement of the items in your report can also influence its overall quality.

Creating numbered lists

By default, the items that are listed in the Access report are usually not numbered. The settings in the Group, Sort, and Total panes determine how the items are listed. The use of number count makes a listing of items in the report more unique and it can also aid in easy identification of items in the list. All the elements in the list on an Access report can have a number assigned to them by using the Access Running sum function. It is always ideal to let the Access query engine handle all of the aggregate functions, even though a large portion of this work may be completed with the use of VBA, which can assist in programmatically adding the data that are produced by the query or a SQL statement in the report's Record Source field. Keep in mind that when Access queries are saved, an automated optimization process takes place.

Creating bulleted lists

If you would rather, you can add bullet characters to a list in place of adding numbers. It is believed to be considerably simpler to concatenate the bullet character control to the control's Record Source property rather than using a separate field to hold the bullet. Usually, the bullet is created via taking use of Windows feature exploits. When using proportionally spaced typefaces, such as Arial, keep in mind that the actual alignment of report items may vary at times. Concatenating the data in a text box helps eliminate any issues that may arise from character spacing. That being said, the following rows will not be indented if there is more content in the text box than just one row. The typeface used in the text fields on the report needs to have indicated characters, which is the only character restriction you may run into while creating an Access report.

Adding emphasis on the run time

By configuring the visible property, you may decide whether to show or hide control for a certain record. If you just need to show a field under some circumstances and conceal it under others, this can be very helpful. When you set the visible property to either False or No, it is optimal to conceal a control throughout the design phase. You should only set the visible value to True when you need to utilize the data that the control contains.

Avoiding empty reports

When a report has been printed, all that will be shown is a blank detail section if Microsoft is unable to locate valid records to enter into the section. This appears to be a problem, but it may be prevented by adding code to the NoData event of the report that, if no data is found, displays a notice and cancels the print event. When Microsoft Access tries to produce a report and finds data in the report's underlying record set, it typically triggers the NoData event. You don't need to search through any of the report's sections to find the NOData event because it is tied to the report itself. Your users won't ever question why they are viewing a blank report if you include this code as the NoData of the report event function.

Inserting vertical lines between columns

With the height of a report section being fixed, you can easily include a vertical line. The inclusion of a vertical line that can grow in height is more difficult. Even though most controls are added during the design phase, there are situations in which controls must be added when the report is being printed. Using the line method in the report to incorporate vertical lines at run time is the most effective way to go about this. The four distinct arguments that are often required for line methods are X1, X2, Y1, and Y2, which serve to identify the line's top and bottom coordinates. Keep in mind that you can draw the horizontal lines using the same process. Note that when you make use of the Line control any time the height is fixed helps to draw the lines for each of the sections faster.

Adding a blank line

Records that are merged without sufficient space between them can be exceedingly difficult to read and understand, and they can also be easily lost. It will be much simpler to read text when a blank line is added to report data, much like when you write in Microsoft Word, and can add blank spaces to make your writing much easier to read. Although Access does not provide a mechanism to create a blank row in the middle of a detail section, you may accomplish this with the help of some programming and some hidden controls.

Even-odd page printing

There is quite a difference when a report is printed on an even or an odd page. When the report is on the odd-numbered page, the page ought to be displayed on the right edge of the page while on the even-numbered side; the page number will be displayed on the left side of the page. Then, how can you adhere to this format? To determine if the current page is even or odd, you can utilize the page footer's Format in the Page Footer section event. The content will then be aligned to the left or right side of the text box correspondingly. You may be sure that you will always be able to choose where the text aligns, even if the Text Align is set to either Left or Right at the time of design, thanks to the Format event.

Using different formats in the same text box

In some report fields, it could be necessary to utilize a different format. Regretfully, a control in a report's Detail section can only have one particular format in its Property Sheet. To set the format property at runtime, there is a workaround available. This method involves using the flex format function, which is often found in the MFunctions module and is also utilized in the rptFlexFormat. It does this by returning a string that shows the format that is specified when the 1 Decimal argument is used. The text with one decimal character count and zero characters overall will also be returned by the string format.

Centering the title

It can be quite difficult to center the title of a report in the middle of a page. The best way to ensure that the title is centered is to stretch the tile from the left margin to the right margin and once you are done simply click on the Center button in the Text Formatting group of the Home tab.

Aligning control labels

Maintaining the correct alignment of text boxes and their labels on reports can be somewhat challenging at times. The label must always be positioned differently to match it with the text box because the text box and its label have separate moving capabilities. When you add a label text to the text box's record source, you can completely erase the label. Once this is completed, the text box, label, and bound record source will all move as one unit whenever you need to move them. The only issue with this technique is that you must always make use of the same format for the text box and its label.

Micro-adjusting controls

The easiest way to make adjustments to the size or position of controls on a report in quite little increments is to hold down either the **Shift or the Ctrl key** and then click **on the arrow keys** according to how you want to make the adjustments.

Adding Data

In this section, you will learn how to increase the confidence users have in a report by adding some touches to the report such that it will help the user know when the report was printed.

Adding more information to a report

Page and pages are report properties that can be added to the report and are made available at run time. To accomplish this, you need also to evaluate the benefits of including a few more report properties in the document. As long as the property is included in square brackets, the majority of report properties can be included in unbound text boxes.

Adding the user's name to a bound report

If a text box is unbound and its control source is set to an unresolved reference, Access may ask for further information to finish the text box. For every parameter in a parameter query, Access displays a parameter dialog box. The report will then display the text that has been placed into the text box. The report's unbound text box and other elements allow you to select a reference as well. Before the report is ready for printing, the provided Parameter Value dialog box will appear. This implies that the data you provide in the dialog box can be utilized in calculations or the VBA code included at the back of the report.

Adding Even More Flexibility

This section talks more about features and some more techniques that can make your report much more flexible for users.

Displaying all reports in a combo box

The MSysObjects system table has all of the names of all the top-level database objects saved in it. You can always run a query against MSysObjects just the same way you run queries against any other table in the database. To perform this operation,

- Choose **Table/Query as the Row Source** Type for the list box and put the SQL statement in the RowSource of your list box to fill up the box with a list of all reports that are in the database.

Take note that using this strategy does not require opening reports. Since MSysObjects is aware of every object in the database, no report will escape detection when employing this method. If your database objects have names that follow a convention, use a prefix to show only the reports that are required. You may easily retrieve the names of the other top-level database objects as well, as MSysObjects stores the names of all database objects.

View the MSysObject table by;

- Choosing **the Show System Objects** check box in the Navigation Options dialog box and you can get there by right-clicking on **the Navigation panes title bar** and then choosing the **Navigation Options** from the shortcut menu.

You don't have to make MSysObjects visible for this trick to work.

Fast printing from queried data

Because forms and reports do not use the same recordset, printing a report based on a query can be very time-consuming. When a user locates the proper record on a form, the query must be run again before the record can be printed. You can create a table with every field that will be printed on the report to address this issue. In this manner, the user can open the report after finding the appropriate entry on the form and copying it to the table. To get the result populated, you only need to run the query once. Since the report is now based on a table, it will open very fast and is then ready to be printed immediately after the report is open.

Using snaking columns in a report

In Microsoft Access, snaking columns are a widely used feature mostly utilized by power users. Microsoft Access reports contain snaking columns, which help to fill up all available space on the page, reducing the number of prints needed and speeding up the process. It is frequently necessary to print some text, which can fit easily on less than half of the page or just about half of it. In situations like this, you can decide to utilize the slithering columns and then utilize all of the available space on your website. When you are making use of snaking columns to print text, you will obtain documents in the form of data stored in phone books or dictionaries. This will not just save paper, but it will be done faster and it is more comprehensive and pleasing aesthetically. To ensure that you can understand all of the information you are receiving from a query that yields a lot of data, you can also utilize snaking. If you plan to print a lengthy report, make sure to have it previewed in multiple formats so you can choose the one with flowing columns that best fits your needs. This will provide you with a clear understanding of the layout that works best for your report and provide you with a glimpse of the aesthetically beautiful result that can be achieved when using snaking columns in your report design.

Exploiting two-pass report processing

Using a two-pass report has the primary advantage of allowing you to include expressions in your reports that essentially rely on data that is present throughout the report. Using the aggregate functions based on the reports of the underlying record source will be possible when using the two-pass report, which is an additional advantage. Group headers and footers may contain information that is not yet known until all record sources have been processed.

Assigning unique names to controls

Access will name the new text box in the report the same as the fields in the recordset underlying report if you utilize the Report Wizard or drag fields from the Field List when creating your reports. For Access to distinguish between the control's name and the underlying field, you must modify the control's Name attribute to something like txtDiscount.

PART VI

MICROSOFT ACCESS PROGRAMMING FUNDAMENTALS

CHAPTER 22

USING ACCESS MACROS

An automated input sequence that mimics mouse clicks or keystrokes is called a macro. A macro is commonly utilized in spreadsheets and certain database applications to modify a recurring sequence of keyboard and mouse operations. The Visual Basic for Applications (VBA) programming language became the industry standard for automating Access database applications as Access was developed as a development tool. Many developers have abandoned macros because they were lacking in variables and error handling in earlier iterations of Access. Compared to earlier versions, this feature is now integrated into macros, making them a far more practical substitute for VBA.

An Introduction to Macros

A macro is defined as a tool that enables you to have tasks automated in Access. With the use of Access macros, you can perform certain defined actions and then include functionality in your forms and reports. Selecting actions from a drop-down list and then populating the action's arguments is the process of designing macros. You can select actions using macros without creating a single line of VBA code. The commands that VBA offers include the macro actions. Developing a macro is frequently much simpler for people than writing VBA code. Supposing that you wish to include buttons on the main form that may be used to access the different forms in your application. One option is to include a button in the form, or you can create a macro that will launch a different form in your application when the button is clicked.

Creating a macro

If you want to build a new macro simply;

- Click **on the Macro button** on the Macros & Code group on the Create tab of the Ribbon.

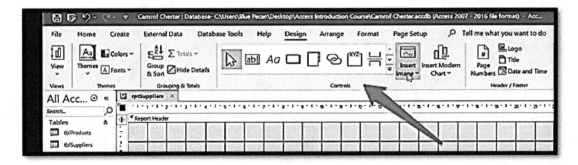

- Click on the **Macro button** which will in turn open the macro builder which contains a drop-down list of more macro options.

To the right side of the Macro Builder is an Action Catalog which contains different macro options and information about the action that should be used for a particular task.

- Click on **MessageBox** from the drop-down list in the macro builder. The macro builder will then change to show an area where you include the arguments like the message, beep, type, and title which are associated with the messagebox action.

Click the **Run button** located in the Tools group on the Ribbon's Design tab to initiate the macro. Access will ask you to save the macro after you develop it; you must do this before Access may run the macro.

Note that macros can also be executed from the Navigation pane.

- Close the **macro builder** and then show the display group on the Navigation pane.
- You can then click **twice** on the mcrHelloWorld macro to execute it.

When the Hello World! Macron has been displayed and you are satisfied with the view.

- Click on **the close button** in the upper-right corner of the macro builder to go back to the main Access window.

Assigning a macro to an event

The only purpose of macros is to automate programs without requiring the writing of VBA code. It is recommended to have your macros attached to an object's event so that the application is relatively simple to use. The most frequent event to which a macro can be assigned is the button click event. **Go through the steps below to build a button that runs the mcrHelloWorld;**

- Choose the **Create tab** on the Ribbon and then click on the Form Design button in the Forms group.
- On the Form Design Tools Design tab of the Ribbon, deselect the **Use Control Wizard's** option in the controls group.
- Choose the **Button control** and draw a button on the form.
- Configure **the name** of the button property to cmdHelloWorld.
- Configure **the caption property** of the button to Hello World!
- Choose the **drop-down list** in the click event of the button's property and choose mcrHellowWorld from the list.

Understanding Macro Security

Not every macro is safe. Almost everything that can be done in the Access user interface can also be done in a macro. Some actions, such as running a delete query, may result in an unanticipated loss of data. With Access's integrated security environment, you can stop malicious and undesired macros from running, so you're covered.

When objects like forms, macros, and queries are being executed, Access uses the Trust Center to identify commands that are safe to execute. The Trust Center does not advise that macros and VBA code be trusted by default since it considers them to be "macros." Unsafe commands may pose a hazard to the computer, alter its configuration, or destroy the workstation across the network environment if they are permitted to be run.

Enabling sandbox mode

A security feature known as a "sandmode box" stops Access from executing certain expressions that are deemed "unsafe." These so-called unsafe expressions are often prevented regardless of whether the database has been trusted. To specify whether Access should be run in sandbox mode or not, use the registry key.

When Access is installed on a computer, the registry key is misconfigured to enable sandbox mode, and the sandbox mode is enabled by default. If you must permit the execution of all expressions, you have the option to change the registry key value to prevent sandbox mode.

To enable the sandbox mode simply follow the steps below;

- Launch Access, click on the **File button,** and then choose **Options**.
- Click on the **Trust Center tab**, and then click on the **Trust Center Settings.**
- Select the **Macro Settings tab.**
- Select either **Disable All Macros without Notification or Disable All Macros** with Notification.

An encrypted security file that is attached to a macro or document is known as a digital signature. It demonstrates that the author of the macro or document is a reliable source. Large enterprises that are prepared to pay for the cost of acquiring and maintaining digital signatures are essentially the ones who use them. Make sure you wait to sign your Access project until after it has undergone extensive testing and you don't anticipate any changes. Any alterations made to the project's code will render the digital signature invalid.

The Trust Center

The Trust Center is where you can get security and privacy settings for Access.

If you would like to show the Trust Center;

- Click on the **File button** then click on **Options** to open the Access Options dialog box.
- Choose the **Trust Center tab** and then click on the **Trust Center Settings**.

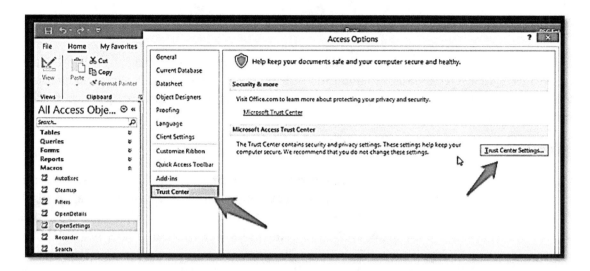

Below is a description of each section in the Trust Center Settings and what it controls;

- **Trusted Publishers**: it shows a list of trusted publishers. If you would like to remove a publisher from this list, choose the publisher and then click on the **Remove option**. Trusted publishers must have a valid digital signature that has not expired.
- **Trusted Locations**: This displays the computer network's trusted locations list. This section gives you the option to add, remove, or modify computer folders that are guaranteed to contain a trusted file. It is possible to open a trusted file in a trusted location without the Trust Center having to verify it.
- **Add-ins**: this gives you the ability to customize how Access handles add-ins. It is up to you to determine if add-ins that have not yet been digitally signed should be notified or if they should be signed digitally from a reliable source.
- **ActiveX Settings**: this allows you to control the level of security for Active X controls.
- **Macro Settings**: this gives you the option of setting the security for macros that are not in a trusted location.

Digital Signature

By adding a digital signature to a database, you may demonstrate your belief in the security of the database and the reliability of its content. A digital signature attests to the fact that the database's macros, code modules, and other executable elements were created by the signer and haven't been changed since. This aids users in determining the level of trustworthiness of the database and its contents. Consider a security certificate as a digital signature pen or as an exclusive wax stamp that you can apply. You have two options for adding a digital signature: either make your own or use a commercial security certificate. Depending on the database version you're using, there are several steps involved in digitally signing a database.

Commercial security certificate

A commercial certificate authority (CA) will provide you with a commercial security certificate if you wish to digitally sign a database and then distribute it commercially. Background checks are conducted by certificate authorities to confirm the legitimacy of content creators (such as database creators).

Self-signed certificate

Using the SelfCert tool that comes with Microsoft 365, you can create a digital certificate for use in personal or small workgroup scenarios inside your organization. When you use a self-signed digital certificate to digitally sign a document and subsequently distribute the digitally signed file, others are unable to independently confirm the legitimacy of your digital signature unless they choose to believe your self-issued certificate.

- Navigate to the folders that have your Microsoft Office program files. There will be a need for you to find the executable file, SelfCert.exe, and the exact location might be different as this is usually dependent on diverse conditions like if you are making use of either a 32 or 64-bit Windows operating system and also if you are making use of Microsoft 365.
- Look for the right folder and click twice on Selfcert.exe. This will then show the Create Digital Certificate dialog box.
- In the box titled Your certificate's name, insert a name for the novel test certificate.
- Double-click on the **OK button.**

Digitally sign an Access package to distribute a database

Distributing and signing a database is quick and simple. The file can be packaged, given a digital signature, and then given to other users in a signed package. Using the Package-and-Sign feature, the database is stored in an Access Deployment (.accdc) file, which is then signed, and the signed package is stored at a location of your choosing. After that, users can work directly in the database (instead of in the package file) by extracting the database from the package. It is worth noting that there is still a possibility of you making use of the packaging feature to create a .accdc file, if or not you also code-sign the database. It should be noted that creating a.accdc file using the packaging capability is still possible regardless of whether you code-sign the database.

Digitally sign an Access database

You can digitally sign components in the.mdb and. mde database formats in any version of Access. Additionally supported are the.accdb and. accde database formats as of Access for Microsoft 365 Version 2211.

To code-sign a database, take these steps:

- Launch the database you would like to sign.
- In the Macro group, on the Database Tools tab, choose Visual Basic to commence the Visual Basic Editor, or tap ALT + F11.
- Choose the database or Visual Basic for Applications (VBA) project that you would like to get your signature on in the Project Explorer window.
- Choose **Digital Signature** on the Tools menu and then the Digital Signature dialog box will be displayed.
- Select **Choose to pick your preferred test certificate.** The Select Certificate dialog box will then be displayed.
- Choose **the certificate** you would like to apply for. Choose the certificate that you designed with the use of the SelfCert if you have adequately followed the steps in the former section.
- Select **OK** to get the Select **Certificate dialog box closed**, and then chooses **OK** once more to close the Digital Signature dialog box.

Lock the VBA project before signing it to keep users of your solution from unintentionally changing it and nullifying your signature. Locking your VBA project, however, does not stop someone else from substituting a different digital signature for the original one. Re-signing templates and add-ins give corporate managers more control over what applications users can execute on their PCs. Avoid digitally certifying the database if your application makes changes to the data that may render the signature incorrect, like adding a new action query. As an alternative, distribute files in a signed package (.accdc) and pair it with a reliable site. Other sections include; the message bar, privacy options, and trusted add-in catalogs.

Multi-action Macros

The ability of a macro to do several tasks with a single button click is the real test of a macro. It is preferable to create a macro that does many queries rather than double-clicking on every action query in the Navigation pane.

If all the action is not being displayed in the Action drop-down list,
- Choose the **Show All Actions command** in the Show/Hide group on the Macro Tools Design tab of the Ribbon.

Certain macro operations require a trusted database or an environment that permits macros via specific security configurations. Additionally, some macro actions are known to be dangerous because they modify database data or carry out operations that could damage the application. When a macro action is deemed risky by the macro designer, a warning icon is always displayed. Access will only display trusted macro operations by default, regardless of security settings.

Submacros

In the Macro Designer box, an alternative macro is defined by a sub-macro declaration in Access. Using the RunMacro action, you can choose to execute the actions listed in sub-macros from another macro. **In the Macro Name argument of the RunMacro action, you can make use of the syntax below to execute the sub macro;**

<Macro name>.<submacro name>

A sub-macro statement can also be used in the definition of an error-handling set of actions within a macro.

To implement a macro with the use of sub-macros;

- Create a **form** with three buttons then configure the **On Click event properties** of these buttons.

With the Sub Macros, you can reduce the number of macros that are being displayed in the Navigation pane and manage more macros with more ease.

Conditions

You can add several single macro objects to a single group using sub-macros, but before the macro can act, it needs to meet specific requirements, as indicated by a condition. The IF macro action requires a Boolean expression; if the expression evaluates to False, No, or 0, the action will not be performed. This is important to note. The action is executed if the expression evaluates to a different value.

Opening reports using conditions

To show conditions and the IF macro condition, use the example of a Report Menu which has three buttons and a frame control with two different button options which are Print and Print Preview.

- When you click on the **Print option**, it will set the value of the frame to 1 and when you click on the **Print Preview option** it will set the frame value to 2. The macro that will be opening the report will make use of the sub-macro as well as the If macro action.

Multiple actions in conditions

If there is a need for you to execute various conditions based on a particular condition, add multiple actions within the If and End If actions. The If macro will then allow you to execute certain actions based on the values that are in your applications. Make use of the If macro action to reference controls on forms or reports and some other objects and then decide on the actions that should be executed.

Temporary Variables

Up to this point in Access history, variables could only be used in VBA codes. Three new macro actions were introduced with Access 2007: RemoveTempVar, SetTempVar, and RemoveAllTempVars. These actions let you create and utilize temporary variables within your macros. These variables can be used in conditional expressions to pass data to and from forms or reports or to regulate which actions should be performed. To transfer data between modules, you can also decide to get access to VBA.

Enhancing a macro you've already created

Any of the previously covered macro actions can be used to obtain a value from the user and then display it in the message box when you need to improve an existing macro. Name and Expression are the two arguments that the SetTempVar action takes. The expression specifies what the temporary variable's value should be, and the name is just the variable's name. Other actions can be used exactly how you would like the macro to be improved, and they each have their own set of requirements. Keep in mind that temporary variables are global and can be used in any VBA method, query, macro, or object property after they are created.

Using temporary variables to simplify macros

With the use of temporary variables, you can make the use of macros quite easier by eliminating certain steps like the need to create a structure of multiple OpenForm or OpenReport actions. You can also choose to make use of more than one variable in a macro.

Using temporary variables in VBA

You can start automating your program with macros, but as time goes on, you can start using VBA code to add functionality to other areas and automate even more tasks. It's not necessary to discard any temporary variables you've previously created using macros; you can use them straight in your VBA code. Keep in mind that any VBA that is written can be used in macros and vice versa. You can no longer utilize variables in your macros that you also remove in VBA, and vice versa. Your macros and VBA code will no longer be independent of one another when you employ temporary variables.

Error Handling and Macro Debugging

The primary reason most developers choose VBA instead of macros to automate their programs is that the latter does not provide error handling. Anytime a macro contains a bug, it may stop working and remain dormant for several hours until the problem is rectified. When you include error handling in your macros, you can select what to do if an error arises while the macro is still executing.

The OnError action

With the ONError action, you can make your decision on what you would like to do when you encounter an error in your macro. There are two arguments in this action which are the Go to argument and the Macro Name argument.

One of the simplest ways to have error handling in a macro is to

- Make the OnError the first action and then configure the **Go to the argument** as the Next. Once this has been done, your macro will keep running non-stop but you will not know the actions that are running and the ones that are not.

The MacroError object

The macro error object has information about the last error that occurred. It also keeps this information until another error occurs or the last one has been cleared with the use of the ClearMacroError action. This object has some read-only properties like ActionName, Arguments, Condition, Description, MacroName, and Number. The MarcoError object can be used to display messages to the user, who can then relay the information to you, or as a debugging tool. Use the Object included in an If action to modify the running actions according to the error that transpired. You may handle errors more effectively, display helpful messages, and provide information to the user and yourself when you utilize the object in conjunction with the OnError action.

Debugging macros

With the use of the OnError action and also the MacroError object, debugging Access macros can be a lot easier.

Embedded Macros

An embedded macro is the part of the object that it belongs to, hidden away in an event property. Since each inserted large scale is free, once you modify an embedded large-scale item, there's no need to stress any other controls that might use the large scale. The macros that have been inserted are not shown in the navigation pane and can only be accessed through the object's Property Sheet. Macro embeddings are reliable. Even if your security settings prevent the code from running, it will always run. Because embedded macros are always automatically stopped from carrying out actions that are not safe, you may always distribute your program as a trusted application.

Macros versus VBA Statements

Macro functions in Access frequently provide an ideal means of handling many fine details, like executing reports and forms. Using a macro will allow you to construct apps and assign tasks more quickly since it displays the arguments for the macro operations. You don't need to remember complicated linguistic structures. Many of the tasks that can be accomplished with VBA statements are better suited for macros.

The actions below tend to be more efficient when they run from macros;

- Using macros against the whole record with action queries.
- Running reports
- Opening and closing of forms.

Choosing between macros and VBA

Although oftentimes macros have proven to be the solution, VBA is the tool to beat at other times.

You will most often want to make use of VBA other than macros when you want to:

- Create and make use of your functions.
- Make use of automation in communication with other window applications or to run system-level actions.
- Make use of existing functions in external Windows Dynamic Link Libraries.
- Work with records one after the other.

Converting existing macros to VBA

Some of your application macros may need to be reworked as VBA methods once you're comfortable writing VBA code. As you begin this process and go over each macro in your various macro libraries, you quickly come to understand how logically difficult the effort may be. The macro cannot simply be copied from the macro builder and pasted into a module window. You must first study the task that a macro completes for each condition, activity, and activity contention before creating the same expressions of VBA code in your function. Thankfully, Access has a tool that can automatically convert macros to VBA code. Convert Macros to Visual Basic is a button located in the Tools group of the Design tab of the Ribbon. It only takes a few seconds to convert a macro to a module with this option.

Activity

1. Create a macro.
2. Assign a macro to an event.
3. Describe macro security.
4. Enable the sandbox mode.
5. Open reports with the use of conditions.
6. Enhance a macro you have created.
7. Make use of temporary variables in simplifying macros.
8. Debug macros.
9. Convert existing macros to VBA.

CHAPTER 23

ACCESS DATA MACROS

It has long been believed that when it comes to managing an application's logic, VBA is superior to macros. Basic issues with Access macros include their incapacity to interact with code, their inability to trap or handle mistakes in macros, and their inability to track how a macro affects a specific form. Because Access data macros are covered in detail in this chapter, Microsoft Access 2024 is currently the recommended version.

Introducing Data Macros

When viewing a table in Datasheet view, data macros are managed from the Table tab and are not displayed under Macros in the Navigation Pane. Data macros can be used, among other things, to validate and ensure the accuracy of data in a table. There are two basic types of data macros: those that are called "event-driven" because they are triggered by table events and those that are called "named" because they execute in response to being called by title.

Understanding Table Events

There are about five various macro programmable table events which are BeforeChange, BeforeDelete, AfterInsert, AfterUpdate, and AfterDelete. In this section, these events will be briefly described.

"Before events

The before events (BeforeChange and BeforeDelete) are quite easy and straightforward and also offer support for just a few macro actions. Comparable to the BeforeUpdate event related to forms, reports, and controls is the BeforeChange event. As its name suggests, BeforeChange fires just before a client, an inquiry, or a VBA code altering data in a table. Additionally, BeforeChange gives you the chance to view newly added values to the record that is presently being used and then make any necessary changes. The BeforeChange event can't hinder the client with a message box or halt the record from upgrading within the fundamental table. All BeforeChange can do is set a field's value or set a local macro variable's value before the record is added or upgraded within the table.

"After" events

Compared to their prior equivalents, the after events—which comprise the AfterUpdate, AfterInsert, and AfterDelete options—are significantly larger. Since all of the aforementioned events are compatible with the entire family of data macro actions, data macros may be based on these events more frequently. Normally, when a record is added to the table, the AfterInsert data macro is called. On the other hand, if you would like to track more table modifications, you can opt to add the data macros to the AfterUpdate and AfterDelete functions.

Using the Macro Builder for Data Macros

The same macro builder used to create client interfaces and embedded macros is also used to create data macros. You'll use the macro builder for all macro progress and administration once you've mastered it. The primary difference is that the Activity Catalog (seen in the other section) offers different activities based on the environment. It's incredibly easy to add data macros to a table. An Access table doesn't have to be in the Design view; if you'd rather, you can add data macros to a table that is displayed as a datasheet. The data macros you create for a table take effect immediately, so you can work on a macro and see its effectiveness without having to compile or switch between the Design view and Datasheet view. You can easily use the data macro builder with your table in the Design view by selecting the Create Data macros command from the Design tab.

Understanding the Action Catalog

The Activity Catalog on the right side of the macro builder serves as the store of macro activities you include in your data macros. The contents of the Activity Catalog depend completely on which table event has been chosen, so its appearance shifts impressively whereas you work with Access macros.

Program flow

At the very top of the Action Catalog is some program flow constructs that can be added to your macros. When you are making use of data macros, the only program flow constructs that can be used are comments, groups, and If blocks.

Data blocks

Properly checking under the Program Flow constructs will reveal Data Blocks. There is a section in each data block construct where one or more macro operations can be included. The data block construct can perform all macro actions as part of its operations. The CreateRecord, EditRecord, ForEachRecord, and LookupRecord are among the data block macro activities.

Data actions

The Data activities are the next group of tasks included in the Activity Catalog; a data macro can do these tasks. As you have already read, a data macro consists of one or more actions that are carried out simultaneously in response to a table event. You would like to have a thorough understanding of the various macro operations that data macros can do.

Creating Your First Data Macro

Now that you have some prior knowledge about macro builders follow the steps below to create your first Data Macro.

- Open the **preferred table** in the Datasheet view
- Choose the **Table tab option** on the Ribbon then click on the **BeforeChange event**.
- Click **twice or move the Group program flow action** to the design surface of the macro.
- When in the newly created group, click **twice** on the Comment program flow action to add a comment to the design surface of the macro.
- To add a new logic check to the macros' design surface, double-click the If program flow action.
- Double-clicking the Setfield action button should edit the record if the given condition evaluates to true.
- The logic for the macro is finished if you have followed the procedures up to this point. The next step is to simply click and save commands.

Managing Macro Objects

This section tells you what you can do in managing macro objects once you have added them to a macro's design.

Collapsing and expanding macro items

Items that collapse can be quite helpful, particularly if you need to study huge macros and display only a portion of the macro at a given moment. Keep in mind that you can also decide to expand or collapse instructions from the Ribbon.

Moving macro items

Macro items can be moved from one place to another with the use of the copy and paste function, as an alternative you can also choose to drag the items with the use of the mouse button.

Saving a macro as XML

The ability to copy Access data macros from the macro builder and paste them as XML into a content editor is a completely hidden capability. Macro storage in Access is done internally as XML, so copying a macro also copies its XML form.

Recognizing the Limitations of Data Macros

Despite their immense strength, data macros are limited in what they can accomplish. They are unable to open a form or report, display a message box, or have a user interface, for example.

They are designed to function at peak efficiency while remaining invisible. Data macros are unable to function in attachment or multi-value fields. VBA, or classic user interface macros, must be used if logic needs to be controlled over certain kinds of data. VBA operations cannot be called by data macros. One of the key goals was to make them particularly transferable to SharePoint when an application was scaled up to a web application. Transactions are not supported by data macros. There is no mechanism to undo multiple table modifications; all field and record alterations are carried out instantly.

Activity

1. What are data macros?
2. What are table events?
3. Make use of the macro builder for data macros.
4. Create a data macro.
5. Manage macro objects.
6. Collapse and expand macro items.
7. Save macro as XNL
8. What are the limitations of data macros?

CHAPTER 24

GETTING STARTED WITH ACCESS VBA

Most Access designers utilize macros almost every time. Even though macros give a speedy and simple way to mechanize an application, composing Visual Basic for Applications (VBA) modules is the most perfect way to form applications. VBA gives data access, looping and branching, and other features that macros essentially do not support. In this chapter, you learn how to utilize VBA to expand the control and value of your applications.

Introducing Visual Basic for Applications

Database developers can create data entry forms, reports, and queries in Microsoft Access using various capabilities that allow users to query current data in the database and enter data that isn't being used. This development method is made easier by various wizard gadgets and inquiry builders. That being said, there can be situations with these devices where the designer wants to incorporate even more features that aren't currently available through the MS Access advancement tools. The engineer could want to automatically correct bad data, for example, before it is stored in the database. Including code that makes use of the Visual Basic for Applications programming language is how this modification is accomplished. In the majority of expert Access programs, VBA is an essential component. Microsoft includes VBA with Access because it provides Access database applications with essential flexibility and control. Access macros would have been responsible for providing a somewhat restricted range of actions for Access programs in the absence of a fully functional programming language such as VBA. Although VBA is considerably easier to deal with when creating complex data-management capabilities or advanced user-interface requirements, macro programming also includes adaptability to Access applications.

Understanding VBA Terminology

Below are terms that are often used with VBA;
- **Keyword**: This is simply a word with a special meaning in VBA. For example, the word Now in VBA refers to the name of a built-in function that sends back the current date and time.
- **Statement**: this is a single VA word or group of words that build an instruction to be performed by the VBA engine.
- **Procedure**: this is a group of VBA statements put together to take up some task. The two basic types of VBA procedures are Subroutines and Functions
- **Module**: procedures are often stored in modules. A module has one or more procedures and some other elements which are put together as just one entity within the application.

Starting with VBA Code Basics

There are an interminable number of distinctive VBA programming statements that seem to appear in an Access application. For the most part, be that as it may, VBA statements are reasonably simple to study and get. Most frequently, you will be able to understand the reason for a VBA statement based on the keywords. Each VBA statement is an instruction that is processed and also executed by the VBA language engine which is built into Access.

Creating VBA Programs

You can work with tables, queries, forms, and reports in Access without ever having to put in a line of code because of its vast range of devices. Even with macros, certain activities cannot be completed via the client interface. You require the power of a high-level programming language like VBA for situations like this. Many of the basic structures available in most programming languages are also available in VBA, an advanced and well-organized programming language. VBA may be extended to call Windows API schedules and can be linked to any Access or VBA data type, as well as ActiveX Information Objects (ADO) and Data AccessObjects (DAO).

Modules

Modules are containers wherein procedures are stored. There are two different types of modules. They are the standard module and classic module. Standard modules don't require any other Access objects, such as reports or shapes. They serve as a place to keep code that is used across your program. Since these tactics apply to every part of your Access application, they are sometimes referred to as global or public. Employ public strategies in expressions, macros, occasion methods, and other VBA codes throughout your application. You sort the title of a public method into another method in your program to use it. Class modules describe how an object behaves. Although you have the option, the most commonly used class module is attached to a report or a form. When you insert VBA code in a form or report, Access automatically creates the class module that is connected to that form or report. The main and most important difference between class modules and standard modules is that the latter support events. Events execute VBA code included in the event strategy in response to client activity.

Procedures and functions

The next step you completed after making a module to hold your strategy was to make the strategy itself. It's a straightforward method that does a little straightforward math and shows the result. Each statement is organized concurrently with the language's syntax, meaning that the spelling of keywords and the order of the words within the statement are critical. Except for one significant exception, a function is quite similar to a sub-procedure: upon closure, a function returns a value. The built-in VBA Now () function, which returns the current date and time, is an example of an easy case. You can use Now() pretty much anywhere your program needs to use or display the current time and date. One way to let the client know exactly when the report was printed is to include Now () in the report header or footer. Among the several hundred pre-installed VBA routines is now(). You may include bespoke capacities that return values needed by your applications in addition to built-in capacities.

Working in the code window

Utilize the Code window to type in, show, and alter Visual Basic code. You'll be able to open as many Code windows as you have got modules, so you'll be able to effortlessly see the code in numerous forms or modules, and duplicate and paste between them.

White space

Within the programming community, white space refers to particular blank lines and indentation. Very few exceptions aside, VBA ignores white space. Certain computer languages require and value white space. With VBA, it isn't the case. White space is used to help your code read more easily. Various software engineers use white space in their code in different ways. The most important thing is to be consistent, regardless of the formatting styles you choose to use. Maintaining a consistent organizational style will help you review and comprehend your code more efficiently, even when you're reading it months or even years later.

Line continuation

The characters used to continue a line are a gap followed by an emphasis. The VBA compiler recognizes that the next line can be a continuation of the current one when it observes emphasis and space at the end of the line. Use the line continuation characters to divide lengthy sentences into many lines. This will allow you to see the entire statement.

Multi-statement lines

Another way to make strides in the clarity of your code is by putting two or more statements on one line. VBA uses the colon to isolate statements on the same line. If you have some brief statements that are taking up a part of vertical space within the code sheet, you'll be able to put a number of them on the same line to clean up the code.

IntelliSense

There are about four different features in Access collectively known as Intellisense and they are used to help you locate the proper keyword to be used; they also determine the right parameters as each line of code is being created. These features are Complete Word, Auto List Members, Auto Quick Info, and Auto Constants.

Compiling procedures

To finish the development process, code needs to be compiled after it has been written. The English-like VBA syntax is converted to a binary format that is performed at run time during the compilation stage. Additionally, during compilation, every line of code is examined for errors in syntax and other faults that could arise when the user interacts with the application. When a client opens an Access program and begins using it, Access compiles the code if you don't compile your applications throughout the development cycle. In this instance, errors in your code could prohibit the client from using the application, which would be extremely burdensome for all parties involved.

Saving a module

Modules are saved by saving the database and reacting to the prompts that Access shows.

- Within the VBE, select **File** then click on **Save** to save the database. You will be prompted to save all unsaved modules and other unsaved objects.

You aren't prompted to save modules that have as of now been saved; nevertheless, in case they've been changed. Those modules are spared with the name you gave previously. Class modules that are connected to a frame or report are saved when the form or report is saved.

Understanding VBA Branching Constructs

The most well-known feature of a programming language is its capacity to make decisions based on conditions that may vary somewhat each time the user interacts with the program. There are two main ways that the VBA operations can be carried out:

Branching

Branching in VBA can simply be described as the ability of an application to view a value and based on that same value, decide the code it will run.

The If keyword

Although the If keyword can be used in a variety of ways, it always checks a condition and then executes an action based on the evaluation. It is necessary to evaluate the condition to a Boolean value (True or False). The program advances to the line that follows the If statement if the condition is True. The program moves on to the statement that follows the Else statement, if it is there, or the End If explanation statement, if the Else clause is absent, if that condition is False.

The Select case...End Select statement

VBA provides the Select Case statement to check for various conditions. Below is the general syntax for the Select Case statement;

> Select Case Expression
> **Case Value1**
>   [Action to take when Expression = Value1]
> **Case Value2**
>   [Action to take when Expression = Value2]

Take note that the syntax is compared to that of the If...Then statement. Rather than a Boolean condition, the Select Case articulation employs an expression at the top. At that point, each Case clause tests its value against the expression's value. When a Case value matches the expression, the program executes the block of code until it comes to another Case statement or the End Select statement. VBA executes the code as if it were one matching Case statement.

.Looping

The ability to execute a single statement or a set of statements repeatedly in VBA is known as looping. Until part of the requirements are satisfied, the statement or set of statements that were performed will also be repeated. VBA has two different kinds of looping constructs: the Do..Loop and the For..Next. DoLoop constructs are primarily utilized when you need to repeat a statement but are unsure of how many times to repeat it while the For loop is running. When repeating a statement is necessary and you know how many times it will be repeated, you can utilize subsequent constructs.

The Do... Loop statement

Do...Loop is utilized to repeat a bunch of statements until a condition is true. This statement is one of the foremost commonly utilized VBA looping constructs. Do...Loop has various alternatives. The While clause causes the VBA statements inside the Do...Loop to execute as long as the condition is true. Execution drops out of the Do...Loop immediately the condition assesses to false. The until clause on its own doesn't work in the same manner, it works such that the code within the Do....Loop will only be executed when the condition is false.

.The For... Next statement

To repeat a statement block several times, use the For Next statement. For the most part, The counter variable is increased by the sum given by the step value in the subsequent loop, which checks upward from a starting value. However, in certain situations, you may need a loop that starts at a high starting value and decreases to the final value. Use a negative number as the step value in this scenario. When looping in reverse, the Step keyword is necessary. If you ignore it, the loop won't be carried out since the for statement will determine that CounterVariable is more important than End.

Working with Objects and Collections

VBA provides several constructs that are primarily meant to be used with individual objects and groups of objects. VBA for Access is sometimes referred to as object-based, even though it's not strictly an object-oriented language. In Access, a lot of the data you work with are objects rather than just plain old numbers and character strings. Generally speaking, an object is a multifaceted material that serves multiple purposes within an Access application. Collections are used by Access to group objects together into a single group. Typically, collections are given names by pluralizing the names of the things they contain. The Form object is part of the Forms collection. The Report object is part of the Report collection. Still, there are certain exceptions, like the Controls collection. Although Control objects are included in the Controls collection, each Control object is also a different kind of object. A Text Box, a Combobox, or any of several other specific object types can be a control object.

Properties and methods

Objects also have properties and methods which are also discussed in the sections below;

Properties

With properties, you can choose to change some values that are the characteristics of that particular object. Properties also can return some other objects.

Methods

Methods are quite different from properties in that they do not return a value.
Methods basically can be in two categories which are;
- Methods with the ability to change more than just one property at once.
- Methods that can act external to the object.

The With statement

You can access an object's methods and properties by using the With explanation instead of always writing the object's name. All attributes or operations applied in the space between With and End With implicitly refer to the object specified in the With clause. Between the With and End With statements, any number of statements may appear, and the With statements may be resolved. The term "properties and methods" refers to the internal protest of a piece that includes them. In any case, the With explanation may improve overall performance when working with large amounts of data. Either way, the With explanation reduces the subroutine's wordiness and greatly simplifies the code to read and comprehend. Additionally, it saves a ton of writing when altering an object's properties.

The For Each statement

The In The You can navigate across the controls collection using any statement. It makes certain that each member of the collection is inspected and that it is accessible for analysis or modification.

Exploring the Visual Basic Editor

In this section, you will learn more about the features of the Visual Basic Editor and how to effectively make use of them.

The Immediate window

The immediate window has to allow you to give your procedure a trial without necessarily having to leave the module. **You can execute the module and also check variables.**

- Click on the **Ctrl+G buttons** to see the immediate window or click on View then Immediate window when you are in the VBA code editor.

The Project Explorer

This is a window that is within the VBE that shows all the modules that are in your project. It also offers a much easier method of moving modules without having to go back to the main Access application. **To view the Project Explorer;**

- Press the **Ctrl+R buttons** or click on **View** then Project Explorer from the menu of the VBE.

The Object Browser

With the Object Browser which is also a window in VBE, you can see all the objects, properties, methods, and events that are in your project. The object browser can be very useful especially when you are looking for properties and methods, the Object browser can help show all the elements that are in a particular string.

VBE options

Below are some of the other options that are available for use within the VBE;

The Editor tab of the Options dialog box

This box has lots of very important settings that influence how you deal with Access as you include code in your applications.

You can access these by

- Clicking on **Tools** and then **Options** from the VBE menu.

The Project Properties dialog box

By keeping track of all the code objects stored in the project—which is essentially distinct from the code included in the program as runtime libraries and wizards—Access takes control of the code in your application. Every Access project contains a few crucial settings. Developers should also pay close attention to the settings in the project Properties dialog box. Assuming that "project name" is the name assigned to your database project, click Tools to open the Project Properties dialog box, then select Project Name Properties.

CHAPTER 25

MASTERING VBA DATA TYPES AND PROCEDURES

A variable can just be a value that you say in your code; as a result, it gets stored in the memory of your machine. You must give your variable a name, and it's a good idea to say what kind of data it contains. Once you declare the Data type, you are instructing the computer as to what kind of data it should store in your variable. The program will also have access to your variable, which you will use in your code. While your code is running, the actual value of your variable may change. The variables you employ have a significant impact on your applications. Regarding the creation and utilization of variables in your Access applications, you have additional choices. Inappropriate use of a variable might cause data loss or slow down an application's ability to run correctly. Everything you want to create and use variables is covered in this chapter; the knowledge here will also enable you to utilize data types most effectively while avoiding the well-known issues associated with VBA variables.

Using Variables

A variable is assigned a name and can be a temporary capacity area for a particular value. Variables can be used to keep user-inputted values, record the outcome of calculations, or read data from tables. Alternatively, they can be used to create controls whose values are accessible to other procedures. You use a variable's name to store the outcome of an expression so that you may refer to it. The = operator is used to assign the outcome of an expression to a variable.

Naming variables

Almost every programming language has its own defined fuels that it uses in naming variables.

In VBA, the conditions a variable name must meet are as follows;

- The name must be unique with a mix of both upper and lower case.
- There must be no space in the names or punctuation characters.
- It must start with an alphabetical character.
- It must not be longer than 255 characters.

Declaring variables

You can add variables to your program in essentially two methods. The first approach, which VBA uses to automatically generate variables for you, is referred to as implicit declaration. This is not a smart idea because it can cause debugging and performance problems. Explicit declaration is the second method. When declaring, this technique makes use of a keyword. Among the keywords are Dim, Static, Private, and Public keywords. Keep in mind that the selection of keywords used will always impact the variable's scope inside the application and will play a major role in determining where the variable can be utilized within the program. Though VBA doesn't need you to declare your variables before you make use of them, it offers several declaration commands. Note that it is a very good practice to always have your variables declared. When a variable is declared it simply means there is a certain type of data that can be assigned to it which most of the time is usually a numeric value or characters alone.

The Dim keyword

The best way to declare a variable is to use the Dim keyword. Please make sure that the variable name is provided when using this keyword. When defining a variable, keep in mind that the variable name will always come after the Dim declaration. Additionally, utilize the Use As Data Type option to provide a specific data type for the variable when naming it. The default data type is variation as it can carry any kind of data; however, this data type is essentially the kind of information that will be kept in the variable. You can also declare variables in the declarations part of the module after which all the procedures in the module will be able to gain access to the variable. The procedures on the outside of the module in which the variable has been declared will however not be able to read or make use of the variable.

The Public keyword

The Public keyword should be used if you want to make every module in the application accessible. Declaring a public variable in a single standard module that is used to store public variables only is the best way to do it. Finding all of the publicly declared variables in one location can make things quite simple.

The Private keyword

Technically speaking, there isn't much of a difference between the Dim and Private keywords; however, it is a good idea to use the Private keyword at the module level when declaring variables that are only accessible by that module's procedure. All procedures in the module will be able to access the variable, but not all procedures in the other module will be able to, thanks to the private keyword.

Working with Data Types

When you declare a variable you ought to specify the data type for each of the variables also. Each variable has its data type and the data type will also determine the type of information that will be stored in the variable. For example, a string variable will only be able to hold a data type of string that can be typed on a keyboard.

Forcing explicit declarations

Access provides a simple compiler order that makes you speak the variables in your apps out loud all the time. When the Option Explicit statement is used at the beginning of a module, VBA is instructed to demand that each variable inside the module have an explicit declaration. Explicit declaration is a terrific idea; therefore you might not be surprised to learn that Access provides a technique to automatically ensure that every module in your application uses explicit declaration.

Using a naming convention with variables

One way to ease the burden of overseeing the code and objects in an application is through the utilization of a naming convention. A naming convention applies a standardized strategy of providing names to the objects and variables in an application. A one- to four-character prefix (a tag) is added to the base names of the objects and variables in a VBA application as part of the standard common naming pattern used in Access applications. Most of the time, the tag is determined by the kind of control for controls, the kind of data the variable contains, or the range of variables. Variable names frequently have a similar structure. A Boolean variable called bActive would indicate whether or not the customer is active, while the strong variable sCustomer would include the customer's name.

Understanding variable scope and Lifetime

Variables are more than just simple data storage devices. Each variable may be used at different points throughout the program's execution and may be a dynamic component of the application. A variable's declaration specifies more information than just its name and data type. The variable may be highly visible to a significant percentage of the application's code, depending on the keyword used to declare it and where in the program's code it is declared. However, a different placement can severely limit how the application's strategies might refer to the variable.

Examining scope

A variable or strategy's scope is how visible it is. A variable is considered public scope if it is visible to and usable by any strategy in the application. A variable is scoped private to a module if it is available to all strategies within that module. A variable is considered to have a limited scope to that strategy if it may be used by only one method. True bugs in many Access applications may have a misconception about variable scope. In an Access VBA project, it is entirely possible to have two variables with the same name but different scopes. Access consistently uses the defined variable that is "closest" when there is doubt.

Determining a variable lifetime

Their lifetime is determined by their declaration, in the same way, that the position of their declaration determines their visibility. The lifespan of a variable determines when the application

309

can access it. Local variables are always present by default, but only while the process is running. The variable will be removed from the memory as soon as the process is complete and won't be available again.

Deciding on a variable's scope

All you have to do to determine the scope of a very is to minimize the scope of your variables. As a result, the majority of your variables will only be declared at the procedure level and will make use of the Dim keyword. Reducing the scope can also limit the number of sites where a variable can change, which can make it much simpler to identify issues as soon as they arise.

Using constants

There is one major difference between constants and variables which is the fact that a constant does not change values. If you at any point attempt to change the value of a constant after it have been declared, it will result in an error.

Declaring constants

Constants are declared with the use of the const keyword. The format for the declaration is as follows;

    [Public | Private] Const constname [As type] = constvalue

Utilizing competitors can help you improve the readability of your code and assist ensure that it is error-proof if a value is used more than once. It should be noted that constants made available only within the same procedure are those that are declared using the private keyword inside the process. It's also important to remember that constants have constant values, so when declaring constants, the static keyword is completely unnecessary.

Using a naming convention with constants

The same naming policy that is applied to variables is a very smart idea. When you prefix a constant's name, it makes it easier for you to understand its scope just before using it. To assist keep the names of your constants unique and error-free, you can also include a prefix when determining the data type of the constant. Any combination of upper- and lowercase characters can be used to declare constants. Constants are named according to the same guidelines that apply to variables and processes.

Working with arrays

An array is a very special type of variable. Rather than just keeping one block of memory, an array keeps various blocks of memory. The size of an array can be fixed or dynamic.

Fixed arrays

The size of a fixed array is specified in the Dim statement at the time of declaration and cannot be altered later. Fixing the upper bound index in parenthesis after the variable name is the simplest approach to declaring a fixed array. If you ever discover that your application seems to be consuming more memory than it needs to or that you are experiencing specific performance issues, make sure the memory in your array is not larger than what you need.

Dynamic arrays

The size of dynamic arrays can be altered considerably later in the process, and they are frequently declared without the use of any indices. When a dynamic array is declared, no memory is allocated until the dimensions are provided to initialize the array. When the array is declared, the data type is also set, and it cannot be altered. Use of the dynamic array is recommended if the size of the array you will be utilizing is unknown until runtime.

Array functions

VBA offers lots of useful functions that can be used with arrays some of which are; boundary functions, the array function, the split function, the join function,

Understanding Subs and functions

A VBA application's code is saved in modules, which are made up of procedures, as was previously mentioned. In VBA, there are two main categories of procedures: functions and subroutines also referred to as subprocedures (or subs). You can run the lines of code for functions and subs alike. The primary distinction between a procedure and a function is that the former will return a value upon call, meaning that the latter generates a value during execution and makes it accessible to the code that invoked it. However, a sub doesn't give back a value.

Understanding where to create a procedure

There are two places where a procedure can be created;

- **In a standard VBA module**: a sub or function is created in a standard module when the procedure will be shared by code in more than one form or report or by an object other than a form or report.
- **Behind a form or report**: if you are certain the code you are creating will be called by just one procedure or form then you should create the sub or function in the form or reports module.

Calling VBA procedures

VBA procedures can be called by their name or Call statement, or they can be placed in modules and called from events hidden behind forms and reports. Only functions are left with the opportunity to return values that could be assigned to variables once subroutines are called and completed. Keep in mind that depending on how the procedure is called, the syntax used to call subroutines with parameters may change.

Creating subs

Oftentimes, forms are always created in forms. Follow the steps below to create subs;

- Choose **the location** you would like to create the sub from the Design view.
- Click on **F4** to show the Property Sheet for the control.
- Click on the **After Update event property** in the Event tab of the Property Sheet and choose Event Procedure from the events drop-down list.
- Click on the **builder button** to open the VBA code editor.
- Close the **VBA window** and go back to the location you chose initially.

Creating Functions

Functions vary from subroutines in that capacities return a value. Although functions can be made behind individual forms or reports, ordinarily they're made in standard modules.

Handling parameters

Generally, the procedure handles parameters the same way it handles any other variable. They are utilized to transmit data to a procedure and have a name and data type. Parameters can also be used to extract data from a method. You may choose whatever name you like for a parameter.

Calling a function and passing parameters

A function call usually comes from a form or report of the event and at other times though rare from another procedure and the call does well by sending information as parameters.

Simplifying Code with Named Arguments

In general, parameters are handled by the procedure in the same manner as any other variable. They have a name and a data type, and they are used to send data to a process. Data extraction from a procedure is another usage for parameters. You are free to give a parameter to whatever name you choose.

Deploy an Access Application

For creating database applications, Access offers a feature-rich platform. A database application is computer software that offers a user interface that adheres to the application logic of business tasks in addition to a means of managing and storing data. Basic deployment planning, database application deployment, packaging and signing, and the Access Runtime environment are covered in this section.

Plan for deployment

The following are some questions you should ask yourself regarding how the application will be deployed before you start.

Should the data and the logic be separated?

Data management and application logic can be combined into a single file in an Access application. This is how an Access application is structured by default. The simplest deployment strategy involves combining data management and application functionality into a single file. However, this approach is riskier and only functions well when a small number of users are concurrently using the application. For instance, if the user accidentally deletes or corrupts the program file, data loss may result. Generally speaking, application logic and data administration should be kept apart. This enhances dependability and performance. Using the Access Database command (included in the Move Data group on the Database Tools tab) is one method of separating data and logic. Your database application will be divided into two Access files by this command: a front-end (for logic) and a back-end (for data). For instance, MySolution.accdb, a database, is divided into MySolution_fe.accdb and MySolution_be.accdb files. The back-end database is stored in a network folder or another shared place. One copy of the front-end file is sent to each user's machine. It is even possible to assign distinct front-end files to various users. Using a database server program (like Microsoft SQL Server) for data administration and Access for application logic is another technique to keep data management and application logic apart.

More reasons for separating data and logic can also include the following;

- **Data integrity and security**: The hazards associated with combining data and logic into a single file extends to the data as well. By utilizing NTFS security features on network folders, an Access application that separates logic and data files can contribute to data integrity and security protection. Permission to read, write, create, and delete must be granted to access users for the folder containing the front-end file. The front-end file itself, however, can have a distinct set of permissions applied to it. For instance, you might wish to give certain users read-only access while granting other users read/write access. Additional security features for your program, including limiting which users can access specific data, can be necessary. In this scenario, you might supply the application logic in Access and store and manage your application data on SQL Server or SharePoint.
- **Scalability**: The largest size an Access file may be is two gigabytes (GB). While 2GB can hold a significant quantity of text data, some programs might not be able to use it,

313

especially those that store attachments in database entries. Your application can handle more data if the logic and the data are kept apart. You may want to use many Access data files if you anticipate users storing a lot of data. For additional details regarding scalability, you should also go over the Access program standards.

- **Network capacity**: When data and logic are merged into a single file and numerous users are required to utilize the application simultaneously across a network, data corruption is more likely to happen. Furthermore, you are unable to optimize the network traffic that Access creates if you merge the data and the logic into a single Access file. You should separate the data and the logic in your application if numerous users will be accessing it concurrently across a network. You can do this by utilizing two or more Access files, or by using a database server product for the data and Access for the application logic.

What will the network environment be like?

A key to its success is selecting the appropriate Access database solution for your network environment. To assist you in selecting the best option for your needs, use the following criteria.

Home network

To share an Access database with a small number of users, you can utilize a single database on a home network that each user opens and uses.

Local Area Network (LAN)

A local area network, or LAN, is an internal network that is typically very fast but is only accessible within a small physical space, like a single room, building, or collection of buildings. It is recommended to partition the database, store the back-end database in a network folder, and distribute a copy of the front-end database to each user when numerous users are sharing the database over a local area network.

Wide Area Network (WAN)

A wide area network (WAN) can be configured in a variety of ways to cover a large geographic area. It is possible to have several offices dispersed throughout a city that are linked to satellites, leased lines, or public networks. A Virtual Private Network (VPN) is frequently used to enable safe remote access when traveling or at home. A WAN can be simply understood as something you use anytime you are connected to a LAN even when you are not inside of it.

Azure file shares

Azure file shares offer a method to use file shares over a network without requiring a file server; they are not a different kind of network. On the other hand, using an Azure file share may cause problems akin to those that occur when utilizing an Access split database across a wide area network.

Will users have access?

Your users can open and utilize the application just like any other Access database file if they have all installed Access on their computers. When you deploy your application, you can also deliver the Access Runtime software to users who do not have Access installed on their computers, if any or all of them.

Deploy an Access application

For the deployment of an Access application, there is a need for you to follow the tasks below.

Prepare the database as an application solution

To get your solution locked down, control navigation and startup, and then configure other very important choices, and then get the following done;

Tasks	More information
Choose whether to utilize a default form, a switchboard, a navigation form, or hyperlinks and command buttons to guide users through the user interface.	Set the default form that pops up when you launch an Access database, design a navigation form, customize the navigation pane, display or conceal object tabs, design, and also make use of a switchboard.
Decide if you would like to get the office ribbon and command menus customized.	Create a custom ribbon in Access, design custom menus and shortcut menus by making use of macros, employ the use of the custom toolbars, and startup configuration from earlier versions of Access.

Apply a consistent Office theme and background	Include an Office background, and alter the Office Theme.
Control database startup	Include a custom title or icon to a database, bypass startup choices when you launch a database, create a macro that executes when you open a database, and then command line switches for Microsoft Office products.
Set important properties and options	Configure startup properties and options in code, see or alter the properties for an Office file.
Modify regional configurations	Alter the windows regional configurations to alter the appearance of some data type.

Get the following done before you deploy;
- Do all you can to get the best performance out of your solution?
- Compact and fix the database.
- Backup the database so you will have an original and safe copy of the original database.
- Employ the use of the database documenter to print the design characteristics of database objects.
- Decide on how you want to have your file secured. There are various approaches you can choose to take;
    - Give the database a security certificate. See Demonstrate trustworthiness by incorporating a digital signature and choose which databases to believe. In the event that you choose to do this, choose the control scheme for your database's Message Bar.
    - If you do not want the front-end database to open in Protected View, store it in a trusted location to evade Trust Center inspection.
    - Get the database file encrypted.
    - To be sure that user cannot alter the design of forms, reports, or VBA code, think about making use of a compiled binary file (.accde).

Decide the file format to make use of;
Note that there are four Access file formats that you can choose to make use of when you deploy an application;

316

- .accdb: This is Access's default file format. When an application is deployed in this format, users have the greatest customization and navigation choices available to them. The. The.accde file format is what you should use if you want to make sure users don't alter the appearance of your program. Furthermore, if you package a.accdb file, it is difficult for a user to tell if it has been altered; to solve this, use the.accdc file format.
- .accdc: Another name for this format is an Access Deployment file. An application file and its digital signature are the two components of an Access Deployment file. Users are reassured by this file format that the application file has not been altered since it was packaged. This format can be used with an Access compiled binary file (.accde) or an Access file in the default format (.accdb). An Access Deployment file can include only one application file. You can package your application's logic and data files independently if they are separate.
- .accde: Another name for this type is a compiled binary file. A database application file that has all of the VBA code built and saved is known as a compiled binary file in Access. A compiled binary file for Access contains no VBA source code. A.accde file minimizes database space, assists with performance enhancements, and stops design and code changes. An Access built binary file can be opened with the Access Runtime. To open the binary file if the Runtime does not recognize the.accde file name extension, build a shortcut pointing to the Runtime and add the path of the binary file that has been compiled.

Installing and upgrade an Access front-end database

Each user must receive access to the front-end database when using a split database design. Take into account the following recommended practices to ensure everything goes smoothly:
- Make sure the front-end database opens in the appropriate version of Access and that each user has the appropriate version of the program. There are 32- and 64-bit versions of Access as well. Incorrect "bitness" settings can impact ActiveX controls, DLL library references, and Windows API calls.
- Make an installation package for any other files that could be needed, such as application-related files, batch files for setup and configuration, and database drivers.
- To enable the user to launch the Access solution fast, provide a Windows desktop shortcut. Add an icon, a description, a suitable shortcut name, and the folder path to the shortcut.
- When upgrades are needed, figure out how to replace the front-end database and redeploy it in an efficient manner. You should also retain file versions to monitor any changes. One possible use for VBA code would be to automatically check for updates and upgrade the program even before users launch it.
- Each client computer must also have the DSN file loaded in order to establish an ODBC connection using a file that provides the connection string. Another method to do away with the DSN file is to use VBA code to create a "DSN-less" connection.

Understand and download the Access Runtime

You can distribute Access apps that don't require users to install Access on their computers by including the Access Runtime, which is free to download from the Microsoft Download Center, with the applications. An Access database opens in runtime mode when you use the Access Runtime to open it. Runtime mode is an Access operating mode that prevents default access to several Access functionalities. On the other hand, runtime mode allows for the availability of certain of these inaccessible functions.

Below are the set of features that are unavailable in runtime mode;

- **Special keys**: keys to circumvent the databases launch options, such as Ctrl+Break, Ctrl+G, and the Shift key.
- **Navigation Pane**: Runtime mode does not provide access to the Navigation Pane. This makes it harder for users to access random objects within your database application. Runtime mode restricts what can be opened to only those things that you make visible to users, such as a navigation form. The Navigation Pane cannot be accessed in runtime mode.
- **The Ribbon**: The Ribbon is not accessible in runtime mode by default. This helps stop users from doing potentially dangerous tasks like connecting to new data sources or exporting data in ways you did not intend, as well as from creating or changing database objects. In runtime mode, the basic Ribbon tabs cannot be accessed. On the other hand, you can make a personalized Ribbon and link it to a document or spreadsheet.
- **Design view and Layout view**: Runtime mode does not provide any database objects with Design or Layout views. This lessens the possibility that users will alter the appearance of items in your database application. In runtime mode, neither Design view nor Layout view can be enabled.
- **Help**: Integrated Help is not accessible in runtime mode by default. Some of the standard integrated Access Help may not be useful to users of your application and may even confuse or frustrate them because you determine what functionality is offered in your runtime mode application. To go along with your runtime mode application, you might make your own unique Help file.

You shouldn't rely just on runtime mode to secure a database application, even though it does restrict access to navigation and design elements. It might be feasible for a user to start a runtime database application on a PC running the full version of Access and then modify its appearance or carry out other unauthorized operations by opening the application with all of its features enabled. You can still allow users to move your database application to a machine with the full version of Access installed and open the runtime database application as a regular database application, even if you only deploy your database application on machines without the full version of Access installed.

Create an installation package

You can make use of the Windows Installer or look for a third-party program that builds installation packages. **Put in mind the following facts as you move to design and also sign a package;**

- Demonstrating trust can be achieved by signing and packaging a database. The signature verifies that the database has not been altered when you or your users receive the package. You can activate the content if you have faith in the author.
- Only databases saved in the.accdb file format are eligible for the Package-and-Sign feature.
- A package can only include one database file.
- Not only macros or code modules, but all the objects in the database file are code signed when you package and sign it. To speed up downloads, the package file is additionally compressed during the packaging and signing process.
- The signed package and the extracted database are no longer connected once the database has been extracted from the package.
- Packages signed with your self-signed certificates will always be trusted if you use one of your self-signed certificates to sign a database package and then select Trust all from the publisher when you open that package.
- When you open the database, its contents will be activated immediately if you extracted it to a trusted location. A default disabling of some database material may occur if you select a non-trusted site.

How to use the database in a signed package file and how to generate a signed package file are covered in the following sections. You need to have at least one security certificate available in order to finish these tasks. If your machine does not already have a certificate installed, you may either get a commercial certificate or generate one with the SelfCert tool.

Design a signed package

- Launch the database you would like to have packaged and signed.
- Choose the **File tab** and then choose **Save As.**
- Beneath Database File Types, choose **Package and Sign and then choose Save As.**
- In the dialog box of **Select Certificate,** choose a digital certificate, and then select **OK.** The Create Microsoft Office Access Signed Package dialog box will be displayed.
- In the list for Save in, choose your preferred location for your signed database package.
- Insert your preferred name for the signed package in the box for the File name, and then choose Create. Access will then design the .accdc file and then position it in the location of your choice.

CHAPTER 26

UNDERSTANDING THE ACCESS EVENT MODEL

You can discover that you have to perform the same tasks again when working with a database system. As an alternative to repeatedly performing the same procedures, you can automate the process with VBA macros. Throughout your application, you can utilize VBA code to automate these tasks. A vast array of commands for working with form controls, table records, and virtually anything else may be found in the VBA language. The work with procedures in forms, reports, and standard modules that was started in earlier chapters is carried over into this chapter.

Programming Events

An access event occurs as a result of or as a result of a user's activity. When a user moves from one record to the next in a form, dismisses a report, or clicks a command button on a form, an Access event happens. Even simply moving the mouse causes a series of events to occur.
You can categorize Access events into seven distinct groups which are;
- Windows events.
- Keyboard events.
- Mouse events.
- Focus events.
- Data events
- Print events
- Error and timing events

Understanding how events trigger VBA code

You can create an event procedure that executes whenever a user executes one of the many different types of events that Access recognizes. Access is able to respond to events because of unique form and control features. Reports contain a similar set of events that have been modified to meet the demands and specifications of the report.

Creating event procedures

Event processes in Access are carried out using an object's event attributes. With Access, you can use event properties to connect VBA code to an object's events. For instance, the On Open attribute is connected to a report or form that displays on the screen. To add an event method to a form or report, choose the event property in the object's Property Sheet. If there isn't an event procedure for the property yet, a builder button and a drop-down arrow appear in the property's box.

Identifying Common Events

Many distinct Access objects can cause certain events to be triggered. Microsoft has gone to great lengths to ensure that these events behave consistently regardless of the object that triggers them. The table below covers some of the most popular events used by Access programmers. The majority of these events are applicable to forms and all of the various controls that you might include in an Access form.

Event	Event Type	When the Event is Triggered
Click	Mouse	When the user presses and then releases the left button of the mouse on an object.
DbClick	Mouse	When the user presses and releases the left button of the mouse two times on an object.
MouseDown	Mouse	When the user presses the button of the mouse while the pointer is on an object.
MouseMove	Mouse	When the user moves the mouse pointer over an object.
MouseUp	Mouse	When the user releases an already pressed mouse button while the pointer is on an object.
MouseWheel	Mouse	When the user spins the wheel of the mouse.
KeyDown	Keyboard	When the user presses any key on the keyboard when the object has focus or when the user makes use of a SendKeys macro action

KeyUp	Keyboard	When the user releases a pressed key immediately after using a SendKeys macro action.

Because the mouse and keyboard are the user's primary way of inputting information and giving guidance to an application, it's no surprise that these events are all linked to them. Not every item responds to each of these events, but when an object does, the event behaves in the same way.

Form event procedures

When dealing with forms, you can design event processes that are based on events that occur at the form, section, or control level. When you tie an event procedure to a form-level event, the action is applied to the entire form whenever the event occurs (such as when you go to another record or leave the form). To make your form respond to an event, create an event procedure and attach it to the form's event attribute. Numerous properties can be used at the form level to initiate event actions.

Essential form events

Many different events trigger access forms. Because of their specialized nature, you'll never develop code for most of these events. However, there are some events that you'll implement in your Access apps over and over again.

Event	When the Event Is Triggered
Open	When a form is opened, but the first record is not displayed yet
Load	When a form is loaded into memory but not yet opened
Unload	When a form is closed and the records unload, and before the form is removed from the screen
Close	When a form is closed and removed from the screen

Active	When an open form receives the focus, becoming the active window
Deactive	When a different window becomes the active window, but before it loses focus
Timer	When a specified time interval passes. The interval (in milliseconds) is specified by the TimerInterval property.

Form mouse and key-board events

Access forms also respond to some mouse and keyboard events. The table below better describes this;

Event	When the Event is Triggered
Click	When the user presses and also releases the left mouse button.
Double Click	When the user presses and releases (clicks) the left mouse button twice on a form
Mouse Down	When the user presses the mouse button while the pointer is on a form
MouseMove	When the user moves the mouse pointer over an area of a form

MouseUp	When the user releases a pressed mouse button while the pointer is on a form
KeyDown	When the user presses any key on the keyboard when a form has focus or when the user uses a SendKeys macro action
KeyUp	When the user releases a pressed key or immediately after the user uses a SendKeys macro action
KeyPress	When the user presses and releases a key on a form that has the focus or when the user uses a SendKeys macro

Form data events

Access forms are mostly used to display data. As a result, Access forms have a number of events that are directly tied to the data management of the form. Almost every time you work on an Access program, you'll come across event routines built for these events. The Current event is fired upon a form's data refresh. This typically occurs when the user navigates away from the form to a different record in the supporting record set. Often, formatting controls or computations based on form data are performed via the Current event. Data can be transferred from a form to an underlying data source using the BeforeInsert and AfterInsert events. When Access is ready to send data, BeforeInsert fires, and once the entry has been committed to the data source, AfterInsert fires. Data can be transferred from a form to an underlying data source using the BeforeInsert and AfterInsert events.

Control event procedures

Events can also be brought about by controls. Control events are commonly used to validate data when the user modifies the control's contents or to change the control's appearance. When a user interacts with a control, control events also influence how the mouse and keyboard function with it. While the BeforeUpdate event of a form does not fire until the form is moved to another record, the BeforeUpdate event of a control fires as soon as the focus leaves the control (that is, before data is transferred from the control to the recordset underlying the form, allowing you to

324

cancel the event if data validation fails). (The form's BeforeUpdate commits the entire record to the data source.)

Report event procedures

Similar to forms, reports use event processes to react to particular occurrences. Access reports support events for each segment as well as the overall report. Access reports with individual controls do not cause events to occur. A report that has an event method added to it will execute code each time it opens, closes, or prints. Every section (header, footer, and so on) contains events that occur when the report is generated or printed.

Event Property	When the Event is Triggered
Open	When the event is opened before printing
Close	When the report is closed and taken off the screen.
Active	When the report receives the focus and hence becomes the active window.
Deactivate	When a different window becomes active.
Page	When the report alters pages
Error	When a runtime error is produced in Access.

Even though users do not interact with reports in the same way that they do with forms, events are nevertheless important in report design. When you open a report with no data, the findings are usually incorrect. A title and no detailed information may be displayed in the report. It may also display #error values for missing data.

Report section event procedures

Access provides three unique event attributes for usage with report sections in addition to the form's event elements.

Event	When the Event is Triggered
Format	When the section has been pre-formatted in memory before it is being sent to the printer.
Print	This is when the section is being sent to the printer.
Retreat	This is immediately after the format event but before the Print event. This usually occurs when there is a need for Access to backup previous sections on a page in order to take up several formatting.

Paying Attention to Event Sequence

An apparently innocent action taken by the user can set off a chain reaction of events. For example, each time a key on the keyboard is touched by the user, the KeyDown, KeyPress, and KeyUp events are raised. Pressing the left mouse button causes the MouseDown, MouseUp, and Click events to be triggered. You have total control over which events you program in your Access programs as a VBA developer. Things don't just happen. Events fire in a pattern that is predictable, depending on whichever control is generating the events. One of the hardest things about working with events can be remembering the order in which they happen. It can seem counterintuitive that the Enter event occurs before the GotFocus event.

Looking at common event sequences

Below are the series of events for the most frequently encountered form scenarios;

- Opening and closing forms
- When a form opens: Open (form) → Load (form) → Resize (form) → Activate (form) → Current (form) → Enter (control) → GotFocus (control)
- When a form closes: Exit (control) → LostFocus (control) → Unload (form) → Deactivate (form) → Close (form)
- Changes in focus

When the focus moves from one form to another: Deactivate (form1) → Activate (form2)

When the focus moves to a control on a form: Enter → GotFocus

When the focus leaves a form control: Exit → LostFocus

When the focus moves from control1 to control2: Exit (control1) →   LostFocus (control1) → Enter (control2) → GotFocus (control2)

When the focus leaves the record in which data has changed, but   before entering the next record: BeforeUpdate (form) → AfterUpdate (form) → Exit (control) → LostFocus (control) → Current (form)

When the focus moves to an existing record in Form view: BeforeUpdate (form) → AfterUpdate (form) → Current (form)

- Mouse events
- o When the user presses and releases (clicks) a mouse button while the mouse pointer is on a form control: MouseDown → MouseUp → Click
- o When the user moves the focus from one control to another by clicking the second control:
Control1:   Exit   →   LostFocus
Control2: Enter → GotFocus → MouseDown → MouseUp → Click
- o When the user double-clicks a control other than a command button: MouseDown → MouseUp → Click → DblClick → MouseUp

Writing simple form and control event procedures

Writing simple ways to verify a form's or control's event sequence is easy. Using the information above, decide which application event should be harnessed. An event procedure associated with an event that happens too late or too early to gather the data needed by the application is usually the cause of unexpected behavior. Recall that you ought to write code exclusively for occasions that are pertinent to your application. Code-free events are ignored by Access and have no effect on the program. Moreover, it is highly probable that at some point you may write the wrong event for a certain task. You may be tempted to add code to the Enter event in order to change a control's appearance. (Many developers change the control's BackColor or ForeColor to make it easier for the user to see which control is focused.) You'll quickly find that the Enter event is not a reliable sign of when control has taken focus.

Opening a form with an event procedure

Most applications need a lot of forms and reports to finish their business operations. In order to facilitate user navigation, applications usually include a switchboard form. This eliminates the need for users to navigate the database container in order to determine which forms and reports fulfill specific duties. A number of command buttons on the switchboard are labeled with the objective of the form or report that is being opened.

Running an event procedure when closing a form

When you close or leave a form, you may want to do something with it. For example, you might want Access to keep track of who has used the form, or you might want the Print dialog box to close every time a user closes the main form. Simply utilize the Form Close event to accomplish this. Although it isn't an error to try to close a form that isn't currently open, it's a good practice to check if an object is available before performing an operation on it.

Using an event procedure to confirm record deletion

Having a Delete button on the form is a better practice even though you may remove a record in a form by using the Delete button on the Records group on the Home tab of the Ribbon. Because it provides a visual representation of how to delete a record, the Erase button is more user-friendly. Furthermore, a command button gives you more control over the deletion process because you may incorporate code to check the deletion before it is completed. Alternatively, to make sure that removing the record won't destroy the link to it in another database table; you might need to do a referential integrity check.

Activity

1. How do events trigger VBA code?
2. Create event procedures.
3. What are the common events?
4. Report event procedures.
5. Report section event procedures.
6. Operate a form with the use of an event procedure.

CHAPTER 27
DEBUGGING ACCESS APPLICATIONS

Like any other programming language, fixing a VBA error or an application issue can be difficult and time-consuming. The amount of organization in the code and the adherence to basic conventions such as giving variables and methods descriptive names can make it challenging to find even minor coding errors. Thankfully, Access includes a full suite of debugging tools to make life simpler. These tools can help you identify where a coding error occurs, save time by assisting in understanding how the code is organized and how it is executed from procedure to process. This will pay close attention to the bugs that seriously impair your application.

Organizing VBA Code

The first step in troubleshooting your code is to avoid coding issues in the first place. It should come as no surprise that your coding practices have a major influence on the kind and quantity of errors you find in your applications. In VBA code, straightforward coding principles can frequently eliminate all but the most challenging syntactical and logical errors.

- **Use a naming convention:** A consistent naming system can aid in the detection of problems that might otherwise go undetected.
- **Limit scopes for variables:** By default, variables are created at the procedure level, and the scope is only increased when the logic of your code necessitates it. Keep your variables with a global scope in their own module. Consider modifying your code when the list of global variables grows too long.
- **Keep your procedures short:** Your code will be much easier to manage if you have many little procedures rather than a few large ones.
  Consider breaking up your operations into smaller ones and calling each one from the main procedure if they get too lengthy to fit on a single screen.
- **Don't repeat yourself:** If you find yourself repeating the same code again and over, think about breaking the code up into separate procedures and passing arguments from the event procedure. It will save you time and prevent mistakes if you need to make changes—you just have to do it once.
- **Compile often:** Do not wait until the full module or project has been written before compiling it. After you've written or updated numerous lines of code, compile your project. When you're writing your process, you'll have a lot of knowledge about what it does and where it's utilized, so it's the perfect time to identify problems.

Testing Your Applications

Each time you depart the VBA Editor to execute code or switch from Design to Normal view on a form or report, you test your application. Every time you edit a property in a form or notification and move your cursor to another property or control, you're testing the property you've altered.

329

Testing is the process of determining whether your program functions as intended or at all. You've found that an application doesn't function properly when you launch it due to a problem. The process of finding and resolving coding mistakes is known as debugging. Most problems with the design of a query, forms, and reports are obvious. You can tell you have an issue when a query returns inaccurate data, a form or report won't open, or it will open with an error notice displayed. Access often produces an error when you execute forms and reports if it finds something that is obviously incorrect. It can be challenging, nonetheless, to locate a VBA code flaw precisely and figure out how to remedy it. With VBA code, you're pretty much on your own when it comes to finding and fixing mistakes. Thankfully, there are plenty of features in the editor to help you.

Testing functions

Functions are much easier to test than other operations because they return values. It is best to test your function exactly as written, as this will identify any problems early on and make them easier to fix. Finding a bug in a function that spreads to a form control could be more challenging. Writing tests also makes you think about your functions' logic from other angles.

Compiling VBA code

There is just one way to compile your complete application;
- Open **the compiler**, and then choose **Debug Compile Database Name** from the Modules toolbar in the VBA editor window. To reach the Debug menu, you must have a module open. To ensure that all code is stored in a compiled state, you should always use the Compile Database Name command.

It may take a while to compile complicated programs, so you should only do so right before releasing your Access applications to end users or running benchmark testing. When you choose Debug Compile Database Name, your project's name shows. When you initially created or saved your database file, you gave it this name. If you later rename the database file, the project name remains unchanged. To change the database name, select Tools Properties in the module window. The database name setting is available in the database Properties dialog box.

Traditional Debugging Techniques

Since Access 1.0, two frequently utilized debugging approaches have been offered. The first is to use MsgBox commands to display variable values, procedure names, and other information. Inserting Debug. Print is the second most frequent technique.

Using MsgBox

The MsgBox keyword causes code to pause while displaying a string in a box that needs to be cleared in order for the code to continue. The message box appears immediately on the user interface, so you don't need to flick to the immediate window or have it open in order to see it. There is just one line of code needed to use the MsgBox statement, making it easy to use.

Using Debug.Print

The Debug is the second most used debugging method.Output messages to the immediate window by printing. Unlike the MsgBox statement, you can hide the Debug with no effort. Print the output from the user interface. Troubleshoot.Print only prints to the immediate window, therefore you don't have to worry about debug messages showing up for end users as they never see the immediate window.

Using the Access Debugging Tools

Microsoft Access includes a plethora of debugging tools in addition to additional capabilities. With the help of these tools, you can monitor the development of your VBA code, do various debugging tasks, and halt the execution of a statement to examine the value of variables at that particular moment.

Running code with the Immediate Window

The Immediate window shows information from debugging statements in your code or commands typed into the window directly.

To open the immediate window, click the button below.
- Select the **Immediate window (CTRL+G)** from the View menu.
- To run code in the immediate window, press **Ctrl+Enter**.

In the Immediate window, type a line of code.
- To run the statement, press **ENTER**.

Use the Immediate window to do the following:
- Problematic or newly written code should be tested.
- While an application is running, you can query or modify the value of a variable. Assign a new value to the variable while execution is halted, just as you would in code.
- While an application is running, you can query or alter the value of a property.
- Procedures are called in the same way they are called in code.
- While the program is running, look at the debugging output.

Suspending execution with breakpoints

You use a breakpoint to halt the execution of a procedure at a certain statement, such as when you think there are problems. When you no longer require breakpoints to interrupt execution, you remove them.

To set a breakpoint
- Place **the insertion point** anyplace in a process line where you want the procedure to stop running.
- Choose **Toggle Breakpoint (F9)** from the Debug menu, or click on the **next button** close to the statement in the Margin Indicator Bar (if visible) or the toolbar shortcut:

The line is set to the breakpoint color selected on the Editor Format tab of the Options dialog box, and the breakpoint is added. When you set a breakpoint on a line with numerous statements separated by colons **(:)**, the break happens at the first statement on the line.

To get rid of a breakpoint

- Place the **insertion point** on any line of the method that has a breakpoint.
- Toggle **Breakpoint (F9)** from the Debug menu, or click next to the statement in the Margin Indicator Bar (if visible).
- The breakpoint has been reset, and the highlighting has been deleted.

To remove all breakpoints from the app

- Clear **All Breakpoints (CTRL+SHIFT+F9)** from the Debug menu.

Looking at variables with the Locals window

To declare a local variable inside a process, use Dim, Static, or ReDim (for arrays only). There may be more than one process that uses the variable temp, but since each variable is specific to its own procedure, it functions independently of the others and can have distinct values. The Dim statement's specified local variables are only good for that part of the process. Static local variables are ones that remain valid for the duration of the application. You'll see an example of how a static variable could benefit your code, and you may want to keep a variable value constant throughout the program. You can change the values of simple variables (numeric, string, and so on) in the Locals window by selecting the Value column in a variable's row and putting in a new value for the variable. This makes experimenting with different combinations of variable values in your application a breeze.

Setting watches with the Watches window

You can declare the variables you want to watch as you iterate through your code in the Watches pane. A monitored variable's value fluctuates dynamically while the code executes. (You'll need to be at a breakpoint in order to truly view the values.) One benefit of the Watches window is that it does not require the variables to come from the local method. In actuality, the variables in the Watch box could originate from anyplace within the application.

Setting a watch involves a few more steps than setting a breakpoint or utilizing the Locals window.

- Select **View** then click on **Watch Window** to display the Watches window.
- Select **Debug** then click on **Add Watch** or right-click **anywhere** in the Watches window and choose Add Watch from the shortcut menu
- Insert **the name** of the variable or any other expression in the Expression text box.

Using conditional watches

While watching variables in the Locals or Watches windows might be entertaining, attempting to see anything unexpected can take up a lot of time that could be better spent on other things.

Generally, it is significantly more efficient to set a conditional watch on a variable and tell the VBA engine to break when the condition you've created is met. Another technique to utilize conditional watches is to use compound conditions (X = True and Y = False) and to trigger a break if a value is different from what is entered in the Expression text box.

Using the Call Stack window

By using the Call Stack pane, you may see the function or procedure calls that are currently on the stack. The method and function calls are shown in the Call Stack window in chronological order. An effective tool for analyzing and understanding an application's execution route is a call stack. The Call Stack window might not be able to display the appropriate information for a piece of the call stack when debugging symbols aren't available for that portion of the call stack.

Trapping Errors in Your Code

Use the Error event to find errors on an Access form or report. When a user tries to enter text in a Date/Time field, for instance, the Error event is triggered. An error event procedure is triggered when you add it to an Employees form and then enter a text value in the HireDate field. The Error event method receives the DataErr integer input. The number of the Access error that happened is specified in the DataErr argument of an Error event function. Checking the value of the DataErr argument within the event process is the only way to find out how many mistakes were made.

Understanding error trapping

VBA raises an error when it discovers an error in your code. When an error occurs, several things happen, the most important of which is that the VBA engine looks for an On Error statement and the Err object is created. When you want VBA to react in a specific way when an error occurs, you use the On Error keywords in your code.

On Error Resume Next

The statement that follows the one that resulted in the run-time error, or the statement that follows the procedure's most recent call out, is where execution resumes when the On Error Resume Next statement is executed. This statement permits the program to run even though a run-time error has occurred. You can put the error-handling method where the error would occur in the procedure, instead of moving control to a different part of it. An On Error Resume Next statement becomes inactive when another procedure is called, thus you should run an On Error Resume Next statement in each called routine if you want inline error handling in that routine.

On Error Goto 0

On Error GoTo 0 disables the current procedure's error handling. Even if the method comprises a line numbered 0, it does not indicate line 0 as the start of the error-handling code. When a procedure is exited without an On Error GoTo 0 statement, the error handler is immediately disabled.

On Error GoTo Label

An error-handling procedure is initiated on the line where the On Error GoTo label statement is positioned. Turn on the error-handling function before the first line where an error might happen. Execution proceeds to the line indicated by the label parameter in the event that an error arises while the error handler is active. The label parameter should indicate the line on which the error-handling procedure should start.

The Resume keyword

Resumes can also be used independently. When Resume is used in isolation, the error is raised once more and the program goes back to the line that caused it. This is useful for handling problems and inspecting the line that caused the error, but if you don't use caution, it might result in an endless cycle of errors being raised and restarted. To point program execution in a new direction, a resume and label can be coupled.

The Err object

A thorough explanation of the problem and a solution should be provided to the user whenever they encounter an error in your program. VBA programmers may easily identify and trigger Microsoft Windows-specific issues with the help of the Err object. In essence, the Err (short for error) object logs any issues that arise during the current process. This information is stored in properties.

The following are the most prevalent Err properties:

- The current error is described in the description field.
- The current error number is contained in the number (0 to 65,535).
- The name of the object that caused the error is found in the source field.

There may be times when an error occurs in your software that is exactly the same as one reported in an error description, but the associated error number is not generated. Errors can be introduced using the Err object's Raise function. When a specific error condition is met, the Raise method shows the user a dialog box. The Raise method receives a number as an argument.

Including error handling in your procedures

Every time your software communicates with the outside world, you should include error handling to handle unforeseen inputs or outputs. One way to provide error handling is to write your own error-handling procedures. The traffic cops in your program are error-handling procedures. These processes are capable of handling any kind of programming problem or error caused by human error that you can think of. They should not only detect the issue but also attempt to correct it or at the very least provide the program or interacting humans the opportunity to do so.

To start error handling in a process;

- Use the **On Error GoTo statement** to indicate that an error-handling function will be used. This statement can be inserted anywhere in your method, but it's best if it's near the top, just after any procedure-level variable declarations.

Executing the Exit Function or Exit Sub instructions is required before program execution moves into the error-handling procedure. If these statements are not present, an error-free procedure also runs the error handler. If there is no Exit statement, a procedure that runs error-free also runs the error-handling mechanism. Typing the error handler's name and a colon (:) is the initial step in handling errors. The error handler's code for handling the error is subsequently created.

PART VII

ADVANCED ACCESS PROGRAMMING TECHNIQUES

CHAPTER 28

ACCESSING DATA WITH VBA

Applications can be created using bound forms and reports, but there is a lot more flexibility when using Visual Basic for Applications (VBA) code to access and modify data directly rather than through a bound application. A small amount of VBA code that retrieves and manipulates data using ActiveX data objects (ADO) or data access objects (DAO) can be used to complete any task that can be completed with bound forms and controls. In-depth examples of working with DAO, SQL, or ADO-based procedures that modify database data are provided in this chapter.

Working with Data

The most popular object model among Visual Basic programmers for accessing databases is ADO. While ADO is an excellent architecture with many benefits of its own, DAO excels in the context of Access databases because it has native database connectivity. Whenever the data or underlying schema needs to be altered, other programming languages, such as Visual Basic, Delphi, and others, must establish an explicit link to the data source in order to make the necessary changes. This is because these applications lack an integrated connection to the data source, in contrast to Access. Through an implicit connection that Access maintains with the Access database engine, ODBC, or ISAM data source it is connected to, DAO enables you to modify data and structure. DAO is simply the greatest solution for accessing Access databases because Access is the only program that has linked tables. In fact, it cannot be done natively with any other data access type. The best paradigm for dealing with and updating the objects and structure of the Access database engine is currently DAO, which has developed in lockstep with Jet and the Access database engine. Because of its close integration with Access, DAO provides faster access to Access databases than either ADO or the Jet Replication Objects (JRO).

This may all sound like marketing hype, but to qualify the advantages of DAO over other models, consider the following:

- ADO connections are limited to one database at a time, but DAO allows you to link (connect) to several databases at the same time.
- The dbDenyWrite option of the OpenRecordset function in the DAO lets you open a table while preventing other users from opening the same table with write access. The ADO Connection object's adModeShareDenyWrite constant operates at the connection level rather than the table level.
- Through the use of the dbDenyRead option in the OpenRecordset function, the DAO permits you to open a table while blocking other users from opening it. Only at the connection level may the ADO Connection object's adModeShareDenyRead constant be set.

- While ADO does not allow you to specify the PID (Personal IDentifier), DAO does allow you to create users and groups.
- While ADO lacks an AllPermissions property and requires you to list every user's group, DAO has an AllPermissions attribute that lets you access an object's implicit privileges.
- A private session of the Access database engine can be launched using PrivDBEngine, something that ADO does not enable.
- DAO lets you construct multi-value lookup fields with new complicated data types. A multivalued lookup field in an embedded record set is a single field that has multiple values that it can store.

Understanding DAO Objects

Working your way down the object hierarchy in code, you refer to objects in the DAO hierarchy. As you may remember from our last meeting, a collection is a container for a set of related objects. You might have to go through a number of collections before finding the item you want to work on because many DAO object collections contain other collections. This is a very predictable and systematic method of accessing data and schema. Every DAO object—aside from the DBEngine object—is housed inside a separate collection. Collections are individual objects when their names end in s when they are named in the singular, but individual objects are collections when their names finish in s when they are named in the plural. A connection to a database or other data source is represented by the Database object. It belongs to the Databases collection of the Workspace object, which is a container for a collection of Database objects that represent connections to one or more databases.

The DAO DBEngine object

The DBEngine object, a property of the Access Application object, represents the top-level object in the DAO paradigm. Unlike many other DAO objects, you cannot create more instances of the DBEngine object, even if it contains all other objects in the DAO object hierarchy. The two primary collections in the DBEngine object are Workspaces and Errors.

The DAO Workspace object

Depending on the database type, a workspace is a specified user session that includes open databases, permits transactions, and offers user and group-level security. All of your workspaces are kept in the Workplaces collection because you can have many workspaces active at once. You can utilize the Microsoft Access database engine in the Microsoft Access workspace to access Microsoft Jet databases (MDB files built in previous versions), Microsoft Access database engine databases (ACCDB files made in Access 2007), and installable ISAM or ODBC data sources. The following groups, items, and features are supported by Microsoft Access workspaces.

The DAO Database object

An open database is represented by a Database object.

To manipulate an open database, you utilize the Database object and its methods and properties.
- You can conduct an action query in any database by using the Execute method.
- To connect to an ODBC data source, set the Connect property in order to establish a connection. .
- To limit the amount of time it takes for a query to execute against an ODBC data source, use the QueryTimeout property.
- To find out how many records were affected by an action query, use the RecordsAffected property.
- To run a select query and produce a Recordset object, use the OpenRecordset function.
- To find out which version of a database engine built the database, use the Version property.

There is no automatic establishment of links to the designated external files when you access a database that has linked tables. Use the TableDef or Field objects in the table, or open a Recordset object. If there is an issue linking to these tables, it becomes a trappable error. The database might only be accessible to another user, or you might need authorization to access it. These circumstances give rise to trappable errors. When a method that declares a Database object is finished, all open Recordset objects and local Database instances are closed. There won't be any trappable errors, but all pending transactions will be rolled back and any outstanding updates will be lost. You should explicitly finish any open transactions or updates and close the Recordset and Database objects before leaving operations that declare. When using the OpenDatabase method, there's no need to specify the DBEngine object.

The DAO TableDef object

The stored definition of a base table or a linked table is represented by a TableDef object (Microsoft Access workspaces only). A TableDef object and its methods and properties are used to manipulate a table definition.

You can, for example:
- Analyze the local, linked, or external database table's field and index structure.
- Use the Connect and SourceTableName properties to set or return information about linked tables, and use the RefreshLink method to update connections to linked tables.
- Use the ValidationText and ValidationRule properties to set or return validation conditions.
- Use the OpenRecordset method to create a table, dynaset, dynamic, snapshot, or forward-only type Recordset object based on the table description.

The DAO QueryDef object

In a Microsoft Access database engine database, a QueryDef object is a stored definition of a query. To build a new QueryDef object, use the CreateQueryDef method. In a Microsoft Access workspace, if you supply a string as the name argument or specifically modify the new QueryDef object's Name property to a non-zero-length string, a permanent QueryDef will be created and appended to the QueryDefs collection before being saved to disk. You can either directly change the Name attribute to a zero-length string or supply a zero-length string as the name parameter to build a temporary QueryDef object. Unlike permanent QueryDef objects, temporary QueryDef objects are not added to the QueryDefs collection or saved to disk. For queries that must be run repeatedly at run time but do not need to be saved to disk, temporary QueryDef objects are helpful.

The DAO Recordset object

The records in a base table or the records returned by a query are represented by a Recordset object. Recordset objects are used to manipulate data at the record level in a database. When you utilize DAO objects, you nearly exclusively manipulate data via Recordset objects. Records (rows) and fields are used to create all Recordset objects (columns).

Recordset objects are divided into five categories:

- **Table-type recordset:** is a coded representation of a base table that can be used to add, edit, or delete records from a single database table (Microsoft Access workspaces only).
- **Dynaset-type Recordset:** the outcome of a query on records that can be updated. A dynamic set of records that you may utilize to add, edit, or remove entries from underlying database tables is called a Dynaset Recordset object. Fields from one or more database tables can be included in a Dynaset recordset object. This type is corresponding to an ODBC keyset cursor.
- **Snapshot-type Recordset:** a static copy of a set of records that you can use to find data or generate reports. A snapshot-type Recordset object can contain fields from one or more tables in a database but can't be updated. This type corresponds to an ODBC static cursor.
- **Dynamic-type Recordset:** a query result set from one or more base tables in which you can add, change, or delete records from a row-returning query.
- **Forward-only-type Recordset:** like a snapshot, with the exception that there isn't a cursor. Only forwarding through records is possible. When you just need to make one pass through a result set, this enhances performance. This type is equivalent to a forward-only ODBC cursor.

Navigating recordsets

A data structure with rows and columns of data is called a record set. Obviously, the columns are fields and the rows are records. DAO offers ways to navigate a record set for convenience of use. When viewing a table or query results as a datasheet, you can navigate up, down, left, and right via the Datasheet view of the recordset using the arrow keys or the vertical and horizontal scroll bars. Recordsets support the concept of a current record pointer. There is never more than one current record in a series of records. Whether you travel through the rows of a record set or make changes to it, your code only affects the current record.

Deleting the record set end or beginning

You can delete an existing record from a table or Recordset object of type dynaset by using the Delete method. You cannot remove records from a snapshot-type Recordset object. When you use the Delete method, the Access database engine removes the current record instantly and without prompting you. You have to use the MoveNext method to move to the next record when you delete a record because it doesn't instantly become the current record. Once you have moved beyond the deleted record, you won't be able to get back to it.

Counting records

It's possible that you'll choose a criterion that produces too many records for you to handle effectively. The number of records in the record set is indicated by the RecordsCount property of the Recordset objects. To find out if a record set has any records or not, RecordCount is a helpful tool. RecordCount penalizes performance on large recordsets, which is its only drawback. The Recordset object pauses execution while it counts the number of records in its collection.

The DAO Field objects (recordsets)

An instance of a data column with a common data type and set of properties is called a Field object. The Fields collections of the Index, QueryDef, Relation, and TableDef objects provide the specifications for the fields that those objects represent. The Fields collection of a Recordset object represents field objects in a row of data, or in a record. To read and modify the values for the fields in the Recordset object's current record, use the Field objects within the Recordset object. In a Microsoft Access workspace, fields are manipulated using Field objects and their associated methods and properties. When you access data from the current record as part of a Recordset object, it appears in the Value property of the Field object. To modify data in the Recordset object, you often make an indirect reference to the Value property of the Field object in the Recordset object's Fields collection rather than directly referencing the Fields collection.

Understanding ADO Objects

Given that it is a programming model, ActiveX Data Objects is independent of any specific back-end engine. But as of right now, the only engine that supports the ADO model is OLE-DB. In addition to an ODBC OLE-DB Provider, there are other native OLE-DB providers available. Programs written in C++ and Visual Basic link to databases such as SQL Server and others use ADO. An Azure SQL Database hosted in the cloud can also be connected to it. Microsoft ActiveX Data Objects (ADO) let your client applications access and modify data from multiple sources using an

OLE DB provider. Its simplicity, quickness, low memory overhead, and small disk footprint are its key benefits. Essential features for Web-based and client/server applications are offered by ADO.

The ADO Connection object

A Connection object represents a single data source session. It may be equivalent to an actual network connection to the server in a client/server database system. Some collections, methods, or properties of a Connection object may not be available depending on the capability enabled by the provider.

The Connection and Recordset objects in ActiveX Data Objects (ADO) can be opened in a number of ways;

- Setting the ConnectionString property to a valid Connect string then calling the Open () method. This connection string is known to be provider-dependent.
- Passing a valid Connect string to the first argument of the Open () method.
- Passing a valid Command object into the first argument of a Recordset's Open method.
- By passing the ODBC Data source name and if necessary, user-id and password to the Connection Object's Open () method.

The ADO Command object

A specific command that you want to conduct against a data source can be described with the aid of the ADO command object. Use a Command object to conduct a bulk operation, change a database's structure, or query a database and return records in a Recordset object. Be aware that, depending on the provider's capabilities, certain Command collections, methods, or properties may cause an error when referenced to.

The ADO Recordset object

The ADO recordset object represents the entire set of records from a base table or the output of a command. The Recordset object always refers to a single record in the set as the current record. To manipulate data received from a provider, recordset objects are needed. Recordset objects are the foundation for almost all ADO data manipulation operations. Fields and records (rows) (columns) make up each object in the Recordset. Be aware that some Recordset features or methods might not be available due to supplier capacity.

Writing VBA Code to Update a Table

Using a form to update data in a database is simple. Simply set controls on the form for the table fields that need to be updated.

Updating fields in a record using ADO

Any changes you make to the current row of a Recordset object or the Fields collection of a Record object are saved when you update fields in a record using the ADO. To save any modifications you've made to the current record of a Recordset object since invoking the AddNew method, or to edit any field values in an already-existing record, use the Update method. The Recordset object must be capable of supporting updates.

Updating a calculated control

To display the results of a calculation, you can utilize calculated controls on forms and reports in Access databases. Whenever the user changes the information, the total sales or tax amount must be recalculated.

Checking the status of a record deletion

Access constantly verifies deletions made by users. Access displays a dialog window asking the user to approve the deletion. The current record is briefly saved in memory and erased from the form's recordset if the user approves the deletion. This allows for the deletion to be undone if needed.

Eliminating repetitive code

Moving identical or nearly identical code to a standard module and calling it from the event procedures can help avoid duplicating the code when it's created in several event procedures. Remember that even while the code may be similar, it may not be identical, so don't just throw it into a standard module because it seems similar.

Adding a new record

A table can be updated or new records can be added with equal ease. Use the AddNew function to add a new record to a table. Editing record set data with the AddNew method is the same as editing it with the Edit method. The AddNew function creates a buffer in preparation for a new record. After you run AddNew, you can set values for the fields in the new record. Before adding a new record into the underlying table, the Update method appends a new record to the end of the record set.

Deleting a record

A record can be deleted from a table using the ADO method Delete. When records are deleted, the deletion confirmation dialog box is not shown. Validating changes made to code-generated data is typically not done since it would interfere with workflow. Once the record is removed, there is no way to undo the modification to the underlying table. Referential integrity is still upheld by Access, though. If you attempt to remove a record that is inconsistent with referential integrity, an error will be raised.

Deleting related records in multiple tables

Before deleting records in multiple tables, you must be aware of the application's relationships while writing code to delete records. It's possible that the table containing the record you're deleting has a one-to-many link with another table.

Activity

1. What are DAO objects?
2. What are ADO objects?
3. Write a VBA code to update a table.

CHAPTER 29
ADVANCED DATA ACCESS WITH VBA

In the previous chapter, you were introduced to DAO and ADO and also how to access data in tables and queries with the use of recordsets. In this chapter, you will bring to play what you have learned and also learn how you can show forms that you have chosen with the use of a combination of various techniques involving forms, Visual Basic code, and queries.

Adding an Unbound Combo Box to a Form to Find Data

When entering data on forms in Access desktop databases, it may be quicker and simpler to choose a value from a list rather than having to remember what to input. Verifying that the value entered into a field is accurate is another benefit of using a drop-down menu. A list control has two options: it can link to existing data or display fixed values that you input when you construct the control. A list box or combo box that can be used to locate a record when a value from the list is selected can be included when constructing a form in Access. It will be quicker for users to locate existing records without requiring them to provide a value in the Find dialog box. The combo box control presents a list of options in a more compact format; the list is concealed until you click the drop-down arrow. You can also use a combo box to input a value that isn't on the list. The combination box control combines the functionality of a text box with a list box in this way.

Using the Find a Record method

The FindRecord method finds a record in the bound record set of a form. This is the same as using the Ribbon's magnifying glass to locate a record in a datasheet.

When searching for a datasheet,

- Start by **selecting the column** you want to search, such as LastName.
- After that, you open the Find and Replace dialog box by clicking the magnifying glass (Find button) on the Ribbon and typing the name you want to find in the record set.
- When you insert the data, Access will move the datasheet record pointer to the row that has the data you must have inserted.

Using a bookmark

Haven mentioned that one effective way to look for data is to use the Find a Record function. Another great method for finding any information you could need is the Bookmark Method. A bookmark is a fixed pointer within a record set to a certain record. The AfterUpdate function locates the entries in the form's record set that meet the search parameters by using a bookmark.

Filtering a form

Although the FindRecord and FindFirst methods help you to rapidly discover a record that meets your criteria, they nevertheless display all of the other entries in a table or query record set, and they don't always keep all of the records together. Filtering a form allows you to see only the record or collection of records you desire while hiding all other records that don't match. Filters are useful when you have a huge number of entries to go through and only want to see a subset of them that meet your criteria.

Filtering with code

Using a code, you can also decide which records to filter. The string that is used as the criteria provided to the FindFirst property of the record set is exactly the same as the one used in the first line of code to construct the form's filter property. The process of turning on the filter is finished by the second line of code. Keep in mind that it's better to include a method for turning off a filter in addition to one for turning it on. Usually, to turn off the filter, press the little button next to the combo box.

Filtering with a query

You might want one form to control the other. Alternatively, you might want a record set to display data based on user-defined criteria. The best method to accomplish this is to utilize a parameter query.

Creating a parameter query

Any query with criteria that references a variable, a function, or a form control is referred to as a parameter query. Create a select query, specify the query's criteria, then run the query to see that it works before changing the criteria to include the question you want to ask.

Creating an interactive filter dialog box

Using a code, you can also decide which records to filter. The string that is used as the criteria provided to the FindFirst property of the record set is exactly the same as the one used in the first line of code to construct the form's filter property. The process of turning on the filter is finished by the second line of code. Keep in mind that it's better to include a method for turning off a filter in addition to one for turning it on. Usually, to turn off the filter, press the little button next to the combo box.

Linking the dialog box to another form

The parameter dialog box has code to open the form containing the value, thus it may do much more than just generate a value that can be referenced from a query. However, if you use the dialog box to search for another record twice, for example, the Requery function makes sure that the form displays new data even if it has already been opened.

Migrate Access data to Dataverse

For citizen developers, the combination of Microsoft Access, Microsoft Dataverse, and Power Platform opens up a world of possibilities in cloud and mobile scenarios. In the following aspects, this combination opens up hybrid solution scenarios that maintain the benefits and usability of cloud-based storage together with Access.

- Mobile and Microsoft Teams scenarios.
- Real-time sharing and modifying of Access data making use of cloud-based data stores and front-end applications designed in Access, Power Apps mobile and Microsoft Teams.
- New security and compliance capabilities via Dataverse storage in the cloud with the use of AAD, and role-based security while having to manage it from Access.

The following methods are available for sharing Access data with Dataverse, a cloud database that powers Power Platform apps, workflow automation, virtual agents, and more for the web, mobile device, or tablet:
- Design a Power platform environment and include a new Dataverse database.
- Migrate Access data to Dataverse or Dataverse for Teams.
- Proceed with the use of Access desktop solution for the synchronization and the editing of data dependent on the linked tables and also making use of existing frontend forms, reports, queries, and macros.
- Construct a multi-device, low-code Power App, automated process, AI-powered Virtual Assistant, or Power BI dashboard that allows you to view and update the same underlying Dataverse data simultaneously.

The foundation of the Power Platform is Dataverse, which has the capacity to hold shared data from several apps. Additional cross-platform opportunities for managing and interacting with shared data in Dynamics 365, Microsoft 365, Azure, and standalone applications are made possible by this capability. Take note Both Access and Dataverse refer to "field" and "column" in the same way. In Dataverse, the terms "table" and "entity" are synonymous.

Below are the various things things you should put in place before you begin migrating;

Begin: quick checklist

Below is a quick checklist to ensure that you are ready;

- Obtain a video overview of employing the use of Access Dataverse Connector with Power Platform for the integration with cloud-based storage.
- If you do not have one already, get a Power Apps license that has Dataverse or employ the use of an existing environment.

347

- If for any reason your Access data has a multivalued field, get it prepared for migration.
- Compared to the Access floating-point data type, Dataverse's floating-point data type has smaller range limitations. Convert any floating-point fields in your Access data to Number data types first, then set the Field Size attribute to Decimal. After that, move the data to Dataverse, where it will be stored as Decimal Number data types.

Begin: obtain needed software licenses

Ensure you get the needed licenses;

- Access: ensure you have a 365 plan which includes Access.
- Dataverse: A PowerApps plan.
- Dataverse for Teams: also a microsoft 365 plan which should now include Teams.

Begin: configure a Dataverse environment

There are basically two ways to employ the use of Dataverse, the full version as well as the Dataverse for Teams.

Dataverse

The complete edition of Dataverse serves a large user base and offers all data types needed for cross-device, low-code apps. After obtaining your Dataverse license, you have the option to migrate your Access data to a new environment or access an existing one. Before importing data into Dataverse, make sure you have the appropriate authorizations. "Environment Maker" is the security job you require, while "Basic User" is the role app users require.

If you are making use of a new environment;

- Sign in to Power Apps from microsoft.
- Choose Settings > Admin Center.
- Choose New on the Admin center page. The New Environment pane will then be opened.
- Insert the name of the environment in the Name box.
- Choose Trial from the ist that drops in the Type box. If you have a production environment of your own, you can choose Production.
- Ensure the default option is the United States in the Region box.
- Insert your preferred description in the purpose box.
- Choose Yes in Create a database for this environment.
- Once the process of migration commences in Access, the Global Discovery Service ought to find out the right instance URL.

Dataverse for Teams

Microsoft Teams makes it easier for coworkers and work groups to communicate in real time through chats, meetings, webinars, and messaging. With the addition of numerous apps, such as Power Apps based on Dataverse for Teams, you can further enhance productivity and personalize Teams. This essentially offers Teams an integrated low-code data platform and one-click solution deployment. Apps, workflows, and virtual agents within Teams don't require a separate license if you have a Microsoft 365 plan with Teams; nevertheless, Power BI apps must. Additionally, the underlying Dataverse has certain functionality constraints, and access to the Dataverse environment is restricted to the owners, members, and visitors of Teams. You must first install an app into Teams in order to provision the Dataverse for Teams environment.

- Launch **Teams**, then click **Apps** in the window's lower-left corner.
- Use the search box to find **"Power Apps"** in the App Marketplace window, and then choose **Power Apps.**
- Click **Add** to add the Power Apps application to Teams. The window for Power Apps opens.
- Choose **Make an application.**
- Pick the squad for your application.
- Click **Start Now** to create an environment for Dataverse for Teams.
- Enter the name of the program in the Power Apps editor, then choose **Save.**

Find the correct instance URL in Power Apps and manually enter it throughout the migration procedure if, for any reason, the Global Discovery Service is unable to find it.

- **Dataverse**: Choose **Settings** at the top right of the page, choose **Session Details**, and the right Dataverse URL will then be listed as the Instance URL.
- **Dataverse for Teams**: Once you are done creating an App for your Dataverse database, choose **about,** and the correct Dataverse URL is listed as the Instance URL.

Migrate Access data to Dataverse

Creating and defining a Dataverse environment, exporting data from Access to Dataverse, choosing tables and related tables, building linked tables in Access to the migrated tables in Dataverse, managing primary keys, names, and relationships, validating the data export, and previewing the results in Access and Dataverse are all steps in the process of migrating Access tables and columns to Dataverse.

Select data source and destination

- Launch **Access**, choose **Account**, and then choose **Switch Account.** The dialog box labeled **"Account" appears.**
- Verify that the login credentials you use for Power Apps are the same ones you use to access Access. You might be required to submit extra security data, like a pin or secondary authentication, depending on your situation.

Take note Permission problems prevent migration from succeeding if you use different accounts for Power Apps and Access.

- To migrate an Access database, open it.

Note Due to the possibility of a lock preventing table transfer, makes sure that any open Access objects are closed.

- In the navigation pane, right-click **a table and choose Export > Dataverse.**
- Choose all the tables you wish to export and remove all the tables you don't want to export from the Export Objects dialog box.
- Click **OK**.
- From the list that the Global Discovery Service has provided, choose an **instance URL** in the Export Data to Dataverse Environment dialog box.

Take note: An instance URL in Power Apps denotes a particular PowerApps environment session. It is not the same as the URL of a web page. "crm.dynamics," a part of the string, is a holdover from earlier Power App iterations.

Migrate: make a decision about related tables, linked tables, and previewing of tables

- Click **Export all associated tables** to export related tables of the tables you have selected.

Take note currently, when you export linked tables, only direct child tables are included. Use the Export Objects dialog box to pick all the tables you wish to migrate if you want to include all relationships.

- Click **See Related Tables** to access these tables. The dialog box for Related Tables opens.
- Two columns show table relationships in a hierarchical view: the linked tables are shown in the right column, and the selected tables are shown in the left column.
- After exporting, choose Link to Dataverse table to build table links in Access for every Dataverse table that was produced by the export operation.
- When you're done, click Open the Dataverse table URL to see the results.
- If you are using Teams to export data to Dataverse, this option is not available.
- Select Select primary name fields and select a field from the drop-down list to formally designate a field as the primary name column.
- The Primary Name column is the first text column from the left if you don't select a different column. A primary name placeholder column with null values is created if there isn't a text column.

Migrate: validate exported data

The moment you see a dialog box with the words "Running Validator..." at the top, the validation process starts automatically. You can choose **OK** after another notice that reads "Validation complete" if the validation process was successful. Access detects unsupported data types or rows that violate limits during the validation process if there are unsupported fields. It then produces a Dataverse column validation errors table and stores the exported table name and the unsupported fields in each row. All supported data types can be migrated, or non-supported data types can be left unmigrated. Should you decide against migrating, the data stays in Access.

Migrate: preview results in Access

If you decide to link tables, be sure the outcomes match your expectations. Keep an eye out for this message. "Retrieving list of tables from the Dataverse environment". The tables are still the same, but their names have been altered. To ensure that all front-end elements function as they did previously, the connected tables should now have their original table names. There is no loss of the AutoNumber primary key for Access. The table name is the column name that has been added, and it correlates to the Dataverse Primary Key (GUID). Additionally, Access adds linked tables from Dataverse called Teams, Users, and Business Units. These tables are quite helpful in providing information.

Migrate: preview results in Dataverse

Examining every table and field in the Dataverse environment is a smart way to verify and review the migration process. The names of the Dataverse tables and fields and the Access tables and columns should match. The first migrated table is automatically opened in the Dataverse environment by Access.

- Access tables have the following table appearances in Dataverse, along with matching display names and data types:
- Within a table, the names of all Access fields should be listed in the "Display Name" column.
- The table name (for example, cr444_) and a prefix are included in the format for a "Name" field. The term "logical name" in Dataverse refers to this.
- The auto-generated GUID and the current Dataverse field data types are adjacent to all migrated Access fields, which show up as "Custom" under the Type column.

Access sets the Dataverse main name to be the first text column (from left to right) by default. Access adds an empty text column as the final field in a table and sets it as the Dataverse primary name if the table does not have any text fields. A certain field can also be designated as the primary name. You may see this column in Dataverse and Access.

CHAPTER 30

CUSTOMIZING THE RIBBON

Similar to other Office programs, Access also features a customizable Ribbon. In contrast to other Office applications, Access is unique software. The main difference is that while Word and Excel are used to create documents, Access is used to create apps. Access offers a unique collection of ribbon customization choices. If you've modified the Ribbon in other Office applications, you'll have an edge with Access as you'll be accustomed to the XML. I'll go into enough depth even if you're entirely new to Ribbon customization so you can comprehend everything.

The Ribbon Hierarchy

The Ribbon is a hierarchical structure with a complex structure. The tabs that go along the top of the Ribbon are at the top level.

Each tab is divided into groups, each of which has one or more controls.

- **Tabs**: Tabs are the highest level of the Ribbon structure. Tabs are used to organize the most basic activities into logical categories.
- **Ribbons**: Groups are ranked second in the Ribbon hierarchy of objects. Logically, operations enabled by a Ribbon tab are divided into groups. They may consist of any of the numerous control kinds.
- **Controls**: Within each group, there are several controls on the Home tab. Although this isn't always the case, controls in a group are typically tied to one another.

Controls for Access Ribbons

Buttons, text boxes, labels, separators, checkboxes, and toggle buttons can all be found on a ribbon. Access has several unique controls that you may utilize on your custom Ribbons. These controls are available in the default Ribbon as well as customized Ribbons you create for your applications.

SplitButton

In Access, a SplitButton is a button that may be split into two independent parts either vertically or horizontally. The left (or top) side of the control responds to a single click and works just like any other button. An arrow on the button's right (or bottom) side, when clicked, presents a list of options with just one choice.

Menu

The SplitButton and Menu are similar in many ways. They both display a list of single-selected items and disclose a list when you click them. The main difference is that a Menu only moves the list downward when clicked, but a SplitButton is separated into two sections—the button that does the default action and the menu.

Gallery

Access makes significant use of gallery controls to display features like formatting controls and font selection.

Button

When you click a button, it acts. It does not provide menu or gallery options, but it can launch a dialog box with additional settings.

ToggleButton

To set the status or condition of the program, utilize the ToggleButton, a special kind of button control. ToggleButtons have two states that can be switched between: on and off. A ToggleButton appears as a standard button on the Ribbon when it is disabled. When a ToggleButton is clicked to turn it on, its background color changes to represent that status. The ScreenTip caption may also change.

ComboBox

The ComboBox control on a form is quite similar to the ComboBox control on the Ribbon. It's a cross between a text box and a list box in that you can input directly into it or use the controls down arrow to see a list of possibilities.

CheckBox

A CheckBox control resembles a check box on a form in appearance and behavior. A check mark displays in a CheckBox when it is clicked; otherwise, the box appears empty.

Special Ribbon Features

There are two unique qualities of the Ribbon that are worth mentioning. Some controls include SuperTips, which can increase the amount of data displayed in a ScreenTip.

SuperTips

A SuperTip is a control that displays the text you define, assisting the user in understanding the control's function.

Collapsing the Ribbon

The Ribbon is always open on the screen. With all of its buttons and tabs, the Ribbon can impede users' ability to work with an application. Alternatively, you can double-click any tab to collapse the ribbon by pressing **Ctrl+F1.**

- A **single click** on any collapsed tab restores the Ribbon, but only for a short time; the Ribbon will "auto collapse" until you **double-click** a tab **(or press Ctrl+F1)** to restore it to its pinned state.

Editing the Default Ribbon

Changes to the Ribbon are saved in Access on the system where they were made; however, the Ribbon Designer has the option to export adjustments.
- To open the Ribbon Designer, **right-click** anywhere on the Ribbon and select **Customize the Ribbon** from the shortcut menu.

Once the menu is opened, you are free to customize the ribbon as you wish. **Note that if you would like to export the changes you must have made simply;**
- Click on **the Import/Export button underneath the Customize the Ribbon list**, this will then export the changes you have made to the Ribbon in the form of an external file.

It's simple to apply custom Ribbon changes to all users working with an Access 2024 application by using a customization file. It's also an excellent way to save a copy of your changes in case you need to reapply them later. For example, you may customize the Ribbon exactly how you want it to appear to your users, export the customization, and then restore the Ribbon to its original configuration so that you have access to all Ribbon capabilities during your design process.

Working with the Quick Access Toolbar

On the main Access screen, the Quick Access toolbar is situated in the upper left corner, directly above the File tab. There is full customization available for the Quick Access toolbar. You can choose to reveal or hide several default controls, some of which are hidden, using the Customize Quick Access Toolbar option.

The easiest way to add a command to the Quick Access toolbar is to

- Locate **the command** on the Ribbon, **right-click it**, and then select **Add to Quick Access Toolbar** from the shortcut menu that appears. Access adds the selected item to the rightmost position in the Quick Access toolbar.

- Select **More Commands** from the shortcut menu to open the Customize the Quick Access Toolbar screen for more freedom when changing the Quick Access toolbar.

You can easily manage which commands users can access when using your Access apps with the Quick Access toolbar. The Quick Access toolbar allows you to perform tasks like backing up the current database, converting it to a different Access data format, viewing database properties, and joining tables. Use the Add and Remove buttons in the Quick Access Toolbar Designer to shift an item from the left list to the right list. A command that has already been added to the Quick Access toolbar cannot be added to it again. The Quick Access Toolbar Designer additionally has up and down arrows to the right of the selected list that you can use to reorganize the Quick Access toolbar commands from left to right.

Developing Custom Ribbons

Customizing the Access user interface is simple with the Ribbon Designer and Quick Access Toolbar Designer. There isn't a programmable object model for ribbons in Access. A unique table called USysRibbons holds XML declarations that explain ribbon customizations. Access uses the data in the XML to create and display the Ribbon on the screen.

The Ribbon creation process

The process below highlights Ribbon creation:
- Design **the Ribbon** and compose **the XML** that defines the Ribbon.
- Write VBA callback routines (described in the following section) that support Ribbon's operations.
- Create **the USysRibbons table**.
- Provide **a Ribbon name** and add the **custom Ribbon's XML** to the USysRibbons table.
- Specify the **custom Ribbon's name** in the Access Options dialog box.

Using VBA callbacks

A callback is a segment of code that is sent to another object for handling. Access's "Ribbon processor," which carries out Ribbon's operations, receives each procedure you create to support Ribbon operations. The event-driven code you've been utilizing in Access is not the same as this. The code in the button's Click event function is immediately activated when you click a button on a form. Although a callback procedure is associated with a Ribbon, it is executed by Access on an internal basis and is not triggered by a Ribbon click.

Creating a Custom Ribbon

There are about five steps used in describing the process of creating a custom ribbon.

These steps are explained in detail in the section below;

Step 1: Design the Ribbon and build the XML

As with other database objects, the first step in creating a new Access Ribbon is to carefully design it. The design you've made should be the same as the XML document you create for your Ribbon. Perhaps the hardest part of writing the Ribbon XML is imagining how the Ribbon will look based on the XML that powers it. There are no visual cues in a Ribbon XML document indicating how the Ribbon will look when it is rendered in Access. Your best resource for Ribbon modification advice will be experienced; occasionally, trial and error will be the only way to get the desired outcome. To create the XML that will define the new Ribbon elements, use your preferred XML editor.

Step 2: Write the callback routines

You must reference the Microsoft Office 16.0 Object Library in the References dialog box before creating any callback code for Ribbon controls, or the VBA interpreter will have no notion of how to handle references to Ribbon controls. In contrast to event procedures, callback routines do not immediately respond to control events. The Ribbon processor needs to follow each callback routine's unique "signature" to identify and utilize it. These callbacks support the same onAction control attribute, but the controls differ, hence the signatures are different. The callback method for control is often named after the control to differentiate it from callback processes for other controls. This procedure's declaration matches the button control prototype for the onAction callback procedure. Although not necessary, this procedure additionally adds a remark that describes the Ribbon control that calls the routine. For the Ribbon process to detect callback functions, they need to be declared in a standard module with the Public attribute. Callback procedures can be called in whatever way you like, provided that the procedure's declaration matches the control's onAction signature. The procedure name must match the value you assign to the control's onAction attribute. It is also very helpful to document the procedure's relationship to a Ribbon control for future reference in case either the Ribbon or the callback needs to be changed.

Step 3: Create the USysRibbons table

To see if there are any custom Ribbons in the current database application, Access looks for a table named USysRibbons. This table is not present by default; if it is, it contains the XML that defines the application's custom Ribbons. The definitions for several custom Ribbons may be present in your Access database as USysRibbons is a table. However, only one custom Ribbon can be in use at once. The USysRibbons table's ID field just keeps track of the Ribbons within the database; in contrast, RibbonName and RibbonXML are Long Text fields that hold the XML that defines each Ribbon, respectively. Make sure that the three crucial fields (ID, RibbonName, and RibbonXML) aren't changed or eliminated if you alter USysRibbons. These three fields need to be present and properly identified in USysRibbons for your custom Ribbons to function.

Step 4: Add XML to USysRibbons

You can now put your XML into the USysRibbons database. In the Datasheet view, open the USysRibbons table. Enter rbnMessages in the RibbonName box and then move the pointer to the RibbonXml field. Copy the XML you prepared in Step 1 and paste it into USysRibbons' RibbonXml field. Open the XML file in XML Notepad and click View Source to output the XML to Windows Notepad if you're using XML Notepad. After that, copy the XML and put it into USysRibbons.

Step 5: Specify the custom Ribbon property

Go to Current Database Properties, scroll down to the Ribbons and Toolbar Options section, and select the new Ribbon name from the Ribbon Name combo box before restarting the application. Neither the name of the new Ribbon nor the names of the custom Ribbons in USysRibbons that were in the table when Access started are listed in the combo box. The combo box's list does not contain the name of the new Ribbon because the names of the custom Ribbons in USysRibbons that were in the table when Access started are not there. You have two options: either restart the application or let Access locate the Ribbon in USysRibbons, or type the Ribbon's name into the combo box. When you close the Access Options dialog box after selecting a new Ribbon Name, Access warns you that the changes won't take effect until you close and reopen the database.

The Basic Ribbon XML

The Ribbon (XML) component allows you to use XML to customize a ribbon. If you want to customize the ribbon in a way that the Ribbon (Visual Designer) item doesn't allow, use the Ribbon (XML) item. From the Add New Item dialog box, you can add a Ribbon (XML) item to any Office project.

Adding Ribbon Controls

In this section, we will be looking at some Ribbon controls that you can include in your document;

Specifying imageMso

For the most part, Ribbon controls have an image that is specified by the imageMso attribute. In the Office 2022 applications, every Ribbon control has an associated imageMso value. These data are inserted into your custom Access Ribbon controls along with a label indicating the purpose of the control. Open a specific Ribbon in the Customize the Ribbon window to locate the imageMso for that particular Ribbon control. Then, from the dropdown menu in the upper left corner of the designer, select the Ribbon category that contains the Ribbon command, and move the mouse pointer over the command's entry in the list.

The Label controls

The Label control is by far the simplest and most straightforward to incorporate into a Ribbon. A Ribbon label is quite similar to a label added to an Access form. It holds text that is either hardcoded or generated via a callback method.

The Button control

The Button control is one of the most basic and useful of all the Ribbon controls. A button has only three attributes: a label, an imageMso attribute for setting the button's image, and an onAction attribute for naming the callback procedure.

Separators

A visual component that divides a group of objects is called a separator. Separators are vertical lines that appear in groups and are text-free. Although they don't have much intrinsic value by themselves, they visually distinguish controls that would otherwise be grouped too closely together.

The CheckBox control

The CheckBox control is useful for allowing the user to choose from a variety of alternatives. The user can select any of the checkboxes inside a group without affecting other selections, as CheckBox controls are not mutually exclusive.

The Dropdown control

Compared to the labels, buttons, and checkboxes that were previously covered, the DropDown control is more intricate. The user can choose from a menu of options provided by it. Consequently, a DropDown has several attributes linked to its look. Before an item is displayed in the DropDown control, the user must choose it from the list. Although the DropDown control seems to be a ComboBox control, the user cannot directly change its value. Except for allowing the user to change the value directly within the control rather than being limited to the list items, the ComboBox control functions similarly to a DropDown. List Boxes and Combo Boxes resemble the CombBox and DropDown controls that you may encounter on a form.

The SplitButton Control

The SplitButton control comes in handy when the user has a variety of options to choose from, but one option is utilized more frequently than the others. The menu> and /menu> tags hold the items on a SplitButton's list. The SplitButton's list includes any controls that appear within these tags.

Attaching Ribbons to forms and Reports

The Ribbon elements you've created thus far are always visible. Often, you will want the Buttons, DropDowns, and Menus that you create on the Ribbon to always be visible. On the other hand, there may be Ribbon elements that you want to display only under specific conditions. Access offers an easy way to display Ribbons when a form or report is active. This may be achieved by configuring the RibbonName field in the field Sheet in the VBA.

Removing the Ribbon Completely

You might need to remove the Ribbon completely; simply follow the steps below.
- Build **a new table called** USysRibbons if you haven't already done so.
- If you will be creating the USysRibbons table for the first time, including the three fields: ID (AutoNumber), RibbonName (Text), and RibbonXML (Memo).
- Create **a new record** with the RibbonName set to Blank. It doesn't matter what you call it.
- Add the following **XML to the RibbonXML column**:
- Restart the **database**.
- Select **the File tab** and then click on the **Options button** in the Backstage.
- Click the **Current Database tab** and scroll to the **Ribbon and Toolbar Options area**.
- In the Ribbon and Toolbar Options area, set the **Ribbon Name to Blank** (the same name you specified for the RibbonName column in the third step).
- Close and have the database reopened.

CHAPTER 31

PREPARING YOUR ACCESS APPLICATION FOR DISTRIBUTION

Not only does properly distributing your application make it easier for end-users to install and use it, but it also makes it easier for you, the application's developer, to update and maintain it. This chapter discusses the challenges that come up when it comes to delivering Access apps.

Defining the Current Database Options

A variety of options exist in Access databases that make the distribution process easier.

These database parameters can be accessed by
- Go to **File Options** and then to the Current Database tab.

Database options allow you to configure certain features of your program, decreasing the amount of starting code required. Before you deploy an Access program, it's critical to organize these settings correctly.

Application options

This section describes the various options that can be explored in the options of an application.

Application Icon

Your application's title bar and Windows task switcher (Alt+Tab) will display the icon you specify in the Application Icon box. If you don't give an icon for your application, Access will use the default Access icon; therefore you may wish to provide an application-specific icon.

Display   Form

When Access starts, the form you choose in the Display Form dropdown list opens automatically. The Form Load event of the display form fires when the form loads, eliminating the requirement for an Autoexec macro.

Display Status Bar

- To remove the status bar at the bottom of the Access screen, deselect the **Display Status Bar check box.**

Document Window Options

In this section, you can choose how the forms and reports will be displayed in your distributed application. The options that are available to you include; Overlapping windows which keep the view of the former version of Access, and Tabled documents which make use of a single-document interface that looks much like the recent version of famous web browsers.

Use Access Special Keys

If you choose this option, users of your application will be able to bypass various security controls by using accelerator keys particular to the Access environment, such as unhiding the Navigation pane. When distributing the application, choose the Access Special Keys check box to prohibit users from bypassing the options you choose; otherwise, users may accidentally reveal the Navigation pane or VBA code, causing confusion and other issues.

Compact on Close

When you check the Compress on Close checkbox, Access will compact and fix your database automatically when you close it. While some Access developers prefer to utilize Compact on Close to undertake this maintenance process every time a user interacts with a database, others believe it is unnecessary. It's important to keep in mind that compacting a huge database can take a long time. Furthermore, Compact on Close does not affect the backend database. The Compact and Repair Database option may be of little use to your users unless your application uses the front end for temporary tables or other procedures that cause the front end to bloat.

Remove Personal Information from File Properties on Save

When you check this box, the personal information from the file properties is immediately removed when you save the file. For this modification to take effect, you must close and reopen the existing database.

Use Windows Theme Controls on Forms

If you check this box, the form/report controls will utilize your system's Windows theme. This option is only available if you are using a Windows theme other than the default.

Enable Layout View

When you right-click an object tab, the Enable Layout View check box shows or hides the Layout View button on the Access status bar and in the shortcut menus that appear.

Enable Design Change for Tables in Datasheet View

The Enable Design Changes for Tables in the Datasheet View check box lets you make structural changes to your tables without having to go to **Design View.**

Check for Truncated Number Fields

Checking this option makes numbers show as ##### when the column is too narrow to display the whole value. Unchecking this option truncates values that are too broad to be displayed in the datasheet, which means that users see only a part of the column's value when the column is too narrow and might misinterpret the column's contents.

Picture Property Storage Format

You can specify how graphic files are saved in the database under the Picture Property Storage Format.

Navigation options

You can define parameters that affect how users explore your database as an application in the Navigation section.

The Display Navigation Pane checkbox

When the Display Navigation Pane option is deselected, the Navigation pane is hidden from the user when the computer starts up.

The Navigation Options button

When the Navigation pane is accessible at startup, Access 2024 allows you to choose which database objects are shown to users.

- The Navigation Options dialog box appears when you click the **Navigation Options button.** It allows you to change the categories and groups that appear in the Navigation pane.

Ribbon and toolbar options

When accessing your database as an application, the Ribbon and Toolbar Options section allows you to design custom Ribbons and toolbars. For any of the options in this section to take effect, you must close and reopen the current database.

Ribbon Name

This option allows you to create a personalized Ribbon. If you don't provide Access a Ribbon name, it defaults to the built-in Ribbon, which may or may not be acceptable for your application.

Shortcut Menu Bar

The default menu for shortcut menus is changed to a menu bar that you select when you set the Shortcut Menu Bar. It is usually preferable to have bespoke shortcut menus with functionality relevant to your application.

Allow Full Menus

When the Allow Full Menus box is checked, Access displays all of the commands in its menus rather than just the ones that are often used.

Allow Default Shortcut Menus

When a user right-clicks an object in the Navigation pane or a control on a form or report, the Allow Default Shortcut Menus setting governs whether Access shows its default shortcut menus.

Name AutoCorrect Options

Various developers have run across issues with altering the names of fundamental database objects regularly. In Access 2024, Microsoft implemented the Name AutoCorrect capability to help developers avoid the difficulties that unavoidably arise when database objects are renamed.

Developing the Application

Defining requirements, establishing database objects and writing code, developing documentation, and testing an application are all common steps in the development process. If you're making an app for yourself, the needs are generally already in your thoughts. You can also not see the necessity to codify the requirements since you're so familiar with the problem you're trying to solve. Consider putting them down anyway to help you clarify your thoughts and spot any potential issues early on in the development process.

Building to a specification

All databases are designed to help people address a certain problem. The issue could be that they are unable to access or obtain data in the format that they require. The easiest way to ensure success is to plan out the application thoroughly before creating any tables, queries, or forms. Only by following a plan will you be able to determine how successfully the app will handle the user's problem.

Creating documentation

It is essential to make proper documentation before creating an application, with this you are sure that nothing will go wrong with the application.

Documenting the code you write

Changes or enhancements to the application may be required over time. Even if you're the one making the changes, the passage of time since you first developed the code may mean you're having difficulty comprehending what it accomplishes. As a result, it's a good idea to have the code you've developed documented.

Documenting the application

The applications you deliver to end-users should come with documentation that explains how to use them. End-user documentation does not require including details of the user interface's core structure or logic. It should, however, clarify how the forms and reports function, give printouts of sample reports, and identify items users should avoid (for example, modifying current data).

Testing the application before distribution

Consider how you'll test the various components of your app as you create it. Because you'll still remember the functionalities of the form or report if you plan your tests during the design phase, this is the perfect time to do so. As soon as it's feasible, carry out your test plans. Then run them once more when the project is finished and you're ready to distribute it. The first time you use them, you can be sure you designed the object correctly. Executing them at the end ensures that no bugs are introduced by future changes.

Polishing Your Application

Spend some time polishing your application after it has been properly tested and appears to be ready for distribution.

Giving your application a consistent look and feel

The first thing you need to do is to establish some visual design guidelines and apply them to your app. If you want your applications to have a professional look and feel, this stage is critical.

The following are examples of design decisions you might want to ask yourself;
- Will the text boxes be elevated, chiseled, flat with a border, flat without a border, or sunken?

- What color should the back of the text boxes be?
- What color are the forms going to be?
- To divide related things, will you utilize chiseled borders or a sunken or raised border?
- What size buttons will there be on the forms?
- When the form opens, which control will be the center of attention?
- What method will be used to determine the tab order?
- For text boxes, what will your Enter key property be?
- Will you make a visible distinction between multi-select list boxes and those that aren't?
- Will you add a visual indicator when the Limit to List property of combo boxes is set?

Adding common professional components

Aspects of most professional applications are similar. The splash screen, an application switchboard, and an about box are the most frequent components. These may appear to be minor features, but they can significantly improve the appeal of your application.

A splash screen

The splash screen not only improves an application's perceived speed but also gives it a clean, professional appearance from the first time a user uses it.

An application switchboard

An application switchboard is a navigational tool that helps users navigate around the application's functionalities and forms. You may also utilize the switchboard as a navigation form, displaying other forms with the help of buttons.

An about box

The About box contains information about your organization and copyright, as well as the name of the application and its current version. The About box serves as a legal notification of ownership and makes it easier to support your application by providing easy access to version information to your users.

The status bar

The status bar displays information about the state of the object you're working on by default. The SysCmd function in Access allows you to display messages in the status bar. You can show your messages on the left side of the status bar using SysCmd. Since it doesn't require any user involvement, the status bar is an excellent area to display non-critical messages.

A progress meter

In the status bar at the bottom of the main Access window, there is a built-in progress meter. This progress meter is a rectangle that extends horizontally while Access executes a long-running process. To set up and use a progress meter, you must first initialize it, and then set the meter to the next value.

Making the application easy to start

To make an application start with ease it's best to have it pinned to the Windows Start screen. When used correctly, a program icon gives the impression that the application is separate from Access and that it has the same status as Word, Excel, or other task-oriented programs.

Bulletproofing an Application

Bulletproofing an application entails making it more stable and less vulnerable to problems caused by inexperienced users. Bulletproofing entails catching user-caused problems including improper data entering, attempting to launch a function while the program isn't ready, and allowing users to click the Calculate button before all relevant data has been entered.

Using error trapping on all Visual Basic procedures

For most data entry errors (for example, characters entered into a currency field), Access has built-in error processing; however, automatic error processing for VBA code errors does not exist. Every VBA procedure should have error-handling procedures. Any untrapped error discovered in your code causes the program to stop completely when executed at run time. Your users will be unable to recover from such a crash, and significant data loss may result. After an application error, your users must restart the program.

Maintaining usage logs

The user's name or ID, the date, and the time are all captured in usage logs. They provide useful information, especially in the event of an error. Although you can quickly accumulate too much data, a well-designed usage log will allow you to discover whether a particular sort of problem always appears when a specific user interacts with the system or when a specific query is conducted. Usage logs are also a great approach to conducting a postmortem on an application that isn't working properly. Instead of relying on the user's explanation of the error, you can observe exactly what happened at the moment an error occurred if you have logged in each subroutine and function that might fail at run time.

Separating tables from the rest of the application

Forms, reports, queries, modules, and macros should all be kept distinct from table objects. Separate code and data database files should be used in all properly distributed programs, especially those designed for network use.

Building bulletproof forms

Below are the steps to be taken to ensure the forms in your application are virtually bulletproofed:
- Consider removing the Control Box, Min, Max, and Close buttons from the form at design time.
- Always put a Close or Return button on forms to return the user to a previous or next form in the application.
- Set the ViewsAllowed property of the form to Form at design time.
- Use modal forms where appropriate.
- Use your navigation buttons that check for EOF (end of file) and BOF (beginning of the file) conditions on bound forms.
- Use the StatusBarText property on every control, to let the user know what's expected in each control.

Validating user input

Simply validating anything the user enters into the database is one of the most important bulletproofing strategies. Error data input can be captured during data entry, which is a crucial safety to include in your apps.

Using the /runtime option

When you open a database in Access' runtime mode, all of the interface elements that allow you to edit objects are hidden. In reality, a user is unable to view the Navigation pane while in runtime mode. If you choose to make use of the runtime option, make sure your app has a launch form that offers users access to any items you want them to see.

Encrypting or encoding a database

When data security is crucial, one of the first steps you should take is to encrypt or encode the database. The data and contents of Access databases are protected by robust encryption.

Follow the steps below to have an Access database encrypted;

- Open an **existing database** exclusively.
- Select the **File button** in the upper-left corner of the screen, and then choose the **Encrypt with Password command** on the info tab.

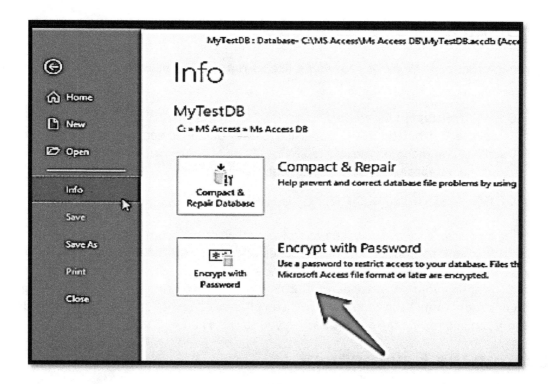

- In the Password field, insert **the password** that you would like to make use of in securing the database.
- Type **the same password again** in the Verify field and then click on the **OK button**.

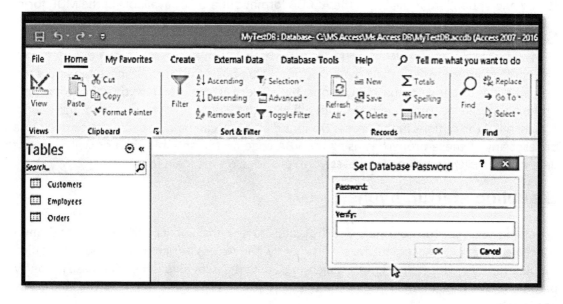

Removing a database password

Run through the steps below if you would like to remove the password from an encrypted database;

- Open **the encrypted database**.
- Select **the File button** in the upper-left corner of the screen and choose the **Decrypt Database command** on the info tab
- Insert the **database password** and click on the **OK button**.

Protecting Visual Basic code

By defining a password for the Visual Basic project you want to secure, you can restrict access to the VBA code in your application. Users are requested to input the database password each time they try to see the Visual Basic code in the database when you specify a database password for a project. Distributing your database as an ACCDE file is a more secure way of safeguarding your application's code, forms, and reports. Access compiles all code modules, eliminates all editable source code, and compacts the database when you save it as an ACCDE file.

Securing the Environment

Unauthorized users must be kept out of a major Access application. Multiple degrees of security are provided via the built-in user-level security mechanism. Note that only the MDB database format supports user-level security. Other methods of data security, such as password-protected strong encryption, are available in the ACCDB format but are not available in the MDB format.

Setting the startup option in the code

The choices you choose in the Access Options dialog box's Current Database tab apply to every user who logs into the database on a global basis There are times when you want to control these options through startup code instead of allowing the global settings to control the application. Almost all of the options in the Access Options dialog box can be changed using code. You can set or reset any of these properties using the VBA code on the splash screen or switchboard form, depending on the username (and password) provided on the login form.

Disabling startup bypass

Bypassing your startup routines, you'll be able to see the application's design and any items concealed behind the user interface. Fortunately, the Access designers foresaw the requirement for bulletproofing an application starting by including the AllowBypassKey database property. This parameter disables (or enables) the Shift key bypasses at the application starting and takes True or False values.

The code to implement the AllowBypassKey attribute is as follows:

- Public Sub SetBypass(bFlag As Boolean)
- Dim db As DAO.Database
- Dim pBypass As DAO.Property
- Const sKEYNAME As String = "AllowBypassKey"
- Set db = CurrentDb
- On Error Resume Next
- Set pBypass = db.Properties(sKEYNAME)
- On Error GoTo 0
- If pBypass Is Nothing Then
- Set pBypass = db.CreateProperty(sKEYNAME, dbBoolean, Flag)
- db.Properties.Append pBypass
- Else
- pBypass.Value = bFlag
- End If
- End Sub

Setting property values

If a startup property does not exist, the following function sets its value, generating and appending the property to the Properties collection:

- Public Function SetStartupProperty(sPropName As String, _
- ePropType As DAO.DataTypeEnum, vPropValue As Variant) As Boolean
- Dim db As DAO.Database
- Dim prp As DAO.Property
- Dim bReturn As Boolean
- Set db = CurrentDb
- On Error Resume Next
- Set prp = db.Properties(sPropName)
- If prp Is Nothing Then
- Set prp = db.CreateProperty(sPropName, ePropType, vPropValue)
- If prp Is Nothing Then
- bReturn = False
- Else
- db.Properties.Append prp
- bReturn = True
- End If
- Else
- prp.Value = vPropValue
- bReturn = True

- ○ End If
- ○ SetStartupProperty = bReturn
  - ▪ End Function

It's simple to use SetStartupProperty(), but you must know the exact property name and data type of the property before calling it ().

Getting property values

It's far easier to determine the worth of a property than it is to determine the value of a property. The property is returned by the Properties collection, while the value is returned by the Value property.

The following is the syntax for getting the value of the AppTitle property;

- ▪ On Error Resume Next
- ▪ GetAppTitle = CurrentDb.Properties("AppTitle").Value

CHAPTER 32

INTEGRATING ACCESS WITH SHAREPOINT

The option to launch your Access application as a SharePoint website is an exciting feature of Microsoft Access 2024. **In this chapter,** we'll look at the different methods for converting Access databases to SharePoint. This chapter explains what SharePoint is and how it can be used to help organizations share and collaborate data.

Introducing SharePoint

SharePoint is an online collaboration platform that facilitates communication between business teams through the use of "list" databases, workflow applications, and additional web components and security measures. Additionally, SharePoint enables businesses to automate workflow processes within corporate groups and control access to information. Information workers in all sizes of verticals may increase their visibility and productivity with SharePoint. The core functionality of SharePoint is its intranet-based cross-collaboration environment, which facilitates secure document sharing, workflow collaboration, and other features. Using the web-based platform SharePoint, users can upload documents and distribute them to immediate recipients. Additionally, customers have the option to have OneDrive, which is a private cloud storage area where they may upload documents and files and keep them private until they "share" or provide other people access to them. Although it doesn't have to be, this makes it easier for a group of coworkers to examine a published document. The workflow and approval technologies listed above can be used to control document exchange and personnel data handling within firms. Email can also be used to send links to shared documents or collaborative areas, making it simple for users to find what they need.

Understanding SharePoint Sites

This section provides an insight into the two commonly used SharePoint sites;

SharePoint documents

SharePoint is an online tool that lets users upload files and distribute them to anyone who requires instant access. Additionally, they can have OneDrive, which is a private cloud storage area where they can save documents and other files. Until they "share" or grant access to other users, no one can view the files they upload. Although it doesn't have to be this way, allowing a group of coworkers to see a published document is made easy by this. The technologies mentioned above for workflow and approval can be used to control document transmission and personnel data handling within organizations. Users can also send links to shared papers or collaborative spaces via email, making it easier for them to discover what they need.

SharePoint maintains track of files from the moment they are added to a list until they are removed or deleted. Anyone with written access to a SharePoint site can share a document. SharePoint maintains track of who made the changes and when a document is checked in or out. SharePoint can even be instructed to reverse document modifications to an earlier version if necessary. The most common application of this document-sharing paradigm is information distribution within businesses, enabling SharePoint site users to work together.

SharePoint lists

Although a SharePoint list is one of the most versatile and potent features of the platform, its potential is not often fully utilized. One reason for this is that lists are sometimes perceived as a feature exclusive to IT professionals or people with extensive technical knowledge, yet power users and citizen developers may use SharePoint lists with no difficulty. SharePoint makes it simple to accommodate multiple lists, so a company can add as many lists as necessary. Sadly, SharePoint lists are not relational like Access tables are; you cannot query multiple SharePoint lists to find pertinent information or link data from two separate lists together. Conversely, listings from SharePoint can be imported or connected to Access. Integration with SharePoint

Sharing Data between Access and SharePoint

Going into an Access program, linking to SharePoint lists, and then building forms and reports based on those linked tables is all it takes to create Access apps with SharePoint data. Access treats a linked SharePoint list like any other linked data source.

Linking to Sharepoint lists

Access can link to a SharePoint list and use the data as it would any other linked data source.

To link to a SharePoint list, follow these steps:
- Click **the New Data Source** then click on **From Online Services >SharePoint List** in the Import & Link group on the External Data tab
- Click on the **"Link to the data source by creating a linked table"** option, and click **Next**
- Insert your **username and password**
- Add a **checkmark** next to each list you want to be linked, and then select **OK.**

Importing SharePoint lists

You can just import the data as a separate, unconnected table into Access after taking a snapshot of a SharePoint list. In contrast to a linked SharePoint list, an imported list will not automatically update with fresh SharePoint data.

Follow the steps below to Import a SharePoint list;

- Choose the **New Data Source** drop-down button in the Import & Link group on the External Data tab.
- Click on **From Online Services >SharePoint List** from the list of online services.
- In the top portion of this dialog box, either selects a recently **visited SharePoint site** or enter **a new destination SharePoint URL**; then select the Import option.
- Insert t**he appropriate permissions** to import a SharePoint list.
- Add a **checkmark** next to each list you want to be imported, and then select **OK.**

Exporting Access tables to SharePoint

Data must occasionally be transferred from Access to SharePoint so that SharePoint users have access to the same information as Access users. **The steps below will show you how to export a table from Access to a SharePoint list.**

- Right-click **the table** you want to export in the Navigation pane, and then **select Export > SharePoint List**.
- Insert or select the **target SharePoint site URL.**
- Choose the **OK button.**
- Select the **Close button** in Access to dismiss the Export to SharePoint dialog box.

Moving Access Tables to SharePoint

Moving every table in an Access program to SharePoint in a single export operation and then linking the new SharePoint lists back to the Access application is an alternative to just exporting Access tables to SharePoint. Every table in the Access database is moved to SharePoint and then linked back to Access in a single procedure. The benefit of moving Access tables to SharePoint is that it lets you develop your data model in Access using all of the basic tools for creating tables, and then scale it up for SharePoint. Once the data is in SharePoint, any changes made there will be instantly apparent in Access.

Using SharePoint Templates

Access 2024's SharePoint templates provide important business features including Contacts, Tasks, Issues, and Events. Rather than exporting pre-existing Access tables to SharePoint or referring to lists on SharePoint, this alternative approach entails building entirely new SharePoint lists inside the Access environment. SharePoint list templates for Access 2024 contain all the details required to construct lists in SharePoint, including column names, data types, and other list characteristics. The main goal of this is to reduce time for users who frequently need to make new lists in SharePoint.

Activity

1. What is SharePoint?
2. Move Access table to Sharepoints
3. What are SharePoint sites?

Conclusion

Even if you're not a database expert, Microsoft Access 2024 gives you the tools to get the most out of your data. And, through newly added Web databases, Access 2024 amplifies the power of your data, making it easier to track, report, and share with others.

Some of the amazing features you are set to experience include;
- New themes and templates
- Access event model
- Distributing access application
- Larger show table dialog
- Query box to easily locate Access tools and features
- Ability to export linked data source information to Excel

Whether you're a large corporation, small business owner, or nonprofit organization, or if you're just looking for more efficient ways to manage your personal information, Access 2024 makes it easier to get what you need to be done more quickly, with more flexibility and with better results.

EXTRAS

SHORTCUT KEYS ON MICROSOFT ACCESS

Frequently used shortcuts

This table itemizes the most frequently used shortcuts in Access desktop databases.

To do this	Press
Select the active tab of the ribbon and activate KeyTips.	Alt or F10 (To move to a different ribbon tab, use KeyTips or the arrow keys.)
Go to the **Home** tab.	Alt+H

Go to the **Tell me** box on the ribbon.	Alt+Q, and then enter the search term
Display the shortcut menu for the selected item.	Shift+F10 or the Windows Menu key
Move the focus to a different pane of the window.	F6
Open an existing database.	Ctrl+O or Ctrl+F12
Show or hide the **Navigation Pane**.	F11
Show or hide a property sheet.	F4
Switch between **Edit** mode (with insertion point displayed) and **Navigation** mode in the **Datasheet View** or **Design View**.	F2
Switch to the **Form View** from the form in the **Design View**.	F5
Move to the next or previous field in the **Datasheet View**.	Tab key or Shift+Tab
Go to a specific record in the **Datasheet View**.	Alt+F5, then, in the record number box, type the record number and press Enter
Open the **Print** dialog box (for datasheets, forms, and reports).	Ctrl+P
Open the **Page Setup** dialog box (for forms and reports).	S

Open the **Find** tab in the **Find and Replace** dialog box in the **Datasheet View** or **Form View**.	Ctrl+F
Open the **Help** window.	F1
Exit Access.	Alt+F4

Navigate the ribbon with only the keyboard

Access's tab-based banner at the top is called the ribbon. Upon selection, every ribbon tab presents a distinct ribbon composed of groups, with each group containing one or more instructions. The keyboard is all you need to navigate the ribbon. Regardless of where you are in Access, you can utilize KeyTips, which are unique key combinations, to rapidly access a command on the ribbon by tapping a few keys. You can use a KeyTip to give any command in Access.

There are two ways to navigate the tabs in the ribbon:

- To get to the ribbon, press Alt, and then, to move between the tabs, use the Right and Left arrow keys.
- **To go directly to a tab on the ribbon, press one of the following KeyTips:**

To do this	Press
Go to the **File** menu.	Alt+F
Go to the **Home** tab.	Alt+H
Go to the **Create** tab.	Alt+C
Go to the **External Data** tab.	Alt+X or Alt+X, 1
Go to the **Database Tools** tab.	Alt+Y, 2
Go to the **Table** tab.	Alt+J, T

Go to the **Add-ins** tab, if present.	Alt+X, 2
Go to the **Tell me** box on the ribbon.	Alt+Q

Use the keyboard to work with ribbon tabs

- Press Alt to navigate to the ribbon tabs. Press the KeyTip on a tab to open it directly.
- Use the Down arrow key to move within the currently selected group.
- You can use the Ctrl+Right or Left arrow keys to navigate between groups on a ribbon.
- To navigate among commands in a group, use the Tab or Shift+Tab keys.
- Various methods exist for activating controls, based on the kind of control:
- If the control you have picked is a button, you can press Enter or Spacebar to make it work.
- You can use the Alt+Down arrow key in addition to the selected control to activate a split button, which is a button that opens a menu of additional options. Use the Tab key to navigate through the settings. To select the option that is now chosen, use the Spacebar.
- Press the Down arrow key to open the list if the chosen control is a list (like the Font list). Then, use the Up or Down arrow keys to navigate between the objects.
- Use the Spacebar or Enter keys to choose the control if it's a gallery. Then, to peruse the items, press the Tab key.

Work with database files

Open and save databases

To do this	Press
Open a new database.	Ctrl+N
Open an existing database.	Ctrl+O or Ctrl+F12
Open the selected folder or file.	Enter
Open the folder one level above the selected folder.	Backspace

Delete the selected folder or file.	Delete
Display a shortcut menu for a selected item such as a folder or file.	Shift+F10 or the Windows Menu key
Move forward through options.	Tab key
Move backward through options.	Shift+Tab
Open the **Look in** list.	F4 or Alt+I
Save a database object.	Ctrl+S or Shift+F12
Open the **Save As** dialog box.	F12 or Alt+F, S

Print database information

To do this	Press
Print the current or selected object.	Ctrl+P
From **Print Preview**, open the **Print** dialog box.	P or Ctrl+P
From **Print Preview**, open the **Page Setup** dialog box.	S
Cancel **Print Preview** or **Layout Preview**.	C or Esc
From the **File** menu, return to your database.	Esc

Navigate in the Access workspace

Switch from tabbed documents to windowed documents

By default, Access databases are shown as tabbed documents. If you want to work with documents in overlapping windows instead, you can change the document window options in the app options.

1. To go to the **File** menu, select **File** or press Alt+F.
2. Select **Options**. The **Access Options** dialog box opens.
3. Select **Current Database**.
4. Under **Document Window Options**, select **Overlapping Windows**, and then select **OK**.
5. Close and reopen the current database for the option to take effect.

Move in the Access workspace

To do this	Press
Show or hide the **Navigation Pane**.	F11
Go to the **Search** box in the **Navigation Pane** when the focus is already on the **Navigation Pane**.	Ctrl+F
Switch to the next or previous pane in the workspace.	F6 or Shift+F6 You might need to press F6 more than once. If pressing F6 doesn't display the task pane you want, press Alt to move the focus to the ribbon, and then press Ctrl+Tab to move to the task pane.
Switch to the next or previous database window.	Ctrl+F6 or Ctrl+Shift+F6
Restore the selected minimized window when all windows are minimized.	Enter

| Close the active database window. | Ctrl+W or Ctrl+F4 |
| Switch between the **Visual Basic Editor** and the previous active window. | Alt+F11 |

Work with menus, dialog boxes, wizards, and property sheets

Learn how to use the keyboard shortcuts to navigate and use menus, dialog boxes, wizards, and property sheets.

Use menus

To do this	Press
Show KeyTips.	Alt or F10
Show the program icon menu (on the program title bar), also known as the control menu.	Alt+Spacebar
With the menu or submenu visible, select the next or previous command.	Down or Up arrow key
Select the menu to the left or right or, when a submenu is visible, switch between the main menu and the submenu.	Left or Right arrow key
Select the first or last command on the menu or submenu.	Home or End
Open the selected menu, or perform the action assigned to the selected button.	Spacebar or Enter
Open a shortcut menu or open a dropdown menu for the selected gallery item.	Shift+F10 or the Windows Menu key

Scroll up or down in the selected gallery list.	Page up or Page down
Move to the top or bottom of the selected gallery list.	Ctrl+Home or Ctrl+End
Close the visible menu and submenu at the same time.	Alt
Close the visible menu or, with a submenu visible, close only the submenu.	Esc

Use dialog boxes

To do this	Press
Switch to the next tab in a dialog box.	Ctrl+Tab
Switch to the previous tab in a dialog box.	Ctrl+Shift+Tab
Move to the next or previous option or option group.	Tab key or Shift+Tab
Move between options in the selected dropdown list box or move between options in a group of options.	Arrow keys
Perform the action assigned to the selected button or select or clear the checkbox.	Spacebar
Open the list if it is closed and move to an option in the list.	First letter of an option in a dropdown list
Select the option, or select or clear the checkbox by the letter underlined in the option name.	Alt+Letter key
Open the selected dropdown list box.	Alt+Down arrow key

Close the selected dropdown list box.	Esc
Perform the action assigned to the default button in the dialog box.	Enter
Cancel the command and close the dialog box.	Esc

Use wizards

To do this	Press
Toggle the focus forward between controls in the wizard.	Tab key
Toggle the focus between sections (header, body, and footer) of the wizard.	F6
Complete the wizard.	Alt+F

Use property sheets

These keyboard shortcuts apply to property sheets for tables, queries, forms, and reports in the **Design View** and forms and reports in the **Layout View**.

To do this	Press
Show or hide the property sheet.	F4
Move among choices in the control selection dropdown list one item at a time.	Down or Up arrow key
Move among choices in the control selection dropdown list one page at a time.	Page down or Page up

Move to the property sheet tabs from the control selection dropdown list.	Tab key
Move among the property sheet tabs with a tab selected, but no property selected.	Left or Right arrow key
With a property already selected, move down one property on a tab.	Tab key
With a property selected, move up one property on a tab, or if already at the top, move to the tab.	Shift+Tab
Toggle forward between tabs when a property is selected.	Ctrl+Tab
Toggle backward between tabs when a property is selected.	Ctrl+Shift+Tab

Work with text boxes, combo boxes, and list boxes

Use your keyboard to navigate and edit content in a text box, combo box, or list box.

Edit a text box

An edit box is a blank text box in which you type or paste an entry, such as your username or the path of a folder.

To do this	Press
Move to the beginning of the entry.	Home
Move to the end of the entry.	End
Move one character to the left or right.	Left or Right arrow key
Move one word to the left or right.	Ctrl+Left or Right arrow key

Select from the insertion point to the beginning of the text entry.	Shift+Home
Select from the insertion point to the end of the text entry.	Shift+End
Change the selection by one character to the left.	Shift+Left arrow key
Change the selection by one character to the right.	Shift+Right arrow key
Change the selection by one word to the left.	Ctrl+Shift+Left arrow key
Change the selection by one word to the right.	Ctrl+Shift+Right arrow key

Use a combo or list box

A list box displays a range of unchangeable values or choices, which are automatically listed. A combo box also displays values or choices, but it does not display them until you select a dropdown arrow. With a combo box, you can sometimes enter a value that's not on the list, as you can with a text box.

To do this	Press
Open a combo box.	F4 or Alt+Down arrow key
Refresh the contents of the **Lookup field** list box or a combo box.	F9
Move down one line.	Down arrow key

Move down one page.	Page down
Move up one line.	Up arrow key
Move up one page.	Page up
Exit the combo box or list box.	Tab key

Work with objects

Use keyboard shortcuts to edit and move within the **Objects** list and to navigate and open objects.

Edit and navigate the Object list

To do this	Press
Rename a selected object. **Note:** You can only rename an object when it is closed.	F2
Move down one line.	Down arrow key
Move down one window.	Page down
Move to the last object.	End
Move up one line.	Up arrow key
Move up one window.	Page up

Navigate and open objects

To do this	Press

Open the selected table or query in the **Datasheet View**.	Enter
Open the selected form or report.	Enter
Run the selected macro.	Enter
Open the selected table, query, form, report, macro, or module in the **Design View**.	Ctrl+Enter
Display the **Immediate** window in the **Visual Basic Editor**.	Ctrl+G

Common shortcuts for the Design, Layout, and Datasheet views

To do this	Press
Switch between **Edit** mode (with insertion point displayed) and **Navigation** mode in a datasheet.	F2
Exit **Navigation** mode and return to **Edit** mode in a form or report.	Esc
Switch to the property sheet (in the **Design View** and **Layout View** for forms and reports).	F4 or Alt+Enter
Switch to the **Form View** from the form in the **Design view**.	F5
Switch between the upper and lower portions of a window (in the **Design View** of queries, macros, and the **Advanced Filter/Sort** window).	F6
Cycle between the field grid, property sheet, field properties, the **Navigation Pane**, **Quick Access Toolbar**, and KeyTips on the ribbon (in the **Design View** for tables).	F6

Switch from the **Visual Basic Editor** back to the form or report in the **Design View**.	Alt+F11
Toggle forward between views when in a table, query, form, or report. **Note:** If additional views are available, successive keystrokes move the focus to the next available view.	Ctrl+Right arrow or Ctrl+Comma (,)
Toggle backward between views when in a table, query, form, or report. **Note:** If additional views are available, successive keystrokes move the focus to the previous view.	Ctrl+Left arrow or Ctrl+Period (.) **Note:** This shortcut does not work under all conditions with all objects.

Use a grid pane

To do this	Press
Move among cells.	Arrow keys, Tab key, or Shift+Tab
Move to the last row in the current column.	Ctrl+Down arrow key
Move to the first row in the current column.	Ctrl+Up arrow key
Move to the upper-left cell in the visible portion of the grid.	Ctrl+Home
Move to the lower-right cell.	Ctrl+End

Move in a dropdown list.	Up or Down arrow key
Select an entire grid column.	Ctrl+Spacebar
Toggle between **Edit** mode and cell selection mode.	F2
Copy selected text in cell to the clipboard (in **Edit** mode).	Ctrl+C
Cut selected text in cell and place it on the clipboard (in **Edit** mode).	Ctrl+X
Paste text from the clipboard (in **Edit** mode).	Ctrl+V
Toggle between insert and overtype mode while editing in a cell.	Insert
Toggle the checkbox in the **Output** column. **Note:** If multiple items are selected, pressing this key affects all selected items.	Spacebar
Clear the selected contents of a cell.	Delete
Clear all values for a selected grid column.	Delete

Move around in tables or cells

To do this	Press
Move one character to the left.	Left arrow key

Move one character to the right.	Right arrow key
Move up one line.	Up arrow key
Move down one line.	Down arrow key
Move one word to the left.	Ctrl+Left arrow key
Move one word to the right.	Ctrl+Right arrow key
Move to the end of a line.	End
Move to the beginning of a line.	Home
Move up one paragraph.	Ctrl+Up arrow key
Move down one paragraph.	Ctrl+Down arrow key
Move to the end of a text box.	Ctrl+End
Move to the beginning of a text box.	Ctrl+Home
Repeat the last **Find** action.	Shift+F4

Get help with Access

The Help window provides all Access help content.

To do this	Press
Open the **Help** window.	F1

Go back to Access **Help Home**.	Alt+Home
Select the next item in the **Help** window.	Tab key
Select the previous item in the **Help** window.	Shift+Tab
Perform the action for the selected item.	Enter
In the Access **Help topics** list, expand or collapse the selected item.	Enter
Select the next hidden text or hyperlink, including **Show All** or **Hide All** at the top of a topic.	Tab key
Select the previous hidden text or hyperlink.	Shift+Tab
Perform the action for the selected **Show All**, **Hide All**, hidden text, or hyperlink.	Enter
Move back to the previous **Help** topic (**Back** button).	Alt+Left arrow key or Backspace
Move forward to the next **Help** topic (**Forward** button).	Alt+Right arrow key
Scroll small amounts up or down within the currently displayed **Help** topic.	Up or Down arrow key
Scroll larger amounts up or down, respectively, within the currently displayed **Help** topic.	Page up or Page down
Stop the last action (**Stop** button).	Esc

Refresh the window (**Refresh** button).	F5
Print the current **Help** topic.	Ctrl+P (If the cursor is not in the current **Help** topic, press F6, and then press Ctrl+P)
Change the connection state.	F6, and then Enter to open the list of choices
Switch among areas in the **Help** window, such as the toolbar and the **Search** list.	F6
In a Table of Contents in tree view, select the next or previous item, respectively.	Up or Down arrow key
In a Table of Contents in tree view, expand or collapse the selected item.	Enter

Miscellaneous keyboard shortcuts

To do this	Press
Display the complete hyperlink address (URL) for a selected hyperlink.	F2
Open the **Zoom** box to conveniently enter expressions and other text in small input areas.	Shift+F2

Copy a screenshot of the entire screen to the clipboard.	Print screen
Copy a screenshot of the current window to the clipboard.	Alt+Print screen
Display the full set of commands on the task pane menu.	Ctrl+Down arrow key
Exit Access.	Alt+F4

INDEX

G

H

I

M

N

O

P

Q

R

S

T

U

V

W

X

Y

Z

www.ingramcontent.com/pod-product-compliance
Lightning Source LLC
Chambersburg PA
CBHW060921060326
40690CB00041B/2835